UNDERSTANDING ANIMATION

Understanding .... is a comprehensive introduction to animated film, from cartoons to computer animation. Paul Wells' insightful account of a critically neglected but increasingly popular medium explains the defining characteristics of animation as a cinematic form, outlines different models and methods which can be used to interpret and evaluate animated films, and traces the development of animated film around the world, from *Betty Boop* to *Wallace and Gromit*.

Part history, part theory, and part celebration, *Understanding Animation* includes notes towards a theory of animation; an explanation of its narrative strategies; an analysis of how comic events are constructed; a discussion of representation, focusing on gender and race, and primary research on animation and audiences. Throughout, Paul Wells' argument is illustrated with case studies, including Daffy Duck in Chuck Jones' *Duck Amuck*, Jan Svankmajer's *Jabberwocky*, Tex Avery's *Little Rural Riding Hood* and *King Size Canary*, and Nick Park's *Creature Comforts*. *Understanding Animation* demonstrates that the animated film has much to tell us about ourselves, the cultures we live in, and our view of art and society.

Paul Wells is Subject Leader in Media Studies at De Montfort University in Leicester.

UNDERSTANDING ANIMATION

Paul Wells

London and New York

First published 1998
by Routledge
11 New Fetter Lane, London EC4P 4EE

Simultaneously published in the USA and Canada
by Routledge
29 West 35th Street, New York, NY 10001

Typeset in Joanna and Bembo by
J&L Composition Ltd, Filey, North Yorkshire
Printed and bound in Great Britain by
Biddles Ltd, Guildford and Kings Lynn

British Library Cataloguing in Publication Data
A catalogue record for this book is available
from the British Library

Library of Congress Cataloguing in Publication Data

ISBN 0–415–11596–5 (hbk)
ISBN 0–415–11597–3 (pbk)

CONTENTS

CONTENTS

CONTENTS

FIGURES

ACKNOWLEDGEMENTS

This is my first book-length discussion, and for some readers this will be self-evident, while others will feel that it offers some interesting topics for discussion and further research. Whatever the response, all of its flaws are mine; all of its enthusiasm for animation mine also.

I'd like to thank a number of people for their help and encouragement. Firstly, I am grateful to the School Of Humanities at De Montfort University in Leicester for granting me study leave to complete the book, and to Tim O'Sullivan, Pat Kirkham, and the staff of the Media Studies subject team for their support. My special appreciation goes to Laraine Porter, my co-tutor on the Animation Studies course from which much of the work presented here was developed. Further, my thanks go to all the students who contributed so much to the course's development and success. For additional help, over and beyond the call of duty, as they say, my gratitude goes to Jayne Pilling, Terry Gilliam, Nick Park, Joanna Quinn, Mark Baker, Barry Purves, Bob Godfrey, Roger Noake, Andy Darley, and especially Marysia Lachowitz and Margaret O'Brien at the British Film Institute/Museum of the Moving Image Education.

A final note of thanks goes to Rebecca Barden and all of the staff at Routledge for all their patience and hard work.

This book is dedicated with all my love to my wife, Joanne.

Further acknowledgements

I am grateful to the following copyright holders for the provision of stills to be used as figures in this book:

Playful Pluto (1934) courtesy of Disney and the BFI

The Haunted Hotel (1907) courtesy of the BFI

Composition in Blue (1940) courtesy of the BFI

Lapis (1965) courtesy of the London Film Maker's Co-operative and the BFI

The Street (1976) courtesy of the National Film Board of Canada and the BFI

Jumping (1984) courtesy of Tesuka Productions and the BFI

The Hand (1965) courtesy of the BFI

Tale of Tales (1979) courtesy of Soyuz Multfilm and the BFI

Feet of Song (1988) courtesy of Lee Stork and the BFI

Pas a Deux (1988) courtesy of the BFI

Special Delivery (1978) courtesy of the National Film Board of Canada and the BFI

Bob's Birthday (1995) courtesy of the National Film Board of Canada, Channel Four, Snowden Fine Productions and the BFI

Tin Toy (1988) courtesy of Pixars Animated Studios and the BFI

Asparagus (1979) courtesy of Suzan Pitt and the BFI

Girls' Night Out (1986) courtesy of the BFI

Every effort has been made to trace copyright holders of the illustrations. In the event of any queries please contact Routledge, London.

INTRODUCTION
'Seeing the brick'

He did several studies of the streetcar and when he held them together and flipped the pages it appeared as if the streetcar came down from the tracks from a distance and stopped so that the people could get on and off. His own delight matched the girl's. She gazed at him with such serene approval that he had a fever to create for her. He bought some more scrap paper. He imagined her on ice skates. In two nights he made one hundred and twenty silhouettes on pages not bigger than his hand. He bound them with string. She held the little book and governed the pages with her thumb and watched herself skating away and skating back, gliding into a figure eight, returning, pirouetting, and making a lovely bow to her audience.

(Doctorow, 1976: 95)

Humankind has always been fascinated by moving images. The desire to make pictures move has provoked some of the most innovative developments in the fields of Science and Technology during the twentieth century. Curiously though, it is this very fact which has inhibited a proper recognition of the animated film and animation as an art form. The profound pleasure, recorded here by novelist, E.L. Doctorow, in the construction and use of an animated 'flip' book, recognises the relationship between the artist and the actual creation of movement that so intrinsically informs the art of animation, an art that *precedes* its recording on film. Doctorow stresses the appeal of making images apparently move – the 'fever to create' which underpins the work of all animators.

'Animation', in this sense – the skill of animating images by hand, 'frame-by-frame' – became only one of the approaches by which pioneering film-makers tried to create and record moving images. The driving imperatives of the pioneers were largely technological in that they were testing the capability of a new medium in a mechanistic rather than aesthetic way. The development of the camera was more important than the things it photographed (though these things became important both to film-makers and historians as the medium progressed). Consequently, the techniques of photography, and the skills of the photographer subsumed the art and craft of animation and surpassed the early

1

achievements of the animator. Pre-cinematic achievements in animation will be addressed in Chapter One, but particularly significant was the work of French professor, Emile Reynaud, who invented the Praxinoscope:

> It consisted of a cylindrical box attached to a pivot. A coloured strip of paper on the inside face of the cylinder showed the consecutive stages of a movement. When the cylinder rotated, these stages were reflected in rapid succession on a mirrored prism mounted on the pivot, and the viewer who looked at the prism would see the drawn image move freely.
>
> (Bendazzi, 1994: 4)

The Praxinoscope soon became a popular children's toy, and anticipated the fate of a great deal of work in animation by being dismissed as a novelty and relegated to a children's audience. Reynaud ultimately modified the Praxino-scope, however, and created the proto-cinema of the 'Théâtre Optique' in 1889. The short, coloured, strips of images required for the Praxinoscope became longer spools of images painted on ribbon which were back-projected on to a screen by means of a primitive projector allied to more mirrors and a bigger light-source. Reynaud's 'films' included his first experimental piece, A Good Beer (1888), The Clown and his Dogs (1892), and Poor Pierrot (1892), the latter, ten-minute entertainments incorporated into theatrical shows, often with simulated sounds to accompany the illusion of narrative action (e.g. the crack of a stick when Pierrot, the clown, was beaten by his master). The most significant point to emerge from these achievements, however, is not concerned with art, but with industry, and characterises the popular view of animation even in the contem-porary era. The very craftsmanship of the animated film became its inhibiting factor at a time when the immediacy of the photographic image was its novelty and its passport to industrial legitimacy, and thus the name of 'cinema' itself. Ralph Stephenson argues that Reynaud's place in the development of the moving image must not be undervalued, however, and suggests, 'He not only invented a technique, he originated a genre and was the first to develop the animated film (indeed the cinema if by cinema we mean movement, not photography) into a spectacle' (Stephenson, 1967: 27).

Live-action film-making in the realist style of the Lumière Brothers' early works quickly became the dominant mode of film-making. 'Animation', as such, sur-vived unnoticed in the guise of 'trick' photography, and informed many of the early approaches to film-making which looked to create fantasy narratives or comedy. This is best exemplified in the magical fantasies of Georges Méliès (see Fraser, 1979) or the comedies produced and distributed by Pathé at the turn of the century and in the early teens. Animators didn't just disappear, of course, but continued working in the medium, developing its forms and techniques, having to accept its apparently less credible position as a second cousin to mainstream cinema. It may be argued that this early setback for animation in film history has been more than remedied by the work of the Disney Studio, who essentially put animation on the map. Equally, it may be argued that such a dominant model for animation has ghettoised the form in itself by overshadowing its early history and creating an orthodox style. Animation, in some ways, has become synonymous with Disney and thus other kinds of animation and other important film-makers in the field have been further neglected.

Understanding Animation not merely wishes to address these issues and reclaim the animated film as an important art form in its own right, but to provide a variety of points of access into the study of the medium. To study animation is to acknowledge its place in cinema history and to properly evaluate its achievements. Clearly, in the contemporary era, the animated film has a much higher profile, chiefly through the continuing domination of the Disney Studios, the proliferation of cartoons on mainstream television, and the popularity of the Japanese manga films (see McCarthy, 1993). In many senses, however, this creates as many problems as it apparently resolves. This scenario still consigns the animated film to its traditional children's audience, defines the animated film as 'a cartoon', and sustains a view of animation as something which merely fills time in the schedules, or appeals to marginalised tastes. The recent proliferation of animation festivals worldwide, however, coupled with enlightened commissioning policies as adopted by Channel Four in Britain, and the reclamation of new national cinemas in the post-Cold War period, has done much to raise the profile and status of the form.

Ironically, even in what may be regarded as a significant development in the reclamation of animation as an important and influential medium, the Robert Zemeckis film, *Who Framed Roger Rabbit?* (1988), still shows 'Toontown' as a place which is disparaged. As Susan Ohmer has noted, 'Toons' are universally disliked, and, significantly, even subject to the kind of segregation suffered by Black people in America in the pre-Civil Rights era (Ohmer, 1988: 97–104). This is clearly an overdetermination, but a significant one if recognised as a representation of the way the film's producers, an alliance of Warner Brothers, Disney, and British-based animators like Richard Williams, view the cultural neglect of the animated film. Inevitably the film frames 'Toons' in this way to illicit sympathy for, and nostalgia about, a golden era of animation in America during the 1930s and 1940s. Animation, it seems, cannot escape the idea that it is a trivial and easily dismissed form, but most significantly, it seemingly cannot escape the view that it is a thing of the past, a bygone art. Thankfully, however, and necessarily, recent scholarship has also reclaimed this period through detailed studio histories, important biographical work on significant animators, books concerned with style and practical techniques, and some critical work on the modes of construction and aesthetic intention at the heart of the films (see Bendazzi, 1994; Frierson, 1994; Klein, 1993; Maltin, 1987; Pilling, 1992; Russett and Starr, 1976; Solomon, 1989). These texts fundamentally legitimise the art of animation and recognise its influence and achievement. Clearly I will be drawing extensively on this ground-breaking material, but first, I would like to recall two examples of

3

the use of the animated film in mainstream live-action films which usefully foreground the rest of my discussion.

'If the story's so cock-eyed, what's the point of it?'

The Blackboard Jungle (1955), perhaps best remembered for the use of Bill Haley's 'Rock around the Clock' beneath the credits, features a sequence in which teacher Richard Dadier (Glenn Ford) uses a cartoon to engage a class of urban delinquents, including Black musician Greg Miller (Sidney Poitier) and sceptical, knife-wielding Artie West (Vic Morrow). Dadier recognises that the language of the cartoon, with its use of comedy, lack of obvious didacticism, and assumed ideological innocence, presents no threat to the class, and gives them amusement and diversion from the formality of normal classroom practice. In one of the first recorded instances of Film Study, Dadier then encourages the class to talk about the cartoon, using the tale of 'Jack and the Beanstalk' as educational stimulus. He essentially invites the class to use the cartoon to interrogate the fairytale. The boys evaluate the story, but simultaneously, if inadvertently, start to make comment upon the cartoon itself and ways in which it might be understood. They talk about narrative implausibility ('This is a fairytale, he just flew !'), the interpretation of character ('Jack, he ain't no hero, he's a pretty dumb hick'), the moral and ethical issues raised by the film ('Look, the way I got it figured, this Jack, he's a square. First off, he don't care if his old lady starves to death'), and who illicits sympathy in the story ('I kinda felt sorry for the giant').

Most importantly, from Dadier's point of view, the boys have the visceral pleasures of enjoying the film and laughing at its jokes, but start to locate the questions raised by the cartoon within their own experience. Confronted with the multiplicity of interpretations that the cartoon inspires, one boy says 'If the story's so cock-eyed, then what's the point of it?', which solicits the inevitable response from Dadier that he should 'Just examine the story, look for the real meaning'. The scene is a turning point in the film because both Dadier and his colleagues acknowledge that, for the first time, an educational breakthrough has occurred with previously disinterested and frequently delinquent students. I am not, of course, suggesting that studying animation is a panacea for all social ills, or that its study should be directed purely at those who seem to be on the edge of a life of crime! However, the scene does endorse the view that 'a cartoon' (read 'animated film') can carry important meanings and engage with social issues. In short, the animated film has the capacity to redefine the orthodoxies of live-action narratives and images, and address the human condition with as much authority and insight as any live-action film.

Preston Sturges' Sullivan's Travels (1941) corroborates this view in its deployment of the Disney short, Playful Pluto (1934). Chained convicts – criminals largely as a consequence of the Depression – are invited to join a black congregation to watch the cartoon as a small respite from their suffering. Among them is film director, John L. Sullivan (Joel McCrea), who has disguised himself so as to

Disney's *Playful Pluto*, like many of the Silly Symphonies, includes sequences which fully exploit the dynamics and extremes of visual humour which are only available in animation

experience life as a hobo in order to make a social-realist film, *Brother, Where Art Thou?*, concerned with social injustice. Sullivan has previously only made light comedies like *Hey, Hey in the Hay Loft* and *Ants in Your Plants*, films which he views as glib and trivial despite their success. Sturges' satire merely exposes Sullivan's naivety when Sullivan discovers that he genuinely knows nothing of real hardship and that those who constantly endure it find some comfort in laughter and the relief afforded by comedy, here explicitly illustrated by their enjoyment of *Playful Pluto*. Sturges was careful to construct the discourse between the audience and the action of the cartoon by choosing a purely visual sequence. As Brian Henderson suggests:

> The church movie scene in *Sullivan's Travels* required alternating brief bits of screen business with gales of laughter in the audience, a tide of mirth that Sullivan finds puzzling at first, then understands and resists, then gives way to. A cartoon scene that achieved its effects through dialogue would have initiated a logic that detracted from the logic of Sturges' own scene. . . . Showing Pluto trying to extricate himself from flypaper only to get ever more entangled fitted the bill perfectly.
>
> (Henderson, 1991: 161)

5

Sturges asks the audience of Sullivan's Travels to address the relationship between the audience in the film and the effects of the cartoon. Sullivan probably represents a certain kind of audience who resist the appeal of the cartoon but ultimately enjoy its mode of expression. Purely in visual terms the cartoon, echoing silent slapstick comedy, has the capacity to amuse but, more importantly, it possesses the ability to absolutely resist notions of the real world. I will address 'realism' within the animated film later in my discussion, but here it should be stressed that Sturges uses the cartoon to promote the idea that its very language represents the world in an intrinsically different way. The animated film creates a narrative space and visual environment radically different to the live-action version of the world. The cartoon here connotes escapism and unambiguous visual pleasure, albeit unthreatening and comforting, but the way Sturges contextualises the cartoon demands that its difference and effect be recognised.

Both Blackboard Jungle and Sullivan's Travels foreground the animated film as the vehicle by which significant moments of revelation and understanding take place. Both films thus invest the animated film with a specific ability to communicate complex, and sometimes contradictory, ideas within the framework of an apparently accessible, yet taken for granted, form. It is my intention in Understanding Animation to determine a number of methodologies which legitimise the analysis and interrogation of what, in the first instance, might seem to be self-evident texts made purely to entertain, and not to carry significant meanings about art and society. Further, it is my contention that animation as a film language and film art is a more sophisticated and flexible medium than live-action film, and thus offers a greater opportunity for film-makers to be more imaginative and less conservative. Blackboard Jungle and Sullivan's Travels implicitly recognise and foreground this in the sequences where cartoons are used. The animated film enables the film-maker(s) to be more expressive and thus more subversive than is readily acknowledged. Almost consciously, animators, in being aware that they, and their works, are marginalised and/or consigned to innocent, inappropriate or accidental audiences, use this apparently unguarded space to create films with surface pleasures and hidden depths. In Blackboard Jungle, the cartoon carries with it the idea that appearance and identity is a relative and constantly changing thing − a key element in all cartoons, while Sullivan's Travels uses the very anarchy and comic extremism of the cartoon to subvert the idea of representing the reality of the Depression in a film. It must be stressed, however, that the subject of my discussion is animation, and not merely the cartoon, which is only one of the forms I wish to address. Indeed, my analysis is an attempt to reconcile certain approaches to a variety of animated films, and to view animation as a distinctive form that works in entirely different ways from live-action cinema.

In using the 'difference' inherent in the animated film to counterpoint live-action, films like Blackboard Jungle and Sullivan's Travels demand that audiences compare the two forms. Animator Alexandre Alexeieff, writing in 1973, addressed this issue, and suggested that 'the repertoire of photographic cinema is limited and close to exhaustion' (Bendazzi, 1994: xxii) thus implying that animation would come to the fore and be recognised as the progressive medium that it is. This is a view wholly vindicated by: the championing of animation by broadcasting companies, commercial industries, museums and educational institutions in the 1990s; the use of animation as part of the repertoire of special effects deployed in mainstream cinema (echoing the use of animation by the pioneers); and the rise of computer animation almost as a new digital cinema in its own right. Alexeieff stressed,

> Contrary to live-action cinema, Animation draws the elements of its future works from a raw material made exclusively of human ideas, those ideas that different animators have about things, living beings and their forms, movements and meanings. They represent these ideas through images they make with their own hands. In the causal con-catenation of their images – a concatenation they conceive themselves – nothing can be left to chance. For this reason, creation requires an exceedingly long time which is out of proportion to live-action cinema. But the repertoire of human ideas is inexhaustible.
>
> (Bendazzi, 1994: xxii)

In emphasising the human aspects informing the uniqueness of animation Alex-eieff ironically highlights the illusiveness of the form. A first inspection seems to reveal that there are as many individual styles and approaches as there are individual animators, all engaged in the creation of an animated film. How then, is it possible, to address 'animation' given its apparent difference and multiplicity? The answer lies not in attempting to compile exhaustive lists of films or to provide profiles of major animators, though this is beneficial and important (see Bendazzi, 1994; Halas, 1987), but to try to suggest a number of ways in which any animated film may be addressed and analysed.

'So, what's the answer? Visual education?'

So asks one of Dadier's colleagues in *Blackboard Jungle* after his triumphant lesson using a cartoon. The study of animation has had to surmount the incredulity of both students and academics who have not recognised the medium as an impor-tant and neglected aspect of film-making practice, despite its obvious popularity and endurance in the face of passing generic and aesthetic trends in other areas of cinema. Animation has been trivialised and ignored despite its radical tendencies and self-evident artistic achievements at the technical and aesthetic level. Ironi-cally, the dominance of the *cartoon* (i.e. traditional 'cel' animation in the style of Disney or Warner Brothers, which is predicated on painting forms and figures directly onto sheets of celluloid which are then photographed) has unfortunately misrepresented the animated film *because* its art *seems* invisible or, more precisely, is taken for granted by its viewers. The *cartoon* seems part of an easily dismissed popular culture; 'animation', as a term, at least carries with it an aspiration for

7

recognition as art and, indeed, the proper evaluation of other animated forms. Importantly, though, scholars and historians have repositioned the cartoon as an art-form (see Adamson, 1975; Cabarga, 1988; Crafton, 1993; Holliss and Sibley, 1988), and provided the platform for the recovery of other kinds of animation, which may not have had the same kind of popular audience or terms of address, but deserve recognition and study nevertheless. This is particularly necessary in regard to the recovery of traditions of animation in other countries and in more experimental styles.

Understanding Animation represents the first tentative steps to introduce some of these agendas to students of animation, and to provide some models by which they may address a highly complex form exemplified in numerous ways by hundreds of animators worldwide. Understanding Animation is, therefore, part history, part theoretical speculation, and part spirited defence of a neglected but important film form. Inevitably, it will be flawed, seeking not to be definitive but provocative, providing the platform for future debate and revision. In many senses, it is a work in progress, half-informed by my own discovery of the form, half-driven by the desire to promote discourse about its achievements. The book is, therefore, divided into a number of areas of study – first, how the animated film may be addressed, both in relation to its history and evolution, and in regard to its modes of construction. Second, the ways in which the animated film possesses distinctive narrative techniques that inform its uniqueness as a medium of expression. Third, the methods by which animation engages with comedy. Fourth, the agendas raised in the animated film in regard to matters of representation and, finally, an engagement with the notion of spectatorship and animation, delineating some of the experiences enjoyed by its audience.

In order to foreground the relationship between the cartoon and other kinds of work, Understanding Animation theorises the cartoon as 'Orthodox Animation' while categorising other work as either 'Developmental Animation' or 'Experimental Animation'. These terms will be defined and illustrated in Chapter Two, but these categories essentially determine cel animation as orthodox animation; other kinds of accessible narrative based films, made in other forms (i.e. clay, puppets, collage etc.) as developmental animation; and finally, non-objective, non-linear or abstract films as experimental animation. Inevitably, some animation crosses over these definitions, but these terms offer general signposts for certain types of work. This is to begin to define the animated film at the level of form (i.e. the way in which it has been made) in the generation of meaning. It should be stressed here that form is being analysed through the text itself and not specifically through its technical preparation, although some attention will be paid to production processes in certain cases involving particularly unusual or imaginative techniques.

When addressing any of these topics, the choices of films constituting case studies are purely subjective, determined often by the availability of the films or the sheer desire to write about them. I have attempted, however, to include: films from a variety of different geographical contexts and historical periods; films reflecting a wide range of subject areas and approaches; films made by men and women, illustrating the increasing presence of women in the field and the creation of a 'feminine aesthetic' unique to animation; films of recognised significance and influence, and films which operate as models for similar kinds of film and thus represent a broader area. Inevitably, because I am writing from a British context, there are a number of British films under discussion in my analysis. For this I make no apology, especially in the light of the recent Oscar-winning achievements of Nick Park (*Creature Comforts* (1990); *The Wrong Trousers* (1994)), Daniel Greaves (*Manipulation* (1991)) and Alison Snowden and David Fine (*Bob's Birthday* (1995)). Similarly, the very dominance of the American cartoon tradition necessitates its prominance but, ironically, its predominance still remains fundamentally uninterrogated and these films will become fresh texts in the light of new theoretical approaches to them. Some areas of theoretical address, however, are only hinted at or partially addressed in the text. This is partly due to the limited space available to follow too many aspects of enquiry, and partly in the spirit of providing models which are are only half-formed in the hope that they will be developed. It is further hoped that ideas and issues raised will provide students with a set of transferable models for the study of animated films of their own choice. What is most significant about the multiplicity of approaches discussed here is that they may enable students to find an appropriate point of access for study in tune with their own interests and expand the discussion.

Animator Robert Breer once said in a revealing comment that, as an in-joke, animators often include a drawing of a brick within the continuity of a drawing of a moving object, for example, a bird flying. Of course, when an audience sees the film, it cannot see the brick as it passes too quickly for the eye to perceive but, interestingly, Breer suggests that once an audience has been told of the presence of the brick they observe the image much more closely. *Understanding Animation* will encourage the viewer of animated films to 'see the brick' in the sense that it will promote and provide the frameworks for a proper engagement with the animated film and the possibilities afforded by animation itself. To understand the particular illusion that is distinctive to animation is to penetrate its magic and its meaning.

1

THINKING ABOUT ANIMATED
FILMS

What is animation?

To animate, and the related words, animation, animated and animator all derive
from the latin verb, *animare*, which means 'to give life to', and within the context
of the animated film, this largely means the artificial creation of the illusion of
movement in inanimate lines and forms.[1] A working definition, therefore, of
animation in practice, is that it is a film made by hand, frame-by-frame, providing an illusion of movement which has not been directly recorded in the
conventional photographic sense. Although this is a definition which serves to
inform conventional cel, hand-drawn and model animation, it has proven insuf-
ficient in the description of other kinds of animation, particularly the kinds of
animation that have been facilitated by new technologies, chiefly those images
which are computer generated or subject to other kinds of pictorial manipulation.
Consequently, in order to reach a more precise definition, it is useful to consider
the view of Norman McClaren, one of the medium's acknowledged masters. He
says, 'Animation is not the art of drawings that move, but rather the art of
movements that are drawn. What happens *between* each frame is more important
than what happens *on* each frame' (Solomon, 1987: 11).

As suggested in the Introduction, McClaren reinforces the notion that the true
essence of animation is in the creation of movement on paper, the manipulation
of clay, the adjustment of a model etc., *before* the act of photographing the image,
i.e. the activity that has taken place between what become the final frames of film.
Animators of the Zagreb School, in the former Yugoslavia, however, seek to
develop this definition further by stressing the aesthetic and philosophic aspects
of the craft. They suggest, that to animate is 'to give life and soul to a design, not
through the copying but through the transformation of reality' (Holloway, 1972:
9). Though recognising the importance of animation as a technical process, the
Zagreb film-makers wanted to emphasise the creative aspect of literally 'giving life
to' the inanimate, revealing something about the figure or object in the process
which could not be understood under any other conditions. Film-makers at
Zagreb, including leading light, Dusan Vukotic, wanted to transform reality
and resist the kind of animation created by the Disney Studios which, for all its

personality and comic energy, conforms to a certain mode of realism concordant with live-action film-making, which in turn conforms to and reinforces a dominant ideological position within the USA. I will address the complex issue of 'realism' in the animated film a little further into my analysis but, at this stage, it is sufficient to say that the Zagreb School perceive animation as a non-realist and potentially subversive form. As if to confirm this point, British based animators, John Halas and Joy Batchelor, posit the view that, 'If it is the live-action film's job to present physical reality, animated film is concerned with metaphysical reality – not how things look, but what they mean' (Hoffer, 1981: 3).

Implicit in the study of the animated form is how 'meaning' is generated by the unique vocabulary available to the animator which is not the province of the live-action film-maker. Czech surrealist animator, Jan Svankmajer perceives this vocabulary as liberating, unique and potentially contentious:

> Animation enables me to give magical powers to things. In my films, I move many objects, real objects. Suddenly, everyday contact with things which people are used to acquires a new dimension and in this way casts a doubt over reality. In other words, I use animation as a means of subversion. [2]

Svankmajer's view probably best articulates the real possiblities available to the animator, in the sense that he stresses how animation can redefine the everyday, subvert our accepted notions of 'reality', and challenge the orthodox understanding and acceptance of our existence. Animation can defy the laws of gravity, challenge our perceived view of space and time, and endow lifeless things with dynamic and vibrant properties. Animation can create original effects – a point well understood by pioneer film-makers like Georges Méliès and early animators like J. Stuart Blackton, Emile Cohl and Winsor McCay.

Flipbooks, frame-by-frame and funny faces

The development of the animated form is specifically related to the early experiments in the creation of the moving image. As early as 70 BC there is evidence of a mechanism that projected hand-drawn moving images onto a screen, described by Lucretius in De Rerum Natura. In the sixteenth century, 'flipbooks', like the one described by Doctorow earlier, emerged in Europe and often contained erotic drawings which, when flicked, showed the performance of sexual acts. It is interesting to speculate that this kind of drawing, pornographic though it probably was, prefigures the type of animation which resists realistic representation, and recognises the possibility in 'animation' of expressing feelings and thoughts about taboo subjects without inhibition. The realisation of movement in these drawings clearly transcribes the acts themselves into another medium and privileges the act of 'looking', but also foregrounds the notions of recognition and complicity. The idea of 'looking' was properly addressed in 1825, when Peter

Mark Roget wrote what was later to be called the 'Persistence of Vision' theory. This theory determined why human beings could perceive movement, i.e. that the human eye sees one image and carries with it an after-image onto the image that follows it, thus creating an apparent continuity. This is of the utmost importance in watching moving pictures in general, of course, but is particularly significant in legitimising the kind of animated cinema that was to be achieved frame-by-frame. The 'persistance of vision', as it were, was the very recognition of the movement achieved between the frames that McClaren stresses is the essence of animation.

With developments like the Phenakistoscope pioneered by Plateau in 1831; the Zoetrope, invented by W.G. Horner in 1834; Coleman Sellers' Kinematoscope in 1861, and the Praxinoscope, described earlier, and patented by Reynaud in 1877, there was the eventual emergence of the cinematic apparatus.[3] Still intrinsic to the understanding of these developments was the idea of the moving image as essentially magical – something colourful, playful and 'miraculous' in its manip-ulation of still images. This notion was essentially eradicated by the realism of early cinema photography, but perpetuated in trick films and forms akin to, and instrumental in, the continuing development of the animated film.

This may be most obviously seen in the comic strip form, which was estab-lished in the American print media industries by the late 1890s. This is important because the comic strip was to help provide some of the initial vocabulary for the cartoon film,

> [. . .] including continuous narration, whereby a single set of char-acters appears repeatedly from frame to frame and the action progresses from left to right; calligraphic caricature, which renders the protago-nists and their adversaries immediately recognisable; facial and gestural schemata, which express the characters' actions and reactions; action abstraction, a pictorial shorthand, universally understood, in which exploding lines indicate sudden impact, stars unconsciousness, light bulbs ideas and balloon puffs thoughts; literary legend, conveyed in a balloon, which clarifies the comic's visual message; and specialised vocabularies, such as 'Banana Oil!', 'Zap!' and 'Pow!' which heighten the extreme emotion or action manifested by the characters.
>
> (O'Sullivan, 1990: 9)

By 1893, the *New York World* and *New York Journal* were using colour printing in their strips and these may be seen as prototypic of later animated forms. Indeed, Richard Felton Outcault, working in the *Journal's* 'American Humorist' supple-ment, created *Hogan's Alley*, which featured as its main character, the Yellow Kid, who was printed yellow as a test for the new tallow-drying process. As Judith O'Sullivan notes, 'Since then the term yellow journalism, popularly supposed to have derived from the Yellow Kid, has been applied to newspapers that feature sensational reporting and conspicuous display as a means of attracting viewers'

(O'Sullivan, 1990: 13). 'The Yellow Kid' anticipates another yellow kid, Bart Simpson, by about one hundred years, but the creator of *The Simpsons*, Matt Groenig, also a cartoonist before becoming an animator, similarly coloured his characters yellow in order to create a conspicuous identity for his animated family and enable 'channel-surfing' viewers to locate the programme with ease.

The relationship between the comic strip and the animated cartoon will be examined further later but, before the formalism of the comic strip became an intrinsic part of animation, 'animation' itself was still in the hands of the magicians. Chief in the development of 'trick effects' in the emergent cinema was Georges Méliès. The story of his accidental discovery of the 'dissolve' (i.e. when one image fades into another) when his camera accidentally jammed, led him to pioneer a whole number of other cinematic effects which have become intrinsic to the possibilities available to animators. These included 'stop motion photography', split-screen techniques, fast and slow motion, and the manipulation of live action within painted backdrops and scenery. Méliès was also a 'lightning cartoonist', caricaturing contemporary personalities, speeding up their 'construction' on screen by undercranking the camera. In many ways animators and animation, during this early primitive period, were the first to self-consciously address the possibilities of the medium in an aesthetic rather than technical way. The divorce between live-action cinema and animation as its own art was imminent.

By 1900, J. Stuart Blackton had made *The Enchanted Drawing*. He appeared as a 'lightning cartoonist' drawing a man smoking a cigar and drinking some wine. By the use of stop motion, one drawing at a time is revealed and the man's face is made to take on various expressions. Various similar films emerged, including *The Vanishing Lady* (1898) and *A Visit to the Spiritualist* (1899). These films can be classified proto-animation as they use techniques that are used by later animators but are not strictly and wholly made frame-by-frame. Blackton achieved full animation of this sort in *Humorous Phases of Funny Faces* (1906). Though using full animation in key sequences, the film was still essentially a series of tricks. Primitive notions of narrative animation followed in the early work of famous comic strip artist, Winsor McCay, who under Blackton's supervision at the Vitagraph Brooklyn Studio made an animated version of his most celebrated strip, *Little Nemo in Slumberland*, in 1911. In an extraordinarily prescient moment, McCay, interviewed in the *Buffalo Enquirer* in July 1912, anticipated the conflation of the graphic arts and cinema that became the animated film industry:

> There will be a time when people will gaze at [paintings] and ask why the objects remain rigid and stiff. They will demand action. And to meet this demand the artists of that time will look to the motion picture for help and the artist, working hand in hand with science, will evolve a new school of art that will revolutionise the entire field.
>
> (Quoted in O'Sullivan, 1990: 26)

Figure 1.1 J. Stuart Blackton's 'trick' film, *The Haunted Hotel*, was vigorously promoted by Vitagraph in order to perpetuate the popularity of such films. Simultaneously, it enhanced the view that the animated short might become more commercially viable

Blackton's influence in the process towards this achievement cannot be understated as he is responsible for distinguishing the concept of the animated film as a viable aesthetic and economic vehicle outside the context of orthodox live-action cinema. His film, *The Haunted Hotel* (1907), a simple narrative piece with impressive supernatural sequences, was instrumental in convincing audiences and financiers alike that the animated film had an agenda and position all of its own, unique in its form and unlimited in its potential. As Donald Crafton has noted, *The Haunted Hotel*, was not significantly different from a number of trick-films and short animations that preceded it, but Vitagraph vociferously publicised the film, and sought to extend the popularity of such films at a time when it was thought to be waning, by deliberately *mystifying* the process of their creation (Crafton, 1993). Similarly, the *un-natural* acts and events that took place in these films chimed with the changes in the cultural climate. Suddenly, the magical agendas of Gothic and Romantic fiction found some basis in the technological possibilities of the newly industrialised Modernist age. In what Crafton describes as a 'turn of the century fascination with self-propulsion' (Crafton, 1993: 32), the reality of the aircraft and the automobile co-existed with the animated fictions of *apparently* moving objects, often drawn from the domestic sphere, and, most usually, toys and utensils. The material and specifically non-human seemed invested with life. As reknowned Russian film-maker and theorist, Sergei Eisenstein, recognised 'if it moves, *then* it's alive; i.e. moved by an innate, independent, volitional impulse' (Leyda, 1988: 54). This sense of *aliveness*, ironically gave animation a particularly

14

enigmatic quality, signifying kineticism yet denying its source and possible intention. The illusion of life in animation was profoundly more challenging than the
seemingly unmediated and recognisable representation of reality in live-action
films, despite their novelty as an emergent popular art. As such, the animated film
was soon perceived as something intrinsically different from the kind of films that
began to constitute popular cinema. The animated film thus became defined by its
distinctive technical and aesthetic qualities, in both two- and three-dimensional
forms.

The Haunted Hotel had been released in the USA and France. In France, French
animator, Emile Cohl, completed his Fantasmagorie in 1908. His later film, En Route,
was released in the United States in 1910. Cohl employed a technique in line
drawing where lines would fall randomly into the frame and converge into a
character or event. Cohl's incoherent cinema was essentially the free flow of seemingly
unrelated images in the stream- of-consciousness style of the Modernist writers.[4]
Further inspection reveals an implied, and more significant, level of relatedness in
the imagery, prefiguring later animated films which trust the elements intrinsic to
animation, chiefly, the primacy of the image, and its ability to metamorphose into a
completely different image. Such metamorphoses operate as the mechanism
which foregrounds this new relatedness by literally revealing construction and
deconstruction, stasis and evolution, mutability and convergence. Such imagery
did not operate as a set of visual tricks or jokes, nor did it constitute a conventional literary narrative, but was a kinetic construction wholly determined by the
choices made by the animator, relating images purely on his own personal terms,
sometimes by obvious association, sometimes by something entirely within the
domain of his own psychological and emotional involvement with the visual
system.

This technique was borrowed by McCay in Little Nemo and informed his other
key works as he translated his comic strip style into the newly established
animated form. Based on one of his 1909 comic strips, Dreams of a Rarebit Fiend,
McCay made The Story of a Mosquito (1912), a mock horror story of a mosquito
graphically feeding on a man until it is so bloated with blood that it explodes.
McCay differed from Cohl, however, in prioritising narrative clarity, even in the
most apparently illogical or irrational dreams that informed his stories. The sense
of narrative sequence in McCay's films is the trait he most obviously maintains from
his comic strips. McCay's most significant contribution to the animated form
though is the development of personality or character animation through his
creation of Gertie the Dinosaur (1914). The playful dinosaur Gertie gleefully hurls a
mammoth into a lake in the film and clearly displays an attitude. This anthro-
pomorphism (the endowment of creatures with human attributes, abilities and
qualities) later informs the work of Walt Disney, and indeed, remains the consistent locus of a great deal of animation, raising questions about the role and
identity of beasts and their behaviour which is discussed in relation to gender
issues in Chapter Five. McCay clearly saw Gertie as 'a woman with her own
mind', and sought to authenticate her identity in its own right by conducting a

15

dialogue with her when he showed his film during his vaudeville act. McCay attempted to sustain the illusion that Gertie was corresponding to his commentary by synchronising his actions accordingly and concluded his film with Gertie apparently lifting McCay up while he, of course, exits stage left. McCay appears to pass into the film, and provides an example of what would become a continuing discourse between animation and live-action film in the medium's early years. It is as if the early animators wanted to constantly expose the limitations of representing 'reality' on film and insist upon the domain of 'fantasy' as: first, the most appropriate mode of expression for the cinematic form and, most specifically, the animated form; second, as the most versatile model by which to create amusement and illusion; and third, as the most expressive vocabulary by which to interrogate the complexities of the human condition.[5]

This may seem too grand a claim for these early vehicles, but it is important to note that McCay's subject matter was deliberately chosen to avoid the notion that its creation was in any way bound up with the achievements in photography. Mythic, extinct, or microscopic creatures, the characters that feature in McCay's work could not be photographed, yet all are characterised by an authentic principle of motion, thus heightening both the belief in the creatures themselves, but also the capability of the medium. McCay's animated films clearly represent a development in animation at the technical and artistic level, using self-conscious exploitation of the codes and conventions of the comic strip form to successfully conjoin the apparently surreal with the conditions of the real world. McCay's comic strips and films aspire to the condition of an interior state rationalised by external mechanisms, constructing narratives which reveal some of humankind's deep-rooted fears in the Modernist era. These are chiefly anxieties about relationships, the status of the body, and advances in technology, all of which evoke threat and disorder, and it is, perhaps, ironic that these kind of themes are only properly acknowledged in McCay's work when he makes the first animated documentary, The Sinking of the Lusitania (1918), which uses a realist mode to engage with the horrors of the tragedy. Interestingly, his approach to animation still corresponds to McCay's, in the sense that this too was an event that was impossible to record. His film, therefore, becomes part informed speculation, part quasi-newsreel, part propaganda, and raises many further issues about animation and the representation of reality, which I will discuss later.

While McCay can claim to have created the first colour cartoon (he hand-tinted at least one of the prints of Little Nemo), and produced a cel-animated film, Winsor McCay Makes His Cartoons Move (1911), (using rice-paper cels), it is John R. Bray who, incorporating similar initiatives by another animator, Earl Hurd, pioneered the cel-animation process using translucent cels in 1913, and made a film called The Artist's Dream. At about this time, Raoul Barre also developed the first production process which enabled animated films to be made by a number of people with specific roles within an industrialised studio base. Bray studios soon developed a similar process and released a series of cartoons with a continuing character, 'Colonel Heeza Liar', a parody of President Teddy Roosevelt, and demonstrated the viability of animation as a commercial industry capable of mass production. This move towards the industrialisation of animation as a film-making process was viable at the economic level but had significant consequences in inhibiting the development of the form itself on purely creative terms. The individual nature of animation was essentially sacrificed to collective production, and this could be achieved by allying the production of animated films with the specific vocabulary of the comic strip, which could be readily understood by all the available animators. 'Individuality', at this stage, could only be properly expressed through the content of the films as the emergent industry quickly rationalised its form in order to maximise efficiency of production and distribution. In essence, this meant that individuality could only be expressed through the primacy of 'gags' and the evolution of a comic vocabulary that has since come to dominate the form (see Chapter Four).

Between 1913 and 1917, the dominant mode of animated film was the adaption of the comic strip. In 1913: Eclair released *The Newlyweds*, based on a strip by George McManus which he had drawn some nine years earlier, animated by Emile Cohl; Essanay released and distributed the 'Dreamy Dud' series, drawn by Chicago Interocean cartoonist, Wallace Carlson; Earl Hurd joined John Bray, and with Gregory LaCava, produced animated versions of popular comic strips like George Herriman's 'Krazy Kat' and Rudolph Dirks' 'Katzenjammer Kids'; and Raoul Barre partnered Charles Bowers in the production of a series of cartoons featuring Bud Fisher's characters, 'Mutt and Jeff'. It is worth noting here that if the aesthetic considerations of animation were still located in the dynamics of movement itself, the industrial aspects determined that animation should concern itself with entertainment values. These were soon consolidated into cartoonal concepts that partly define the first apotheosis of animation yet also determine the limits that the industrial process was implicitly placing on the further development of the form.

Case study: Early comic strip cartoon concepts

Soda Jerks (1920) by Hurd and Barre, serves as an interesting example of the early cartoon form in the sense that it represents how the comic strip creates a vocabulary for the animated short. Mutt, a gangly authoritarian straight-man, and Jeff, a small, balding, clown-figure, with a handlebar moustache that stretches right across his face to his sideburns, are two characters already established in the public mind by H.C. 'Bud' Fisher's popular comic strip. Fisher's work was often characterised by moments of comic reversal. In one example, Jeff tells Mutt that he has invented a pair of spectacles that enlarge things to enormous proportions and that he intends to sell them to baseball players on the basis that the ball will appear so large no player will ever fail to hit it. Mutt counters that the same glasses will make first base seem miles away and the ploy will backfire. Defeated Jeff exits, leaving Mutt longingly examining a tiny 'New York steak' made huge by wearing the glasses. The strip defines the relationship between the

17

two characters and demonstrates a comic logic that simultaneously enjoys the physical comedy around the issue of size and shape, the manipulation of expected outcomes to develop the comedy, and the satiric edge which implicitly critiques New York butchers and restaurateurs.

In *Soda Jerks*, Hurd and Barre cast Mutt as the owner of a soda parlour and Jeff as his underdog counter assistant. The parlour and, indeed, many figures throughout the cartoon remain static, revealing Barre's 'slash' method of animation in which only the aspects of each frame which moved were actually animated. This involved creating a sequence of movements already drawn on sheets and placed in a pile, the areas designated to move, 'slashed', or torn, as it were, from the top image to reveal the next movement, while the background remained unchanged. This perpetuates the look and style of the comic strip, and the sense of linear progression in the narrative that comic strip readers were accustomed to, but it also privileges the narrative importance of certain movements, and the function of the movements in the creation of physical comedy.

Jeff tries to impress a lady customer, not merely by serving her, but by standing on a box jerkily posing and dancing. He blushes, graphic hearts appearing over his head popping with embarrassment, before Mutt pushes him away, whereupon he receives a blow on the head with an umbrella from another irate lady customer and falls into a box. The influence of silent slapstick comedy is readily apparent here, but is exaggerated yet further by the elasticity of the animation and the accompanying convention of spinning stars around Jeff's head. Hurd and Barre attempt to reduce the number of speech 'bubbles' which characterise the comic strip, preferring to tell the story visually, and employ title cards for important lines of dialogue. Mutt says 'Boy, get me some syrup' which angers Jeff, who, feeling humiliated, exacts his revenge by filling the syrup tank with 'Pep – A Powerful Tonic', a bottle of which stands incongruously among the syrup bottles. This is essentially the establishing premise of the narrative, which then becomes a sequence of 'spot gags' based on the consequences of different characters mistakenly drinking the tonic. This structure is also common to many later cartoons which prioritise 'gags' over story and deploy what Gerald Mast calls 'riffing' in improvising a number of comic events within a given situation (Mast and Cohen, 1974: 462).

The cartoon becomes faster; the woman who first drinks the tonic dances frantically, puts a glass on Mutt's nose (which Jeff breaks with a mallet), and tumbles into the street, her vocal wails of 'Whoops' and 'Whee-ee' literally written on the image. Bystanders, and particularly a standard silent cinema coupling of a small man and a tall woman, venture into the soda parlour to find out what is happening. They too, take the tonic. The tonic, in being the chief catalyst for the action, and the mechanism by which any notion of 'realism' may be disrupted, legitimises Hurd and Barre to use the narrative space purely for a display of the possibilities available to the animated form. For example, once the couple drink the tonic, their heads become subject to the squash and stretch technique, whereby given the supposed effects of the tonic, their heads elongate

18

and compress in the comic fashion of a body reflected in a hall of mirrors. These movements are accompanied by 'action abstraction', i.e. quivering white lines which accentuate the physical changes. The sequence climaxes with the couple emitting puffs of smoke – their bodies apparently having boiled over or exploded. Notions of the body becoming mechanistic will be discussed in my analysis of comic modes in animation which, in themselves, are clearly a major factor of the evolution of the animated film.

The couple, like the first woman, pirouette into the street, and it is here that the cartoon demonstrates its capacity not merely to construct comic effects, but to legitimise the breaking of taboo, an important factor that is to characterise the development of the animated film. The very language of animation seems to carry with it an inherent innocence which has served to disguise and dilute the potency of some of its more daring imagery. I will return to this issue throughout my discussion but, in this instance, it is sufficient to say that the actions of the couple in Soda Jerks – the exposure of the woman's frilly undergarments, tying the policeman's truncheon in a knot, ripping the policeman's uniform and biting his shin – all operate, despite their apparent comic innocence, as subversive acts. Though it may be argued at this point that these events merely echo the comic business of the silent movies, it is important to recognise that as the animated film progresses, its acts of subversion become more complex and radical but seemingly remain innocent by virtue of the form in which they are created Issues of gender, sex and sexuality, and law and order are being played out in this comic scenario, but they are essentially ignored because they are part of 'a cartoon'. The transgressive possibilities available to the cartoon, therefore, seem limitless, and this has not been lost on animators since the evolution of the form. A cartoon like Soda Jerks is just the beginning.

Like many later cartoons, as well as employing 'spot gags', Soda Jerks uses a 'running gag'. In this instance it is the recurrence of a policeman's attempts to telephone the police station in order to report the anarchic events emanating from the soda parlour. The station sergeant remains asleep (naturally signified by closed eyes, his hand propped on his chin and numerous accompanying 'z's) even though he sits directly next to the phone. The phone, of course, quivers when it rings while its sound is signified once more by the action abstraction of white lines emerging from it. The policeman finally wakes the sergeant by taking the cartoon option of literally reaching through the phone and hitting him on the head. This operates as a piece of comic logic which becomes a typical part of the cartoon, i.e. the literal appropriation of space which, in reality, either does not exist or cannot be physically attained. The assumption here is that the policeman can extend his arm, reach through an object, follow the route of the assumed phone line, and completely violate and compress any notion of time and space. The creation of 'impossible' events becomes, of course, the stock-in-trade of all animated films.

Meanwhile, the man from the couple dances in the street in front of a group of

19

bystanders who, not surprisingly, marvel when the man's shoes dance on their own. The importance of 'dance' in animation must not be understated as, even in its comic form here, it anticipates sophisticated use in later work which allies the choreographic possibilities of physical expression with the open agenda of the principle of motion as it exists in animation (see Chapter Three). After climaxing his street performance by diving into his own hat, the man tells the crowd about the parlour, and all trample over him in their desire to try the soda for themselves. They too pirouette and cartwheel into the street – a heavily bandaged man on crutches miraculously tumbles down the road seemingly uninhibited by his condition while another man jumps out of his clothes, only to see his clothes jump along the road of their own accord. Another woman dives into a water wagon, and a dog who licks the tonic becomes endowed with ever-stretching legs and empowered to chase the dog-catcher, metamorphosing into a lion, a tiger, a rhinocerous, and an elephant as he does so! The comic reversal of the dog chasing the dog-catcher is a clever ploy, but even more engaging is the use of animation to enable the dog to literally change into other creatures in order to signify his aggression and power. I will address metamorphosis as an important aspect of animation later, particularly in regard to its use as a narrative as opposed to a 'magical' device.

The cartoon concludes by directly referencing the style of comedy epitomised by the Keystone Cops in the silent era. Hundreds of police tumble into a tiny police patrol van – the kind of comic exaggeration common in the cartoon – but a signifier also of animation's capacity to engage with and interrogate the viewers' willing suspension of disbelief. As I will suggest throughout my discussion, the tension between belief and disbelief is integral to the achievement and effect of animation as a form. Here the action is taken for granted as a joke but serves to operate in other ways as the medium develops. Once the soda parlour is barricaded and padlocked by the police, Mutt finally has the revelation that Jeff has done something to the syrup fountain. Mutt sniffs the air, his nose gesture accompanied by the word 'sniff', and punishes Jeff by making him drink the rest of the tonic. Jeff, of course, merely fights back, leaving Mutt with stars spinning around his head, and having broken down the parlour door, he takes a piece of wood to the police in the van who flee down the street. Hurd and Barre use the speech balloon common to the comic strip for the first time in a particularly humourous way as it is the policemen who cry 'Help!' and 'Police!' as Jeff continues to attack them. In an escalatory style – later employed by Tex Avery – Jeff throws first a tyre, then a big wooden box, then the whole van, at the police, before spinning Mutt around over his head in what was later to be true Popeye style. The final gag in the cartoon also becomes one of the commonest in later Warner Brothers cartoons, when Mutt defies gravity, hovers in the air temporarily, and finally crashes to the floor with imperfect grace but perfect comic timing. Mutt's humiliation is complete.

20

Disney and the realist principle

Cartoons emerged into the market place in the USA at the same time that more experimental abstract animation was beginning to surface in Europe, particularly through film-makers such as Oskar Fischinger and Walter Ruttmann. This kind of work developed from a more experimental tradition in the graphic and fine arts and, essentially, has come to represent the notion of the avant-garde in animation. I will address this tradition later in this chapter. Clearly though, animation, in whatever form and whatever context, was an expressive vehicle with Modernist credentials – simultaneously, animation was developing its own aesthetic language, and seeking new technologies to facilitate its future progress as both an industry and an art form. Donald Crafton describes Felix the Cat as 'the quintessential cartoon of the 1920s' (Crafton, 1993: 301) chiefly because of its growing popularity and its comic invention (see Chapter Four). Otto Messmer's Chaplinesque cat spoke to an American public willing to fully immerse themselves in fantasy, but a fantasy properly understood to be the product of the medium, and not merely the representation of the free imagery of a dream-state. As Crafton has noted,

> Felix's everyday world is already in excess of anything that we might find in a dream. To show him awakening at the end of a film would have been superfluous. When other animators indulged in irrational imagery, they seemed compelled to draw back from accepting its consequences. The dream-framing device, one of the most important animation codes, acts to establish the limits of rational thought. In American cartoons, as in American art in general, the demarcation between fact and fantasy was usually heeded scrupulously. Felix, however, never shies away from the irrational. He accepts it as ordinary.
>
> (Crafton, 1993: 342)

The free agenda of Felix vehicles most often rendered the character as a heroic outsider, who, for example, in Felix Revolts (1924) becomes a political activist campaigning against the maltreatment of cats. This free expression was legitimised by the openness of Messmer's style of animation. Felix could do anything. He was the master of both the narrative space and the graphic space. This meant that he could straddle the line between rational and irrational discourse without self-consciousness. As Crafton suggested, this was unusual in the American creative context because its very style refuted moral and ideological certainty (Crafton, 1993). Felix did not live in the 'real world', and thus could operate outside its moral and ideological constraints. Sometimes, Felix's environment was significantly enough like the 'real world', however, for him to represent alternative and radical agendas. Animation legitimised the social and political ambivalence of such narratives by simultaneously approximating some of the conditions of real existence whilst distancing itself from them by recourse to the unique aspects of its own vocabulary. It was this potentially subversive aspect of the animated form that was enjoyed by Sergei Eisenstein:

> In a country and social order with such a mercilessly standardized and mechanically measured existence, which is difficult to call life, the sight of such 'omnipotence' (that is, the ability to become, 'whatever you wish'), cannot but hold a sharp degree of attractiveness. This is as true for the United States as it is for the petrified canons of world-outlook, art and philosophy of eighteenth century Japan.
>
> (Leyda, 1988: 21)

Eisenstein effectively equates the apparent freedom of the animated form with personal and ideological freedom. He implicitly suggests that audiences recognised that animation succeeded in demonstrating liberation from social constraint and the fulfilment of personal desire. The freedom of expression sustained in animation was essentially a utopian language, appealing because of the 'rejection of once-and-forever allotted form, freedom from ossification, the ability to dynamically assume any form' (Leyda, 1988: 21). This condition, which Eisenstein called *plasmaticness*, resisted being fixed and stable. In his view, this mutability, the very condition of the animated film, recalled primal states, and relocated contemporary culture within the context of its own evolutionary development. The animated film offered comfort in its unconscious echo of the evolutionary principle *and* demonstrated quasi-revolutionary conditions. Eisenstein felt that it was this sense of changeability and reformation that was lost in a Modernist era driven by the imperatives of the machine. Whilst Eisenstein championed the *aesthetic* principles inherent in the language of animation, and most particularly in Disney's early works, Disney himself became more preoccupied with the development of animation as an *industry*, and most specifically in the development of new technologies. As Merritt and Kaufman note, 'the story of Disney's silent film career is not so much a struggle for artistic expression as it is a fight for commercial stability' (Merritt and Kaufman, 1993: 15).

Disney established Walt Disney Productions in 1923, making his *Laugh-O-Grams*, which were mainly adaptations of popular fairytales like *Puss in Boots*, before embarking on his part animation, part live-action *Alice in Wonderland* films, which featured all the quasi-revolutionary *form* and *content* which so enamoured Eisenstein. This was best expressed in *Alice Rattled by Rats* (1925), in which Merritt and Kaufman suggest 'Nowhere is Disney more exuberant or inventive in showing underlings gloriously taking over the master's domain', a condition also reflected in other *Alice* films in which Disney 'shows kids cutting school, shoplifting and playing hookey, hoboes free from having to work, prisoners escaping prison, or simply Alice running away to have adventures' (Merritt and Kaufman, 1993: 20). In 1927 though, he began working on his 'Oswald the Rabbit' series of cartoons, and this may be seen as the turning point, not merely in Disney's career, but in the development of animation in general. *The Mechanical Cow* (1927), the first cartoon featuring Oswald, may be seen as the moment when Disney left behind the surrealist tendencies of Otto Messmer and the Fleischer brothers, and prioritised the idea of *mechanism*, in regard to both form and content. His films increasingly demonstrate the relationship between the organic and the machine, a relationship that was also of paramount concern to Disney in the very making of animation. During this period, he developed 'the pencil test' (i.e. photographing a pencil drawn sequence to check its quality of movement and authenticity before it proceeded to be drawn on cels, painted etc.). A year later, in 1928, Disney premiered *Steamboat Willie*, featuring Mickey Mouse, which was the first synchronised sound cartoon.[6] Disney then introduced Technicolor, the three-colour system into his Silly Symphony, *Flowers and Trees* (1932), which later won an Oscar. Disney's concentration on innovations in the apparatus to facilitate the animated film ultimately had the consequence, however, of undermining the distinctive aspects of animation itself. Eisenstein admired Disney's films because they represented the attempt to force 'the self-contained objective representational form to behave as a non-material volitional play of free lines and surfaces' (Leyda, 1988: 99). With each technical development, however, Disney moved further away from the plasmatic flexibility of many of the early Silly Symphonies, and coerced the animated form into a neo-realist practice.

Even though Disney dealt with what was a predominantly abstract, non-realist form, he insisted on verisimilitude in his characters, contexts and narratives. He wanted animated figures to move like real figures and be informed by a plausible motivation. As Disney's studio grew and embarked on ever more ambitious projects, most notably the creation of a full-length animated feature, Disney's animators undertook programmes of training in the skills and techniques of fine art in the constant drive towards ever greater notions of realism. Animals had to move like real animals but it was important that the complexity of this movement must be unnoticeable, a condition achieved through the dexterity of the artist's skill in drawing the creatures. Simultaneously, the *ideological* freedoms of animated films displaying both graphic and narrational anarchy, gave way to the overtly moral confrontations within *realistic* scenarios.

This level of reality was further enhanced by the development of the multi-plane camera. Traditionally, in the two-dimensional image, the illusion of perspective had to be created by the artist. As the camera approaches an image like this – for example, cattle grazing outside a farmhouse on a moonlit night – the image loses its perspective as the elements merely enlarge and the moon becomes as big as the farmhouse or cattle. The multi-plane camera stops this from occuring because the image is painted in perspective on different panes of glass that are placed directly behind each other, but have the ability to move. To use my example, the cattle would be painted in the foreground, the farmhouse behind the cattle in the field, and the moon in the background, so when the camera moves through the image, all the elements stay in perspective. Disney's Silly Symphony, *The Old Mill* (1937), successfully demonstrated this technique, but it found its most advanced and persuasive use in the first full-length animated feature, *Snow White and the Seven Dwarfs* (1937). In many senses, Disney had aligned animation with aspects of photographic realism, and misrepresented the form's more distinctive characteristics.

The animated film had reached maturity, but in doing so had established Disney as synonymous with 'animation'. This has led to animation being understood in a limited way. Disney perfected a certain language for the cartoon and the full-length feature which took its model from live-action film-making.[7] This overshadowed other types of innovation and styles of animation which have extended the possibilities of the form and enabled other kinds of film to be made. Consequently, and ironically, Disney's dominance of the medium places the issue of 'realism' at the centre of any discussion of animation. Disney rightly concluded that a full-length feature could not be sustained upon the limited premises of a sequence of gags, which, of course, characterised the animated short, but in aspiring to the conditions of the live-action feature he creates conditions by which the intrinsic qualities of animation are overlooked. First then, before I address those particular qualities, it is important to define the notion of realism in animation in order to readily perceive how the form's specific claims are measured against it.

Case study: The problem of realism

Any definition of 'reality' is necessarily subjective. Any definition of 'realism' as it operates within any image-making practice is also open to interpretation. Certain traditions of film-making practice, however, have provided models by which it is possible to move towards some consensus of what is recognisably an authentic representation of reality. This may range from the non-fiction film (i.e. travelogue, documentary etc.), through to neo-realist fictions (i.e. the films that emerged from post-war Italy or the 'kitchen sink' dramas made in Britain in the early 1960s). It may be argued that this type of apparently objective film-making is only concerned with external reality and the representation of ordinary, everyday existence. Other kinds of cinema, principally the work of the surrealists, therefore, prioritised psychological approaches, suggesting that 'reality' is a matter of how it is perceived or unconsciously mediated. 'Realism', it seems, is a relative thing, but the kind of film which seems to most accurately represent 'reality' is the kind of film which attempts to rid itself of obvious cinematic conventions in the prioritisation of recording the people, objects, environments and events which characterise the common understanding of lived experience. Any film-making practice, however, is necessarily self-conscious, and this is where any attempt to define 'realism' in the cinema comes unstuck. Principles of organisation and manipulation intervene with any notion that a film has shown unmediated reality. Similarly, any film that claims to be 'true' or merely showing the facts is probably going to be challenged on the grounds that it is 'false' or just fiction. The animated film, inevitably, complicates these issues even further.

Significantly though, animation immediately extricates itself from these kind of

24

debates by already being a medium which is informed by self-evident principles of construction. Animation does not share the same method and approach of the live-action film. Rather, it prioritises its capacity to *resist* 'realism' as a mode of representation and uses its various techniques to create numerous styles which are fundamentally *about* 'realism'. As Eco notes, apropos of Disney's theme parks, 'to speak of things that one wants to connote as real, these things must seem real. The "completely real" becomes identified with the "completely fake". Absolute unreality is offered as real presence' (Eco, 1986: 7). In many senses this view defines animation in general (i.e. animation is a 'completely fake' medium by virtue of the fact that it does not use the camera to 'record' reality but artificially creates and records its own), but it most particularly defines the kind of animation which aspires to the creation of a realistic image system which echoes the 'realism' of the live-action film. This, using Eco's term, is 'hyper-realism', and fundamentally defines the films of Disney, and those who emulate the studio's style. For Disney, and others working in this way, to connote 'reality', however, the construction of, and the contexts created within, the films, must necessarily aspire to verisimilitude, even when making films with fairytale narratives or using animals or caricatured humans as the main characters.

'Realism' as I have already suggested is a relative term, but within animation it is useful to locate the 'hyper-realism' of the Disney films as the yardstick by which other kinds of animation may be measured for its relative degree of 'realism'. In other words, the animated film may be defined as non-realist or abstract the more it deviates from the model of 'hyper-realism' located in the Disney film, and principally a full-length feature like *Bambi* (1942), which even as ardent a supporter of Disney's work as Eisenstein found too lyrical and unrepresentative of the language of animation in which Disney's previous work had revelled (Leyda, 1988: 98–9). Consequently, the relativity of 'realism' within the context of animation may prove to be a valid analytical tool because some films may be categorised as more 'realistic' than others, or may work in a style that connotes a greater degree of 'realism' than another style etc. Informing the hyper-realist style are some key codes and conventions which enable these kind of comparisons to take place. These are:

- The design, context and action within the hyper-realist animated film approximates with, and corresponds to the design, context and action within the live-action film's representation of reality.
- The characters, objects and environment within the hyper-realist animated film are subject to the conventional physical laws of the 'real' world.
- The 'sound' deployed in the hyper-realist animated film will demonstrate diegetic appropriateness and correspond directly to the context from which it emerges (e.g. a person, object or place must be represented by the sound it actually makes at the moment of utterance, at the appropriate volume etc.).
- The construction, movement and behavioural tendencies of 'the body' in

25

the hyper-realist animated film will correspond to the orthodox physical aspects of human beings and creatures in the 'real' world.

Clearly, these conventions transcend the subject matter of the films and the style and techniques employed to make them. They are the codes by which verisimilitude is achieved. The more the animated film corresponds to these codes the more hyper-realist it will seem, whether it be Disneyesque in construction or like the subjective-documentary 'lip-sinc' series made by the Aardman studios in England. The more an animated film deviates from these conventions the more it will demonstrate different kinds of approach and purpose. By focusing on the issue of 'realism' in animation it is therefore possible to begin the close analysis of any one animated film. Already, it is clear that the use of such conventions may determine the degree and extent of the non-realist agenda of the 'cartoon'. It is necessary, however, to interrogate this issue and establish some additional criteria by which the animated film might be analysed.

Roger Cardinal suggests 'the whole ideal of the animated film is to suppress the categories of normal perception; indeed its logic might even be to suppress all differential categories, and annihilate the very conditions of rationality' (Hames, 1995: 89). Clearly, animated films which do move towards a realist ethos have to be evaluated on other terms. Former Disney chief, Jeffrey Katzenberg says of *Pochahontas* (1995), the studio's most live-action oriented cartoon feature, that it is *exaggerated* reality, where the real possibility of Pochahontas diving 100 feet from a cliff into a pool of water may be made be more spectacular if she were to appear to dive 300 feet, a feat enacted in entire safety, and with persuasive plausibility, in the animated form. At one and the same time 'the very conditions of rationality' have been challenged but made to comply to a different, yet convincing, realist rationale. It may still be the case that this perspective on realism will ultimately be unsatisfying. As Kuenz notes, a little boy watching *Beauty and the Beast* (1989), didn't like the supposedly happy ending, because he said 'everybody turns back into real people' (The Project on Disney, 1995: 72). In his eyes, the realist agenda was evidently an abnegation of animation's capacity to authenticate fantasy.

Importantly, though, in the case of *Pochahontas*, The Disney Studios felt a strong commitment to depict its lead characters as believably as possible because, for the first time in a Disney animated feature, the story was based on real-life people and events. As Peter Biskind notes, though, 'with realism, however, comes sex, a no-no in the Disney universe' (Biskind, 1995: 85), and a scene in which a topless John Smith passionately kisses the Native American Indian girl, Pochahontas, was cut as inappropriate. The limits imposed on the animation by the imperatives to achieve a plausible, yet highly selective, realism left Disney animators divided about the wisdom of undertaking the project. Glen Keane, one of the studio's leading animation directors, counters by saying, 'I disagree with the argument that if it's animation, it has to be subject matter that you can only do in animation. If that's the case, why not just have everybody stop doing landscape paintings because of Ansel Adams?' (Biskind, 1995: 85). This argument, citing

Adams' photographic realism as a definitive view of landscape imagery, suggests that Disney animators believe that they do move beyond traditional modes of realist representation in their work, and maintain a hyper-realism which is neither a completely accurate version of the real world nor a radical vindication of the animated form. Andy Darley, apropos of certain kinds of computer-generated imagery, has usefully suggested that this may be defind as *second-order realism*,[8] where every object and environment, though recognisably 'real', precise in its construction, and logical in the execution of its own laws, becomes essentially *over-determined*, moving into a realism which is simultaneously realistic but beyond the orthodoxies of realism. It may be argued, therefore, that the mode of realism in animation could be understood as *over-illusionism*.

Supporting this view is the idea that the principles of movement themselves are necessarily over-enunciated in the animated vocabulary. Disney's mode of 'squash-n-stretch' animation[9] necessarily over compresses and elongates character movement to give it an over-determined and often comic style, but it remains that moving figures within the Disney canon correspond more directly to 'realistic' movement than work informed by other approaches. Indeed, the very subjectivity involved in producing animation, as it is played out through the medium's intrinsic capability to resist realism, means that any aspiration towards suggesting reality in animation becomes difficult to execute. For example, the intention to create 'documentary' in animation is inhibited by the fact that the medium cannot be objective. Having said that, the medium does enable the film-maker to more persuasively show *subjective reality*. Marjut Rimmenen's film *Some Protection* (1987), documents the deep anxiety of Josie O'Dwyer, using her own troubled recollections of abuse, petty crime and the brutalities of imprisonment, and effectively shows the *perception* of reality as it is experienced by O'Dwyer. Arguably, this is a more truthful reality and one which is only possible to document in animation. O'Dwyer's view of the experiences she goes through are clearly authentic, but sometimes the credibility of the first-person address may be viewed as a questionable credential in the pursuit of documentary truth. Subjective views, opinions and recollections are the staple of many live-action documentaries but, in a medium as fluid as animation, these vocabularies more readily support a subjective approach to animated film-practice as any authored piece. Paul Vester's *Abductees* (1994), for example, uses recollections by people who claim that they have been abducted by aliens. Whilst being highly amusing, the idea of 'documentary' is compromised not merely by the implausible nature of the subjective voice, but by animation which uses so much imagery from the pulp sci-fi fictions like *Astounding* and *Amazing Stories*, produced throughout the 1930s and 1940s. The film certainly operates as a case in which 'realism' can only be viewed as an imaginative rather than a factual premise.

Peter Lord's *Going Equipped* (1989) is perhaps closer to what might be a more commonly held view of the realist agenda, using animation to emphasise the taken-for-granted aspects of the fly-on-the-wall, 'talking head', variant of documentary practice. So much so that, whilst being 'realistic', it also operates as a perfect example of the art of acted performance in animation, which is addressed in Chapter Two. So thorough is the naturalism that the film almost begs the question of why it was necessary to animate the work and not merely see it in live-action. The animation does draw the viewers' attention to significant, and sometimes unnoticed aspects of the character, however, and once more demonstrates its usefulness as a different medium. Such work, which so aspires not only to naturalistic representation but to the engagement with social reality, may be usefully termed 'animation with documentary tendency,' the first example of which would be Winsor McCay's The Sinking of the Lusitania (1918) which, ironically, still fits in with McCay's fundamental working premise of animating subjects would could not possibly be filmed. The quasi-newsreel 'feel' of the piece is powerful and emotionally affecting, but it is as much allied to autobiography and propaganda as it is to the realist mode required for documentary.

Indeed, it may be suggested that Tex Avery's mock travelogues, like Cross-Country Detours (1940), or Disney's quasi-educational films like Jack Kinney's How to . . . series, featuring Goofy, also demonstrate the documentary tendency, only to subvert their informational or instructional tone by the use of cartoonal humour. Interestingly, a number of Disney shorts allude to the documentary tendency, or the realist mode, to authenticate certain ideological or didactic principles. A sequence from Bambi, one of Disney's most hyper-realist features, for example, was released in 1978 as an educational short called Bambi − A Lesson in Perseverance. The realistic attempts of Bambi to stand up and walk are indeed over-determined, but the sequence only moves beyond realist orthodoxies through the anthropomorphised exchanges between the animals. Ultimately, most attempts to engage with the documentary tendency result in what Jan Svankmajer has called 'Fantastic Documentary' (Hames, 1995: 112), which are works based in reality, but which reveal intrinsic truths through the machinations of animation used as a subjective tool. Reality in animation, therefore, can only be a comparative and relative form, half-dedicated to representational authenticity, half-dedicated to the narrational forms which heighten and exhibit the fluid conditions of the real world.

True animation?

No animation film that is not non-objective and/or non-linear can really qualify as true animation, since the conventional linear representational story film has long since been far better done in live-action.

(Moritz, 1988: 21)

Film historian, William Moritz, here defines what may be regarded as a purist view of what properly constitutes 'true animation'. Clearly, he is suggesting that the animated form is best represented by the creation of films which concentrate purely on using and developing the unique vocabulary available only in animation which, therefore, distinguishes it from any other style or approach to film-making. This effectively locates animation as an experimental or principally *avant-garde* form of expression. Further, it suggests that animation works best as an abstract form, where it fully demonstrates its intrinsic capability of moving non-representational lines and materials which fall outside the orthodox domains of 'realist' constructions and agendas. Animation of this sort may be recognised as more specifically bound up with the desire to express profoundly personal, sometimes conscious, sometimes unconscious, aspects of human thought, feeling and experience. The liberating freedom of the medium has a direct correlation with the variety of work achieved by certain animators and artists, who are not merely seeking to find the most appropriate means by which they express their vision, but to progress the medium itself.

New Zealander, Len Lye, for example, used batik methods directly on film, influenced by his belief that the forms of aesthetic expression exemplified in the art of primitive cultures were more directly in touch with the actual neurological and physiological experiences of humankind. He believed that the lines and shapes painted on walls or etched in pots and vases were the direct expression of primal feeling, and thus sought to replicate this approach in both his sculpture and his film-making. His last film, *Particles in Space* (1979), is an attempt to project the cellular life of his brain and body directly onto film, in the hope that its abstract pattern and movement was a document of the dissolution of his neuro-physiological state as he neared death. Norman McClaren worked in a similar way, but with more cheerful intent, in a film like *Boogie Doodle* (1940), in which he literally painted on to the cells of film in response to the boogie-woogie piano of Albert Ammons. This approach places the emphasis and purpose of the expression less in the realm of the body's actual physical life, and more on the unmediated emergence of unconscious forms of response to external stimuli. McClaren's lines, shapes and patterns correspond to the syncopated beat and rhythm of a boogie tune, colliding, conjoining, expanding, contracting, speeding up, slowing down, changing in tone and definition, resisting any coherent mode of narrative or representation, yet somehow expressing a mood, an idea, an experience.

Most notable in this field of non-objective, non-linear expression is Oskar Fischinger, whose initial designs and animation were used to complement Bach's 'Toccata and Fugue in D Minor' in Disney's *Fantasia* (1940). Fischinger later left the project, feeling that his individual approach did not fit the studio ethos. This is hardly surprising, in the sense that while *Fantasia* was clearly Disney's attempt to legitimise the animated film by working in a more abstract, highly aesthetic, supposedly 'cultured' way, it did not properly encompass Fischinger's vision of purely visual music. Once again, like Lye, Fischinger recognised animation as a form which could accomodate fluid, primal, expressions of thought and feeling. His desire to synchronise music and movement was primarily driven by his view that few questioned the abstraction of sound. It was merely accepted for what it was, stimulating its own associations and reactions. Fischinger felt that this could also be achieved in purely visual terms. Shapes and forms need not represent anything at all and would provoke a variety of responses in the viewers who received them.

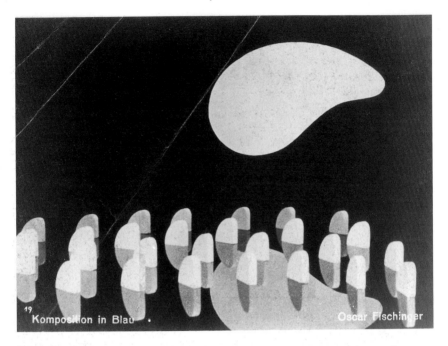

Figure 1.2 *Composition in Blue*, an abstract 'visual poem' expresses the *joie de vivre* of moving colour, shape and form in its own right, illustrating the dynamics of experimental animation

By directly synchronising music and movement in his 'Studies', made during the 1930s, and most notably in *Composition in Blue* (1935), Fischinger hoped, however, that the accepted abstraction in the music would enable the acceptance and understanding of abstraction in the animation. Such abstraction was further systematised in the rhythms and repetitions of Victor Eggling's films which more closely approximate to programmed patterns of construction and deconstruction, and are clearly informed by logical schemata and almost mathematical precision. A film like *Diagonal Symphony* (1925), which works entirely on the basis of a formal geometric pattern constantly mutating in part-organic, part-mechanistic fashion, anticipates similar constructions in contemporary computer animation by more than fifty years.

While these achievements are startling, and fully demonstrate the range of possibilities in animation, they are, in many senses, difficult to relate to and even harder to understand. Even innovators like John and James Whitney, who, in the 1940s pioneered the first examples of quasi-computer animation, and who had a distinct approach to the idea of visual music in addressing the emotional implications of abstraction, produced work that was not particularly accessible. James Whitney, especially, had a particular interest in allying spiritual themes to his film-making practice. His film, *Lapis* (1965), is named after the philosopher's

Figure 1.3 *Lapis* is a film which uses primal forms of expression to encourage a different level of engagement in an audience which is not predicated on narration or humour but the contemplation of spiritual life

stone in the practice of alchemy and encourages notions of contemplation and a fuller understanding of the place of humankind within the cosmos. The film, a relaxing, visual *tour de force* of fluid particle movements, is entirely composed of hand-drawn dots, and it is in this that the viewer may find a point of access to the modes of expression and intended meaning. All of the artists cited above sought to work out of more primitive forms, and thus have a specific understanding of how these forms evolved, and what they ultimately represent. It is useful, there-fore, to consider the specific vocabulary these artists are primarily working in as animators.

What, for example, is 'a dot'? It might be the beginning of a line, the end of a line, a mark in space, a point that designates perspective etc., but more impor-tantly, it is the smallest, most direct, completely determined, graphic mark that the artist can use. In other words, it is the primary, most intense symbol of expression that relates the artist to the artwork. The dot is a *primal* form that is only rationalised as a *geometric* form much later in its application. This is the case for all of the orthodox shapes and forms:

31

Primal form	Geometric form
Point (dot)	Point/points with specific meaning
Scratch	Straight line
Wavy line	Grids/nets
Spiral	Circles

The method of graphic expression which merely uses primal forms is concordant with the animator's *atavistic* intentions. In other words, the approach, and its subsequent achievement is a direct attempt to get in touch with different kinds of expression which precede Formalism. Sergei Eisenstein suggests that 'heartless geometrizing and metaphysics . . . gave rise to a kind of antithesis, an unexpected re-birth of universal animism' (Leyda, 1988: 35). Animism, a concept which may be defined as a pre-rational, pre-scientific state of relatedness to the organic inter-connectedness of the natural world and primordial conditions, may be seen to inform the kind of animation which prioritises subjectivity and resists orthodox modes of representation.

The first acts of animist animation come in the form of cave drawings, in which expression is not a consciously creative act but an automatic physical engagement which reveals hand/eye co-ordination and the ability to affect a stroke-drawing or mark (Leyda, 1988: 43). This physical act may be defined as the mechanism which enables humankind to draw, even in the most crude terms, and demonstrates that 'drawing' itself is, in Eisenstein's words, 'brought to life' (ibid. 43) operating outside the constraints of representation. It is clear then, that animation intrinsically provides the opportunity to express the life within drawing/sculpting etc. on its own terms, before expressing the obligation to narrate or make representational associations. It may be argued that this kind of artwork corresponds to *sensual* rather than *rational* interpretation, prioritising an active engagement with the pre-logical. Significantly, Eisenstein suggests that the key agenda of these primal forms is the idea of something that is *coming into being* (ibid. 69) and it is in this state that the artwork is at its most expressive. He fears, however, that the imperative which insists upon exactitude or absoluteness, or in his word, *generalisation*, will finally render the artwork inexpressive (Leyda, 1988: 82).

Primal forms exhibit simplicity without overt meaning; geometric forms rationalise lines and shapes in a way which universalises graphic expression and moves it towards particular codes and conditions of interpretation. The tension between these two polarities is resolved in an experimental film by Hans Richter called *Rhythm 21* (1921), of which he says: 'I used the square (or rectangle) as the simplest way of dividing the square *film-screen*, after I had discovered that our scrolls were paintings and followed the laws of painting not of filming. The simple square gave me the opportunity to forget about the complicated matter of our drawings and to concentrate on the orchestration of movement and time' (Russett and Starr, 1976: 49). Crucially, this simple decision delineates another way in which these abstract films may be addressed. If atavistic expression prioritises the free movement of the primal form, and the act of *coming into being*, Richter's animation rationalises it to the extent to which the free play of abstract forms may be understood through the division of space. Such division enables the viewer to comprehend the relationship between oppositional ideas and contexts, i.e. the play from right to left and left to right; the play between above and below; the tension across the diagonal or foreshortened spaces etc. This may be extended into an interpretation of forms in relation to light and dark, or even the gendering of lines and shapes, if the viewer accepts a tension between masculinity as vertical and femininity as horizontal. Immediately, the vocabulary of possible access is extended.

Computer animator, Larry Cuba, calls this general principle of abstract expression within a particular spatial context, 'design in motion', and stresses the importance of the apparatus with which he is working. He says:

> If you think about the process used in abstract animation, it does become important that you're using a computer, in a way it affects your vocabulary. Because if you start with these mathematical structures, you can discover imagery that you've not pre-visualised but have 'found' within the dimensions of the search space.
>
> (Russett and Starr, 1976: 28)

Cuba effectively articulates how new technologies help to create greater expressive freedom within apparently fixed mathematical and geometrical structures. Suddenly, unanticipated 'found' relationships between shapes and forms within the computer program create aspects of the 'pre-visualised' in ways that echo the primal spontaneity and expressiveness cited earlier. This clearly demonstrates that the tension between: conscious and unconscious creation; primal and rationalised forms; and the movement between non-representative and associative images, remains in place whatever the means of creating abstract animation. The concept of 'the dimensions of the search space' described by Cuba is of further use, however, in suggesting ways in which the animator uses a particular context, drawing the viewers attention to: the size and shape of forms; their graphic and technical quality; their rhythm and counter-rhythm; their symmetry or asymmetry; their movement towards, or away from, the edge or centre; their relationship and effect upon each other, and perhaps, most importantly, their openness or closure as a form. By addressing these aspects of abstract animation it is possible to create a variety of ways in which non-linear or non-objective works can be narrated.

As animator, Alexander Alexeieff has noted, it is the imperative of such works to engage the spectator's imagination and sensual apparatus at a different level, and to provoke the recall of physical movement and playfulness in childhood (Russett and Starr, 1976: 94). This idea best exemplifies the purpose of the abstract film and once more calls attention to the space *between* the representation/figuration and abstraction/decoration. Once primal forms become geometric they become familiar, rationalised, and narrowly symbolic. By maintaining the notion of coming into being, or subverting formalism, animators create the possibility not merely of narrational perspectives, but of ways in which the lines and shapes themselves may be identified in expressive terms which describe the nature of their movement, e.g. explosive, erotic, expansive etc.

So, from a point where abstraction may seem alienating, it has been established that primal forms may be read as an expression of their progress towards rational and associative forms, and may be understood by the narration which may be given to the division of space, the kinds of movement occuring within a particular context, and in relation to what may be termed the energy or suggestiveness of the line or shape itself. Clearly, such work may be read in a variety of ways. Psychoanalytic theory lends itself readily to an interpretation of the narrational agendas raised by this methodology. Interestingly, Norman McClaren's Love on the Wing (1938), a surrealist film in the guise of a publicity short for the new airmail service, was actually prevented from being shown by the Minister of Posts for the Government during World War II in Britain, because it was believed to be 'too erotic and too Freudian' (McClaren, 1978: 13). Obviously, the Minister had made the transition from the narration of primal forms to the interpretation of shapes and lines at the level of symbolic and submerged associations. McClaren's sexually charged imagery did not sit well with the propagandist and informative agendas of the film. In simple terms, psychoanalytic readings offer the possibility of relating the abstraction within the films to certain modes of rationale that attempt to explain subjectivity and its expression. The methods of interpreting abstract animations that have been described, precede the application of such theories, but provide a vocabulary which helps to delineate them in opposition to the quasi-realist animation defined earlier. This antithesis between the realist and abstract models of animation is pursued, and further defined in regard to construction and intention, in Chapter Two.

2

NOTES TOWARDS A THEORY
OF ANIMATION

Styles and approaches

It may be argued that Disney's art and the hyper-realist animated film remain the dominant discourse of animation. The proliferation of mass-produced 'cel' animation has done much to overshadow the styles and approaches adopted by other animators in other contexts. Inevitably, the amount of cheaply produced, highly industrialised cel animation made in the USA and Japan has colonised television schedules, and perhaps, more importantly, the imaginations of viewers. Although this is to discredit the quality and variety of work in cel animation, it seems necessary to reclaim, re-introduce and re-validate animation made with other materials, with different creative impulses and aesthetic interests, outside the context of mass production, to properly evaluate the achievements of the animated film. It also provides an opportunity to theorise the textual apparatus of different forms of animation which, for the purposes of this discussion, I haved called *orthodox animation*.

Developmental animation and experimental animation

These tentative definitions attempt to address certain modes of expression and construction in the animated film linking these aspects to the techniques employed.

The table on p. 36 represents a definition of orthodox and experimental animation as opposing but related forms. Developmental animation operates as a mode of expression combining or selecting elements of both approaches, representing the aesthetic and philosophic tension between the two apparent extremes.

Cel animation remains the most convenient technique for the mass production of cartoons and, therefore, the most commonly seen form of animation. Consequently, it constitutes what may be understood as *orthodox* animation, and is most associated, even in its most anarchic or fantastical form, at the level of narrative, along with the hyper-realist style discussed earlier. This may seem extraordinary to the viewer who sees the cartoon as an intrinsically non-realist form, but as will become clear, this sense of unreality only operates with regard to the representation of events in a cartoon, and not the 'realist' conventions by which it is understood. Significantly, these kinds of films are usually storyboarded first, after

Table 2.1

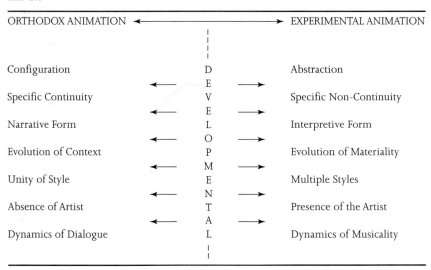

ORHODOX ANIMATION ◄———————————► EXPERIMENTAL ANIMATION		
Configuration	D	Abstraction
	E	
Specific Continuity	V	Specific Non-Continuity
	E	
Narrative Form	L	Interpretive Form
	O	
Evolution of Context	P	Evolution of Materiality
	M	
Unity of Style	E	Multiple Styles
	N	
Absence of Artist	T	Presence of the Artist
	A	
Dynamics of Dialogue	L	Dynamics of Musicality

the fashion of a comic strip (and thus, its linear mode of story-telling), and animated when synchronised to a pre-recorded soundtrack. The animation is achieved when 'key drawings' are produced indicating the 'extreme' first and last positions of a movement which are then 'in-betweened' to create the process of the move. After 'pencil-testing' (now often computerised), the images are drawn on separate sheets of celluloid, painted, and photographed frame-by-frame against the appropriate background. The music, dialogue and effects correspond to the images. This method enables a large number of animators to be involved and facilitates an industrial process.[1] It also results in a certain creative intention which characterises the criteria for orthodox animation.

Terms and conditions: Orthodox animation

Configuration

Most cartoons featured 'figures', i.e. identifiable people or animals who corresponded to what audiences would understand as an orthodox human being or creature) despite whatever colourful or eccentric design concept was related to it, i.e. Donald was recognisable as a duck whether he wore a sailor's suit or khaki togs and a pith helmet!

Specific continuity

Whether a cartoon was based on a specific and well known fairytale or story, or was based on a sequence of improvised sight gags, it had a logical continuity even

36

within a madcap scenario. This was achieved by prioritising character and context. For example, in a structure like that of the Mutt and Jeff cartoon cited earlier, Disney's Goofy was given an establishing premise for a following sequence of gags – most often his perpetual attempts to succeed at a task and his consistent failure. He is thus contextualised in the continuing imperative to complete the task, but simultaneously creating slapstick comedy through his failure. Further, and most important, he creates sympathy for, and understanding of, the fundamental aspects of his character, the chief bonding agent in the scenario.

Narrative form

It is important to stress the importance of narrative form. Most early cartoons echoed or illustrated the musical forms of their soundtracks. This provided proto-narrative before particular scenarios were later developed. These were most often based on character conflict and chase sequences, where common environments became increasingly destabilised as they became subject to destructive forces (see Klein, 1994: 164–166). However notional, the idea of 'a story' was essentially held in place by the 'specific continuity' of establishing a situation, problematising it, creating comic events and finding a resolution, mainly through the actions of the principal character that the audience had been encouraged to support and sympathise with throughout.

Evolution of content

The orthodox cartoon only occasionally draws the audience's attention to its construction, especially in the case of the Disney hyper-realist text.[2] Rarely also does it tell the audience of its interest in the colour, design and material of its making. Instead, it prioritises its content, concentrating specifically on constructing character, determining comic moments and evolving the self-contained narrative. This is not to say that the colour, design and so forth are irrelevant, but that they constitute a particular kind of style which merely reinforces the 'cartoon-ness' of the animation and, thus, the 'invisibility' of its aesthetic achievement and its industrial context.

Unity of style

The formal properties of the animated cartoon tend to remain consistent. Cel-animated or hand-drawn cartoons remain in a fixed two-dimensional style throughout their duration and do not mix with three-dimensional modes as later, more experimental, animation does. Visual conventions echo those of live-action cinema in the 'hyper-realist' sense, deploying establishing shots, medium shots and close-ups etc., but camera movement tends to be limited to lateral left-to-right pans across the backgrounds or up-and-down tilts examining a character or environment. One consequence of camera movement across a drawing, though, can be the illusion of a change of perspective or angle to facilitate an unusual context for the character. This often happens, for example, when Wile E Coyote chases Road Runner and finds himself in an impossible predicament. An apparently safe rock formation suddenly presents itself at an impossible angle and becomes a dangerous landscape that defeats him once more (see George, 1990). Narrative and design conventions like these inform most cartoons which mainly operate on the basis of a repeated formula – one of the most obvious of these is the chase.

The chase informs the pace of these narratives, privileging speed and frenetic action and creates its own action abstraction conventions, like visible movement lines around moving limbs and the blur of fast-moving bodies. Sound conventions (like 'the crash' or 'the boing' or the ascending and descending scale), orthodox cinematic conventions (like the cut, dissolve, use of ellipse etc.) and even conventions unique to the animated form (like 'metamorphosis' – see Chapter Three), do not disrupt the unity of style and, despite using all these conventions, colour, scenic design, and character formation, tend to remain consistent.

Absence of artist

The early development of the cartoon form was characterised by an overtly signified tension between animation and its relationship to live-action. This resulted on many occasions in films combining animation and live-action, often depicting the creation of an animated character by the artist who drew it, and the activities of the animated character within the working environment of the artist. Clearly, these early efforts foreground the art of animation as an artist-led activity with a distinctive language – the Fleischer brothers enabled Koko the Clown to emerge 'Out of the Inkwell' into the real world (see Cabarga, 1988; Frierson, 1993), while Disney's early work reversed the process, and showed 'Alice' in an animated environment (see Merritt and Kaufman, 1993). Many of these imaginative initiatives were simply extensions of the work of the pioneers, who reconciled the idea of the live-action 'lightning cartoonist' with the capacity of the medium to record and ultimately show the evolution of the cartoon itself. With the emergence of the industrial cel-animation process, the role and presence of the artist was essentially removed and, consequently, cartoons/orthodox animation prioritised narrative, character and style, rarely privileging the signification of their creation, unless as a system to create jokes (see the following analysis of Chuck Jones' Duck Amuck (1953)). Later cartoon animation but, most specifically, more personal 'auteurist' animation,[3] does signal its codes and conventions and thus reveals the presence of the individual artist in creating the work. Also, the reclamation and recognition of specific artists working at Disney, for example, Vlad Tytla (see Canemaker, 1994) and Warner Brothers, for example, Tex Avery (see Adamson, 1975) and Frank Tashlin (see Garcia, 1994), has enabled interested viewers to relocate the artist in apparently conventional cartoons. For the purposes of this discussion, though, such initiatives will be used more in regard to the thematic or stylistic influence achieved by the artist, rather than as a mechanism by which the cartoon can be seen as an overtly personal film which obviously challenges the general criteria for orthodox animation defined here.

These general principles remain consistent even when the contributions of individual artists are acknowledged because the creation and perpetuation of a studio 'style' became more important than those who created it.

Dynamics of dialogue

Even though the fundamental appeal of the cartoon lies in its commitment to action, character is often defined by key aspects of dialogue. Disney's use of dialogue tends to initiate action or be used in moments of admonishment or conflict, chiefly when Mickey disciplines Pluto, or Donald rails against the world, but joke-orientated dialogue was a particular feature of the characters created at Warner Brothers Studio for the 'Looney Tunes' and 'Merrie Melodies' cartoons. Bugs Bunny's laconic sense of superiority is established by his carrot-munching proposition, 'What's up, doc?', or his call-to-arms when his current adversary temporarily gains the upper hand and he confirms: 'You realise, this means war!'

Specifically based on the verbal dexterity and confident delivery of Groucho Marx, Bugs also qualifies any minor error in his plans by claiming: 'I should have taken the right turn at Albuqererque!' Equally, Daffy is characterised by his consistent babble, arrested only when he has experienced complete humiliation and lispily claims 'You're despicable!' Elmer Fudd always insists on quiet as he hunts 'wabbits,' while Yosemite Sam overstates his position when he says 'I'm seagoing Sam, the blood-thirstiest, shoot-em firstiest, doggone worstiest, buccaneer that's ever sailed the Spanish Main!' All these verbal dynamics served to support the visual jokes and create a specific kind of 'noise' which is characteristic of these films. Philip Brophy suggests that the Disney soundtrack moves towards the symphonic while the Warner soundtrack embodies the cacophonic. The symphonic is informed by classical aspirations towards the poetic, balletic and operatic, while the cacophonic is more urban, industrialised, beat-based and explosive in its vocabulary (see Cholodenko, 1991: 67–113). The role of sound is crucial in the animated film and will be more specifically addressed in Chapter Four.

Case study: Deconstructing the cartoon

Duck Amuck (1953), directed by Chuck Jones at Warner Brothers Studio, though in a sense untypical of the kind of style and unity in orthodox animation described earlier, is the perfect example of a cartoon subject to its own deconstruction. As Richard Thompson points out:

> It is at once a laff riot and an essay by demonstration on the nature and conditions of the animated film (from the inside) and the mechanics of

film in general. (Even a quick checklist of film grammar is tossed in via the 'Gimme a close-up' gag).

(Thompson, 1980: 231)

Daffy Duck begins the cartoon believing himself to be in a musketeer picture and swashbuckles with due aplomb until he realises that he is not accompanied by suitable scenery. He immediately recognises that he has been deserted by the context both he, and we as the audience, are accustomed to.

He drops the character he is playing and becomes Daffy, the betrayed actor, who immediately addresses the camera, acknowledging both the animator and the audience. Perceiving himself as an actor as real as any in any live-action movie, he localises himself within the film-making process, and signals its creative and industrial mechanisms, all of which are about to be revealed to the audience.

Trooper that he is, Daffy carries on, adapting to the new farmyard scenery with a spirited version of 'Old Macdonald had a farm' before adjusting once again to the arctic layout that has replaced the farmyard. The cartoon constantly draws attention to the relationship between foreground and background, and principally to the relationship between the character and the motivating aspects of the environmental context. Daffy's actions are determined by his comprehension of the space he inhabits. These tensions inform the basic narrative process of most cartoons. All Daffy wants is for the animator to make up his mind! Each environment is illustrated by the visual shorthand of dominant cultural images – the Arctic is signified by an igloo, Hawaii by Daffy's grass skirt and banjo. The white space, however, becomes the empty context of the cartoon. Daffy is then erased by an animated pencil rubber and essentially only remains as a voice, but, as Chuck Jones has pointed out, 'what I want to say is that Daffy can live and struggle on in an empty screen, without setting and without sound, just as well as with a lot of arbitrary props. He remains Daffy Duck' (Peary and Peary, 1980: 233).

This draws attention to the pre-determined understanding of Daffy as a character, and the notion that a whole character can be understood by any one of its parts (see *Synecdoche* p. 80). Daffy can be understood through his iconic elements, both visually and aurally. No visual aspects of Daffy need to be seen for an audience to know him through his lisping voice, characterised by Mel Blanc. We need only see his manic eyes or particularly upturned beak to distinguish him from Donald Duck and all other cartoon characters, all of which have similar unique and distinguishing dimensions in their design.

At the point when Daffy asks 'Where am I?', even in his absence, the audience knows of his presence. When he is re-painted by the anonymous brush as a singing cowboy we anticipate, of course, that Daffy will sing, though the genre probably prohibits him singing 'I'm just wild about Harry', which remains one of his favourites! Initially, Daffy experiences no sound and in post-Avery style, holds up a small sign requesting 'Sound please', thus drawing the audience's attention to the explicit vocabulary of sound necessitated by the cartoon form, and one immediately familiar to the anticipated viewer. When Daffy attempts to play the guitar it sounds first like a machine gun, then a horn, then a donkey, which simultaneously shows the necessity of sound and image synchronisation for narrative and hyper-realist orthodoxy and the creation of comedy through the incongruous mismatching of sound and image. This is developed after Daffy breaks the guitar in frustration – a standard element of the cartoon is the process of destruction – and attempts to complain to the animator about his treatment, especially as he considers himself 'a star'. He is given the voice of a chicken and a cockatoo, and just when he is at his most hysterical with the attempt to speak, he is allowed his own voice, but at increased volume. Daffy is visibly humiliated and his attitude once again reveals to an audience his helplessness in the face of the power of the animator. The animator is at liberty to completely manipulate the image and create impossible and dynamic relations which need not have any connection with orthodox and anticipated relations.

This manipulation of Daffy's image and identity also tells an audience about his essential character traits – egotism, ambition, frustration, anger and willfulness. These traits are constantly challenged in most of the narratives involving Daffy by the resistance offered up by the world around him. In Duck Amuck, he is also defeated by the context he exists within. He pleads with the animator for orthodoxy and is greeted with a child's pencil drawing for a background, slapdash scenery painting and an absurd reconstruction of his own body in wild colours and a flag tied to his newly drawn tail indicating that he is a 'screwball'. Ironically, it is at this point that Daffy is arguing for Disneyesque hyper-realism in regard to the need for a linear narrative and consistency in the design of character and environment but, clearly, the condition of the cartoon here remains subject to the animator's desire to destabilise these orthodoxies.

Despite protestations that he has fulfilled his contract, Daffy continues to be treated with contempt. Just when he seems granted the legitimacy of 'a sea picture' – an obvious reference to both Donald Duck and Popeye – Daffy is subjected to further humiliation. Jones self-consciously addresses the capacity of the cartoon to both disrupt orthodox hyper-realist conventions and enjoy predictable conventions that are a standard part of the cartoon vocabulary. For example, like Mutt in Soda Jerks, and hundreds of other cartoons, Daffy is suspended in mid-air, recognises that he is temporarily defying gravity, and drops into the sea as soon as he has realised. Seconds later he is on an island, but the image is merely a small frame within the normal frame, this time drawing the audience's attention to the compositional elements of the cartoon, and indeed, of film language itself. The audience can hardly hear Daffy as he calls for a close-up. He is then rapidly animated into an apparent close-up, as the frame fills only with Daffy's eyes.

Jones, once again, calls upon the audience's recognition of the frame as a potentially three-dimensional space as Daffy tries to cope with the sheer materiality of that physical space when he tries to support the black scenery that falls upon him like a heavy awning. He eventually tears up the 'screen' in sheer frustration and demands that the cartoon start even though it has already been running for several minutes. A screen card stating 'The End' comes up accompanied by the Merrie Melodies theme. Whatever Daffy expects, or wishes to experience, he is countered by its opposite. Like a true professional, and in an apparently independent act that attempts to defy and refute the conditions to which he has been subjected, Daffy then attempts to take control of the film. He returns to the key notion of himself as an entertainer outside the context of a cartoon and performs a vaudevillian soft-shoe shuffle. He is, however, trying to reclaim the idea of the cartoon as a medium for entertainment. All this, of course, is another method by which Jones can establish further premises to deconstruct the cartoon. Daffy's song and dance routine is interrupted by the apparent slippage of the frame of film in the projector. It appears to divide the screen in half and exposes the celluloid frames of which the film is supposedly composed. The two frames, of course, reveal two Daffys, who immediately start to fight and disappear in a blur of drawn lines – the fight merely becomes a signifier of cartoon movement; a symbol of kineticism unique in embodying character and signifying form.

Narrative life improves for Daffy as 'the picture' casts him as a pilot. This is merely another device, however, to demonstrate a series of conventional cartoon gags, including an off-screen air crash, the fall, the appearance of the ubiquitous anvil as a substitute for Daffy's parachute, and an explosion as Daffy tests some shells with a mallet. By this time, however, he is a gibbering heap, devoid of dignity or control, the two chief qualities Daffy most aspires to. As he tries to assert himself one last time, Daffy demands to know 'Who is responsible for this? I demand that you show yourself!' The frame, as the audience perceives it, is then completely broken as the scene changes and the camera pulls back to reveal the drawing board and 'the animator' – Bugs Bunny, Daffy's arch-rival. As Thompson remarks, 'Duck Amuck can be seen as Daffy's bad trip; his self-destruction fantasies and delusions, with their rapid, unpredictable, disconcerting changes of scene and orientation, are the final extension of ego-on-the-line dreams' (Peary and Peary, 1980: 233). This is an important point in a number of respects. It locates Daffy as a character in his own right, the subject of a relationship between form and meaning.[4] In Duck Amuck, Jones demonstrates the dimensions of the animated form and shows its capacity to support a number of meanings, particularly with regard to character construction, modes of narrative expectation and plausibility, and the conditions of comic events. It is a model which usefully reveals the range of possibilities within the animated cartoon and, as such, the readily identifiable conventions of orthodox animation. These aspects will be interrogated further when placed in a different context of enquiry later but, in order to clarify the meaning of orthodox animation it is important to define and illustrate experimental animation as its antithesis.

Experimental animation embraces a number of styles and approaches to the animated film which inevitably cross over into areas which may also be termed *avant-garde* or 'art' films (see Wees, 1992), which may only partially display aspects of animation in the form I have previously discussed. Of course, there has been experimentation in all areas of animation, as is clearly demonstrated by a cartoon as apparently orthodox as *Duck Amuck*, but in this area I am prioritising animation which has either been constituted in new forms (computer, xerox, sand-on-glass, direct on to celluloid, pinscreen, etc.) or resists traditional forms. The dominant aspects of experimental animation listed in Table 2.1 on p. 36, provide useful criteria for further analysis.

Terms and conditions: Experimental animation

Abstraction

This kind of animation tends to resist configuration in the way audiences most often see it (i.e. as an expression of character through the depiction of a human being or creature). Experimental animation either redefines 'the body' or resists using it as an illustrative image. Abstract films are more concerned with rhythm and movement in their own right as opposed to the rhythm and movement of a particular character. To this end, various shapes and forms are often used rather than figures. As historian, William Moritz, suggests:

> Non-objective animation is without doubt the purest and most difficult form of animation. Anyone can learn to 'muybridge' the illusion of representational life, but inventing interesting forms, shapes and colours, creating new, imaginative and expressive motions – 'the absolute creation: the true creation' as Fischinger termed it – requires the highest mental and spiritual faculties, as well as the most sensitive talents of hand.
>
> (Moritz, 1988: 25)

Specific non-continuity

While initially seeming a contradiction in terms, the idea of specific non-continuity merely signals the rejection of logical and linear continuity and the prioritisation of illogical, irrational and sometimes multiple continuities. These continuities are specific in the sense that they are the vocabulary unique to the particular animation in question. Experimental animation defines its own form and conditions and uses these as its distinctive language.

Interpretive form

The bias of experimental animation is aesthetic and non-narrative, though sometimes, as I will illustrate, aesthetic conventions are deployed to reconstruct a different conception of narrative. Predominantly, though, experimental animation resists telling stories and moves towards the vocabulary used by painters and sculptors. Resisting the depiction of conventional forms and the assumed 'objectivity' of the exterior world, (and indeed, the conditions of hyper-realist animation), experimental animation prioritises abstract forms in motion, liberating the artist to concentrate on the vocabulary he/she is using *in itself* without the imperative of giving it a specific function or meaning. As Cubist painter, Leopold Survage, wrote as early as 1914,

> I will animate my painting. I will give it movement. I will introduce rhythm into the concrete action of my abstract painting, born of my interior life; my instrument will be the cinematographic film, this true symbol of accumulated movement. It will execute 'the scores' of my visions, corresponding to my state of mind in its successive phases . . . I am creating a new art in time, that of coloured rhythm and of rhythmic colour.
>
> (Quoted in Russett and Starr, 1976: 36)

This kind of subjective work has therefore necessitated that audiences respond differently. Instead of being located within the familiarity of formal narrative strategies (however illogical they are made by the inclusion of comic events), the audience are required to interpret the work on their own terms, or terms predetermined by the artist. As William Moritz insists, though, these acts of interpretation should not be inhibited by trying to force the abstraction to directly equate with some known quantity or meaning. He says:

> The true abstraction and the true symbol must have an intriguing spirit and integrity of its own, and it must suggest more meanings, various, almost contradictory depths and speculations beyond the surface value; otherwise, why bother to obfuscate? If the viewer comes to the point of saying, 'Oh, that represents the police and that represents freedom,' then that revelation is about as interesting as, 'Gee, Donald Duck drives a car and mows his lawn just like an average American; he must represent the average irascible American!'
>
> (Moritz, 1988: 29)

Moritz, in determining the necessary requirements for the truly abstract film, and the role of its audience, simultaneously distinguishes the kind of film which, in my analysis, would constitute developmental animation in the sense that it would be deliberately using animation in a directly metaphoric way and not working in the realms of the purely abstract.

Evolution of materiality

The experimental film concentrates on its very materiality, i.e. the forms in which it is being made, and the colours, shapes and textures which are being used in the creation of the piece. These colours, shapes and textures evoke certain moods and ideas but, once again, film-makers working in this way are suggesting that these aspects should give pleasure in their own right without having to be attached to a specific meaning or framework.

Experimental animation thus privileges the literal evolution of materiality instead of narrative and thematic content, showing us, for example, how a small hand-painted dot evolves into a set of circles, where the audience recognises the physical nature of the paint itself, the colour of the dot and its background, and the shapes that emerge out of the initial design.

This sense of 'materiality' goes hand-in-hand with the emergent technologies which have liberated more innovative approaches to animation.

Multiple styles

If orthodox animation is characterised by a unity of style, experimental animation often combines and mixes different modes of animation. This operates in two specific ways – first, to facilitate the multiplicity of personal visions an artist may wish to incorporate in a film, and second, to challenge and re-work orthodox codes and conventions and create new effects.

Presence of the artist

These films are largely personal, subjective, original responses, which are the work of artists seeking to use the animated form in an innovative way.

Sometimes these 'visions' are impenetrable and resist easy interpretation, being merely the absolutely individual expression of the artist. This in itself draws attention to the relationship between the artist and the work, and the relationship of the audience to the artist as it is being mediated through the work. The abstract nature of the films insists upon the recognition of their individuality. Sometimes, however, individual innovation is localised in more accessible ways which have a relationship with dominant forms, however tenuous the link. It may be, for example, that the experimental animation will try to create something aspiring to the condition of the dream-state, which, of course, has its own abstract logic, but conforms to a common understanding of 'the dream', and thus may be subject to scrutiny through psychoanalysis. It is often the case that experimental animation is closely related to philosophic and spiritual concerns and seeks to represent inarticulable personal feelings beyond the orthodoxies of language.

Dynamics of musicality

Experimental animation has a strong relationship to music and, indeed, it may be suggested that if music could be visualised it would look like colours and shapes moving through time with differing rhythms, movements and speeds. Many experimental films seek to create this state, and as I have already suggested, some film-makers perceive that there is a psychological and emotional relationship with sound and colour which may be expressed through the free form which characterises animation. Sound is important in any animated film, but has particular resonance in the experimental film, as it is often resisting dialogue, the clichéd sound effects of the cartoon, or the easy emotiveness of certain kinds of music.

Silence, an *avant-garde* score, unusual sounds and redefined notions of 'language' are used to create different kinds of statement. It may be said that if orthodox animation is about 'prose' then experimental animation is more 'poetic' and suggestive in its intention.

Case studies: Non-objective and non-linear animation

A Colour Box (1935)

Len Lye's A Colour Box, is a completely abstract film in that it is created with lines and shapes stencilled directly on to celluloid, changing colour and form throughout its five-minute duration. It has dominant lines throughout with various circles, triangles and grids interrupting and temporarily joining the image, until it reveals its sponsors, the GPO film unit, by including various rates for the parcel post (i.e. 3lbs for 6d, 6lbs for 9d etc.). Interestingly, the addition of the parcel post rates define the film as an advertising film, but its image system requires further interpretation. Films like A Colour Box, raise questions about purpose and intention which the glib coda of merely including obvious signs (i.e. numbers and letters) do not answer. It would appear that the film is more *about* the relationship between the artist and modes of expression than what is ultimately expressed.

The dazzling, dynamic images are set to a contemporary jazz-calypso score which has the effect of bringing further energy and spontaneity to the piece. Lye believes that this kind of work should be seen as 'Composing Motion' as it reveals the 'Body Energy' which connects the music and the images (Curtis, 1987: 5). In other words, the lines, shapes and colours that move in relation to the music represent the spontaneous physical response of the artist during the moment of expression. Their 'narrative' is entirely bound up with the psychological and emotional state of the artist in relation to social and environmental stimulus, the background and experience of the artist, and the artist's knowledge and use of the medium. Importantly, this method of making animated films corresponds even more directly to McClaren's notion that what determines the proper understanding of animation is the action that takes place between the frames, since in Lye's case that may be subject to intense variation given the conditions he imposes upon himself in making the film.

The genuine abstraction within the film serves to provoke viewers, who must find 'sense' in the imagery on a personal level, perhaps by association, perhaps by empathy with the rhythm of the piece or perhaps by something altogether more personal. Listeners have little trouble with the 'abstraction' of music in this way; viewers must find their own relationship with imagery and its determinate meanings on their own terms.

The Nose (1963)

Former engraver, Alexander Alexeieff, invented the pinscreen technique in animation during the early 1930s, in association with his partner, Clare Parker. This involved a 3 by 4 feet board in which a million headless pins were placed, with the capability of being pushed backwards and forwards. Black and white images were created by gradating the pins in the fashion required and lighting them in a specific way. Each image was created and photographed frame-by-frame. Hard black, bright white and various tonalities of grey could be achieved and as images dissolved and metamorphosed one into another a unique sense of dream-like continuity and mood was created. This proved particularly appropriate to the kind of work Alexeieff was interested in producing – animation which prioritised the ways in which light redefined solid materials rather than animation concerned with line-forms or surfaces (Bendazzi, 1995: 107–114). More importantly, Alexeieff wished to slow the pace and timing of the animated film, which was already dominated by the speed and frequency of events epitomised in the emergent cartoon. Alexeieff's emphasis upon 'shade' in his imagery was essentially related to his interest in creating stories with narrative ambiguities and destabilised environments. His films seem dream-like and render the viewer uncertain and vulnerable, yet encouraged to participate in the dream logic which seems to define parallel worlds, like that of The Nose.

The Nose is a free adaption of Nikolai Gogol's surreal short story of a barber who finds a nose in his loaf of bread, a noseless young man, and a nose that wants a life of its own. It is the very 'unnaturalness' of the story and images which appealed to Alexeieff in the creation of his free-flowing animated film. In the same way that Lye (and artists like him) could articulate the inarticulable through animation, Alexeieff used animation to create 'the unnatural' and address 'the uncanny'. Alexieff shows a sofa slowly changing into a rowboat in a dream sequence and also a streetlight becoming a policeman. Objects disappear, the nose transforms in size and shape, and time speeds up and slows down, all in the spirit of resisting an obvious 'story' in order to create mood and atmosphere. The film was made as a silent film, but music was added later to punctuate aspects of it rather than to create a specified emotional response.

Experimental animation, as may already be seen by the two chosen examples, has strong links with painting and sculpture, and is often closely related to particular movements in fine art. *The Nose*, and other animated films made in a similar style, demonstrate strong Surrealist tendencies, and it is important to note that animators like Alexeieff recognised the capacity of animation to properly facilitate and develop the principles of Surrealism (and indeed, other schools of artistic thought) in a new medium. When French poet, André Breton, launched the Surrealist movement in October 1924 with the publication of his 'Manifesto of Surrealism', he recognised that certain modes of rationalist expression were inadequate in the post-war period, and that other kinds of philosophic and aesthetic approaches to art were necessary. Indebted to the work of Freud, he determined that art should emerge uninhibited from the unconscious mind, recovering the imagination to engage with notions of the supernatural and the re-creation of myth. Whatever the final achievements and influence of the Surrealist movement were is arguable, but Alexeieff's film, *The Nose*, rejects a particular kind of rationalism in the construction of its narrative, challenges the surfaces of existence and requires that an audience engage with the film at the level of finding fresh responses to new relationships between humankind and its physical environment. It is certainly the case that psychoanalytic thought becomes a useful tool to address the aims, objectives and possible meanings inherent in this kind of film. Especially useful to note in this instance is Freud's essay, written in 1919, titled 'The Uncanny', as I wish to argue that the notion of the 'uncanny' is central to the whole art of animation as well as its more surreal manifestations (see Freud, 1986; O'Pray, 1989).

Freud essentially discusses 'The Uncanny' in regard to E.T.A. Hoffman's 'Sand Man' story (see Hoffman, 1952), focusing on the ability of certain supernatural stories to inspire dread and foreboding, largely through the reader's inability to reconcile tensions between the familiar, domestic and intimate ('heimlich') and the sudden, irrational emergence of secret repressed forces within the familiar ('unheimlich'). The feeling of the 'uncanny' is most provoked, he suggests, by dolls, automata or, most specifically, the notion of an unconscious mechanistic force informing certain kinds of human thought and behaviour. Freud places special emphasis on the way this informs artistic practices:

> . . . an uncanny effect is often and easily produced when the distinction between imagination and reality is effaced, as when something that we have hitherto regarded as imaginary appears before us in reality, or when a symbol takes over the full functions of the thing it symbolises, and so on. It is this factor which contributes not a little to the uncanny effect attaching to magical practices.
>
> (Freud, 1986: 367)

It is not difficult to see how animation has the ready capacity to facilitate 'the uncanny' by effacing the imagined and the real in creating an environment where inanimate lines, objects and materials have the illusion of life, impossible relations can take place, and representational modes of expression become fully accepted aspects of the 'real' world. The Nose creates a strange world which conflates the real and the imagined so that the viewer is uncertain of the status of either. 'Characters' slip in and out of a fluid physical environment and have a temporary narrative status, seemingly operating as figments of the imagination. Other films which employ what are hitherto drawn or constructed 'symbols' in animation (Bugs Bunny, Will Vinton's 'Claymation' figures, Ladislas Starewicz's puppets etc.) take over and sustain more consistently the complete function of what they apparently symbolise (a rabbit, a California raisin, an insect etc.) and, as such, literally become embodiments of the familiar and the unfamiliar which conjoin to provoke the 'uncanny' effect. This effect, clearly, may manifest itself in different, and sometimes apparently opposing, ways. It may be the kind of dread and fear evoked by Alexeieff's images or the comic strangeness evoked in cartoons, but the 'uncanny' can materialise through the acknowledgement and acceptance of the power and effect of any animated image. In many ways, this is illustrated by its most obvious example. It is surely 'uncanny' that Mickey Mouse, an animated drawing, became acknowledged as one of the world's great movie stars in the same way that any live-action actor or actress did. Further, although given his global presence this may be now less affecting, Mickey Mouse is a real character who meets and greets tourists in any Disney theme park or store. Magical practices indeed.

Deadsy (1990)

British animator David Anderson's Deadsy is an example of the combination of xerography and puppet animation, and is included in this brief introductory set of examples which define experimental animation for a number of reasons. First, Deadsy represents the desire to find an innovative technique to express complex ideas. Second, the film addresses the idea of language in animation and third, the film deliberately foregrounds its interest in the dream-state.

The technique Anderson employs – xerography – in this particular instance, involves the filming of a live performance by an actor, followed by the transfer of still images of his performance on to videographic paper. These images are then xeroxed (photocopied) and enlarged, and then rendered and drawn on before being re-filmed on a rostrum. The effect is to distort and degrade the image to create a haunting and hallucinatory quality to 'the character' known as 'Deadsy', a symbol of apocalyptic despair and shifting sexual identity.

Deadsy is introduced as one of the 'Deadtime stories for Big Folk', thus signalling its relationship to the vocabulary of the dream-state and, most particularly, the nightmares experienced by adults. The film creates the dream-state of deep sleep and reveals profound anxieties about the fear of death and the instability of gender and sexuality in its central character, 'Deadsy', who oscillates between being represented by a skeletal model and a distorted human figure. The film continually blurs lines in regard to its representation of 'life' and 'death', masculinity and femininity, and the physicality of sex and violence. Particularly effective in reinforcing this uncertainty and ambiguity is the use of writer Russell Hoban's monologue for 'Deadsy', which echoes the corrupted nature of the images by creating a post-apocalyptic language which slurs and mixes words together, for example:

When Deadsy wuz ul he like din do nuffing big

He din do nuffing only ul ooky-pooky Deadsy

Byebyes like he do a cockrutch or a fly

He din do nuffig big. He werkin his way up tho after wyl

He kilia mowss o yes my my.

This kind of language *suggests* meaning, it does not formally fix meaning in the way that English-speaking peoples might readily understand it. It alludes to the escalation of violent behaviour in the development of humankind and the inevitability of the apocalypse. 'Deadsy' as a character becomes aligned with the personality of a rock star motivated by inner voices and instinctive drives and aroused by the spectacle of destruction.

This sense of arousal either inspires or informs the shifting gender positions 'Deadsy' represents. Anderson shows the phallic relationship between male genitals ('sexothingys') and missiles, illustrating the masculine imperative to violence. 'Deadsy' has a desire to change sex, however, to justify these actions. 'Deadsy' assumes that if he becomes feminised, i.e. 'Mizz Youniverss', then 'ewabody will luv me'. These gender shifts become symptomatic of the complex relationship between sexuality and violence and the socially unacceptable thoughts and feelings each individual may experience and repress. Anderson is suggesting that this kind of complexity underpins the fundamental anxiety that humankind will inevitably destroy itself. The language of animation is particularly enabling in the way that it can blur the lines of gender representation – an issue to be addressed in Chapter Five – so that the notion of being a man or a woman is merely alluded to through the ambiguous traits associated with masculinity and femininity. Animation also reduces the status of 'the body' and, in doing so, extends its vocabulary of representation, thus using it as an infinitely malleable property less fixed by biological or social constraints. The body here is uncertain but obviously politicised.

The film is clearly trying to break into the viewers' preconceived ideas about both animation as a form, and gender, death and global politics as a set of issues. Instead of adopting a more discursive form, Anderson is attempting to re-engage an audience with its deepest fears, using an abstraction of visual and verbal languages, which resist rationalist interpretation and evoke a primal 'babble' of the unconscious mind directly expressing the taboo and the repressed aspects of the human condition. Clearly, like *The Nose*, the film invites Freudian and Jungian analysis but, merely using the criteria that define experimental animation, it is possible to illuminate Anderson's position. 'Deadsy' is a notional configuration but is characterised by differing representations as a form (i.e. as a photographed image and a model) and, as stressed earlier, in regard to gender and expression. 'Deadsy' is simultaneously alive and dead, a figure and an abstraction, a symbol and a cipher for a multiplicity of interpretations. Dialogue is abandoned in favour of a voiceover monologue in order to privilege a corrupted language that is difficult to understand, but betrays a half-relationship to known quantities and perceptions, thus enabling the viewer to engage with its possible implications. Styles are mixed, narrative and continuity are blurred and ambiguous, sometimes deliberately resisting interpretation, and even the artist, whilst clearly present, is also elusive, but this is clearly an attempt to disorientate and provoke the viewer. Anderson wishes to confront his audience with the possibility of what a post-apocalyptic dream-state may look like, and thus deploys the only form that could properly facilitate such an ambition. Animation, like no other aesthetic language, here bridges the gap between the apparently unknowable, seemingly unimaginable, imagery of the unconscious mind, and the apparently knowable, seemingly unthinkable vision of a future world.

At its most simplistic level, experimental animation can picture such psychological and emotional states but, perhaps even more importantly, it properly interrogates dominant perceptions of 'reality' and the received imagery which apparently represents it. Consequently, it may suggested that if orthodox animation attempts to retain some sense of 'the real', experimental animation refutes and invalidates it, insisting upon the medium's capacity to create different and unique image systems with their own inherent form and meaning. Developmental animation sits between the two polarities and, perhaps, represents a high proportion of the work done in the animated field in the sense that it works with the hyper-realist space but subverts it through the use of different techniques, different modes of story-telling and, most significantly, different approaches to issues and themes.

Backward looking, forward thinking: Case studies in developmental animation

Developmental animation, by definition, harks back to traditional aspects of the animated film but also seeks to embellish or reform these traditions with contemporary approaches. Having established that cel animation both dominated the form of, and significantly established, the hyper-realist agenda in the animated film, it is important to consider how animators have resisted or redefined the inherent vocabulary within orthodox animation. This has been achieved in a number of ways, most notably through the move from two-dimensional to three-dimensional animation as a working practice (i.e. clay or puppet animation), or through a re-working of the ideological premises of the animated film that have been established by (white) men within the studio ethos and which have essentially created and defined orthodox animation. Both these issues considerably inform the rest of this discussion as it is not only the intention to validate the cartoon ethos but to question its dominance and promote models of other kinds of animation. These case studies require the viewer to recognise dominant forms but also to realise that certain films re-position the viewer in order to mount a critique of the assumed limits of the medium and the attendant values and attitudes determined by these parameters. An initial example of gentle subversion occurs in the British animation, Girls' Night Out.

Challenging hyper-realist ideology: Girls' Night Out (1986)

Joanna Quinn's Girls' Night Out, made with particular attention to the fluidity of its 'drawn' style, tells the story of Beryl, an ordinary Welsh housewife, who goes out for 'a quiet drink with the girls', and ends up enjoying a male striptease routine. Quinn is careful to prioritise Beryl's warm and engaging character and encourage the audience's empathy with her by stressing the authenticity of the character through the identifiable mundaneness of her existence. It is the very ordinariness of Beryl and her environment, exemplified in the design of the film, which locates it in the 'realist' mode, but it is this sense of quasi-documentary which enables Quinn to manipulate the accepted notions of orthodox animation and the hyper-realist text. The soundtrack is a constant babble of conversation as the film opens, establishing the 'reality' of factory life by focusing upon the image of a conveyor belt with a passing line of cakes. These cakes are endowed, however, with a particular 'bounciness' and are being individually topped with bobbling red cherries. Quinn caricatures and accentuates the 'cartoon-ness' of action abstraction and, as such, subtly implies the image of breasts and this, along with the chorus of chatter, determines that the factory and, indeed, the narrative form of the animation, is gendered feminine. (see Chapter Five). This is important as the film is attempting to reclaim the language of film (live-action and animation) which is predominantly gendered as masculine by the prominence of male characters, modes of action and adventure, and the relegation of women to subordinate roles and narrative functions.

Quinn further subverts the language of the cartoon by prioritising its customary 'speed' for her female characters and her 'feminised' imagery. The sheer vitality of the film is expressed by endowing objects and figures with an excess of drawn movement – telephones shake and jump when they ring, drinks rattle fervently on a tray matching Beryl's bouncing bosom, figures literally blur into shapes which embody the visual dynamics of excitement and laughter. This energy drives the narrative and underpins the sexual agenda of the film. Beryl, for example, fantasises that the macho man of her dreams 'will take her away from all this' and make love with her on a desert island. These fantasies which have deployed the thought bubbles of the comic strip in the first instance, then become the whirring blur of lines and shapes as Beryl kisses her dream man, exhibiting not merely sexual frenzy but uninhibited joy. The notion of 'speed' and the kind of imagery which resists the hyper-realist text (i.e. representational lines and movements) has been gendered feminine, and thus subverted the masculine norms. These 'norms' are satirised by Quinn's clever use of static, hyper-realist images of domestic boredom, characterised by Beryl's couch-potato husband and the family cat who sit drowsily and unmoving in front of the television. Quinn skillfully keeps the scene static while giving it a visual interest, however, by changing the look of the image through the look of the flickering light emanating from the television set. Beryl's husband ignores her when she tells him she is going out and, clearly, the audience's sympathy and encouragement lie with Beryl. It is she who has energy and life. It is she who becomes the embodiment of the capacity for animation to illustrate such tendencies.

She speeds off in a car which leaps across a street map representing the town where she lives. This juxtaposition is a good example of narrative and visual condensation, a concept to be addressed more fully in Chapter Three, but which is essentially an economy of representational ideas compressed within one image. As Beryl speeds along, the pub-sign of 'The Bull' swings in anticipation, and provides a punctuation in the construction of her journey. When she arrives at the pub, Beryl buys her drinks and, as she returns to her seat, the film emphasises the 'wobble' of her body and its obvious size, especially when she settles her large bottom on a creaking bar-stool. In a similar way to which Daffy is viewed in *Duck Amuck*, the audience is invited to inspect and interrogate Beryl's body in a spirit of acceptance and not judgement, an issue Quinn develops in her later film about Beryl entitled *Body Beautiful* (1989) (see Law, 1995). Beryl is an ordinary, working-class woman with a pedestrian experience who is looking for some excitement in an otherwise dull and oppressive life. Quinn shows, however, that there is good humour and vitality in a large, middle-aged woman; someone, perhaps, who is under-represented in the media and to whom the language of animation can call particular attention. The sheer shape and size of Beryl can be manipulated to ambiguous effect. Humourous aspects may be drawn from her character, in the conventional execution of jokes concerning comic size but, more importantly, the exaggeration in her design calls attention to the fact that there are many women like Beryl who are, ironically, rendered 'invisible', or misrepresented by other notions of womanhood and ideas about femininity which are prioritised and endorsed in the media, for example, youth, slimness, sexual passivity/availability etc. The film is suggesting that the audience see life from Beryl's point of view by sharing Beryl's point of view.

Laura Mulvey's groundbreaking work in this area is especially interesting when applied to the more fluid imagery available to the animator (Mulvey, 1992: 22–35). Writing in 1975, Mulvey posited that the 'ease and plenitude of the narrative fiction film' had to be negated in order to re-orientate image-making which merely endorsed patriarchal norms. She suggested that:

> The alternative is the thrill that comes from leaving the past behind without rejecting it, transcending outworn or oppressive forms, or daring to break with normal pleasurable expectations in order to conceive a new language of desire.
>
> (Mulvey, 1992: 24)

Using certain aspects of psychoanalytic theory, she highlights the 'scopophilic' (the sheer pleasure of 'looking', primarily at an object of desire) and the 'identificatory' (the pleasure of identifying with, and endorsing the image of, a screen character) within the practice of engaging with film images. The 'to-be-looked-at-ness' that she then identifies as intrinsic to the image of women in films is cleverly manipulated by Quinn, who plays out a number of interesting reversals in the body politics implicit in the text. Further, Quinn recognises the inherent subversiveness of animation as a medium to facilitate the necessary changes Mulvey promoted. Animation becomes the 'alternative' by constructing 'a new language of desire' located in laughing at the codes and conventions by which women have been represented.[5]

Beryl's body is an ironic take upon the 'squash-n-stretch' characters which populate Disney films in the sense that Quinn constantly draws attention to the 'roundness' and 'compression' of Beryl's figure as a statement about 'the body' and not merely a convenient mode of animated movement. Quinn thus subverts the notion of 'to-be-looked-at-ness' by using the apparent innocence of the animated film to locate Beryl as a woman to be looked at but in a way that *de-sexualises* her at the level of physical spectacle and male fantasy, and *re-sexualises* her at the level of gender. It is in this way that Quinn challenges what Mulvey terms the 'phallocentric order'. This is further enhanced by playing out Beryl's body against the stereotypical ideal of the macho body as it is expressed through the male stripper.

Clad in a black vest and a leopardskin G-string, the moustached, muscle-bound stripper reveals his hirsute chest and rotates his hips as the image concentrates on his bulging codpiece, toying with the idea of the exposure of his penis. The stripper simultaneously operates as comic caricature for the viewing audience and as sexual stimulus for the audience of women in the film. Interestingly, Quinn focuses on parts of his body in the same way that parts of women's bodies have been fragmented and fetishised in mainstream cinema. This cleverly uses the 'filmic' aspect of animation to draw attention to the convention but simultaneously uses caricature and exaggeration in the drawing style to de-eroticise and find amusement in what Mulvey describes as 'the primordial wish for pleasurable looking'. The soundtrack consists of screams of delirium and encouragement – 'Get 'em off!' roars Beryl, as she sprouts horns of bedevilment and mischief, a moment where, once more, animation uses the hyper-realist context but demonstrates Beryl's emotions and attitude through a simple embellishment of the image. The girls enjoy both their excitement and their embarrassment as the stripper dances with increasing confidence and physical bravura. Quinn carefully composes her images to enable the viewing audience to laugh at the stripper's antics by sharing the point of view of the women who are watching him. The stripper echoes the performance of such entertainers in real life but Quinn endows him with an impossible physical dexterity as he bends over and wobbles his buttocks or moves across the stage balanced on one finger! In

Figure 2.1 Joanna Quinn's film, *Girls' Night Out*, neatly reverses the expectations of the spectatorial gaze by illustrating, and ultimately undermining, the voyeuristic pleasures of observing the body of a male stripper

parodying this performance she mocks the supposed sexual prowess identified with over-determined muscular bodies.

Quinn also draws attention to the voyeuristic instincts of the viewer, and reverses the tendency of mainstream cinema for women to be the object of the sexualised male gaze by showing women and, by extension, the viewing audience, the image of a male figure who, by definition, has the specific role of inciting sexual arousal and pleasure. Quinn's ultimate joke, however, is that while it is important for women to be represented in this way, and for men to be portrayed in this light, the final outcome is not worth looking at or taking seriously! This is confirmed by the final moments of the film, which endorse two further areas of Mulvey's analysis. First, her use of Jacque Lacan's work on the 'mirror phase' of human development. She says, 'The mirror phase occurs at a time when the child's physical ambitions outstrip his motor capacity, with the result that his recognition of himself is joyous in that he imagines his mirror image to be more complete, more perfect than he experiences his own body'

(Mulvey, 1992: 25). The cinema has long been seen as the 'mirror' by which the mature spectator continues to re-imagine himself in the light of the models offered by films but, clearly, different kinds of cinema, and here obviously, the animated form, offers different models with different intentions which go some way towards addressing the second aspect of Mulvey's concern, the 'castration complex':

> . . . the female figure poses a different problem. She also connotes something that the look continually circles around but disavows: her lack of penis, implying a threat of castration and hence unpleasure. Ultimately, the meaning of woman is sexual difference, the absence of the penis is visually ascertainable, the material evidence on which is based the castration complex essential for the organisation of entrance to the Symbolic Order and the Law of the Father.
>
> (Mulvey, 1992: 29)

It may be argued that to use these psychoanalytic modes of analysis is to over-burden a delightful and highly amusing animated film, but this is to undervalue the animated film *per se*, and the capacity of Girls' Night Out to support and subvert these theoretical agendas. The image of the stripper in Quinn's film is clearly offered as a parodic epitome of the perfect male form, a form that the women in the film take delight in, but recognise as 'other', not merely at the level of gender, but at the level of the expression of excess. The desires of the women may be measured in their appreciation of the stripper's body and their recognition of his performance as a demonstration of the 'more complete' form which they lack. Instead of accepting this notion of 'deficiency', however, Quinn uses her female characters, chiefly Beryl, to challenge the 'Symbolic Order' and the 'Law of the Father'. Towards the end of the film, the stripper's shadow looms over the initially terrified Beryl, who offers him a drink – the drink in essence being offered to the camera, and the mechanism by which Beryl's actions are disguised as she tugs at the stripper's G-string. Once more, in a frenzy of action abstraction, reaction lines are drawn around the stripper's face and body, which destabilises his previously certain sense of himself and the representation of his masculinity, and consequently, operates as a moment when the film foregrounds itself as a woman's film. The audience has identified with the heroine and enjoys how she undermines the sexual posturing of the stripper (which by extension is a metaphor for arrogant, oppressive masculinity) by tearing off his G-string, exposing a small penis. In psychoanalytic terms, the stripper undergoes 'castration' through the revelation that the power of the 'phallic' male which he physically and metaphorically embodies, in Quinn's terms, is really the comedy of the flaccid penis.

The stripper is humiliated and the women, most obviously Beryl, feel empowered by the moment. Beryl gleefully swings the G-string around after the fashion of the stripper himself, and clearly enjoys her moment of triumph and difference.

Temporarily, Beryl, in the symbolic act of challenging male dominance as it is coded in the stripper's sexual confidence and sense of superiority, undermines the patriarchal norms which constitute the 'Symbolic Law' and the 'Law of the Father'. What Beryl achieves in the narrative, Joanna Quinn achieves in her manipulation of film form and the reclamation of particular image systems which have privileged the male position and rendered women as either absent or merely passive subjects. *Girls' Night Out* fulfils Mulvey's wish to encompass the past but revise 'outworn or oppressive forms' (which we may recognise here as a certain view of orthodox animation), and create new models which foreground female pleasures and desires. Quinn's film becomes the 'language of desire' because it privileges and illustrates a 'feminine aesthetic', a concept to be addressed in Chapter Five.

Continuities in clay: Creature Comforts (1990)

Before addressing Nick Park's Oscar-winning animation, *Creature Comforts*, it is important to stress the emergence of 'clay animation' as an alternative to cel animation and, thus, as a form which is intrinsic to the notion of developmental animation as it is here defined. Clay animation, like animation employing other materials (i.e. models, puppets, objects, cut-outs etc.), is made frame-by-frame but extends the vocabulary of animation into the three-dimensional form and satiates what Art Clokey (the creator of American television's 'Gumby' character) calls the audience's 'Spatial Hunger' (Frierson, 1993: 24). Far from arguing, as has been suggested here, that cel animation constitutes 'hyper-realism' in the animated film, Clokey believes that any intrinsically 'drawn' film is an abstraction, and that an audience recognises its two-dimensionality as a visual deficiency. Three-dimensional animation, in his view, is therefore, more 'real' as it is executed in a real world space and enables animators to work in essentially 'live-action' conditions, but with greater creative freedom and control. This is a persuasive argument, and had it not been for the early industrialisation of the cel-animated process, clay animation may well have come to enjoy a more prominant role. As it is, clay animation, in a similar way to that of animation itself in relation to the live-action film, has been sidelined, while cel animation has come to constitute what has been described as orthodox animation. Indeed, only recently has the first proper history of the clay-animated film emerged. Michael Frierson's work (see Frierson, 1993) only addresses the development of clay animation in the USA, but it provides valuable information and insight to which the following brief contextual history is indebted.

Following his invention of Plasticine in Britain in 1897, William Harbutt published a book entitled *Harbutt's Plastic Method and Use of Plasticine in the Arts of Writing, Drawing and Modelling in Educational Work*, which, as it suggests, provides models for working with Plasticine in educational contexts, and in many key respects also provides models for the proto-animation of clay. Inevitably, the first use of clay emerged in trick films, and *Fun in a Bakery Shop* (1902), whilst not

57

animating clay itself, followed the model of other early films which featured 'lightning cartoonists' in providing a short showcase for a 'lightning sculptor'. Two of the first animated films to actually feature clay animation took their model from Winsor McCay's comic strip, *Dreams of a Rarebit Fiend*, and were titled *A Sculptor's Welsh Rarebit Dream* (1908) and *The Sculptor's Nightmare* (1908), which features a number of 'busts', of Teddy Roosevelt, and prospective presidential candidates who might replace him. The 'bust' and the *tableau vivant* ('living sculpture') are dominant motifs in clay animation – 'the statue that comes to life' was a staple of vaudeville entertainment and continues to be of significant use in many forms of clay animation because it serves to establish a number of useful dramatic and ideological tensions. A statue is, by definition, fixed and still, so when it moves it violates physical laws which means that the statue either operates in the spirit of the uncanny, noted earlier, or as the catalyst for comic farce. Further, a statue is most often a tribute to a well-known figure, and thus carries with it particular notions of status and recognition. Even in *The Sculptor's Nightmare*, Roosevelt is constructed in classical rather than overly caricatured style and, as Frierson notes, this places 'the film's sculpture in the grand humanist tradition: a half-realistic, half-idealised bust that transforms low matter into high art, a timeless rendering of a popular American leader, that elevates the film beyond its slapstick narrative' (Frierson, 1993: 54). These aesthetic and political tensions are more fully utilised by later animators, for example, Will Vinton in *The Great Cognito* (1982), who concentrates on the bust-like head of a stand-up comedian to critique the postures of the American military, and Jan Svankmajer, in *The Death of Stalinism in Bohemia* (1990), who literally uses a number of busts of former Soviet leaders to both represent and discredit communist rule.

J. Stuart Blackton, pioneer of the early cartoon form, also made one of the first clay animations in 1910 titled *Chew-Chew Land* and, by 1916, clay animation regularly featured in the *Universal Screen Magazine* with Willie Hopkin's 'Miracles in Mud' series. Fulfilling Harbutt's intentions to see Plasticine used in educational arenas, Helena Smith Dayton created *Romeo and Juliet* for distribution through the Educational Film Corporation of America in 1917 and, clearly, her role as one of the earliest woman animators is an important, if evidently neglected, milestone.

In many senses, though, this is as much about the lack of recognition for animation in its own right as it is about gender politics. Clay animation doubly suffered from neglect, though its appearance in the Fleischer brothers' 'Out of the Inkwell' short, titled *Modeling* in 1921 was an important step in the recognition of clay animation as a generic form. Previously it had been understood only as the recording of the act of sculpture and not as a mode of expression with its own unique aesthetic codes and practices. Developments in this sub-genre were slow, however, largely because of the work-intensive aspects of producing clay animation and the rapid escalation of the cartoon form. Frierson cites that the key aspects of progress within the form were (perhaps unsurprisingly) the creation of films involving animals, but particularly prehistoric creatures, like the dinosaurs in Keaton's *The Three Ages* (1923) and Virginia May's *Monsters of the Past* sequences for the Pathé Review in 1928, which echoed the work of celebrated stop-motion puppet animator, Willis O'Brien in *The Dinosaur and the Missing Link* (1915) and *The Lost World* (1925).

With the exception of experimental efforts by Leonard Tregillus in the 1940s, and the emergence of Art Clokey's 'Gumby' in the early days of American television, it was not until Will Vinton's Oscar-winning *Closed Mondays* (1974) and the trademarking of 'Claymation' in 1981 that clay animation was a fully consolidated, semi-industrialised, wholly recognised, sub-genre of animation. Vinton's documentary, *Claymation* (1978), usefully addresses some of the key aspects of clay animation and serves as an introduction to the later work of Aardman Studios, and most particularly, Nick Park's *Creature Comforts*. Vinton cleverly uses clay animation to illustrate the processes and pitfalls of making a clay-animated film. He essentially demonstrates the 'materiality' of clay by illustrating its malleability and consistency, and its capacity to literally evolve from a coloured mass into solid and articulated forms. Vinton is careful to show how clay animation shares many of the same processes as the live-action film by animating a film set populated by clay characters and objects, lit like real actors in a studio environment. Some of the key differences, however, lie in the work that precedes the animation. Real actors do, in fact, perform the roles of the animated characters, providing a reference track for the animators. Music is added to the track before the animation team synchronise the action with it. Even preceding this stage, though, is the storyboarding of events, and the plotting of specific movements for both the animated characters and the camera to make. This is crucial in the sense that both aspects must occur frame-by-frame. In one sequence, for example, in which several characters fly a kite, the camera both pans across and cranes vertically upward as the kite rises, eventually tilting apparently above the kite, all at the same time as the characters look upward, facially gesture and wave their arms. Numerous events take place simultaneously in any one frame of film, especially as Vinton's work is populated by characters with a high degree of gestural expression and entire environments are constructed from clay.

Aardman Studios in England developed the tradition of clay animation through their deployment of the opinions, monologues and dialogues of real people, instead of using scripts performed by actors. Thus, while American animators like David Daniels perfected 'Strata-cut' clay animation, Joan Gratz extended the range of 'clay painting', and Vinton continued to innovate with 'clay replacement' techniques,[6] Aardman developed the clay animation with documentary tendency. *Creature Comforts* essentially develops the anthropomorphic tendencies of the Disney cartoon into three dimensions by using Plasticine models of zoo animals. These animals are voiced by real people, however, talking about their own living conditions and those of animals in a zoo.

Dissatisfied with the initial recordings of people's views about zoos, Park quizzed them on their own living environments, and skillfully blends the two kinds of responses on his soundtrack. The humour in the film derives from the tension between the very ordinariness of these varied points and opinions and the visual jokes, achieved first, through the design of the characters, and second, by the activities which take place alongside the main character speaking. The film is constructed in short segments in which each animal is apparently being interviewed by an off-screen reporter.

Numerous things take place while the main character is speaking, however, including a hippo going to the toilet behind an interviewee, a highly coloured bird having its beak 'twanged' as if it were a paper cone on an elastic band stretched around someone's face, or a beach ball which bounces on screen on to the head of an unsuspecting tortoise. These visual jokes are directly drawn from Park's enjoyment of It'll be Alright on the Night, which is a programme composed of 'out-takes' from other programmes, featuring mistakes and unanticipated situations.[7] Park found particular amusement in those out-takes where a reporter is talking about a serious subject, only to be unknowingly undermined by an animal copulating or defecating in the background!

The soundtrack is characterised by people of different age groups speaking in various dialects, and these voices are skillfully matched to an appropriate animal. An old lady's voice, for example, is given to a koala as it perches on a eucalyptus tree. The koala is endowed with huge glasses so as to foreground its large eyes and its difficulty in seeing. This reinforces the vulnerability and 'cuteness' of the creature and the old lady which it represents. This is especially so when, in one of Park's favoured visual jokes, the koala insists she feels very secure just when the branch she is sitting on creaks in anticipation of breaking.

Creature Comforts prioritises a more static image system than Vinton's Claymation work, concentrating on the particularities of small gestures and details for specific comic or narrative effects rather than as a concentrated aspect of 'real' expression. Inevitably, a quasi-documentary approach, however, is closely related to the 'hyper-realist' form, and Park, like Vinton, uses a wider filmic vocabulary 'like camera movements, effects of lighting and complex sets that exist in real space'.[8] He also uses a conventional, diegetically appropriate, soundtrack in respect to the zoo/jungle 'atmosphere' and sound effects to accompany jokes in the style of the cartoon. The 'dynamics of dialogue' that characterise orthodox animation are here substituted with the dynamics of monologue, carefully editing voices together for juxtapositional tonal and thematic effects. The result is an intrinsic 'Englishness' which, like his later Oscar winner, The Wrong Trousers (1993), featuring Wallace and Gromit, is gentle in tone, but ironic in style. Though influenced by the British comic book, The Beano, and Monty Python animator, Terry Gilliam, Park dilutes the craziness and surrealness of these comic-book styles, preferring an unpretentious whimsical approach which highlights the eccentricities of everyday life, and defers to a nostalgic belief in the common but unaddressed aspects of the ordinary. His cause has also extended the progress of clay animation as an important area of developmental animation.

Out of the puppet tradition: Daddy's Little Bit of Dresden China (1987)

If Girls' Night Out represents a re-working of the ideology embedded in the cel-animated image system, and Creature Comforts operates as a sophisticated three-dimensional version of cel-animated forms, another British animation, Daddy's Little Bit of Dresden China, represents an example of an animated film combining different styles which serve as a reflection of the achievements in Puppet Animation and the use of cut-out collage materials. Animator Karen Watson's graduation film once more looks to some of the general principles of orthodox animation, but deploys alternative traditions of animation which have emerged from other cultures resistant to the cel animated mode. Watson's film is particularly appropriate to this analysis because her approach uses materials which L. Bruce Holman suggests are particularly allied in their 'difference' from cartoon animation. He says:

> Less well known are the techniques of flat-figure and silhouette animation in which two-dimensional figures are moved and photographed on a horizontal surface. The figures are two-dimensional like those of cartoon animation, yet in method of movement and in spirit they are more closely related to puppet animation.
>
> (Holman, 1975: 11)

Watson sophisticatedly blends two- and three-dimensional animation in a powerful address of child abuse that took place in her own family life. As she explains, 'For me, Daddy's Little Bit of Dresden China, acted as a form of therapy, enabling me to express feelings I could not have expressed otherwise. Feelings I didn't have words for, and forbidden feelings such as anger' (Pilling, 1992: 96).

The different 'spirit' Holman locates in the puppet, flat-figure and silhouette forms enabled Watson to express the inarticulable and the unspeakable aspects of her experience. It is important to note in relation to this achievement that the puppet form, in particular, is especially significant as a mode of expression because of its specific function as automata. The puppet plays out a complex tension between being like a human being whilst being non-human in form; at once, the puppet is the embodiment of some degree of living spirit and energy but also inhuman and remote. This tension enables the puppet to operate at the symbolic level and simultaneously represent a variety of metaphorical positions. The puppet differs from the clay figure in being less malleable and recognisably 'soft', but does bear a strong relationship to the style and construction of dolls. Many puppet-animation films play upon this similarity to locate their stories in the context of childhood and the memory of formative years. As early as 1898, J. Stuart Blackton and Albert Smith used puppet animation in a stop-motion film called The Humpty Dumpty Circus, of which Smith remarked:

> I used my little daughter's set of wooden circus performers and animals, whose movable joints enabled us to place them in balanced

positions. It was a tedious process in as much as the movement could be achieved only by photographing separately each change of position. I suggested that we obtain a patent on the process. Blackton felt it wasn't important enough.

(Quoted in Thompson, 1994: 17)

Ten years later, an Englishman, Arthur Melbourne Cooper, also animated children's toys in a film called Dreams of Toyland and, in 1911, the Kalem Company made Tragedy in Toyland. These films largely fall into the category of the early trick film, however, and do not represent some of the more specific innovatory work in the puppet/model animation field that was to follow.

Before addressing Watson's appropriation of the puppet for specific symbolic effects, I wish to foreground her work with a discussion of the use of puppets in other modes. Although French animator, Emile Cohl, had made a puppet version of 'Faust' as early as 1910, and became an important influence, the first significant animator in the field was the Director of the Museum of Natural History at Kovno, in Russia, Ladislas Starewicz, who used puppet models of insects and creatures as his animated characters in such films as The Grasshopper and the Ant (1911) and The Revenge of the Kinographic Cameraman (1912). The latter is particularly effective in reflecting early cinema's preoccupation with itself, and the voyeurism that seemed to be afforded by the new medium. Starewicz depicts a tale of love, deception and betrayal using insects as his main characters which, to the modern viewer, may seem to invest the story with a greater degree of sordidness and brutality. This was probably not the intention in Starewicz's mind given his love for nature. Starewicz initially started out making live-action quasi-natural history films showing the intricacies of insect behaviour. The insects, however, died in the unnatural studio conditions, thus denying him the opportunity of showing such detail. He therefore decided to fully control the process by animating models of insects and soon progressed from notions of making a kind of documentary into the creation of modernised versions of traditional fables populated by puppet characters.

Leaving Russia at the time of the Revolution, he went to France, preferring to continue his work as an individual artist rather than join the assembly line processes already emerging in the USA. His work in France is characterised by the development of puppet animation as a vehicle for allegory and satire. Frogland (1922) mounts an implicit critique of inappropriate modes of leadership and the contradictions inherent in an apparently democratic society and, clearly, echoes the complexities of the situation in Post-revolutionary Russia, while Love in Black and White (1923) both pays tribute to the comedy of Chaplin but gently satirises Chaplin's use of sentimentality. Starewicz's work constantly displays this resistance to sentiment and anything which infantilised the form in which he was working. Whilst creating narratives which could be enjoyed by children, Starewicz's films have distinctly adult themes, especially in their depiction of underlying passion (e.g. Tale of the Fox (1930)) and corruption (e.g. The Mascot (1933)). Brought up by his mother and her six sisters, then married with two daughters, Starewicz was often the lone male in his living space and although too much should not be read into his films as a consequence of this, his daughter confirms that this does inform aspects of the representation of sex and sexuality in his films, citing a sequence in Town Rat, Country Rat (1926) where a rat has his tail irreparably injured as a symbol for the kind of impotence, castration and feminisation Starewicz must have felt.[9]

Common to all Starewicz's films is a playing out of the tensions between animality and humanity, where he sometimes invests creatures with particularly sympathetic anthropomorphic characteristics only to surprise the viewer by then depicting their baser animal nature, for example, when costumed, aristocratic, highly posturing 'humanised' rats become wily vermin once they are pursued by a cat in Tale of the Fox. This enables Starewicz to reveal both the attractive and repulsive aspects of his characters. In not completely transforming 'a rat' into a consistently hyper-realist creature, he can manipulate his narratives to operate on a more surreal plane, using his puppet rat to compel an audience to recall its natural feeling of disdain or contempt for vermin which has previously been displaced by an empathy for an apparently 'human' character. This simultaneously reveals the contradictions of both the human condition and the animated film. It also complicates the notion of what is 'human' by not privileging overtly humanised puppets at the centre of the narrative while the narrative invariably operates as a fable about the foibles of human interaction. Starewicz's insects and creatures thus resist the conventional order of civilisation and reveal its chaotic undercurrents. His sophisticated use of puppets to achieve this demonstrates both their versatility and their particular qualities, and his work remains enduringly influential.

Major works in puppet animation inevitably developed in countries which already had a strong tradition of puppet theatre, largely those of Eastern Europe. Willis O'Brien's work in stop-motion puppet animation was subsumed into the special effects of mainstream cinema, most notably in King Kong (1933), but in the former Soviet Union, Alexander Ptushko created the 'Bratishkin' stories, and was instrumental in the creation of a version of 'Gulliver's Travels' in a full-length feature called The New Gulliver (1935). This in turn influenced Czechoslovakian animators, Karel Dodal and Hermina Tyrlova, the latter of whom withstood the interference and oppression of wartime Nazi occupation to continue her work, completing Ferda the Ant (1942), and an anti-Nazi film in the tradition of animated toy films, called The Revolt of the Toys (1945). Though Tyrlova's contribution is substantial in the development of the puppet-animated film, it is another Czechoslovakian, Jiri Trnka, who, following in the tradition of the puppet theatre created by the renowned Josef Skupa, started his own theatre whilst also illustrating children's books, and eventually translated these skills into animated film-making. L. Bruce Holman believes that Trnka's contribution should not be undervalued:

A true genius, and often the centre of artistic controversy, Trnka's contributions to puppet film-making are many. He provided the world with the most delightful puppet films that have been made. He set standards for artistry and quality which forced all other puppet film-makers to evaluate their work in the light of that produced in the Prague studio. And, using a production team method of working, he trained other puppet film-makers who worked with him.

(Holman, 1975: 37)

Trnka's films, *Springer and the SS* (1946) and *The Hand* (1965), signify Trnka's preoccupations with the role of the artist, the importance of social and artistic freedom, and the need to resist the erosion of tradition and preserve the particular nature of Czechoslovakian national identity and its expression. These would also be the key agendas of those who worked with, and followed, Trnka, chiefly Bretislav Pojar and Jan Svankmajer, who both extended the vocabulary of the puppet-animated film by using puppets in different contexts and mixing puppets with other forms of animation.

It was in raising the technical and aesthetic status of the puppet-animated film that Trnka made his most valuable contribution, however, because this enabled the sub-genre of puppet animation to move away from being merely a quaint medium of children's entertainment to become a medium which could support significant social and political meaning. Puppets and models could be used in a more sophisticated way and fulfil their capacity to mediate the 'consciousness' of the animator through their metaphoric role as neo-humans. Studios across Eastern Europe, particularly in Poland and the former East Germany, were particularly attracted to the puppet medium for this reason. Working in oppressive, often authoritarian regimes, animators needed their work to represent their point of view but remain ambiguous enough not to incur the wrath and intervention of the authorities. The puppet can carry metaphoric and symbolic meaning, universalising its apparently 'human' credentials, whilst disguising the personal and political agendas of the artist controlling it. Ironically, though, the puppet is 'non-human' enough to be the bearer of its own meaning, yet 'human' enough to apparently distance itself from the working sensibility of the actual artist. These ambiguities make the puppet-animated film unique in the realm of developmental animation, particularly, as it has become the mechanism by which to engage with the representation of human thought, human creativity and human feeling in what may be described as its most alienated form, somehow disjunct from its 'human-ness', yet best expressed through its 'non-human' abstraction in the puppet.

Western European puppet animation has been more preoccupied with using this disjunctiveness of the puppet as a vehicle for aesthetic rather than political purposes. In *Odd Ball* (1968), for example, a puppet animation by Co Hoedeman, the Dutch animator, puppets are used to interact with various coloured balls of differing sizes in what has been described as a balletic routine similar in style to the sequence in Chaplin's *The Great Dictator* (1940) in which Chaplin, playing a Hitler figure, lyrically dances with a balloon, which is actually a globe of the world, to metaphorically illustrate his world domination (Holman, 1975: 44–5). Though Chaplin's intentions are clearly symbolic, Hoedeman's are more about demonstrating the possibilities of lyrical movement in puppet animation. Metaphoric implications, could, of course, be read into the film, but Hoedeman's work moves more towards being experimental animation whilst still rooting itself in aspects of the orthodox. Orthodoxy, if it can be termed as such, in the puppet-animation field may be located in the films of George Pal, who pioneered certain techniques in the 1930s and 1940s which are still used in the contemporary era.

The great puppet animator, George Pal, was a truly international figure who worked in Budapest, Berlin, Eindhoven, and finally, in the USA where he made the renowned *Puppetoons*, perfecting his 'displacement' technique in animation. This technique required that all the parts of a puppet that actually moved in any one cycle of movement be made in advance so that instead of moving a model a little at a time between each frame, the moving part could be replaced with the following part that progressed the movement of the puppet until the sequence was complete. This was particularly useful as such a system enabled some scenes to be filmed from varying angles in the sure knowledge that a solid object occupied the same space at any chosen point in the sequence. The drawback, of course, was that a wooden puppet did not have the capacity to squash and stretch in the style of cartoon animation and became highly stylised and Cubist as a result. Pal still managed to invest his puppets with great personality, however, and these puppets represent some of the finest examples of gestural acting in puppet animation. Though criticised on racial grounds (see Chapter Five), Pal's characterisation of Jasper, a backwoods black child constantly in trouble, invests a wooden figure with genuine pathos.

His approach became progressively more 'realist' in the propaganda film, *Tulips Shall Grow* (1942), in which a little girl is depicted with a more overtly human head in the face of the highly mechanised marching bombs with screws for necks ('the screwballs') who represent the Nazis. This innovation continued in *And To Think I Saw it on Mulberry Street* (1944) which coupled a child's highly imaginative rhyme with various shifts from black-and-white into colour footage. And, most especially, in *John Henry and the Inky Poo* (1946), which used bigger, armatured puppets with more facial detail, to tell a darker tale about the death of John Henry after he had defeated a locomotive train in a contest to see if humans could conquer machines by driving a number of steel-pins into a railroad line. Pal's emphasis on three-dimensional hyper-realism moved his later work towards more orthodox animation, and the literal expression of the tale.

At this point, Karen Watson's film, *Daddy's Little Bit of Dresden China*, is re-introduced, for it has absorbed the traditions embodied in the work of Starewicz, Trnka and Pal, and sought to develop aspects of them. Watson uses three-dimensional models which operate with a greater degree of representational complexity than many puppet or model figures in the sense that they are made out of materials which have symbolic connotations. The Father figure in the film is constructed out of metal with glass for a head and razor blades for a mouth. He is clearly coded as cold, remote and dangerous, and this seeks to alienate the audience from him in the comparative way that Starewicz calls upon the repulsive aspects of his vermin/insect characters. It is the Father figure, of course, who has been responsible for the abuse of his daughter. She is a small figure composed of feathers and bandages, with a china vase for a head to suggest her vulnerability and fragility. Her mother is made from dried flowers and has a wooden spoon for an arm. The dried flowers represent the loss of nature and fertility while the wooden spoon connotes her domestic role.

These figures are located in the artificial setting of the theatre, illustrating the polite façade of domestic life which, once the curtains are closed, hides a multitude of sins. This has already been signalled in the prologue which deploys the fairytale as a narrative form, casting Father, Mother and Daughter as King, Queen and Princess Snow White.

The voiceover concludes this establishing piece of story-telling with the ominous words, 'Unfortunately for Snow White, no-one ever questioned the King's love for her. The mother was blamed, the father forgiven and the daughter silenced'. This use of the fairytale form returns it to its more complex and sinister origins in the oral tradition, reclaiming it from the ideological and censorial manipulation to which it has often been subjected, particularly in its use within the traditions of orthodox animation epitomised by the Disney Studios (see Peary and Peary, 1980: 66; Zipes, 1989: 24). Watson supports this subversive mode of story-telling by rejecting dialogue, preferring to use the real testimony of other victims of child abuse, a considerable degree of silence, and music which reflects the sub-textual foreboding of the fairytale. The film places its emphasis, though, on playing out its key agendas through its conflicting image systems.

Watson resists a unity of style in order to broaden the canvas of the issues she is implicitly and explicitly addressing. In using a variety of styles – scratched film, drawn animation, collage, puppet/model animation – Watson draws attention to those approaches, most importantly to foreground their narrative and thematic purposes. The piece demonstrates the personal crises of child abuse and domestic violence through its use of the symbolic puppet figures, but also shows the broader social context through its use of collage. The two dimensional flat-figure animation Watson uses reveals the hypocritical attitudes of men with regard to their treatment of women by aligning particular images which endorse the idea of women as sex objects and commodities with male voiceover which illustrates the ignorance of men in their view of sex and sexual abuse. Watson juxtaposes the physical materiality of the symbolic 'human' figures with the disposable fragments of paper that constitute the public misrepresentation of women and which implicitly encourage improper behaviour in the private domestic space. Once the tiny vase that represents the head of the little girl breaks it is clear that unspeakable acts have taken place and Watson uses the disjunctive aspect of the puppet, so valued by Eastern European artists for political purposes, to make a profound statement about the capacity for a 'human' being to commit socially unacceptable 'inhuman' sexual acts. Watson uses developmental animation to express the psychological, emotional and physical damage incurred by the individual in both the private and public spaces in a way that could not have been achieved in the live-action field. The use of symbolic puppet figures, in particular, extends the duality of the bestial and humane explored by Starewicz, the political meta-phor located in Trnka's work, and the gestural stylisation in Pal's films, to reveal the truly subjective aspects of a taboo area of human existence.

Further examples of orthodox, developmental and experimental animation will be addressed throughout the rest of this book, but each film will now be contextualised within a different approach. This does not negate, however, the terms and conditions for each of the conventions of animation which have been addressed. These are merely one set of tools by which to interrogate the animated film and will support any additional focus of analysis which will further reveal the multiplicity of levels and modes of interpretation and enquiry available to enrich the understanding of animation.

3

ONCE UPON A TIME:

Narrative strategies

As is clear from some of the points and issues raised in the first chapters of this book, animation is a medium which makes available a multiplicity of styles and approaches in the telling of a story or the expression of particular thoughts and emotions. Such is the nature of animation, a high degree of preparation is necessary to make even a short film. In the pre-production process, the development of a script, the recording of a soundtrack and a storyboarding of a version of the film, illustrating the specific mise-en-scène of the image and the requirements of the camera, is often a necessity, though not always common practice (see Halas and Pivett, 1958; Culhane, 1988; Noake, 1988). Each animator works in a personal way and any, if not all, of these aspects may be subject to differing emphases, or not adopted at all. Belgian animator, Raoul Servais, believes, however, that whatever the methodology informing the construction of the film, and no matter how short it is, it should always have a story of some sort (Canemaker, 1988: 66).

The idea of 'a story' may be understood as a sequence of events taking place over a particular period of time. These narrative events are informed by a chain of causes and effects, both subtle and explicit, the ultimate outcome of which is a specified moment of resolution. Such events may play out in a number of ways – in a straightforward linear progression, as a parallel series of related scenes, as past events (memories, dreams etc.) re-told in the present context, as implied 'offscreen' occurences etc. In animation, what is particularly significant is the *presentation* of these events and, most specifically, how the order, or number, or extent of the events finds unique purchase and execution in the animated form. It is the aim of this chapter to delineate some significant methods of construction which inform the ways animation can 'tell the tale'. Some narrative strategies, will, of course, be similar to those encountered in live-action film, for example, the implicit positing of narrative questions which are answered within the development of 'the story'. Equally, animation possesses the capacity to create new modes of story-telling, often rejecting the notion of a plot with a beginning, a middle and an end, in favour of *symbolic or metaphoric effects*, a distinguishing characteristic to be discussed throughout this chapter. This analysis will, therefore, address the key devices used in many animated films, or define an approach to staging a sequence of events, and for each approach some particular case studies which use these elements will be provided.

DEFINITIONS AND DEVICES

Metamorphosis

One particular device is unique to the animated form, and some would argue that it is the constituent core of animation itself. *Metamorphosis* is the ability for an image to literally change into another completely different image, for example, through the evolution of the line, the shift in formations of clay, or the manipulation of objects or environments. As Norman Klein suggests apropos of the work of the Fleischer studios' output, 'an image transmutes as if by alchemy, into many others; its atomic structure seemingly comes unglued' (Klein, 1993: 64). The ability to metamorphose images means that it is possible to create a fluid linkage of images through the process of animation itself rather than through editing, although, of course, editing may also be employed in the same film. Metamorphosis in animation achieves the highest degree of economy in narrative continuity, and adds a dimension to the visual style of the animated film in defining the fluid *abstract* stage between the fixed properties of the images before and after transition. Metamorphosis also legitimises the process of connecting apparently unrelated images, forging original relationships between lines, objects etc., and disrupting established notions of classical story-telling. Metamorphosis can resist logical developments and determine unpredictable linearities (both temporal and spatial) that constitute different kinds of narrative construction. It can also achieve transformations in figures and objects which essentially *narrate* those figures and objects, detailing, by implication, their intrinsic capacities. In enabling the collapse of the illusion of physical space, metamorphosis destabilises the image, conflating horror and humour, dream and reality, certainty and speculation.

Case study: The Street (1976)

Caroline Leaf's film *The Street* uses the technique of manipulated ink on a flat plate of glass, lit from beneath, and filmed from above. It is, on the surface, a simple story, based on the autobiography of Mordecai Richler and his experiences in St. Urbain Street in Montreal during the 1940s. The son of a Jewish family, he recalls the experience of the last days of his grandmother's life. This is lived out in the family home and proves to be the catalyst for different kinds of behaviour and emotional response in each of the family members and the extended community. It is the film's very simplicity, however, which creates its effect because Leaf allies the idea of the son's memory to the fluid particularities of the form she employs. The shifts in the figures and shapes formed by the manipulation of the ink consistently redefine the image. Most of the film is a sustained metamorphosis in which images literally flow on from one another. Leaf carefully manipulates her imagery to make this process as invisible as possible. For example, early in the film, when the grandmother pulls up her bed-covers, this also operates as a mechanism to create a black screen by which other forms are defined in the bedroom. These shifts in ink-shapes are only recognisable through the way the film is lit, and the images are essentially constituted by the play between light and dark and the relationship between lines and space. The film does employ some edits and fade-outs, however, although 'dissolves' are achieved by the film using the movement of the ink to create a black out before it forms the next image.

The story begins with the grandmother lying in bed sleeping while the rest of the family have dinner. The son's memory is necessarily selective and places emphasis on particular events and this echoes the narrative conception of Leaf's film. Significance is placed upon the details of the domestic environment and everyday processes. This sense of the ordinary is encroached upon by the onset of death and necessitates that the family evaluate themselves and accomodate the intrinsically ambivalent nature of existence. 'A nurse came everyday' to visit the grandmother, her movement signified by the direction of the ink as it apparently moves towards the background of the image while the nurse's head grows larger as it seems to get closer. The turn of her head provides a black background from which her movement up a flight of stairs is depicted. This is a typical example of metamorphosis as narrative transition, using the device to elide the time and space the nurse covers as she approaches the bedroom. As her legs 'disappear' at the top of the stairs the ink moves to form faces out of the black screen. In the first instance, the face is defined by its dominant features, the eyes providing the foremost aspect of expression and engagement. The form in which Leaf works necessitates that figures remain simple and project their attitudes and emotions in the most direct way. As Thelma Schenkel suggests, 'The roughness of her gestures contributes greatly to the presence of the memories, to making it seem as though the child whose story we are hearing painted these images himself' (Canemaker, 1988: 44). This informs the fluidity of movement in the bodies as they move from operating as figurative representations and transpose into illustations of specific actions. For example, when the children imagine their grandmother dead, it is suggested that 'after she dies her hair will go on growing for another twenty-four hours', and the image demonstrates this process as if it was happening. The representation of reality metamorphoses into a representation of a thought, a thought which, in itself, is a consideration and projection of an action.

The style of the film also enables Leaf to suggest the magical qualities which arise from remembering a certain occasion in a particular spirit or mood. The son recalls, for example, his older sister making a picture frame with her hands using her forefingers and thumbs, the shadow of which remains on the wall even after she has moved. Such an image economically draws attention to the form by recalling shadow theatre and the act of looking, framing, focusing and shaping a scene. It also suggests an uncertain but imaginative recollection coloured by the

Figure 3.1 Caroline Leaf's ink-on-glass animation, *The Street*, a *tour de force* of stylistic innovation, was initially shelved for its frank portrayal of children's responses to a relative's death

intensity of the emotion informing the memory. Once more, as the children pull the blankets over their heads to sleep, this constitutes a blackout, which immediately becomes a door opening – the boy opening the door to his grandmother's room and, by extension, the next phase of the narrative, in which he covets her room, having shared one for over seven years. He kisses his grandmother but wonders if she knows that his affection is tempered by his desire to attain the room, and the fact that he is merely waiting for her to die. This is not highlighted as a particularly selfish or callous objective and, indeed, slips into the mundane fabric of existence, reinforced by the next transition, in which the boy's figure remains in the frame while the bedroom disappears and the next scene of his mother working in the kitchen builds into the remaining space. This becomes an especially significant scene because the metamorphoses between the mother mixing a cake in a bowl, combing her daughter's hair and washing the floor delineate a seamless domesticity which defines her life. Beneath this utilitarian existence is a deep anxiety about her mother, however, and an increasing recognition that her mother's illness will, indeed, result in her death. She hugs her mother, the naïve shape of the characters adding an additional poignancy to the over-determinacy of the embrace. Having to care for her mother, however, results in her own hospitalisation with a gallstone condition, the additional consequence of which is the placement of the grandmother in an old people's home. The intensity of these events is juxtaposed with the playfulness of the children, unaware of the seriousness of the situation, and remote from its emotional implications. The son and his older sister fight about their own concerns and, as Schenkel describes, provide another example of Leaf's ability to condense narrative action yet create an almost tactile effect:

> The energy of the fight itself is conveyed through the strokes of Leaf's painting. We see fists flying, faces with tongues sticking out, hair being pulled, all surging out of the sepia-toned strokes. The energy of the childhood battle is mirrored by the energy of Leaf's improvisation. Her fingers and their arms become one. The motions of the fight and the gestures of the painter, the storyteller and the story, fuse.
>
> (Schenkel, 1988: 45)

This sense of the improvisatory is very important in that the metamorphoses operate as the mechanism in suggesting immediacy. Similarly, the timing of the metamorphoses can serve to create a more delayed sense of change. For example, the father's response to the moment when his wife, having recovered and returned home from hospital, visits her mother in the home, is played out in a protracted manner, suggesting the anxiety of waiting. The image metamorphoses from viewing the father front-on to a side-on position, eating and staring out of the window, before changing to a view of him from outside the window. This anxious wait only heightens the typically Jewish sense of irony when he says 'I was born lucky, and that's it'. In a further moment of condensation, an ambulance arrives returning the grandmother to the family home, clearly indicating that the mother could not accept that the grandmother would live out her days in a home uncared for by her immediate family. There is a strong sense of guilt and obligation in these actions, prefiguring the ultimate catharsis of the grandmother's death.

The death itself is recorded only after the fact, as it is signified by the son's return home (as he catches a ball, is passed by cars, and vaults over a water-hydrant) only to observe crowds gathered outside his home. He moves through the people, and the sequence uses each metamorphosis as a projection of the boy's own point of view as he enters the building. As he turns, the top of his head becomes the 'screen' by which the image transposes to the top of the stairwell and, finally, into the darkness of the living room. The viewer sees the people at his level, as well as glimpsing the details of the room, like the pattern of the wallpaper. He talks to his mother, two still figures in front of apparently moving shapes and forms behind them. This focuses the scene and the important moment when the mother gives her son the grandmother's necklace and ring. The personal and private aspect of this moment is contextualised by the following scene in which Dr Katzman, a family friend, and the son's uncle, a rabbi, smoke out on the balcony and consider the relativity of life. 'Your heart is broken', says Katzman, 'and yet it's a splendid summer's day'. Leaf's images reflect that life goes on and urbanity remains unchanged in the street, yet this seems curiously affirming instead of indifferent. In order to reinforce this optimism, the concludes with another scene of the innocent preoccupation of the children. They go about their normal routine of retiring for the night and, when they are settled, the older sister teases her brother by pretending to be her grandmother's ghost, whispering 'Who's been sleeping in my bed?'. In the son's memory, it is this moment of terror that signifies the event, only highlighting his self-centredness in wanting the room, and the idea that the child's world had not yet been intruded upon by too many harsh realities. The metamorphoses essentially narrate these emotional moments and heighten them through a tactile immediacy and a simple focus.

Case study: Betty Boop's Snow White (1933)

Dave Fleischer's version of the Snow White story is a representative example of the possibilities achieved in metamorphoses beyond the notion of narrative continuity and suggestion. Fleischer's metamorphoses take on a more surreal, and often sinister purpose, disrupting the rationality of a scenario and challenging the very premises of a stable environment. Snow White is, of course, a fairytale, and within the context of the literary form there are already elements which make it especially fitting to the animated form. As Marina Warner suggests,

> Shape-shifting is one of fairytale's dominant and characteristic wonders: hands are cut off, found and reattached, babies' throats are slit, but they are later restored to life, a rusty lamp turns into an all-powerful talisman, a humble pestle and mortar becomes the winged vehicle of the fairy enchantress and the slattern in the filthy donkeyskin turns into a golden-haired princess. More so than the presence of fairies, the moral function, the imagined antiquity and oral anonymity of the ultimate source, and the happy ending (though all these factors help towards a definition of the genre), metamorphosis defines the fairytale.
>
> (Warner, 1994: xv–xvi)

In many ways, Fleischer's deployment of metamorphosis is a resistance of the 'moral function', and enhances the modernity of animation itself beyond the constraints of mere story-telling. Whilst Disney's version of Snow White changes and distorts the premises of the original fairytale, it does this in order to bring clarity to an extended narrative and to create an optimistic resolution. Even its most memorable metamorphosis – the transition of the wicked queen into the old witch – has a narrative function, that of disguise. Fleischer's Snow White has little interest in such plausibilities, using the fundamental structure of the fairytale as an exercise in the construction of dark humour and sensual fantasy. His version compresses the story into a few minutes, (mis)casting the highly sexualised Betty

73

Boop as the supposedly virginal Snow White, aided by Fleischer stalwart Koko the Clown, and the dog, Bimbo, in the face of a prototypic Olive Oyl character as the Queen.

The Queen consults her mirror in order to discover who is the fairest in the land, whereupon the mirror becomes a blackface character answering in the affirmative (a little implausible, given the excess of caricature in the design of the Queen, but that's cartoons for you!). The apparently racist aspect of the film in making the mirror a blackface character seems reinforced by the role of the mirror as slave to the Queen, and in its connotation of 'black magic', but is contradicted by the use of black singer/orchestra leader, Cab Calloway, in both the performance of 'St James Infirmary Blues', and as the rotoscoped moving figure accompanying the song (see Cabarga, 1988; Langer, 1993). These contradictions will be explored in Chapter Five, but it is perhaps enough to say here that the Fleischers were men of their time, preceding the more enlightened eras of production which exhibit greater sensitivity in regard to representation. Caricature, in their eyes, was merely a convention of cartooning, and did not carry with it overt political agendas. This is also a partial defence of the film's apparent sexism, but Betty Boop was also a product of male artists who felt they were properly reflecting their admiration of, and attraction to, the female form, in their depiction of the child-woman. For them, this was not a misrepresentation, though, of course, it wasn't innocent either, because Betty's design deliberately foregrounded taboo aspects of sex and sexuality, later challenged by the censor.[1] Betty is literally a male fantasy figure contextualised in a masculinised animated space which constantly demonstrates its fascination and preoccupation with her body. It is this fact alone which legitimises the Fleischers' use of Betty as the Snow White figure. She is the fairest in the land because she is the most physically attractive in regard to the overt projection of her sex and sexuality. As Betty enters the castle singing 'I wanna see my stepmama', stalactites coil upwards, knights become upright as she passes, and the whole physical space becomes alive with her rhythm. Betty always seems subject to the male gaze and exists within a phallic environment, a situation which anticipates the primal motives of Tex Avery's narratives (see Chapter Four) but to more surreal (erotic) rather than comic effects.

The Queen resents Snow White because the mirror revises its initial view and suggests Betty is now the fairest in the land. Absurdly, her face metamorphoses into a pan while her eyes change into two fried eggs, signifying, and calling attention to her extreme reaction. 'Off with her head!' she cries, illustrating her order by snipping off the tip of one of her fingers with two other fingers configured like a pair of scissors. Betty is taken away by two guards, who ultimately turn out to be Koko and Bimbo (effectively the huntsmen of the original tale) who tie her to a tree, sharpen an axe blade and clean a tree stump ready for her execution. The phallic nature of the scene is beyond question, but contemporary audiences may also perceive further sexual connotations in Betty's bondage. Affected by Betty's rendition of 'Always in the way', the two knights show compassion and grind the axe and shovel away completely, simultaneously falling through a hole in the ground with the grinder. The tree releases Betty and places a wreath on the now snow-covered space intended to be her grave. These implausible events parody the fairytale and use its illogical qualities to foreground the possibilities inherent in animation to recall some of the darker aspects of fairytales before they have been bowdlerised or made innocuous by contemporary mores. Metamorphosis, in this sense, thus becomes a subversive tool, revealing previously rationalised qualities, and undermining physical orthodoxies.

The narrative literally slides into its darker agenda when Betty trips, rolls herself into a snowball and passes through a gate which reshapes the snow as a box. The box then plunges into a frozen lake, only to emerge as an ice 'coffin' which slithers to the front of the house occupied by the seven dwarves. These transitions drive the narrative in a way which fully demonstrates the capacity of animation to create and justify its own story-telling premises unencumbered by logic or rationality. The dwarves, once more the undifferentiated group of the original tale, elongate their necks to view Betty and, in the time that it takes for the box to pass through their house, become the pall-bearers transporting the coffin to the depths of the mystery cave. The Queen reaffirms her claim as the fairest in the land and uses the mirror to change her clothes as well as to convert Koko into a ghost. The ghost sings 'St James' Infirmary Blues' as the coffin passes into the dark cavern of the underworld, populated by skeletons and decorated with fatalistic symbols such as dice and cards. The loose fluid movement of the ghost was created through the direct rotoscoping of the dance-walk made famous by Cab Calloway. The dips and loops that characterise the movement enable the character of the ghost to operate as if it were a flowing set of tubes or ropes which configure into a ring chain connected to a 20 cent piece, and a bottle, as a literal illustration of the lyrics. These metamorphoses intensify the adult nature of the imagery employed in the blues idiom and locate the cartoon not merely in a demonstrably hellish environment but also in the underworld of vice and criminality. These images are a long way from the safe ideological dislocations of the later Disney version and foreground the dark agendas which define the Fleischer output as a genuine contemporisation of the fairytale form. The Fleischer brothers use their metamorphoses to reveal and emphasise the ease with which social destabilisation and collapse may occur. Their fantasy worlds only heighten the fragile premises of law and order, routine and process, expectation and fulfilment.

As the cartoon reaches its climax, the Queen's tongue turns into a snake as she reaffirms her status, but with that her mirror explodes, turning her into a dragon. In the film's final chase sequence she pursues the now risen Betty, Koko and Bimbo from the cave. Her mouth becomes a horn while three snakes on her head become trumpets as her body literally plays and illustrates the music. In a final visual tour de force, Betty tugs on the dragon/Queen's tongue and pulls its skeleton completely outside its body. The trio escape and dance in a circle in the snow. What then, is an audience to conclude about the deployment of such imagery? It may be argued that two concerns inform this latter sequence. First, the desire to maintain the ambiguities and magical distortions of ancient fairytales, which foreground the relationship between *interiority* and *exteriority*, and treat the psychological and emotional with the same *physical* equivalence as the material world. Second, a formal need to demonstrate the capacity of animation to literally create impossible events and determine new relationships between representative forms and imagined conceptions within ephemeral modes of expression. In this, metamorphosis is the guiding and necessary principle.

Condensation

Animation predominantly occurs in the short form, and manages to compress a high degree of narrational information into a limited period of time through processes of condensation. These primarily include the *elliptical cut* and *comic elision*. The elliptical cut works in the same way as live-action film-making in the sense that cuts are made between the depiction of events that signify the passage of (often undetermined) lengths of time. Adding to this process, may be the *fade out and fade in*, the *dissolve* from one image to another, and the *wipe*, where one image appears to cover and replace another. Such is the nature of the animated form, though, it can signify its own processes of continuity by directly referring to the idea that the film is made by constructing one image at a time which is then photographed one frame at a time. Numerous films include 'page-turning', apparently revealing the next image or event in the story.

Comic elision is essentially the construction of a sequence of comic events which operate as a self-determining process informed by the particular timing and relationship of the visual and verbal jokes. This will be discussed at length in Chapter Four. Condensation in animation prioritises the most direct movement between what may be called the *narrative premise* and the *relevant outcome*. This may be the movement between establishing context and problematising it; creating a comic structure and determining its 'pay-off'; defining dramatic conflict through the relationship between character and event; locating a tension between representation of the past (memory/myth/historical fact) or future (projection) with the representation of the present; or privileging the status of the abstract (symbol/metaphor) over the identifiable and figurative (hyper-realism). Conflating premise and outcome is the defining feature of temporal condensation in animation.

Case study: Home on the Rails (1981)

Paul Driessen's film Home on the Rails creates an environment which deliberately conflates particular kinds of imagery associated with stories concerning trains, most specifically in this case, the opening up of the American West and the melodramatic 'suicide on the rails'. A train track literally runs through the living room of an ordinary couple, who base the whole of their daily routine around the times when a train comes through. In many ways the film is fundamentally an absurdist comedy about waiting. The pace of the piece is slow and the condensation processes as outlined on p. 76 are employed as the occasional events of the film. Driessen cleverly uses the predictable choreography of his couple, however, to create significant visual practices which conflate space and time. Always interested in the visual space itself – in *David* (1977), he uses an unseen character, and only defines action on the screen by voiceover and small narrative events – Driessen recognises that his couple define themselves by the limitations of their movement, so he uses fade-outs and fade-ins to signify the process of their anticipated course of action. They essentially appear, disappear and reappear in a new place. Similarly, he deploys a faint transparent illustration of the train as a set of anticipation lines before the train actually passes through the room. This heightens the predictability of the piece and, most particularly, calls attention to the banality of everyday events in relation to the absurdity of the comic situation. The predictable pattern established by the couple, however, is slightly disrupted by the antics of the cuckoo figure in the cuckoo clock who, in a series of sight gags, punches a small figure out of the clock, empties a bucket of water, excretes on the carpet, guillotines his own head off, and jumps up and down before closing his door. The character is essentially defined by the condensation of the comic event. Each time he appears, therefore, the viewer recognises his abstract comic purpose in relation to the mock-realism of the couple's routine.

While the woman knits, her husband goes out and pans for gold. She routinely opens the living-room doors ready for the train to pass through; he regularly returns with a bag of gold, and contentedly smokes his pipe. One day, he returns without any gold, and anticipates the coming of other people will signal his further demise. After a last cup of tea, therefore, he lies down on the rails and commits suicide when the train comes. Only a broken cup remains, which his wife, in deadpan style, sweeps up. The coming of civilisation, as predicted by the man is not long away though. The supposedly romantic conception of the meeting of East and West at a promontory point in the mid-West is played out as the unseen crashing of trains into the side of the couple's house, jettisoning it into the sky and, finally, into the sunset. Things may have been different if the woman had opened the doors as usual! Driessen's achievement here is considerable. He condenses one of America's greatest myths into an implied off-screen event, only knowable by the banal cruelty of its impact. The narrative premise of illustrating the consequences of change as the defining principle of progress is subverted by Driessen's re-working of the clichéd 'happy ending', as the couple's home is literally projected into the sunset, rather than the latter being the location which happy couples walk off towards.

Driessen's narratives are often informed by such tensions, and his use of condensation effects only serve to heighten the dark premises which underlie seemingly simple, if sometimes absurd, events. His characters are defined by their narrative events and not their psychological and emotional complexity; they are also the embodiment of their individual problems, for example, in this case, an inability to change. They occupy a world, however, which conflates past and present and, as such, becomes a fluid environment subject to its own laws. Driessen's condensation effects, therefore, suit his fundamental purpose of locating the abstract within the possibility of the real, and to redetermine 'realism' in an abstract light.

Case study: Jumping (1984)

Osamu Tezuka, one of Japan's most celebrated animators, was also one of its foremost exponents of the comic-strip manga films, in which he drew stories in a highly cinematic style, aping the compositions and camera angles of contemporary live-action films. Tezuka's work, though, was often informed by philosophic intentions, and his deployment of condensation effects in Jumping are important in redefining the audience's perspective both in relation to what they see and its implications and consequences. The viewer sees the film from the same point of view as its omnipotent but unseen central protagonist – a figure that has the capacity to jump up extremely high and traverse long distances with every leap. As Tezuka has suggested, 'Those who jump are you, the public, humanity. We humans have the tendency to go too far with what we do. Often this becomes a dilemma or a catastrophe' (Bendazzi, 1994: 415).

The narrative of the film is defined by thirty jumps. Each jump takes the viewer high into the air and back down to the ground. As the figure ascends and descends the viewer sees different events which signify both a temporal and spatial progression. This progression may also be read at the metaphoric level as a journey – a psychological rite of passage, the development of human ambition and endeavour, the inevitability of humankind's drive towards its own self-destruction. The 'up and down' aspect of the piece redefines the notion of linearity in narrative progression, and characterises human perception as selective, random and incidental. Suddenly, the whole order of existence is rendered as relative and ephemeral, temporary and cursory. The figure leaps over woods and lakes; clashes with birds; passes an ASIFA sign in an animation in-joke[2]; encounters factories, schoolyards and skyscrapers; passes a man committing suicide on the railway tracks, an irate taxidriver, a naked lady on a roof garden, some fishermen, and cannibals preparing to eat a white explorer. The interaction with the figures is predominantly (and unsurprisingly) shock at the jumper's sudden intrusion, but the figure also affects situations (for example, he/she knocks over a glass of orange on a ship's table) and provokes actions (for example, the cannibals throw their spears after him/her). The cannibals' attack serves as a gentle prefiguring to the jumper's entry into a war zone, his/her projection into the mushroom cloud of an atomic bomb and his/her descent into hell, where he/she encounters demons who attempt to keep him/her there. The gender ambivalance is important in sustaining the view that the narrative is addressing the foibles of all humankind, and that any human being constitutes the viewing audience.

Figure 3.2 *Jumping* exhibits an innovative and amusing sense of narrative development by exaggerating a child's leaps across time and space while literally illustrating animation's ease in showing shifting perspectives

From the film's simple beginning on a plain road, right through to its cyclic conclusion where the jumping figure has emerged from hell back to the place where the narrative began, *Jumping* deploys condensation devices for shock effect. The narrative passes from the comparitive innocence and openness of the natural world through to an apocalyptic world analoguous to hell itself. The comic perspectives encountered early in the film – the continuing irritation of a bird that keeps clashing with the jumper, the surprise of a naked woman sunbathing on her roof garden – soon gives way to a view of the world which implicitly demonstrates its inequalities and its inclination towards conflict and destruction. Tezuka's narrative conceit essentially enables him to privilege a set of observations which operate as images with the same symbolic relevance; in other words, a glimpse of a blue teddy bear in the woods becomes as important as a team of flying war planes. This merely illustrates the *relativity* of existence, and draws attention to the ways in which humankind ignores or dismisses things, refusing to distinguish between what is important and what isn't.

Tezuka is essentially saying that the progression towards Armageddon is inevitable because humankind will not value its very *humanness*. The image that best illustrates this, of course, is (once again) the man committing suicide, who, like everything else experienced by the jumper, is merely glimpsed, and not considered, until it is too late. The implication is that humankind is so preoccupied by elevating itself and moving forward – jumping ahead, that it doesn't consider the cost. The jumper is clearly relieved to be back on the road at the end of the film but, ominously, starts to move forward in exactly the same way as at the beginning as the final credits roll. Tezuka condenses time and space to metaphoric effect, simultaneously commenting on aspects of the Japanese experience and suggesting, with admirable economy, the deep flaws that characterise humankind's ill-considered ambition. This is condensation as critique and warning; by using the point of view technique and the jump as physical and metaphorical ellision, the narrative operates as a historical lesson with contemporary immediacy.

Synecdoche

Another of the chief devices instrumental in the condensation process is the use of synecdoche, literally a device by which the depiction of part of a figure or object represents the whole of the figure or object. (In some respects this is also similar to the use of metonymy, which is the substitution of an image for its action, e.g. a symbol of a bottle instead of the act of drinking.) This can be used in two specific ways. First, to signify the specificity of a narrative event (i.e. the close-up of a hand opening a safe), and second, to operate as a metaphor within a narrative (i.e. the hand becomes a cipher for the idea of a character or a specific associative meaning). Clearly, this device compresses the logic of narrative progression and its dominant meanings into a single image.

The second methodology of the synecdoche is particularly suited to the animated form because the 'part' operating as a representation of the 'whole' is often used as a particular 'whole' in its own right, whilst still recalling the associative aspects of its source. To pursue the example, 'the hand' may become *a character* without negating its relationship to 'the body'. The functional aspects of 'the hand' (the ability to grasp things, gesture, indicate etc.) become the heightened primary aspects of its *personality when it is defined as a character*, but 'the hand' still retains its correspondent set of meanings in relation to the rest of the body, which inform its secondary functions as a narrative form. The synecdoche is particularly effective in drawing attention to the qualities, capacities and associations of 'a part' and its fundamental role within the 'whole', working as both an emotive and suggestive shorthand for the viewer.

Case study: Use Instructions (1989)

Guido Manuli's film, *Use Instructions*, is an extremely direct indictment of the ills of contemporary life, sparing little in its brutal satire. Simply, the film uses a human bottom as its synecdoche and central metaphor, beginning by suggesting that 'we have lost the instruction booklet for its use'. The tone is set by the following credits sequence in which a mosquito is seen sucking from a Killer Spray can before breaking wind and expelling poisonous fumes as it flies past a baby. The baby catches the mosquito, but is transported away by it until it is unceremoniously dumped back into its pram. From here the film operates as a catalogue of the ways in which humankind abuses itself and its environment. This is symbolised by the use of an excreting bottom as the 'part' which best embodies the 'whole' of humankind in its more inappropriate endeavours. For example, the baby points out a car in which the back of the vehicle is a bottom expelling fumes. A ship with a bottom excretes into the sea killing fish; a tap shaped like a bottom pours polluted water which turns a man's hand green and hairy; a television in the shape of a bottom shoots its viewers, likening the anal passage to a gun firing faeces; and bottom-shaped cigarettes exhale smoke-rings which ultimately strangle the baby.

Though these images essentially operate as a one-joke sight gag, they do have an accumulative and escalatory effect, by stressing the exploitative behaviour of humankind. Factories excrete bins of rubbish; Tarzan swings directly into the bottom which defecates a road through the jungle; and a deer is shot and squashed by the bottom of a soldier. Manuli indicts major institutions like big business and the military and, by implicition, the governments of developed countries who exploit the developing world. The use of economy in raising these issues and offering explicit criticism is entirely enabled by the deployment of the synecdoche. When Tarzan swings into the bottom that lays a road through a jungle, an extraordinary compression of ideas takes place. The native of the jungle, and the erstwhile embodiment of a certain primitive heroism, is literally overwhelmed by the exigency of the technological machine, which brings industrialisation and urbanity where nature used to be. The bottom merely substitutes for the technological machine and debases the idea of progress that it apparently represents. To reinforce this agenda, later in the film, a plane drops an aid parcel to a Black developing nation, which is merely a bin of developed world rubbish. The explicit critique of rich capitalist nations is perhaps best embodied, though, by the excretion of a Coke-bottle from a super-drink fountain. Coca-Cola, one of the major global commodities, carries with it a specific corporate identity which signifies a notion of business achievement. To present it as an excretion is to undermine its success, the worth of the product, and the conditions of its production.

Manuli is careful to suggest, however, that the desire to debase and abuse is an intrinsically human quality, exemplified by the fact that a mountaineer still defecates on a snow-peak previously untouched by human presence. At the moment when humankind appears to achieve something it seeks to undermine or destroy it. Human progress is defined by bottom-shaped rockets and, most poignantly, by an atomic cloud, invested with extra significance by the overt visual resemblance between the mushroom cloud and a bottom. The idea of progress is ridiculed on a smaller scale too, when a robber exposes his bottom in a bank-raid, or when a bottom-shaped syringe plunged in a man's arm causes his face to metamorphose also into a bottom. Manuli's persistent point is one of suggesting that these notions of progress are *unnatural*, and misrepresent human-kind. Animation enables him to define and illustrate this 'unnaturalness'. When a plastic surgeon cuts off two bottoms and attaches them to a woman, she has the capacity to excrete from her head and chest (both still overtly represented as bottoms) and her own bottom. The body, it is implied, is an organic and not a falsely constructed thing. Natural functions become the agent by which to recognise the debasement of the physical form.

Such imagery starts to hint at another of Manuli's targets – human sexuality. Even the Red Riding Hood stories in a book in the baby's pram feature a wolf who exposes himself to a baby; his genitals, however, are yet another bottom. A man's hand grabs a woman's bottom and disintegrates. The baby, the film's central figure, then defecates, and is beaten and hit by his parent for doing so, before being kicked into an orbit which reveals that the whole of the planet is a bottom. Manuli's camera dollies out to reveal the planet is in a toilet. The lid closes to the strains of 'Use Instructions' and the film concludes. The film may be accused of being unsubtle and repetitive, but no viewer will be left in any doubt of the ability of the synecdoche to signify specific ideas in a highly condensed way. Manuli suggests that our future children are the ultimate victims of humankind's systematic abuse of the planet in the name of progress and that, as such, the planet is literally 'down the toilet', if it doesn't come to terms with a proper way of disciplining itself and undoing its ills. Much of life is 'shit' suggests Manuli; his economic use of the bottom as a synecdoche conjoined with the physical and material constructions of late industrial capitalism makes this point in a most emphatic and indisputable way.

Case study: Gwee (1992)

Francis Pik Ching Yeung's student film, *Gwee*, is an exemplary example of synec-doche at its most economic. On a backdrop which resembles the downy hair of a fur pelt, a dream-thought tumbles from a window, showing a playful wild animal playing in a stream. The juxtaposition of these images signifies the natural demeanour of the creatures and their ultimate fate at the hands of the fashion industry. The fashion industry is symbolised by the synecdoche of a red sewing machine needle which simultaneously stitches a pelt with red thread whilst appearing to chase the terrified animals away. The stitching sounds like machine-gun fire which only amplifies its destructive intention. The blood-red needle embodies the blood of the creatures and signifies the cost to the natural world as a line of pelts emerges behind the screaming, fleeing animals. Ironically, the synecdoche here works to illustrate the tension between destruction and creativity, and foregrounds the power of the machine over the vulnerability of the physical world. The use of synecdoche minimalises the image vocabulary but intensifies the level of suggestion, further informing the symbolic and metapho-ric possibilities available in narrating the animated film.

Symbolism and metaphor

Symbolism, in any aesthetic system, complicates narrative structure because a symbol may be consciously used as part of the image vocabulary to suggest specific meanings, but equally, a symbol may be unconsciously deployed, and, therefore, may be recognised as a bearer of meaning over and beyond the artist's overt intention. In other words, an animated film may be interpreted through its symbolism, whether the symbols have been used deliberately to facilitate meaning or not. This can, of course, radically alter the understanding of a film, arguably making it infinitely richer in its implications, or misrepresenting its dominant project altogether. The status of the symbol in animation is further complicated by the fact that the symbolic effects in the live-action text are always measured against the literal aspects of 'the real'. As was suggested in Chapter One, the symbol in animation can operate in its purest form, divorced from any relationship to the representation of the real world, finding its proper purchase in the realms of its primal source. The symbol itself can go through many transitions and eventually operate in a variety of ways. It is, therefore, useful to distinguish between the symbol and the sign, and to engage with the idea that the symbol can function in different ways dependent upon its context and the specific historical moment in which the symbol is defined and, subsequently, called into the image system. Peter Munz suggests that 'a sign merely duplicates the thing it signifies' (Munz, 1973: xi), while the symbol,

> . . . is an altogether different kind of substitute. A symbol is more specific and precise in its meaning than the thing it symbolises. Since the symbol has a more specific meaning than the thing it symbolises, the thing benefits from a feedback and receives a new and more specific meaning from its symbol than it originally possessed.
>
> (Munz, 1973: xii)

The symbol *invests* its object with meaning. A useful example, here, is the phallic symbol. A tower, for instance, in literal terms is a tall building, but if it were understood as a representation of the power structures in business, and a particularly dominant figure at the head of such a business, it may be understood as a phallic symbol, relating the material world to physical potency. This enriches the image and extends its meaning, but such a meaning may only be determined by where the viewer participates in what Munz describes as the *historical seriality* of the symbol. He notes that, 'Each symbol is part of a series in which the more specific symbol feeds a meaning back to a less specific one and receives a meaning from another still more specific' (ibid.: xii). The symbol, then, is defined by a series of substitutions, Once more, to pursue the example, the tower motif may have been preceded by other architectural motifs like a spire, or a chimney, or logs, sometimes in cabin structures, or a tree-house, all locating phallic *resemblance* within the image system and relating it to the increasing power and effect of a figure associated with these images. Another way of viewing this historic seriality in the symbol is to see it as a specific narrative progression where developments in the image equate with changing meanings within the story structure. Many animated films rely on these kind of progressions, because they prioritise the role and continuing recontextualisation of the symbol in both figurative and abstract scenarios. Animation liberates the symbol and its attendant meaning from material and historical constraint, enabling evocation, allusion, suggestion and, above all, *transposition*, in narrative strategies.

Metaphor essentially grows out of symbolism and serves to embody a system of ideas in a more appealing or conducive image system. The use of metaphor simultaneously invites interpretation but insists upon openness. The meanings that may be determined from the use of metaphor resist specificity because they emerge from a second-order notion of representation. Metaphors make the literal interpretation of images ambiguous and sometimes contradictory because they invite an engagement with the symbolic over and above the self-evident. This second order of construction offers a parallel narrative to the specific one which merely deals with the construction of logically determined and contextualised events. Whilst the symbol invests an object with a specific, if historically flexible, meaning, the metaphor offers the possibility of a number of discourses within its over-arching framework.

Case study: The Hand (1965)

Argentinian novelist, Jorges Luis Borges once commented that 'Censorship is the mother of metaphor' (Manea, 1992: 30), clearly foregrounding the necessity to *smuggle* meaning into a creative text that would otherwise be prohibited by the authorities. Metaphor has thus characterised many works which have emerged out of an Eastern European or Latin-American context, operating as a means of resistance to oppressive ideological practices. Jiri Trnka's puppet animation, *The Hand*, remains one of the most affecting studies in the recognition of the role of the artist and the importance of free expression in the face of totalitarian regimes that the animated form has seen. It effectively summates the experience of animators attempting to make films free of social and political constraint. Essentially an autobiographical work that engages with the difficulties of making films in Czechoslovakia in the face of intervention and oppression by the Soviet authorities, the film uses a hand as its chief symbol, and the relationship between art and authority as its presiding metaphor. Using the most dominant contextualising metaphor in Eastern European animation, that of an everyman figure within a domestic environment, encroached upon by destructive external forces, Trnka casts his puppet in a more symbolic light by dressing him as harlequin. Harlequin as a character is 'infinitely repeated, theatrically pervasive'[3] and, as such, embodies numerous discourses which exist outside social orthodoxies. Physically dexterous, self-aware, consciously (satirically) humorous, Harlequin often plays out scenarios of moral contradiction, mixing elements of the faithful servant, the knowing child and the occasionally amoral rascal. Trnka uses his figure, however, to express the enforcement of servitude, the expulsion of innocence, and an immoral social universe.

Norman Manea, writing of his experience as an artist under the oppressive Ceaușescu regime in Romania, and recalling Italian film director Federico Fellini's aesthetic polemic on clowns, makes some engaging points which are appropriate in the analysis of Trnka's work. Also recognising the tension between artist and authority as one of perpetual 'masquerade', Manea reads Fellini's conception of the White Clown as Ceaușescu (in a similar way as the White Clown may be understood as Hitler, or Stalin, or indeed, any other despotic dictator) while casting himself as his chief adversary, the artist as wise clown, Auguste the Fool. Trnka valued Bohemian folk-traditions and the theatricality best embodied in peasant wise clown characters like Bottom and the mechanicals in his own adaptation of Shakespeare's *Midsummer Night's Dream* (1959), and clearly views his own Harlequin character in this spirit, casting him as a sculptor and pot-maker, at home with nature, tempering aesthetics with the earthiness of the common people. Harlequin and Auguste share similar qualities, and it is tempting to see Trnka's artist puppet as Auguste and the omnipresent white-gloved hand as the White Clown. Auguste is described by Manea as 'a bizarre bungler who dreams of other rules, other evaluations and rewards and looks for solitary compensations', while his 'weakness suddenly may be seen as an unconventional and devious strength, his solitude as a deeper kind of solidarity; [and] his imagination becomes a shortcut to reality' (Manea, 1992: 35). These ambiguities and contradictions effectively *narrate* the puppet character in *The Hand*, and inform the metaphoric construction of the story.

Trnka's film begins with the juxtaposition of the sound of heavy unseen footsteps with the lively tumbling athleticism of Harlequin, who bows before a pot-plant, suggesting the 'other evaluations and rewards' available through the appreciation of a *natural* rather than imposed order. It is not long, however, before a gloved hand breaks through Harlequin's window, and destroys the pot and the plant, before manipulating the clay on the potter's wheel into a sculpture of a pointing finger. The hand is clearly a tyrannical figure. 'The tyrant', says Manea, 'is someone who manipulates, gives orders, enforces discipline, punishes and rewards according to the sovereign and sadistic laws of evil, ugliness and mendacity' (Manea, 1992: 36). The hand's first actions in the determination of such a set of principles, are resisted, however, when Harlequin merely re-pots the flower, cleans up and pushes the hand away. A box arrives at Harlequin's home, though, which tests his resolve further. Submerged beneath a number of gifts in the box is a ringing telephone, which Harlequin answers. The conversation which takes place is envisaged in images above Harlequin's head which function as three-dimensional thought-bubbles in the style of the comic strip. A hand drops coins into Harlequin's coffers, representing an offer of work in which Harlequin would make small statuettes of the pointing finger on behalf of the authorities. Harlequin refuses the offer and kicks away the phone in his anger. A

Figure 3.3 Jiri Trnka's puppet film, The Hand, cleverly uses symbolism and metaphor to 'smuggle' subversive political statements into a seemingly innocent fable concerning the suppression of art and free speech

number of important narrative principles are established in these early scenes, most notably, the symbolic value of the plant pot and the statuette of a pointing finger. The plant pot is both functional and aesthetic, a necessary container for an indoor plant, itself defined by its beauty and organic nature. The statuette of the pointing finger, however, is merely ornament; a conformist symbol which casts the pointing finger as a gesture of both enlightenment and stricture.

The ambivalence of the gesture is a useful symbolic device that anticipates Trnka's uses of the historical seriality of his symbol, discussed by Munz earlier, later in the film. The hand operates as the physical mechanism for symbolic movement and gesture in its own right, but also accomodates the symbolism of the glove. When a television set arrives at Harlequin's house, the next day, it broadcasts images of a bejewelled glove, a hand holding the scales of justice, the Olympic torch or the torch of liberty, Napoleon's hidden hand, an iron-fist from a suit of armour, a boxing glove, a hand with a gun, gesturing hands, an X-ray of a hand, a handshake and a shadow figure of a rabbit configured by a hand. The deployment of different historically determined representations of the hand constitutes the hand as a symbol while the representations themselves operate as a metaphor for totalitarian propaganda. The benefits of an apparently democratic society, liberty and justice, are actually illusory in the face of those in power who merely enforce their will by any means necessary – aggression, repression and digression. Trnka's Harlequin, in true Augustian style, merely mocks the hand and when it, once again, crushes a pot, he chases the hand away with a mallet, undeterred by the hand's obvious power.

If the Harlequin 'dreams of other rules', he is soon reminded that a totalitarian regime is at the heart of all its communications systems with the arrival of a newspaper, and the emergence of a hand from within it. At this point, the gloves come off, both literally and metaphorically, as the hand resorts to overt brutality in the attempt to enforce his will over Harlequin. Even though he, yet again, resists the actions of the clenched fist, he succumbs to the charms of a female hand in a lace glove, who seduces him into the nooses which render him a stringed marionette rather than a free-moving puppet. Clearly, Harlequin's weakness is his desire; he answers the sexual temptations offered by the beckoning finger of the female hand and becomes trapped, stripped not merely of his dignity but his innocence. Trnka cleverly uses the difference between the puppeteer and the animator to reveal how the state literally pulls Harlequin's strings while the individual artist (i.e. Trnka himself) liberates Harlequin's movement for his or her own aesthetic ends. The hand places Harlequin in a cage and makes him sculpt a huge statue of a pointing finger, the ultimate tribute to, and acceptance of, state authority. He is awarded medals and honours as if he was, indeed, an artist willingly in the service of state propaganda, as all notions of his resistance, and ideological difference, are ignored.

His weakness and capitulation become the sources of his strength, however, when he uses his working candles to burn away his strings, and pushes the huge hand through the bars of the cage in order to make his escape. Suddenly, state authority is overturned in two unexpected gestures, projecting him into a void in which he is pursued by the hand, crashing through images of the bejewelled glove, the boxing glove, the X-ray and the iron-fist, to once again reach his home, and the supposed security of the domestic space. He barricades his home and re-pots a plant as a mark of solidarity, placing it on top of his wardrobe beyond harm's reach. His endeavours to barricade himself further result, however, in Harlequin knocking himself out and breaking the pot-plant himself. This may be read as a deliberate act of suicide or an ironic accident caused by the absurdity of his situation, and the inevitability of further state oppression. Indeed, the hand breaks in, and in finding him dead, uses his wardrobe as a coffin, tidies his home, rouges his cheeks, and honours him with a state funeral, where he receives a salute, and his pot-plant is approved as a proper symbol of his apparent achievement. The state utterly manipulates the social perception of the artist figure for its own ends. There is no sense that the artist had been anything other than in the service of the state apparatus. Trnka's tale reveals that Harlequin's imagination does 'become a shortcut to reality', operating as it does, both as a vehicle to challenge convention and as the mechanism which is necessarily repressed because it does not fit with the politics of the 'real world'.

While Trnka holds up the hand to ridicule, he ultimately acknowledges the horror of its true power. As Manea, an artist subject to the same kind of persecution suggests:

> It is, however, not just a question of the ridiculous but also, first and foremost, of the horror, the destruction of the last enclaves of quotidian normality, the daily risk of physical and spiritual death. It was impossible to escape from that 'rest' [of existence beyond artistic endeavours], which had become the all encompassing, aggressive, absurd, and suffocating *whole*.
>
> (Manea, 1992: 49)

Trnka's deployment of symbol and metaphor effectively implies these conditions, showing the tension between the artist and authority in specific as well as ambiguous terms. His use of animation reinforces the view that it is necessary to use personal forms of expression in the *abstraction* of alternative ideas, and further, that symbol and metaphor, by definition, embody discursive concepts, and not narrational certainty. The language of animation, therefore, works as a system of images which interrogate social conditions, and resist the *fiction* of reported fact, and the selective representations of reality available through the state-controlled systems of mass communication. This is art about the repression of art; a vision of inhibited process and misrepresentative outcomes; a triumph of resistance.

Case study: *Balance* (1989)

While *The Hand* offers a degree of specificity in regard to the interpretation of its symbols and metaphors because it locates itself in a particular context informed by an obvious conflict, *Balance*, made in Germany by Christoph and Wolfgang Lauenstein, seeks a greater openness in its construction of meta-narrative. Five gaunt puppet figures, wearing long grey overcoats with numbers on the back, stand on an oblong slab, apparently suspended in mid-air. Each steps forward, extending a rod, with which they 'fish' over the sides of the platform. One catches a box, which he hauls on to the platform, thus disturbing the balance of the slab as it has previously been determined by the equal distribution of the figures on it. Wherever the box slides, the figures have to move in the opposite direction in order to compensate for the additional weight, and keep the platform in a balanced horizontal position. One of the figures cleans the box and attempts to open it, discovering a wind-up key which, when turned, appears to be the mechanism by which the box plays music. The real function of the box remains ambiguous, however, because it is never opened, and its meanings, therefore, remain open. Each of the figures ultimately covets the box, and begins to calculate how to move, in order to slide the box towards them, and force the others to move to a point by which they balance the platform and preserve their own lives.

88

Balance must also be maintained in order to keep the box, and co-operation becomes a necessary requirement if the box is to be equally enjoyed by all the figures. One sits on it, one dances, but inevitably one wishes to keep the box only for himself, and so begins a frantic choreography in which some figures slip and slide off the platform or are callously pushed or kicked off. One figure remains on the platform after this skirmish. He stands on one side of the platform while the box balances him on the other; to move is to unbalance the platform and fall. The film concludes with this irresolvable situation.

This then, is the ostensible narrative of the piece, but clearly the film invites interpretation, and begs important questions. At one level, the film's meaning is simple and direct – co-operation between people is necessary if they are to benefit from their possessions and conditions of existence. One may argue that this is the film's *preferred* meaning, but with this interpretation comes *attendant* meanings. The film suggests that selfishness and material ambition result in aggressive conduct and, consequently, cause social instability and disruption, which has the further effect, when pursued to its extreme, of possible social collapse. This reading already assumes that the platform is a metaphor for (Western) society, and that the puppet figures participate in a quasi-capitalist culture. The box, in this interpretation, operates as a symbol for material gain. It is clearly something which the figures wish to possess, presumably because it invests them with status and supposed superiority. Certainly, by having it, any one figure disrupts the balanced social harmony that begins the film.

What though, of the status of the platform in mid-air, the design of the figures, and the consequences of their movements, as signifiers which challenge the preferred reading, and suggest *alternative* interpretations? By creating an environment which has no tangible relationship to the real world, the platform has clear metaphoric implications and, as such, also redefines the space around it. The platform may indeed represent society, but it may equally represent the planet earth, or a mythic space, like purgatory, or even, a prison. The film's clear distantiation from 'the real', refuses exactitude and invites the viewer to engage in the collation of evidence to support a particular point of view. If the platform represents the planet earth, the five figures may represent the five continents, but if the platform operates at the mythic level and this is the purgatorial state between heaven and hell, all the figures literally and/or metaphorically fall from grace. To support the view that the platform is a prison, the viewer may cite the figures' clothing and the numbers on their backs, which have associations with convicts. The same grey uniform may also be seen as a death shroud, the number merely an Orwellian indication of statistical conformity. The figures in themselves seem skeletal and ghostly, supporting the view that the platform may represent some notion of life after death, or, as one student recently suggested, a concentration camp. What of the fishing rods? – humankind's desire for change, the inevitable disruption of a harmonic status quo, the need to acquire more things, the mechanism by which the idea of permanent entrapment might be challenged?

All these views emerge from the symbolic and metaphoric agenda posed by the film which essentially narrates its plot and its purpose. Echoing the absurdist theatre of Samuel Beckett, popular in Germany, the film constructs a minimal dramatic space within which it intensifies its modes of suggestion by merely playing out its own conditions of existence, without recourse to an explanation in relation to the conventions of the real world. The film does, however, suggest particular kinds of relationship to the real world by still employing the recognisably figurative, and stylising possible models of behavioural action. These grounding structural features enable the viewer to understand the film as a comment on human agency, and not as a piece of purely abstract choreography though, arguably, the film may be enjoyed at this level too. Beckett's plays are often concerned with the conditions of entrapment, a period of self-recriminating limbo in the afterlife before the peace of death itself, and the pointless, repetitive, and ultimately destructive codes which characterise human existence. *Balance* echoes these themes and foregrounds some of its relationship to the absurdist school through its dark resolution. Symbol and metaphor still render narrative as open-ended, though, because their deployment enables multiple discourses which may, at any point, contradict or support dominant readings.

Fabrication

Three-dimensional animation is directly concerned with the expression of materiality, and, as such, the creation of a certain *meta*-reality which has the same physical property as the real world. This *fabrication* essentially plays out an alternative version of material existence, recalling narrative out of constructed objects and environments, natural forms and substances, and the taken-for-granted constituent elements of the everyday world. In a certain sense, this is the *re-animation* of materiality for narrative purposes. Jan Svankmajer, says of this process:

> For me, objects are more alive than people, more permanent and more expressive. The memories they possess far exceed the memories of man. Objects conceal within themselves the events they've witnessed; that's why I've surrounded myself with them and try to uncover those hidden events and experiences, and that relates to my belief that objects have their own passive lives which they've soaked up, as it were, from the situations they've been in, and from the people who have made them.[4]

In what he describes as 'a magical rite or ritual', Svankmajer, projects the inner life of the object into his animated scenarios. The tangibility and malleability of clay; the hardness and weight of stone; the fragility and smoothness of china; the living essence of wood; the colour and texture of textiles; and the physical mechanism of the human body *become* the narrative imperatives of Svankmajer's work and serve as an important example of fabrication, creating stories through rediscovered and redetermined discourses. Three-dimensional animation relies upon the complicity of the materials in the construction and representation of particular kinds of personal world.

Svankmajer is an important influence on the American Quay Brothers, working in Britain, who take this approach to its logical extreme, essentially *re-animating* materials, bringing to life matter which has all the appearance of merely being detritus or dead. Fabrication in films like *Street of Crocodiles* (1986), *Rehearsals for Extinct Anatomies* (1988) and *The Comb* (1990) comes from the idea of redefining the material or object as if it still possessed an intrinsically organic life. This is the movement from decomposition to recomposition. Incomplete puppet figures, screws and bits of metal, pieces of fluff, wood-shavings etc. all become subject to a reclaiming of kinetic energy that survives within the very materiality of the form. As Jonathan Romney has noted, 'Quay puppets are not alive but *undead*; they don't have lives but afterlives' (Romney, 1992: 25). Consequently, Svankmajer and the Quay Brothers essentially animate apparently still and enigmatic environments which are provoked into life by the revelation of their *conditions of existence* as they have been determined by their evolution and past use. This gives such environments a supernatural quality, where orthodox codes of narration are negated and emerge from the viewer's personal reclamation of meaning. As the Quay Brothers have suggested:

> Narrative to us is always tangential; it just filters in from the side and creates this climate. In the end you feel this conspiratorial climate that makes you think, 'I'm at the centre of something and I don't know what it is'. You come out at the other end still looking in the rear view mirror and thinking, 'I haven't arrived yet'.
>
> (Romney, 1992: 27)

Despite this apparent enigma, however, the fabricational aspects of the work offer up associational meanings with common *historic* dimensions. These aspects of signification create the climate of the uncanny (see Chapter Two) yet maintain the essential *concreteness* of objects rather than place them in transition. The meaning of the object etc. is determined by the understanding of how it has absorbed its historic form and function and created the associational climate for the viewer. Simultaneously, the object etc. is both alien and familiar; familiarity is a mark of associational security while alienation emerges from the displacement of use and context. A child's doll, therefore, would stimulate comforting memories of childhood, whilst embodying the formal distantiation from childhood. The doll narrates itself at the historic level but is estranged from its contemporary context, and thus seems threatening by still seeming to possess the life it was invested with by the child during its period of heightened function. Such issues are central to this mode of animation and are explored in detail in a number of Svankmajer films

(see O'Pray, 1989; Wells, 1993; Lawrence 1994; Hames, 1995), but also characterise most animation using specific objects.

Case study: Jabberwocky (1971)

As Michael O' Pray notes:

> [*Jabberwocky*] begins with a pixillated sequence of a wardrobe in a forest,
> juxtaposed with a modern urban landscape, and then cuts to a theatrical
> tableau. The movements between different types of space and reality, in
> which neither seems to achieve any status over the other, exemplifies
> the tension, and at the same time signals the alienated and narcissistic
> aspects of the film. Svankmajer depicts a world which we cannot
> occupy and have never occupied, except perhaps in dreamstates.
>
> (O'Pray, 1989: 60)

Jan Svankmajer's *Jabberwocky* uses fabricated modes to create related but distantiated
worlds, perhaps half-remembered, half-imagined, but certainly reconstructed
through the repositioning of objects and materials from a *fantastic* past. Couched
within a *perverse* childhood context, Svankmajer's film concentrates on found
objects (seeds, stones, shells etc.), toys (dolls, tin soldiers, building blocks, a
rocking horse), artefacts (chamber pots, a pram, a penknife) and synthetic
materials (a sailor suit, paper etc.) as they interact as part of an over-determined
child's game. Svankmajer essentially plays out the ways in which a child would
uninhibitedly imagine the life in each of the objects which shares the child's
physical, psychological and emotional space. The sailor suit flies, a hat leaps
and dances, a penknife pirouettes and bleeds, tin soldiers march, but this liberated, fluid world is constantly impinged upon by the presence of a real cat which
pushes through a wall of building blocks, and by the fantasised brutalities of a
child's imagination untutored by socialised codes of morality and behaviour –
dolls are placed in a grinder, their heads are 'cooked' etc. Outside, trees encroach,
apples fall and become riddled with maggots, and nature endures in parallel to
the magical fabrications of the playroom, with its sinister undertow of strange
pleasures and unusual pains. Essentially, Svankmajer enjoys using the very sub-
stantiveness and function of an object as its specific identity but fundamentally
challenges the historically determined associations invested in it, by subjecting
the object to the *enactment of redetermination* in the light of subconscious desires *not*
repressed by socialisation processes. Fabrication in animation may, therefore, be
understood as the redefinition of materiality and the physical world by the pre-
conscious imperatives of the artist/film-maker. A child's playroom is thus, not
merely the location of childhood experience, but the context where all the
anxiety and trauma of becoming a human being may be expressed by the artist
through the reappropriation of apparently innocent objects.

Associative relations

Associative relations are principally based on models of suggestion and allusion which bring together previously unconnected or disconnected images to *logical* and *informed* rather than *surreal* effect. Often, though, apparently impossible relationships are created through the fusion of contrary figures and forms, placing formerly disjunct or unrelated elements into new conjunctions. This essentially opens up a *narrative dialectic* between the two image forms. Very much in the spirit of Eisensteinian montage, the collision or fusion of previously unconnected or undirected images creates new narrative impetus, which is not about overt story-telling (or even ideological critique) but the development of *visual* dialogues. Tensions emerge from design strategies, representational associations, and the redefinition of space, completely challenging the dominant orthodoxies of visual perception. Even in the most hyper-real, stylised or simulated of animation, the reproduction of the physical, or the seemingly non-tangible, in a material way, is provocative and incisive in illustrating apparently inarticulable *essences* of meaning that are extraordinarily difficult to communicate in any other form.

Case study: Tale of Tales (1979)

Voted as the best animated film of all time by animators and critics at the 1984 Los Angeles Olympic Arts Festival, Yuri Norstein's *Tale of Tales*, is a personal, and often profound, statement of atavistic recollection. Norstein uses the animated form to recall primal and ancestral sources of human feeling and experience. Fusing folk-tale, memory and personal symbolism, Norstein achieves associative relations which move beyond the realms of standard representations of time and space, privileging the psychological and emotional as the focusing agents in relating images, rather than using orthodox modes of story-telling. As Norstein himself suggests, 'The sanctity of the image, or rather its construction, seems to move in gradually from all sides; the elements that coagulate create the image'.[5]

Whilst the workings of an artist like Norstein may, in the first instance, seem impenetrable to the viewer, it is important to recognise that such methodologies foreground the idea of image-making as a tension between conscious and unconscious experience. This may be understood as a process which accepts and includes images which emerge from a number of sources and which seem at first to have no particular relationship. Further, such images, whether they are perceived constructions of real physical space, fragmentary recollections of dreams, half-remembered visions, hallucinations and fantasies, or pictures without past or purpose conjured in the mind, are not forced into a coherent *story*, though they do possess their own *narrative* which informs the relational conception of the film. The images possess an ontological equivalence (see Chapter Four), and in being valued as equally valid and important whatever their source, occupy a narrative space which refuses to categorise any one character or event as its presiding or dominant element. *Tale of Tales* refuses all obvious signposts of plot,

93

preferring instead a system of leitmotifs, recurring images that play out their own subtle differences and developments as part of a wider scheme of recollection. It may be useful to stress that Norstein's work is *recollection*; a gathering of images which define the psyche and the act of memory as an act of creativity. As Mikhail Yampolsky has noted, 'What confronts us is not simply a film about memory, but a film built like memory itself, which imitates in its spatial composition the structural texture of our consciousness' (Yampolsky, 1987: 104).

Fellow Russian film-maker, Andrei Tarkovsky, made films in a similar style, and suggested ways in which the viewer may find an entry into these kind of texts:

> Through poetic connections feeling is heightened and the spectator is made more active. He becomes a participant in the process of discovering life, unsupported by ready-made deductions from the plot or ineluctable pointers by the author. He has at his disposal only what helps to penetrate to the deeper meaning of the complex phenomena presented in front of him. Complexities of thought and poetic visions of the world do not have to be thrust into the framework of the patently obvious. The usual logic, that of linear sequentiality, is uncomfortably like the proof of a geometry theorem. As a method it is incomparably less fruitful artistically than the possibilities opened up by associative linking, which allows for an affective as well as a rational appraisal.
>
> (Tarkovsky, 1986: 20)

Animation is especially suited to the process of *associative linking*, both as a methodology by which to create image systems, and as a mechanism by which to understand them. Understanding these images only comes from an active participation in the images as the repository of meaning in their own right, and not necessarily, in direct connection to other images. Norstein and Tarkovsky create works which ultimately require the viewer to *empathise* as well as *analyse*, and this dimension of feeling – what Norstein calls the 'spinal cord' of emotional recognition – is the quality which lyricises the image. The 'deductions' that are made possible by this kind of involvement are those which relate the personal to the universal. Norstein essentially engages with his childhood during the war, and through the accumulation of the everyday details and events (real and imagined) of his past life, given special emphasis by the selectivity of memory, he creates a text which elevates the expression of the psyche's own sense of history to the level of poetic insight and spiritual epiphany.

Tale of Tales establishes its chief motifs early in the film – an apple glistening with raindrops; a baby suckling its mother's breast observed by a wolf cub; an old house bathed in autumn light; a group of figures on a summer picnic, established as a poet, a fisherman, a mother and child, and a child skipping with a Picasso-like minotaur. The sense of tranquility and reassurance offered by these half-remote, half-familiar images emerges out of the alchemic relation between them

– the association between the elemental world and natural development; the sense of sustenance and nurture; the notion of mutual support and shared time, past fusing with present, recalling ancient processes. The sense of timelessness possesses a mystery in itself; these small scenarios, it seems, are eternal, harmonious, somehow utopian in their insistent relevance. A number of things occur, however, which disrupt this sense of harmony. A wind of change blows beneath a tablecloth, blowing it away, as a train passes. Norstein's pastoral peasant idyll is disrupted by the onset of war, and the strange by-products of industrial progress. The old house is suddenly surrounded by cars, a wolf cub viewing himself in the mirror of a hubcap, uncertain of his own identity. The house is set ablaze, birds fly away, and the cub plays on an old sewing machine. Innocence and freedom, it seems, subject to the whim of political events, somehow surviving in a greater, more sacred, less obviously extant, chain of being.

In one of the film's most memorable sequences, the men are seen to be almost snatched away from their wives and girlfriends as they dance in the twilight, becoming shrouded soldiers, floating away like ghostly figures, going off to war in the rain. The motif of the wind beneath the tablecloth and the passing train are reiterated as the women receive notification of the deaths of their husbands and fiancés. Leaves scatter in the wind, and life goes on, somehow accommodating its tragedy yet insisting on continuity. The house becomes the locus for this perpetuity, offering light, heat and comfort, as seasons pass, and the smallest things constitute the most significant of memories. A boy eats an apple and watches crows perch on a snow-laden tree. His mother sits on a park bench next to her drunken husband, who finishes his drink, dons his Napoleonic hat, and pulls his wife, who in turn pulls the boy, away from the scene. 'Children's dreams', Norstein suggests, 'can be squelched in a moment, as we try to compensate for our inadequacies by means of petty triumphs over other people'.[6] The juxtaposition of this incident in the park and the scene of the men going to war serves to illustrate how the consequences of a small incident and the effects of a major catastrophe can have the same weight and implication in the psyche. The associative relation is achieved because animation, in Norstein's words, can show 'the material can possess a quite different specific gravity, a different impact'.[7] Norstein deliberately heightens the aesthetic and emotional persuasiveness of each scene so that their particular effect will equate – the 'specific gravity' of one moment as intense and affecting as any one other moment as it is registered in the memory.

The wolf cub plays an especially important role in the film. Perhaps a child's toy, invested with life by memory, the cub's domesticity combined with its very animality, enables it to simultaneously embody the vulnerability of home and family and also the enduring qualities of self-preservation and natural succour. The cub is seen at the hearth warming himself, but, when the house sets ablaze, presumably destroyed in the war, he recalls his experience and builds a fire in the forest to cook some potatoes, but fails to keep it alight. Undeterred, he hums and dances, comforted despite his solitude. The cub, in many ways, is the associative link of the narrative, for example, disappearing into the luminous light emanating from the house, which operates as a transitional link back to the picnic scene at the beginning of the film. Memories submerge within memories, fantasy underpins the flawed or revised recollection of real events. The picnic is observed from afar, but is narrated through, what Norstein terms, a 'musical exchange of gestures'.[8] A man walking past is called back to the picnic and offered some food, for example, and all such small events are understood through the detail of gesture and physical expression. Observed from this remote position, the images have the aura of a child's picture book, an image system which partly reinforces the metaphorical dimensions suggested by the poet figure carrying a lyre, the biblical connotations of the fisherman, the presence of the minotaur playing as part of a child's fantasy, and the relationship between mother and child, echoed in the following sequence when the wolf cub observes a baby suckling its mother's breast. The relationship between the dynamics of light (the central preoccupation of Norstein's work, betraying the influence of Rembrandt), poetic revelation, and the special qualities embodied in the child are further played out through the wolf cub when he steals the shimmering paper belonging to the poet but discovers it to be a baby wrapped in swaddling clothes. Rocking the baby in a cradle, the wolf cub hums a lullaby about a bad wolf carrying off a child that was first heard at the beginning of the film, which here operates as an ironic counterpoint to the wolf cub's caring and protective actions in the face of his new charge. The recurrent motifs in the film gain further purchase and clarity as the film develops, becoming enriched by the accumulative associations of the imagery.

The apple, the image that began the film, also recurs, but chimes with images of falling apples disturbing the winter crows, and the little boy eating his apple, imagining he is feeding them. The falling apples echo the movement in the recurrent images of the soldiers marching away and the skipping minotaur, the processes of nature, history and myth allied in an eternal continuum. The house survives the seasons of memory and the reality of its destruction, the train continually passes, and night falls once again. Cycles of events refuse closure and insist on recognition as the repository of enduring human values. This is a post-lapserian memory which tries to resist the implication of its over-arching motif of 'the fall'.

Animation legitimises the illustration of what might be regarded as the *process of thought* as it deliberates upon this issue, an image system achieved, by the associative relations which inform what Yampolsky calls the 'hyper-cinematographisation' of the animated form. He suggests:

> Norstein . . . has preferred to build a whole constellation of semi-illusory, but osmotically connected worlds, the relations between which are emphasised by the camera, by the creating eye, whose point of view possesses a magical vacillation and inner contrast.
>
> (Yampolsky, 1987: 116)

Figure 3.4 Yuri Norstein's profoundly personal and dream-like film, *Tales of Tales*, uses the distinctiveness of the animated film to move fluidly between images drawn from the unconscious, vivid memories of childhood, and the perceived pictorial-ness of the natural world

Norstein combines the familiarity of the language of live-action film (close-ups, lateral pans across space, dissolves, depth and perspective movement, 'invisible' editing etc.) with the language of animation (metamorphosis, condensation, synecdoche, symbol and metaphor etc.) to authenticate the images preserved by memory, defined by history, located only in the mind.[9]

Sound

The soundtrack of any film, whether animated or live-action, tends to condition an audience's response to it. Sound principally creates the mood and atmosphere of a film, and also its pace and emphasis, but, most importantly, also creates a vocabulary by which the visual codes of the film are understood. 'Sound' in film may be composed of a number of elements:

1 Voiceover [omnipotent narrator] (non-diegetic)
2 Character monologue (diegetic)
3 Character monologue (non-diegetic)
4 Character dialogue (diegetic)
5 Character dialogue (non-diegetic)

6 Instrumental music (diegetic)
7 Instrumental music (non-diegetic)
8 Song [music with lyrics] (diegetic)
9 Song [music with lyrics] (non-diegetic)
10 Sound effects (diegetic)
11 Sound effects (non-diegetic)
12 Atmosphere tracks

There are a number of tensions that are generated at the narrative level between sound which is added to the visuals from without and the sound directly correspondent to the events within the film itself. The early Fleischer Brothers' shorts and the initial output of the Warner Brothers Studio are essentially early forms of the music video in the sense that the cartoon events often directly accompany, and take their narrative imperatives from, a song.[10] This necessitates different modes of performance from animated characters and choices concerning whether the cartoon should literally interpret the words of a song, deviate from the song's story, or partially integrate the content of the lyrics with other narrative concerns developed through the imagery alone. The use of music is entirely related to its appropriateness in the determination of mood or the timing of a sequence, but what is also important is the idea, noted by Philip Brophy, that music essentially operates as a 'present tense' in most animated vehicles (Cholodenko, 1991: 81). This sense of *now-ness* suggested by different kinds of music consistently informs the implicit emotional narrative of a piece. Music may be normally interpreted through the feelings it inspires, and is deployed to elicit specific emotional responses in the viewer and define the underlying *feeling bases* in the story. The music, and its role as a catalyst for the emotive dynamics of an animated film, fundamentally informs how an audience may interpret the film.

Voice remains an intrinsic aspect of most story-telling, and in animation, is used in a number of ways. From the use of 'real', un-scripted, non-performance voices through to the overt mimicry and caricature in the vocal characterisations by such revered figures as Mel Blanc and Dawes Butler, the tone, pitch, volume, and onomatopoeic accuracy of spoken delivery carries with it a particular guiding meta-narrative that supports the overall narrative of the animation itself. In the same way as music, the voice, in regard to *how it sounds*, as much as what it is saying, suggests a narrative agenda. This is particularly important in hyper-realist texts because the emotional synchrony of the voice is reinforcing modes of naturalism — a naturalism, exemplified by Disney, which in defining itself so precisely took on lyrical qualities. The soundtrack of the hyper-realist film prioritises diegetic naturalism but uses the non-diegetic mode to heighten the emotive aspects suggested by the vocal 'performance' of the characters and the implied nature of their context in sound terms. Disney's pre-dominant output, and hyper-realist animated films, in general, seek to ally the tenor and implication of the voice (speaking or in song) with the *atmosphere* tracks that help to define their environment, but as Brophy points out, this is challenged in the post-war period by the Warner Brothers Studio, who heightened the influence and effect of the sound effect:

> If Disney is splashing liquid, Warner Bros. is crashing metal; if Disney mobilised the animatic apparatus, Warner Bros. revved it up to full throttle; and if Disney aspired to the organic life of music, Warner Bros. capitalised on the unnatural presence of sound effects.
>
> (Brophy, 1991: 88)

Chuck Jones confirms this view in his praise of Warner Brothers sound effects editor, Treg Brown:

> . . . he had a wonderful, surprising sense of humour in the editing of sound effects, and that was, whenever possible, never use a sound effect that you'd expect. It should have the same effect on your ears but should not be the same sound effect. And in one [. . .] of the Road Runner cartoons, where the Coyote tries to harpoon the Road Runner and the Coyote's on the rope and he's dragged across the desert, well, you'll notice not one sound that is correct. There's a broken bottle, there's a spring, metal filings falling on a drum and all kinds of other sounds. So your eye sees one thing and your ear says just the opposite.
>
> (Jones, 1991: 61)

Such, of course, was the extent and excess of the visual imagination in these cartoons, that actions and events were depicted which it was impossible to imagine *actual* sound for. What, for example, does a falling boulder or horse or sink actually sound like? Sounds had to be created to match certain events, and as such, became amusing through their incongruousness in relation to 'real world' sounds applied faithfully to their visual source. This inevitably affected the construction of narrative, and within a comparatively short period of time defined its own set of story-telling conventions. (Interestingly, I played just the soundtrack from a 1956 Warner Brothers cartoon, *D'Fightin' Ones*, to a group of students, and from the sound conventions and signifiers alone, they were able to determine the narrative of the film.) The prioritisation of the sound effect in the cartoon did not displace the song or demote the importance of some character dialogue, but it did constitute a sound/image relationship unique to the animated film, particularly with regard to the comic imperatives it placed within the narrative structure. Though all the elements that construct any film are important, the *mutuality* of the constituent elements of the animated film all call attention to themselves as the bearers of *significant* information because of their place within the short form. This is even more the case with sound in the animated film because all the dimensions of sound used do not merely operate as the signifier of authentic atmospheres and environments but delineate specific narrative information. Voice, music, song and sound effect may all be evaluated separately for the particular contribution each makes to the collective aural vocabulary that simultaneously illustrates, interrogates, comments upon and *narrates* the visual image.

Case study: Gerald McBoing-Boing (1951)

Leaving the Disney Studio as a consequence of the strike in 1941, Stephen Bosustow, along with Dave Hilberman and Zack Schwartz, formed United Productions of America (UPA), with a talented rosta of animators that included John Hubley and Bob Cannon. UPA was to revolutionise American animation by working in a completely different style to the hyper-realist conventions established by Disney. UPA employed minimalist, often expressionist backgrounds. They used 'smear' animation (pioneered in Warner Brothers' *The Dover Boys at Pimento University* (1942)), where fewer frames are used to create the movement of characters, so figures appear to jump from pose to pose, increasing the pace of the film. They also created characters configured as apparently crude lines and shapes. At all points, UPA attempted to create a distinctly aesthetic reduced animation style, legitimising an almost surrealist *mise-en-scène* in which staircases lead nowhere and light fittings hang from non-existent ceilings. Particular attention was paid to the language of animation itself, in order to liberate it not merely from Disney's hyper-realism, but Warner Brothers' and MGM's comic anarchy, to achieve more aesthetic and philosophic effects, or an altogether more self-conscious style of humour. UPA essentially represent a quasi-Europeanisation of what had become an intrinsically American art-form. This ultimately resulted in a film called *Gerald McBoing-Boing*, which directly addressed the role of sound in the animated cartoon.

Bob Cannon's film begins with a boy figure wearing yellow dungarees emerging on the screen as if it was being drawn. A mother-figure sewing is also drawn into the design, before a father-figure sitting in a chair reading a newspaper, is faded into the image to join the mother and boy. The opening image signifies itself as a self-conscious construction. This is reinforced by the voiceover which accompanies the action speaking in contrived rhyming couplets, written by 'Dr Seuss'. The style of the film is expressionist with few formal representations of objects as signifiers of a particular space. Simple lines, shapes and colours constitute the environment. The young Gerald is more specifically defined, however, by his incapacity to speak and his ability to communicate only through sounds. His first 'boing-boing' results in his parents phoning Dr Malone in a panic. His arrival is characterised by Gerald's father holding the door open, fixed in mid-air, and having his extended leg used as a hat stand. The figures are characterised by over-extended loose movements, for example, Gerald's parents stretching over the figure of Dr Malone as he examines the boy. When Gerald makes a noise they over-react with shock, and are projected out of the frame, frozen with fright. When 'Gerald got louder and louder, like a big keg of powder', the scene shows the effects of an explosion, most particularly, his father clinging to a chandelier before falling on to a chair spring in an extended sight gag. The key aspect of this sequence, however, is the self-conscious deployment of a cartoon cliché, the explosion, in a fresh context, drawing attention to the consequences of the sound itself as the substitutional representation of an action. There is no narrative vehicle for the explosion except Gerald's capability to make the sound. The noise essentially narrates the scene and determines its visual possibilities.

The film uses a system of fade-outs to link its scenes, accompanied by short pieces of perky flute music to suggest a slightly discordant sense of narrative transition as Gerald's experience becomes increasingly undermined by his gift, rather than enhanced by it. He feels estranged from his family, and increasingly alienated from his school and his classmates. The school authorities 'have a rule that little boys must not go "cuckoo" in our school', while the boys playing marbles in the playground send him away for making a sound like a horn, and a little girl is frightened by his capacity to sound like a bell. A veiled and gentle critique of conformism, the film suggests that society finds it hard to accomodate difference, perhaps also implying that UPA wished to establish itself as a mode of animation that legitimately differed from, and extended the form as it had been previously understood. As well as viewing the soundtrack in a different light, for example, UPA also changed the design of each scene to match its dominant mood. Feeling rejected, Gerald runs off into a dark blue background, and when Gerald's father then sends the boy to bed (his voice, a piece of music, instead of a real voice or a sound effect), Gerald mounts an impossibly steep staircase shrouded in dark red tones, to suggest his disconsolate and alienated mood. In his attic room, Gerald decides to run away, and climbs down a rope of blankets into a dark, snowy night. An almost transparent figure, Gerald runs through an increasingly threatening mise-en-scène of trees and blizzard, before attempting to jump on to a moving train. Gerald's transparency is both a signifier of his lack of identity, and a necessary design strategy to increase the oppressive colour quality of the night-sky. He is finally stopped by an apparently huge figure, drawn to suggest that this is how such a figure would be viewed from a frightened little boy's point of view, who wishes him to come and do all the sound effects on his radio station.

Radio, the most significant embodiment of the vitality and significance of sound, is used as the context by which the film can illustrate the capacity of sound to tell a story. In a vibrant yellow studio, an obvious signifier of optimism and happiness, Gerald performs all the sound effects in a radio play, telling a typical story from the American Old West. Gerald performs the sound of a galloping horse, a cowboy dismounting, his footsteps towards a saloon door (defined predominantly by the jingling of his spurs), some gun-fire and breaking glass, a body dropping to the floor, and the cowboy's exit from the saloon until he gallops away. None of these actions are animated. The viewer merely witnesses Gerald's performance and imagines the scenario. Joined by his family in an extra-ordinarily long limousine, Gerald enjoys the plaudits of the crowd for his achievements and is once again accepted within the community.

The film successfully foregrounds the language of sound as a narrative tool, defining its central character through the non-diegetic apparatus of the voiceover and musical interludes and, most importantly, through the shift from sound-effects as a non-diegetic imposition on a scenario to a diegetic voice within the scenario. It may be argued that sound, in relation to animation, is always a non-diegetic element because sound is not specifically created by the characters or contexts which are being filmed. Sound, it may be suggested, is always imposed. To a certain extent this remains true, but it ignores the very issue that *Gerald McBoing-Boing* implicitly addresses – the pertinent use of sound as a specific signifier for the purposes of narration and characterisation. The role of sound inevitably informs any debate concerning realism in animation because it often defines the hyper-realist premise of a situation, but what it offers more specifically is a mode of *authentication* to the nature of the narrative preferred by the animator. In other words, animators working in abstract forms may prefer to use music alone to help define narrative space, while other animators seek to make films which more directly echo the real world. Such animators may wish to deploy sound in a way that makes characters speak as if they were live-action actors, use music as the barometer of mood in the fashion of live-action narratives, and only employ sound effects to properly represent or enhance the real sounds present in an environment. *Gerald McBoing-Boing* recognises sound as a mode of *authentication*, and implicitly illustrates the relationship between the impositional animator and the requirements of the text. In many senses, sound is the chief mechanism by which this relationship may be properly evaluated.

Case study: *Beauty and the Beast* (1989)

The role of sound in the opening sequence of Disney's *Beauty and the Beast* is especially important in determining the narrative premises upon which the story is to unfold, not least because there are significant shifts in the mode of narration from the delivery of the story-teller through to the execution of a song. The film begins with a prologue in which an omnipotent narrator provides a non-diegetic narration which establishes the conditions preceding the story that is to follow. These are essentially the words of the story-teller creating the premises for a fairytale, but are especially important in this particular case, because they also establish some of the key differences the Disney team make in adapting the original tale (see Warner, 1994: 298–318). The prologue itself is an innovation, in the sense that it essentially makes the film Beast's story, rather than Belle's, even though she represents one of Disney's most persuasive heroines, and later occupies over 30 minutes of screen time within a 75-minute film. By illustrating why the Beast is a beast, the film provides the story with an establishing premise, and a dominant thematic, that only evolves in the original tale, after the initial transgression by Beauty's father, a transgression which is also portrayed differently in the Disney version, and changes some of the earlier tale's narrative devices.

This is particularly the case with regard to the role and purpose of the rose. In the original Le Prince de Beaumont tale, the rose is merely used for the purpose of providing the mechanism by which the old man transgresses. He unknowingly steals a rose from the Prince/Beast to give to his youngest daughter, but this ultimately means that he must forfeit her to the Prince/Beast as punishment. In the Disney version, the rose that was offered to the Prince by an old beggar woman, and disdainfully refused by him, becomes the mechanism by which he is turned into a beast, and also, as director, Don Hahn, puts it, 'the ticking clock' (Thomas, 1991: 147) by which the rest of the narrative plays out. The narrator says:

> The rose she had offered was truly an enchanted rose, which would bloom until his twenty first year. If he could learn to love another, and earn her love in return by the time the last petal fell, then the spell would be broken. If not, he would be doomed to remain a beast for all time. As the years passed he fell into despair and lost all hope. For who could ever learn to love a beast?

The voiceover is of paramount importance in providing the framework for the revisions in the tale, working to foreground the romantic agenda which is to inform the later narrative. Unusually in a Disney film, despite the studio's trademark use of the multi-plane camera to move towards the Beast's castle at the beginning of the film, the narrative is mainly conducted through the voiceover as it accompanies a number of dissolves, in which a series of static stained glass windows (common within the tale's location, the Loire valley) illustrate his words. These images, of course, possess their own narratives, but are not specifically dwelt upon, though they do signify the archaic fairytale context as well as a moral and spiritual dimension underpinning the tale.

As the film moves into its action, the storm that loudly proclaims the Prince's fate, becomes the bird-song of a late summer day, as Belle begins her walk into the town. Sound, in this sequence, essentially reinforces Disney's usual hyper-realist context, using diegetic authentication, before Belle breaks into song, which effectively disrupts the realist mode, imposing the conditions of the musical. Musical narrative, and the particular narrative of the song, is a self-conscious expression of the tension between the realist mode and the performance mode, where the musical presupposes the translation of speech into song, walking into dancing, objects into props, and any environment into a version of a stage. Belle's 'opening number', effectively narrates her frustration, living in a little town with its repetitive routines and small-mindedness. Further, though, it dictates the pace and rhythm of the action, in the movement of the chorus of characters who surround her, and through the use of the structure of the song (verse, chorus, musical breaks between verse and chorus, extended musical break etc.) as a plotting device for the specific placement of monologue and dialogue. While Belle expresses that 'There must be more than this provincial life', the town goes about its business while expressing a number of attitudes about her, from open attraction to critical bewilderment.

During the song, small scenes take place, the first, in the library, where Belle returns her copy of *Jack and the Beanstalk* and borrows *Cinderella*, both a recognition of her literary imagination, and the film's self-conscious recognition of its own status as a fairytale. She reads the book seated at a water fountain, and in the time-honoured tradition of the Disney heroine, finds allies in the animal kingdom (on this occasion, sheep) rather than the ready engagement of the townsfolk. Typically, some characters operate as comic caricatures, in order to create slapstick sight-gags, but others, and most specifically, Gaston, remain in an (exaggerated) realist mode to maintain some of the more serious, if sometimes ironic, aspects of the narrative. Gaston, in fact, takes up the song, suggesting 'In the town there's only she, who's as beautiful as me', before three blonde girls sing and swoon their appreciation of his physique. The townsfolk also sing various lines before gathering as one chorus, following Belle as she concludes her walk through the town, which occurs as the song reaches its crescendo. A central tension is established by the sequence which extends the initial premise determined in the prologue. Belle wishes to expand her horizons and seek out new things while Gaston insists that he will marry Belle. Clearly, the Beast is the fulfilment of Belle's implicit desire, and Gaston's romantic adversary.

The role of a song in the soundtrack may, therefore, legitimise the use of lyrics to *illustrate* thoughts and emotions, and/or *extend* narrative questions and issues. It may also provide a structural device for the specific choreography of a scene or the background for other exchanges. Further, it may be an expression of both diegetic and non-diegetic information, and the stimulus for particular kinds of imagery.[11] The narrational value of music and song becomes of prime importance when, as in *Gerald McBoing Boing*, it also defines aspects of character, particularly those concerning motivation. Narration, in this sense, locates itself in modes of performance, and the execution of particular acting styles.

Acting and performance

'Acting' in the animated film is an intriguing concept in the sense that it properly represents the relationship between the animator and the figure, object or environment he/she is animating. The animator must essentially use the techniques employed by the actor to project the specificities of character through the mechanistic process of the animation itself. In fact, the animator must consider all the possibilities available to the actor in order to create and develop 'character' long before the actual process of animation begins. Like actors in the theatre or live-action film, the animator develops the character from a script, considering the narrative implications of the role in the determination of character design, the range of movement available to the character, and the character's predominant motivation, which inevitably informs modes of expression and behaviour. The animator, like the actor, though, is seeking to extend the possibilities of the character beyond the information given or suggested in the initial text.

Though animated characters ultimately seem fairly limited in their motives, their range of physical expression is extraordinary. It seems, then, that 'character' is defined first by the conditions and possibilities of the medium and its capacity to express and extend the formal capabilities of external, readily perceived, existence. The character may be understood through its costume or construction, its ability to gesture and move, and the associative aspects of its design. The 'internal' aspects of character often seem one-dimensional or subject to the excessive overstatement of particular attitudes or moods, and these singular imperatives become the simple devices that drive the narrative, for example, Donald Duck's frustration or Goofy's ineptitude. Character, in this sense, is merely a cipher for a particular quality, often expressed in exaggerated gestures which echo some of the overt posturing and explicit signification of acting in the era of silent live-action cinema. Characters, in the developmental years of the animated form were essentially expressions of the possibilities of drawing itself, or defined as *performers* and not actors, often modelled explicitly on vaudevillian comics and speciality acts. This aspect of acting in the animated film is explored in Chapter Four. The drives towards hyper-realism in animation, did, of course, lead to the direct mimicking of the (highly exaggerated) naturalism of live-action film. This still prioritised the external aspects of expressing thoughts and emotions, and relied on the camera itself to privilege the extent and emphasis of the thoughts and emotions through the use of close-ups, medium shots etc. This *exteriority* was entirely appropriate to animation in the sense that its main priority is to express the *graphic outcome* rather than the *representational process* of creating character.

The mere recognition of graphic outcome, does not, however, properly recognise the fact that the animator has conducted his work as if he/she was an actor, and that the process of acting through animation requires some proper analysis. There are, of course, a number of theories of acting, but one of the most widely known and used, is the system created by Constantine Stanislavski. It is useful to deploy some of Stanislavski's principles with regard to how the animator invests his animated character with some basic acting technique by using that very technique in the execution of the process of construction. The Stanislavskian system is as complex and self-conscious as the process of animation, but it is the very fact that it is a conscious technique with particular processes, that make it another useful tool in the perception and understanding of the animated form.

If one remembers that the animator is an actor, some of the techniques suggested by the Stanislavskian model are appropriate to the analysis of the construction of character in relation to narrative. If the basic principle of the Stanislavskian actor is to create the 'inner life' that provokes and legitimises external consequences, it is a necessary requirement of the animator to project his/her 'inner life' into the narrational consequences of character construction and development. This is more than a technical process and invests the animated characters with *experience*. There are a number of aspects in this process that echo the Stanislavskian system, not least the use of personal 'sense memories' to inform moments of narrational action, the importance of detailed observation in the nuanced creation of specific characteristics, and the overt concern with matching inner feeling to outer expression. Perhaps the most important part of such a process, however, both for the actor and the animator, is the necessity to re-educate the senses in how the body executes simple mechanistic acts. Discipline and control are the core aspects of the actor's performance and the animator's skill, and these qualities are crucial in the relationship between character and narrative.

Stanislavski suggested that the play text should be broken down by the actor into units and objectives, each unit of the text having a specific set of objectives which fall into three categories: (1) external or physical objectives; (2) internal or psychological objectives; and (3) rudimentary or mechanical objectives (Stanislavski, 1980: 119). The animator, like the actor, breaks down the text into sequences/units, and constructs the exact movements of the character in relation to specific events as they are determined by the character's objectives. Clearly, the animator must prioritise the physical objective because he/she is investing the character with movement per se, and the sequence of movements between one extreme position and the second extreme position that the character moves to must represent the proper relationship between the flow of the weight of the body through time and space (see 'Choreography' p. 111). Such movements normally have a particular imperative, though, which may be understood as mechanical if it is habitual and functional, or psychological if it is informed by an obviously determined motive. Stanislavski's system here proves particularly useful in being able to address the minutiae of a sequence because it addresses both the movement itself and the specific reasons for it. This becomes of specific narrational interest because these elements define the more detailed secondary aspects of story-building so often neglected in the desire to determine the primary imperatives of the narrative overall. These primary imperatives may be understood as the over-arching structure and purpose of the story which finds echo in Stanislavski's super-objective (i.e. the dominant narrative determinant which the actor is working towards). By analysing the units of animation in regard to how a character plays out particular objectives it is possible to establish the complexities of how a character is created and animated, and how narrative develops as a consequence of specific actions.

The Stanislavskian system was especially developed, of course, to encourage the greatest authenticity in naturalistic acting, and it may be argued that the aspects of his system I have addressed are only appropriate to hyper-realist animation which aspires to this quasi-naturalism. It is important to recognise, though, that these procedures are common to the actor and the animator and may only be partially observed in the animated character. I would suggest, however, that the correspondence between these elements of the system and the work of the animator provides a way in which the narrational process of character work may be better understood. In other words, the projection of the animator through his/her character, and the units and objectives that define the process of animation and the actions of the animated character itself, is just as appropriate to the madcap surrealism of the early Daffy as it is to the maturity of Belle in Disney's Beauty and the Beast. The method suggested in the Stanislavskian model, by which an actor constructs a character role, finds close correspondence with the way an animator works. Stanislavski even used the metaphor of the work of a graphic artist to reinforce the system's fundamental principle. Describing the actions of his director figure, he says:

> Next he drew some accidental and unrelated lines on a piece of paper, and asked if that were a design. When we denied that it was he drew a few, long, graceful, curving patterns which we readily admitted could be called a design. 'Do you see that in every art we must have an *unbroken line*? That is why, when the line emerges as a whole, I say the creative work has begun.'

He continues:

> 'On the stage, if the inner line is broken an actor no longer understands what is being said or done, and he ceases to have any desires or emotions. The actor and the part, humanly speaking, live by these unbroken lines. This is what gives life and movement to what is being enacted. Let those lines be interrupted and life stops. Let it be revived, and life goes on. But this spasmodic dying away and reviving is not normal. A role must have continuous being and its unbroken line.'
>
> (Stanislavski, 1980: 254)

Stanislavski, presciently, but effectively, uses the metaphor of the work of an animator to constitute the inner working of the actor. He uses the line to represent the relationship between the actor and the continuity and cohesion of the part – animating the line, as it were, constitutes the creation of a character. Animators essentially echo the same process, but in literally animating the line, and creating character, they become actors. The process and narrative consequence of an animator 'acting' may be understood, therefore, by some of the Stanislavskian technique discussed, and will be illustrated in the following examples.

Case study: Screenplay (1992)

The great Japanese model animator, Kihachiro Kawamoto, suggests that, 'A puppet is an idealised expression of the part it plays', immediately locating the puppet as an actor heightened in its actions by the process of animation. British animator, Barry Purves, plays out the role of the actor in two distinctive styles in his extraordinary film, Screenplay. The first, and extended, part of the film is a highly choreographed piece of limited Noh theatre, telling the story of the tragic love of Takoko and Naioki, two lovers torn apart by the demands of Naioki's father, but eventually reconciled by the enduring faith in their love. The second, much briefer, part of the film, breaks the established story-telling codes established in

107

the first half of the film, extending the action into a quasi-live-action context, in which highly naturalistic brutalities occur. The stylised control and discipline of the mannered Noh theatre gives way to the uncontrolled primal physicality of hyper-realist violence. The juxtaposition of one style set against another benefits the narrative tension in the film, liberating the repressed tensions within the story, and imposed by the very structures of story-telling itself.

Acting in the Noh theatre style is characterised by specific moves and gestures. Purves heightens this approach through the use of a visible story-teller who is also signing the story for the deaf. The specificity of this language of signs fits well with the mannered gestures and dynamic points of action in the Noh theatre vocabulary. The pace of the Noh story is traditionally slow, with escalating emotional tensions released in very precise actions, for example, Naioki's oppressive lady-in-waiting slaps Naioki in the face when she attempts to defy her father. Another similar moment occurs when Takoko is punished for his transgression with Naioki by being stripped naked and impaled while a primitive flesh-ripping device is pulled down his body from a wire-noose round his neck. These acts of violence are contained within the highly controlled staging of events, at once distantiating yet precise in its effect. All the movements are absolutely specific in their function. Instrumental or expressive movement is subject to the same level of control because it operates in the same way as the minimalism of the costume, scenery, and properties, signifying very particular details or conditions of narrative within limited scenes or events. The Noh style is predominantly concerned with staging and the limitation of the acting space. Purves' telling of the tale plays close attention to these choreographic aspects and the capacity of his models to extend the range of the actor in the animated film.

Though the film is too long to properly apply aspects of the Stanislavskian system in full, the final sequence of the film may be addressed by looking at the ways in which some of its principles may be deployed as tools for the specific analysis of acting in animation. The final scene is particularly conducive because it reflects the transition from stylised gesture into hyper-realist naturalism. In Stanislavskian terms, this final scene is a unit with a number of objectives, chiefly, from the point of view of the Warrior assassin, serving Naioki's father, the murder of Takoko, and the attempted rape of Naioki; and, from the point of view of Naioki, the response to the murder of Takoko, her attempt to escape from the Warrior assassin/rapist, her murder of the Warrior assassin, and her own suicide. Takoko has a limited role in the final scene because he is shot down by the Warrior's arrow, falling bloodily through a screen door. The super-objective of the scene from Purves' point of view is to play out the inherent tragedy of the lovers by extending the premises of his story-telling mode. The tale appears to have concluded happily, the story-teller revealing himself as a wise old man, the facilitator of moral fables. Almost at once, however, the Warrior assassin breaks through the screens which signify the limits of performance, and decapitates the story-teller, breaking the frame and the previous codes of staging. He pursues the near naked lovers and kills Takoko with an arrow.

The Warrior assassin and Naioki play out the action and counteraction of their specific acting objectives. These objectives are carried out through the precise execution of movement in regard to motivation. When Takoko is murdered, Naioki is shocked, frightened and overwhelmed with grief. Her *external/physical* movement is limited but affective, prompted by her *internal/psychological* need to express her despair. She places her head next to Takoko's bloodied face, but her next *rudimentary/mechanical* move is wholly prompted by the necessity to escape from the approaching Warrior assassin. She opens the screen door and steps out, placing her back to the wall, constantly looking from right to left in order to see where the Warrior will approach from next. These moves are clearly motivated by her uncertainty of where exactly the Warrior is, and the desire to survive in the face of overt threat. The Warrior, in seeing her uncertainty, approaches her and pushes her to the ground, his psychological motive betraying an opportunist imperative, not merely to assault her, but to rape her too. Naioki's movement is entirely informed by panic and anxiety as she pushes herself backwards to move away from the Warrior's body encroaching on top of her. There is no merely functional movement, it is all directly provoked by specific psychological needs. Her desire to escape his grasp does, however, move from being a defensive necessity to an offensive strategy, as she reaches for his sword, pushing upward to ultimately stab him in the throat. Her first objective in the scene is complete; she has successfully overcome the Warrior.

Her second objective in the scene, though, is to properly express her reaction to the death of Takoko. This occurs in a number of stages and seeks to reconcile the principles of dignity and control inherent in their shared passion with the ultimate defeat of death. Takoko's naked body is rendered absurd by its bloody wounds and ghastly abandon; this is diametrically opposed to the highly postured control of the courtier. Naioki's psychological motivation, therefore, is to give the body dignity by lifting it on to the bed. This necessitates a physical act of strength beyond the norms of rudimentary actions. Her recognition of the hopelessness of her plight, however, is signified in three further conscious moves, highly reminiscent of the Noh theatre principle, yet informed by three specific naturalistic looks. She looks away at the now burning house and then looks at the sword which she ritualistically brings to the level of her head. Looking upward, she plunges the sword into herself and falls against Takoko. The looks operate as a recognition of hopelessness, the possibility of redemption and dignity in self-sacrifice, and the acceptance in herself of the necessity to actually commit suicide. These are *highly conscious* motivations, signalled by specific actions that may properly constitute the presence of the animator as actor determining the absolute detail and specificity of the puppet's performance.

Case study: Going Equipped (1989)

Peter Lord's quasi-documentary, *Going Equipped*, mixes animation and live-action to illustrate the confessional thoughts of a real convicted criminal as he recounts his views about his childhood, his crimes and his experience of prison. The principal acting in the piece is executed through a lone clay figure sitting in a sparsely furnished room talking to an implied interviewer. The live-action sequences are essentially a camera interrogating abandoned environments which the audience assumes the ex-convict has once inhabited, whether they be the family home, or a prison cell. Lord authenticates the documentary mode through his use of a real person's actual experiences and his close attention to naturalistic detail in the expression of gesture and attitude in the clay actor. It may be argued that even though *Going Equipped* represents the closest approximation to the realist mode addressed in Chapter One, and indeed, operates as an important example of the subjective-documentary in animation, it is the very use of animation which betrays the necessary requirement in the film to use and address *performance*. The same documentary in live-action would not directly draw attention to the coded language of physical expression in the way that the animated actor in this context necessarily does. His every gesture and action become a poignant illustration of the nature and implication of his thoughts.

Lord's 'super-objective' as an animator/actor himself, is to authenticate the ordinariness of 'the villain', so often glamorised and mythologised in other fictions. Every objective that he plays out in his clay actor, therefore, must signify the small unheroic, undynamic gestures of a petty criminal, and not the exaggerated actions of a comic-strip outlaw. Animation can legitimise the concern with this sense of small revealing details in a way that live-action can only achieve through the use of the close-up, directing the audience to notice a particular gesture or expression. Lord's clay actor is wholly defined by his vocabulary of physical postures and movements which signify as much about his lack of motivation as they do about his conscious intentions. Dressed in a dull jacket, shirt and jeans, he slouches in his seat, half-bored, half-engaged with this opportunity to try to express himself. Lord clearly concentrates on the profound effort the ex-convict makes in trying to describe, evaluate and come to terms with his particular experience. The difficulties of verbally articulating unpleasant events is matched by the physical unease of attempting to do so. Without the sound, Lord's clay actor displays all manner of subtle physical distress.

He gesticulates towards the camera, a rudimentary mechanical action that accompanies his desire to emphasise points and make observations. As he leans his head to one side, propping it, apparently distractedly, on his hand, however, Lord's objective for his actor is to signify through his body that it is impossible to be at ease when about to deal with the trauma of his childhood, in which he felt unloved and neglected. He fiddles with a pack of playing cards, picks up a can, rubs his hands together etc., all in the same spirit of not knowing what to do with his body while talking so self-consciously about himself. Yet, at the same time, these small movements constitute a vocabulary by which he can appear to be engaged with something in spite of the fact that he is primarily concerned with talking to an unseen figure. Lord, as animator/actor, *consciously* uses his actor to perform apparently *unconscious* acts which represent his lack of assurance and insecurity in being watched and listened to. Ironically, he becomes more direct in his gesticulation as he talks about 'creeping', and gaining recognition and reward as a thief. He addresses the camera/interviewer with more authority, which he reinforces by standing up, and leaning on the table. The move negotiates the staging for his next speech, which focuses on his punishment for burglary – the 'short, sharp shock' of three months imprisonment, which he hated. A small hand-gesture indicates his nervousness as he begins to properly remember and recount his experience in a spirit of regret. He says that he was given twelve months imprisonment for 'going equipped', whereupon he picks up a playing card, at once a rudimentary mechanical act of personal preoccupation, and yet an expression of the psychological act of shame and disillusion. Lord shows the anxiety experienced by the man through the tension in his body as he leans on the table, and increases the intensity of the piece, by focusing the gestural aspects of the character into an almost direct 'pointing out' of what prison is really like. This is principally illustrated by his recall of slopping-out with other prisoners or watching them urinate or defecate around him. His face contorts into gaunt withdrawal as the full implications of his experience affect him, and the viewer watching.

The film concludes with a final, more relaxed confession, in which he admits that his way of making a living is still not legitimate, but is justified in his own eyes by the fact that he is 'not doing crime crime', i.e. robbery, assault etc. He gives a resigned half-smile, and with a distinctly more open body posture, gestures outward, and distractedly rubs the table top, a physical motif occuring throughout the film. This is essentially acting in animation as heightened naturalism, designed to call attention to that naturalism of movement which betrays real psychological and emotional life. Peter Lord successfully uses the animated form to properly focus attention upon someone who in the live-action context may have been merely dismissed or ignored as 'a criminal'. Here, the very same criminal is noticed and listened to because he is reconstructed as a character and physically performed as if by an actor, in a style which draws attention to the necessity of artifice to properly represent aspects of reality.

Choreography

Hundreds of animated films can provide evidence of good 'acting', but even more can illustrate the prominence of the dynamics of movement itself as a narrative principle. Curiously, this obvious choreography, a direct extension of theatrical staging, has not been properly allied to theories of dance, an anomoly made even more strange given the proliferation of animated films which directly use dance. Norman McClaren made Pas de Deux in 1967, an abstract ballet, showing the specific movements of two dancers as a set of multiple images but, for McClaren, every animated film echoed dance 'because the most important thing in film is motion, movement. No matter what it is you're moving, whether it's people or objects or drawings; and in what way it's done, it's a form of dance' (Bendazzi,

1994: 117). The most useful and appropriate ideas for the purposes of inter-rogating the animated film and dance are those written by the pioneer of modern dance theory, Rudolf Laban, in the sense that his work pays special attention to the dynamics of movement itself, a crucial dimension common to the working process of the animated film. Both contemporary dance and animation create narrative through the *ramifications* of movement. As John Hodgeson and Valerie Preston-Dunlop suggest, 'understanding movements and their functions can therefore be a means of understanding people. If they move to satisfy a need to express, then by observing and analysing movement one can discern the need, and also the aims and intentions of the movement' (Hodgeson and Preston-Dunlop, 1990: 17).

I have already suggested that movement may carry specific objectives deter-mined by character, but animation, in prioritising movement of itself, beyond the restrictions of character, uses the *figurative* as part of its determinant vocabulary. That is to say, narrative is often played out purely through the movement of the body as it is represented in the animated film. The 'body' here, may be under-stood as an obvious representation of the human/animal form, an abstracted version of the human/animal form, or the purely abstracted shape that finds correspondence with the dynamics of movement available to the physical form. Laban delineates sixteen basic movement themes which inform contemporary dance, stressing aspects of the *construction* of movement which echo the processes shared by animators (Laban, 1963: 25–51). These include:

1   *Awareness* of the body
2   Awareness of the body's *resistance* to weight and time
3   Awareness of space
4   A recognition of the flow of the weight of the body in time and space
5   The need to *adapt* to the movement of others
6   A recognition of the *instrumental* (functional) use of limbs
7   An increased awareness of *isolated actions*
8   An understanding of *occupational rhythms* (work-related movements)

These eight elements place special emphasis on *weight, space, time* and *flow,* and are especially interesting if seen in the light of animation because, for example, while the animated form clearly moves through 'time', and inherently illustrates 'flow', it can only give the impression of 'space' and 'weight'. It may be argued, though, that animation is liberating because it can manipulate the illusion of space and needs no recognition of weight unless it wishes to draw attention to the implica-tions of a figure or an object actually being light or heavy. Once more, these issues become particularly important in respect to hyper-realist animation, or animation which is using three-dimensional materials and spaces. Clearly, a clay figure moving through time and space has an actual weight, though whether it is the weight that the animator wishes to imply that the figure actually has, will be subject to the movement of the figure. This, of course, is also the case in two-dimensional animation, and relies on the viewer's understanding of the actual weight of figures and objects in the 'real world' and the ease of movement of those figures and objects through material space, and in relation to other figures and objects. Simultaneously, this calls attention to the rhythm and function of movement, to which Laban's second group of eight movement themes adds further levels of engagement:

9   The ability to create different *shapes* of movement
10   The deployment of the 8 basic *effort actions*
          Wringing
          Pressing
          Gliding
          Floating
          Flicking
          Slashing
          Punching
          Dabbing
11   Orientating the body in space, playing out the following key tensions:
          Firm   ◄─────► Light
          Sustained ◄─────► Sudden
          Direct   ◄─────► Flexible
          Bound   ◄─────► Free
12   Relating *shape of movement* to *effort action*
13   The ability to elevate the body from the ground
14   To create group *feeling* through the expression of movement
15   To create group *formation* through movement (e.g. circles, rows etc.)
16   To determine *action moods* through the expressive qualities of movement

This second group of thematic conditions is especially useful in the detailed address of choreographic movement in animation because the elements successfully focus upon the specific vocabulary of any one movement. This helps to distinguish the source of the movement, and the impulses from which it arises; the direction of the movement and its purpose; and the final outcome of the movement, either as it completes its own process, or informs the following cycle of movement. Some specific dance-oriented examples will be addressed later in this discussion but, in order to focus upon some of the aspects of Laban's system, it is necessary to include animator Richard Williams' view of the whale in Disney's *Pinocchio*:

> Bits of it do look like storm-high waves, and the *weight* in that whale when he's angry! When it's on the surface and they've lit the fire inside and the mouth is filling with smoke, and it's shunting like an engine – that was seven years after *Three Little Pigs*! To go from crude cartoons in seven years to that whale, which reads like a monstrous *real* whale,

113

about to sneeze, with tremendous authority and weight, and you feel the push of the water, is incredible. They stop being drawings. It's not real either, but the whole idea of trying to animate weight like that. Nobody's been able to do it since.[12]

Williams clearly focuses on *the flow of weight of the body in time and space, articulating the effort action* of 'pressing' by the whale suggested by the movement of the water. Across the whole sequence, however, from when Geppetto and Pinocchio light the fire in the whale's stomach to the final crash of the whale against the rocks, the whale also moves from a 'floating' effort action to a 'punching' effort action as it goes from a static position to fast penetrative actions along, through and beneath the water.

But, even within this structure of movement, there are other patterns taking place. Williams highlights the *action moods* experienced by the whale as it moves from passivity to the height of anger, caused by the literal fire in its belly. From this source, the impulse of the movement is the implied heat of the fire and the congestion caused by the smoke. As the whale prepares to sneeze, it plays out a tension between a 'bound' state and a 'free' state of movement in the sense that the weight of the body maintains its position and its stillness right up to the second where the sneeze causes the body to completely relocate itself, simultaneously 'freeing' itself to move. Similarly, in another reading of this movement, the 'sustained' stillness of the whale relinquishes itself to the 'sudden' ejaculatory speed of the sneeze. This changes the space orientation of the whale who moves through several different planes of space, especially when he pursues Geppetto and Pinocchio, once they have used the sneeze as the method by which they exit the whale's stomach. The intake of the whale's breath that precedes the actual sneeze creates the 'direct' movement of the characters, fish, etc. *backwards*, while his exhalation creates the 'flexible' movement of Geppetto, Pinocchio and the schools of fish once they have reached the furthest point away from the *forward* projection of the sneeze. An engaging juxtaposition of rhythms and functions then occurs between the whale and the fleeing characters. The viewer becomes aware of the *instrumental* use of limbs by Geppetto and Pinocchio as they attempt to paddle their raft clear of the whale. These *occupational rhythms* inform a set of light, frantic, 'slashing' moves by the characters which directly oppose the heavy, smooth, 'punching' moves of the whale. The sequence reaches its climax as the whale falls back into the water after failing to catch Geppetto and Pinocchio when they are washed up on the shore. The final outcome of this aquatic chase, informed by movement and counter-movement, is stillness and quiet.

Clearly, the deployment of Laban's movement thematics enable an animated sequence to be analysed as a piece of choreographic narrative. By addressing the different and conflicting modes of movement in any one sequence, it is possible to reveal the inherent qualities of the animation itself in the determination of time, space, weight and flow. This formalist approach engages with the implicit meanings of movement and serves to add another dimension to the understanding of animation as a medium over and above its capacity to capture the thrill of the chase or a moral and ideological conflict. The animated dance film may be understood as a small sub-genre of animation in its own right, and the following examples will serve to further engage with Laban's movement theories, and address their more philosophical implications.

Case study: Feet of Song (1988)

Erica Russell's film, Feet of Song, illustrates the relationship between dance and animation to particularly good effect because it is a film showing abstracted human figures engaging in a number of dance oriented movements correspondent to a soundtrack of calypso music.[13] The figures are made up of simple lines and shapes – circles for heads, triangles for torsos, loins and limbs with lines as connecting sinew and muscle. Laban suggested that the first thematic was a specific awareness of the body, and Russell essentially establishes this through her construction of the body and the opening images which prioritise symmetry and balance in the upright form, before slowly giving way to small movements in the shoulders and hips. Russell's figure then demonstrates the awareness of space by negotiating a simple circular turn in which one leg remains still, pivoting the movement, and signifying the maintenance of the body's centre and the movement into space achieved by extending limbs. Taking up Laban's concern with necessary adaptation to partners, Russell multiplies her figures, showing them 'pushing' to the left as a recognition of the flow of weight of the body in space and time. All the figures are shown as if abstractly linked together and are compressed to indicate the centre of the body as the key instigator of movement, both through the horizontal and vertical planes.

The instrumental nature of the pushing movement is extended when five figures stretch out their arms, moving from a high top-left position down through to a low bottom-right position, and two further figures stretch up and down, and from right to left, redetermining movement as expressive rather than functional. A number of figures then crouch behind each other, precisely in step, drawing attention to the collective expression of an isolated movement, and reconfiguring the shape of movement. A figure then demonstrates aspects of Laban's basic effort actions by 'gliding' from a central position to an outstretched position where the arms begin 'slashing' through the implied space. Through this method, the viewer becomes increasingly aware of the relationship between the movement of the body and the animated shapes and forms which represent and illustrate the movement. The body is given depth by moving as a silhouette shadowing a dominant line – curvature represents muscle, triangular shapes represent the weight of bodily form, lines represent the direction and extent of movement itself. The body has an abstract, highly stylised design that foregrounds its abstraction as much as it does its embodiment of the rhythm and creativity of dance. Simultaneously, it calls attention to the illustrative and

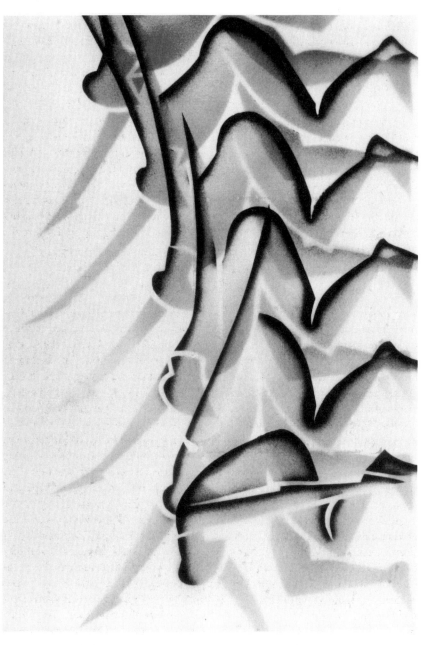

Figure 3.5 Like her later film, *Triangle*, Erica Russell's *Feet of Song* demonstrates her ability to fuse the dynamics of animation, dance and music into post-modern expression of the contemporary body at its most physically expressive and erotic

choreographic elements of both animation and dance, essentially defining their intrinsic relationship.

This becomes even clearer as the film plays out different aspects of interactive dance as a fusion of different shapes and forms. The synecdoche of torso, legs, arms and loins, is deployed to represent the whole movement of the body, and as a method by which to emphasise the particular movement vocabulary of any one part of the body, another of Laban's thematic preoccupations. The final turn and crouch from the top-right to the bottom-left quickly extends and compresses the body, bringing a dramatic movement to a still conclusion in exact time with the music. The overall mood of the piece is one of optimism and joy, the free expression of the body through animation as a celebration of movement for its own sake. The body is narrated through the vocabulary of dance and the expressive design schemata of the animated form. Russell has not subjected her bodies to the demands of realistic movement and 'a story', but used her bodies to narrate the inarticulable abstraction and satisfaction of rhythm and movement. Laban's movement thematics enable the viewer to penetrate this language and define the mood and meaning of physical expression.

Case study: Pas à Deux (1989)

Erica Russell's film, like McClaren's Pas de Deux, explores dance as the free expression of the body, uninhibited by the intricacies or specifities of orthodox dance steps. Canadian, Frederic Back, in his film, Crac (1981), uses dance as the expression of community and ritual, while Zdenko Gasparovic, working at the Zagreb studio in former Yugoslavia, uses the piano music of Erik Satie as the stimulus for the extended dance-oriented movement of Satiemania (1978). Gasparovic's erotic, grotesque, and lyrical images of naked women, clowns, gangsters and piano players represent a psychological choreography, half-dance, half-illustration of the stream-of-consciousness, which begin to suggest metaphorical implications. Monique Renault and Gerrit Van Dijk take this to its logical extreme by using recognised modes of dance as the carrier of multiple discourses in Pas à Deux. This is largely achieved through the use of metamorphosis, where the image and identity of each of the dancers in a couple is rapidly changing, signifying particular shifts in relationship and possible discourse. The dancing figures are predominantly well-known figures with specific cultural and ideological purchase. Renault and Van Dijk's work is characterised by political agendas and it may be inferred that certain critical agendas are being played out through the metaphor of the dance. Renault's feminist leanings emerge in To You (1975), which features a man as a soluble tablet, while Van Dijk's polemicism occurs in his anti-war film, CubeMENcube (1975), his attack on the Ayatollah Khomeini, Tale of 1001 Murders (1978), and his campaign film to release a black American woman who had been wrongly imprisoned, Letter to Carter (1979). Their combined talents use the idea of dance to represent conflict and conduciveness, correspondence and continuity.

Figure 3.6 *Pas à Deux*, Monica Renault's and Gerrit Van Dijk's dance film, plays out political issues concerning gender, power and identity

The film begins with a set of cabaret dancers going on-stage, but quickly cuts to an Apache dance between a girl and a French sailor. The girl becomes Brigitte Bardot while the sailor becomes Popeye. This is the first of a number of associational transitions that signify particular ideological shifts. The aggressive sexuality of the French sailor is satirised by the mock-macho yet bashful figure of Popeye who, faced with the overt sexuality of a 'real' sex siren in Bardot, flushes red, and exposes his limited masculine credentials. Popeye then metamorphoses into the entirely asexual Mickey Mouse, a cartoonal as well as satiric shift, who engages with a peroxided version of Betty Boop, the Fleischer Brothers' fantasy of the child-whore, and a persuasive continuum of the sexuality epitomised in Bardot. Renault and Van Dijk self-consciously play with the tension between the supposed innocence of animated characters and the sexual agenda they embody which is half-revealed, half-masked in the dance metaphor. Significantly, the dance becomes a tango as Betty, heaved to the floor by Mickey, becomes the prone figure of a fig-leafed Eve, man's first temptress, who dances with Fred Astaire, the epitome of gentlemanly sophistication, and the acknowledged master of a particularly precise and lyricised movement. Eve becomes an ordinary woman enjoy-

118

ing her flirtation with the romantic ideal embodied in Astaire, but soon changes into the Liza Minnelli featured as Sally Bowles in Bob Fosse's *Cabaret* (1972), a feisty counterpoint to Astaire's metamorphosis into John Wayne, who, speaking on the soundtrack says 'I am a divided American', a view illustrated here by a rapid transformation between his role as Ethan Edwards in *The Searchers* (1956) and the tough sergeant in *The Sands of Iwo Jima* (1949).

The couple dance through a phone box and Wayne becomes Superman, who is the logical mythical extension of Wayne's role in American culture. Superman's role as a superhuman figure who fights for truth, justice and the American way, triggers Minnelli's metamorphosis into the Statue of Liberty, and a rapid sequence of changes to match a number of dance-spins. Liberty becomes Florence Night-ingale, Mother Theresa, and finally, the Virgin Mary, while Superman becomes Che Guevara, and ultimately, a crucified Christ figure. The sequence implicitly suggests discourses about the relativity of heroism and political achievement and the status of women as maternal protectors, often defined by the success or failure of men. The film demonstrates an easy mix of the sacred and the profane, the religious and the secular, the classical and the popular, using the language of dance/animation as a system which negates difference and illustrates tension.

The Virgin Mary emerges from the twirling coupling with a small child. The viewer assumes the child to be the baby Jesus, but his metamorphosis into a baby Oliver Hardy, complete with small bowler hat and suit, serves to ridicule the sacred, and Hardy's words on the soundtrack, 'She's the sweetest girl you ever saw', only serve to undermine the divine beauty of the Virgin Mary. As Oliver Hardy becomes Winston Churchill, the film makes its most audacious transition, turning the Virgin Mary into a jiving Miss Piggy from *The Muppet Show*. The metamorphoses of the male figures are essentially governed by iconic associations. Hardy to Churchill is based mainly on the similarity between the size of the men and their formal identity in suit and hat. Churchill becomes Chaplin in a similar progression, while Miss Piggy, taller than her puppet incarnation, becomes Marilyn Monroe. Freely playing with notions of size, weight, and dimension, the film uses characters to express the spirit of the dance rather than their dominant behavioural traits or attitudes. The figures become free-floating signifiers, bringing with them an ephemeral identity that simultaneously defines a particular expression of gender or sexuality, and expresses passing phases of fad and fashion. The dance essentially represents the passage through time and space; the metamorphosing couples, the superficial trends reflected in highly mediated social figures.

Chaplin becomes James Dean, a passage from sentiment to cynicism, before Dean becomes Elvis gyrating with Monroe as she metamorphoses into Shirley Temple. In such juxtapositions, the film constantly foregrounds its playfulness, conflating different eras as the mechanism for incongruous comic pairings, which illustrate the capacity for animation to create impossible relations, not merely through the form, but through the representation of characters. This has important consequences with regard to cross-species, cross-genre, gender-challenging relationships, which will be explored in Chapter Five. Even in

Renault's and Dijk's film, though, it may clearly be seen that it is entirely possible for fictional characters to dance with representations of real people, ignoring the boundaries of time, space, gender and species, but perhaps more importantly, the rigours of taste and appropriateness. Elvis becomes Tintin, whose dog, Snowy, jealously tears at Shirley Temple's dress until she, in turn, becomes a blindfolded girl dancing with Don Quixote. This image best illustrates the film's central metaphor, in the sense that it expresses the dilemma experienced by women in finding an appropriate partner in the face of being wholly defined by male romantic and sexual fantasy. Cervantes' Don Quixote, the epitome of the inept romantic obsessive soon metamorphoses into the primal figure of Tarzan, however, who, abandoning Olive Oyl, engages in one of the few appropriate matches in the film when he dances with Jane. Tarzan's primitive physicality, expressed in the ease with which he rolls female figures over his back, prompts the emergence of primal women out of Jane, chiefly, Donna Summer (dressed in Monroe's iconic billowing dress, as she was on one of her album covers) and Tina Turner. This primacy of the physical directly emerges from the energy of rock 'n' roll, but is given an ironic twist when Turner becomes Snow White, her dance with Tarzan observed by Bashful, one of the seven dwarfs. Tarzan then tumbles towards the foreground of the frame, tumbling back into the frame as Grace Jones. This transition in part parodies Jones' androgyny and aggression, but also signals a change of music and a shift in address.

The film's final sequence is played out against contemporary dance music and hip-hop, and self-consciously signifies its previously implied commentary concerning social and aesthetic representation. Jones remonstrates with Santa Claus before placing an artist's canvas in front of her face and body, metamorphosing into the Mona Lisa. Significantly, when the frame passes to Santa, he pulls it over his head and becomes a monkey, who pulls strings attached to his own feet as he evolves into Leonardo Da Vinci's famous symmetric line-drawing of a male figure. The Mona Lisa becomes an equally enigmatic Egyptian Queen, whose neo-geometric construction as a moving graphic is likened to the highly stylised movement of the robotic break-dancer. The most important aspect of these changes, though, is the idea that men and women are now dancing separately. If the previous dances allied, conjoined, linked men and women in a number of ways, expressing relatedness in anything from conflict to coitus, the dance now merely acts as a metaphor for *difference* and estrangement. A break-dancing Pope is juxtaposed with Joan of Arc, a wry comment on the difference between the personal and spiritual faith and the circus of organised, ritualistic notions of religious credo. Jack the Ripper and Louis XIV are matched against a woman in a black dress and a woman in a basque. Van Gogh shares the image with Botticelli's Venus. The Michelin man back-spins with a bunny girl, and they finally evolve into images of an ordinary man and woman, who may be Renault and Van Dijk themselves. The final juxtapositions fundamentally illustrate the limited conception of women in the eyes of men. Art, it is suggested, is complicit in mis-representing women as physical phenomenon, reinforcing their limited social identity. Equally, the film implies that the self-awareness of women means that they are fully able to 'dance' alone in full recognition of the limitations of men.

Though clearly *Pas à Deux* is more concerned with its metaphoric purpose, the choreography that effectively narrates the piece should not be undervalued. The tools offered by Laban's dance thematics may be as useful in determining aspects of meaning in Renault's and Van Dijk's film as it self-evidently was in *Feet of Song*. Clearly, in *Pas à Deux*, the body defines identity, and is allowed an uninhibited space in which to move and change formation. Particularly important in this instance, though, is Laban's concern with the physical adaptation to partners, which in *Pas à Deux* largely signifies the emotional relationship between the characters as it is defined through their connective movement. The spin shared by Liberty and Che Guevara is essentially a call-and-response movement where the circular movement is maintained by the two figures holding on to each other and moving in opposite directions. The spin becomes the perfect metaphor for the *closeness* of the figures with regard to what they represent and the fact that, even though the conception of freedom that each represents is informed by different ideological concerns, the notion of *interaction* is still fundamental to apparently polarised positions.

Equally, Laban's concern with the awareness of isolated action is important when viewing the spins of the break-dancers towards the end of the film, which are wholly about personal dexterity and gratification, and have nothing to do with the idea of relationship at all. In redefining the posture of the body, and the particular execution of movement, it changes the *shape* of movement as it is defined by the choreography of upright couples (though jive does disrupt this orthodoxy), and places emphasis on the individual. If the tension between couples dancing together may be characterised as the play between being bound and being free, using direct movement or exhibiting more flexibility, moving in sudden short moves or in long sustained moves etc., then the movement of an individual alone is assessed by what Laban described as its effort actions. The robotic dancer may be defined by the stylisation of small 'flicks' and 'dabs' and the limited 'slashing' through the air, which has a wholly different connotation to the 'pressing' and 'punching' action of the body in a back-spin. The uncertain, if highly controlled, movement of one action, gives way to the uninhibited free movement of the other. This may be read as the movement from repression to revolution, from passivity to activity, from misrepresentation to self-expression, but in whatever way, this is an individual conception, unencumbered by partnership.

Animation and dance are closely related and effectively narrate the possibilities and meanings of movement. Different theories of dance may be applied to the animated form, but here the basic principles of Laban's theories have been used to provide an initial vocabulary to tell a tale not available in words.

Penetration

> One of the outstanding advantages of the animated film is its power of
> *penetration*. The internal workings of an organism can easily be shown in
> this medium. The depths of a man's soul is more than a phrase to the
> animator: it can also be a picture.
>
> (Halas and Batchelor, 1949: 10)

John Halas and Joy Batchelor, here writing in 1949, focus on the crucial aspect of
penetration in the animated form, chiefly, the ability to evoke the internal space and
portray the invisible. Abstract concepts and previously unimaginable states can be
visualised through animation in ways that are difficult to achieve or which remain
unpersuasive in the live-action context. Penetration is essentially a *revelatory* tool,
used to reveal conditions or principles which are hidden or beyond the comprehension of the viewer. Instead of transforming materials or symbolising particular
ideas, penetration enables animation to operate beyond the confines of the
dominant modes of representation to characterise a condition or principle in
itself, without recourse to exaggeration or comparison. It becomes the very
method which defines or illustrates particular kinds of experience which do
not find adequate expression in other forms. It is often the case that difficult
concepts or unusual codes of existence can *only* be expressed through the vocabulary available to the animator because they are in many senses inarticulable in
words but intrinsically communicated through the visual and pictorial.

This mode of penetration is particularly effective for film-makers seeking to
align the condition of the experience with the condition of the animated film
itself. That is to say, those film-makers who wish to make a film which illustrates
an experience of life led in a distinctive and potentially unknowable way to
others, seek the most direct creative method by which this condition can be
expressed. In the two case studies that follow, animation facilitates the expression
of what it may feel like to be blind or autistic, two conditions among many,
which it may be impossible for others to know about. Animation in the penetrative mode thus becomes a *mediator* of possibilities, offering as close to a visceral
revelation of the condition as a medium of expression can offer. Narration in this
mode is very much determined by the intention to reflect the immediacy of
sensual experience as it characterises the ability to conduct everyday lives taken
for granted by others. This is not the sensual immediacy of creativity, therefore,
but the unique sensual experience which underpins the struggle to live an
ordinary life. The penetrative mode usefully narrates the repositioning of orthodox events in the light of a different experience of them caused by comparatively
rare or unique personal physical conditions or states of mind. Animation of this
sort largely attempts to reconcile and illustrate abstraction within the orthodox
and knowable rather than create a set of purely abstract images which invite
interpretation.

Case study: Blindscape (1994)

Stephen Palmer's graduation film, Blindscape, produced at the Royal College of Art in London, attempts to show how a blind man psychologically and emotionally envisages the landscape he inhabits through the senses of touch and hearing. Palmer illustrates the relationship between the blind man and the environment at the moment when the blind man directly experiences it. Only when he hears something or touches something does a colour image of the place or object etc. actually materialise on the white screen. The blind man himself begins the film as a faceless body, sleeping curled up in a foetal position. He remains a transparent black-and-white line-drawing throughout the film, only gaining colour or definition when he touches his own face or body. Interestingly, even though the man continually rubs the place where his eyes should be, it never becomes a discernable pair of eyes; an image, thus, only confirming the permanency of his blindness. He hears various sounds which evoke a woodland context whilst his hands reach out touching trees and grasping leaves. Palmer accentuates the blind man's feelings by placing emphasis on the immediate intensity of experience as it is highlighted by the animated image. With each attempt to know the space in front of him emerges both the pictorial revelation of his environment and the penetrative revelation of his struggle.

In essence, Palmer's method also stresses the now-ness of animation, because his blind figure exists in a perpetual present. His experience is drawn in a way that eliminates the contextual space and movement in his past, and also refuses to anticipate the contextual space or necessary action required in the future. Though Palmer's background still acknowledges a woodland environment for the benefit of the viewer, the blind man himself only knows of trees by the shocking suddenness of touching them as he desperately moves forward trying to negotiate what is, to him, an endless void. The amplified sound of a bee constitutes threat, and provokes panic in the man, who flails his arms around, only to fall and hit a tree. Once more, the bright colour and movement of the bee serve to heighten the idea of the threat as the man is perceiving it. He constantly seeks reassurance by continually trying to engage with his surroundings, but each movement only provokes a heightened terror of the imagined space. Though the viewer knows that the place where the blind man appears to be is fundamentally safe, Palmer develops his narrative by extending the penetrative mode to further render the physical environment as a purely psychological space. Fluttering birds suggest the presence of someone; a grass snake is imagined as a hideous serpent; a police dog is envisaged as a grotesque demon. The blind man himself metamorphoses into a howling demon tortured by his own frustrations. Penetration in animation has revealed and depicted the deep anxiety of sensual deprivation and lack of control experienced by the man.

Finally, a voice enquires, 'Sir, can you hear what I'm saying?', and is seen to be a policeman leading a search party. At first, the helpers cannot reach the blind man, and he must negotiate a terrifying balancing act on a tree branch in the attempt to reach them. The concluding images concentrate on his desperate struggle to climb towards the policeman – his hands and the final grasp made by the officer to prevent the blind man's fall, operating as a penetrative synecdoche for the moment of acceptance by the blind man in reconciling the hopelessness of his condition with the need for help. Palmer's narrational selection of penetrative illustration properly depicts a physical, psychological and emotional state unimaginable by many viewers. This kind of animation, therefore, readily facilitates an inarticulable experience into a conceivable image system, a process heightened further through other kinds of unusual condition, like autism.

Case study: A is for Autism (1987)

Tim Webb's extraordinary film, A is for Autism, is actually a collaborative effort between film-makers, teachers and students to explain the condition of autism through the medium of penetrative animation. Animation is a particularly appropriate medium with which to reveal the condition of autism because it can represent in itself the introspective results of self-absorbed imaginative activity which is part of the distantiated psychology of autistic thinking. The total preoccupation with, or obsession about, particular things which characterises autism and results in an apparent dislocation or refusal of reality, may be directly expressed through creative acts, and most particularly, drawing. Autistic people sometimes develop a solipsistic view of existence, and find expressing themselves verbally, or through orthodox channels of communication, extremely difficult. This is not to say that the condition remains entirely problematic, because even in spite of having moderate or sometimes severe learning difficulties, autistic people can have extraordinary talents with regard to creative abilities, acts of memory, and the understanding of difficult abstract concepts. Webb's film successfully negotiates the terrain between the chaotic alienation of the autistic state of mind and the unique qualities and experiences which also characterise the same sensibility.

Child psychologists, Lewis and Greene, suggest, 'Feelings that a child is unwilling, or unable, to put into words can often be expressed more easily through drawings and paintings. Emotions too powerful or too confusing to think about, clearly can find release through the use of paint on paper (Lewis and Greene, 1983: 14–15). A is for Autism usefully combines the verbal descriptions of what it is like to be autistic with the vivid drawings of autistic children. The drawings, which become animated sequences, like those of Blindscape, reveal how the world is perceived by a person, but here it is the autistic person themself who is recording that perception, sometimes allying it with their voiced contribution, but also, at other times, attempting to draw the feeling of the experience. In what seems, at certain moments, like an expression of psycho-therapeutic intensity, images evoke the pains and possible pleasures of the condition. Prominent colours, distortions and omissions in representative forms, over-elaborated or scarcely detailed figures and objects, or the mere spontaneity of the line, all reveal aspects of a condition which few can understand or engage with.

Drawing is very much recognised as the expression of action in the film, and such an expression of action as it occurs in individual drawings is extended in *A is for Autism* to accommodate the development and depiction of particular experiences. Constantly, voices tell of the difficulties they have to try and negotiate when their sense apparatus apparently betrays them. Autistic people see and hear things differently; sometimes cannot talk, and often perceive space in a distorted or threatening way. One person stressed that this gave her a fear of small shops, while another talked of the anxiety experienced in merely being out on an ordinary street attempting to negotiate the traffic. Their drawings illustrate the confusion and fear inherent in everyday acts, simultaneously, if unconsciously, aestheticising the representation of their experience. The psychology of feeling like 'an untuned TV' is matched with images of an underground train going into tunnels and emerging into stations only to move back into the dark again. The idea of the collapse of psychological clarity into utter discord is perhaps best expressed, though, through the animation of a number of sentences being written in chalk on a blackboard which the viewer is able to read until the sentences merge with each other and obscure the means of communicating effectively.

Successfully mixing live-action contexts with animated drawings, the film seeks to properly place the condition of autism within the 'real world', refusing to let the simplicity and innocence of the drawing style distract from the serious purpose of using this kind of material. This is best exemplified in two sequences of metamorphosis. First, the opening sequence of numerous portraits whose changes signify growth and development and second, a sequence later in the film, when a drawn paper child held in a mother's arms reduces in size until it disappears. The latter use of penetrative animation is primarily concerned with the identity of the autistic child, both in its own eyes, and the eyes of others, and directly challenges the notions of growth and development suggested earlier. Autistic people, it is suggested, feel that they and their condition are invisible in the social context. It is this very invisibility that penetrative animation defines and illustrates.

The film necessarily narrates the nature of obsessional thinking, but successfully uses this as a symbolic image system, for example, using a series of images which reflect individual preoccupations but which also extend the premises of narration. These include the fascination with counting numbers, the presence of calendars, and the concern with times; the engagement with spinning objects like coins and records on a record-player; the absorption with trains and train times. These conditions often betray abilities of memory and understanding, however, uncommon in others. One boy animates sequences of his favourite trains, which he believes have a particular direction and purpose, but his attempt to animate a similar sequence for a road, only leads him to conclude that the road leads nowhere. His fascination with trains has a purpose for him which is practical, engaging, and relevant, and thus serves as an example of someone coming to terms with himself and his needs. This is particularly enhanced by his creative pride in completing the animation itself. Though there is little doubt that autism is profoundly debilitating, and that the film gives a persuasive account of the destabilised interior world of the autistic person, it is clear too, that creative expression through the language of penetrative animation is crucial in maintaining communication with a world that the autistic person may feel continually estranged from. Animation, in this instance, is a critical expressive and democratising language. When the environment is experienced like 'the unbearable noise of an on-rushing train' to the autistic sensibility, such a film may help society understand how that might feel.

4

25 WAYS TO START LAUGHING

You get to be an impish God. You get to reform the world. You get to take the piss out of it. You turn it upside down, inside out. You bug-out eyes. You put moustaches on Mona Lisas. You change the world and have for a brief moment a bit of control over it. At least you get to humiliate it for a moment, and that's what all cartoonists get their kicks from![1]

Terry Gilliam, film director and animator of the linking sequences in Monty Python's Flying Circus, describes the capacity for animation to recreate and laugh at the world; to challenge its orthodoxy and pretention; to explore the boundaries of taste and expression; to suggest that things could be different. This chapter is concerned with comedy in the animated film. Comedy is assumed to be at the core of most animated films, seemingly, its intrinsic but largely uninterrogated vocabulary. Theories of comedy have proliferated ever since humankind started to laugh, and no one is any closer to knowing why human beings make absurd noises in response to the innumerable things that amuse them. Everyone would claim to have a sense of humour, but it seems that everyone does not possess the same sense of humour, so what is funny remains an entirely relative thing. In whatever shape or form, comedy can be silly or subversive, purposeful or perfunctory, observational or offensive, but always possesses energy and 'life', the intrinsic imperative of animation.

The apparent ambiguities and contradictions inherent in attempting to under-stand comedy as a genre should not mean, however, that comedy should not be addressed in the very particular way that it informs animation, for, as Gilliam has already implicitly suggested, the animated form extends the vocabulary of humour within the live-action film. No analysis could, therefore, be exhaustive, but in the spirit of the rest of this book, the following 'twenty-five ways to start laughing' constitute an attempt to both chronicle the evolution of humour in the animated film and create a typology of the 'gags' and comic structures that emerge in a representative cross-section of films from cartoon capers to computer comedy.

1 Magical surprises

As has already been stressed, early cinema was characterised by the development of live-action cinema and the emergent visual orthodoxies of photographic realism. This was countered by the tradition of the 'trick' film, which was essentially evolved as the consequence of experimenting with the new medium and finding that extraordinary effects could be achieved through stop-motion, frame-by-frame, photography. The early Edison and Pathé films, as well as those of Méliès, thus provide examples of proto-animation which amuse because of the sheer divergencies in imagery from representations of the 'real'. Trick films invested human beings with extraordinary capabilities, anticipating the animated film's preoccupation with the deconstruction and manipulation of the body. In investing human beings and their environment with magical properties, these films constantly surprised their audiences, who laughed in disbelief and wonder. These kinds of images soon constituted visual conventions. In manipulating the image in this way, film was able to demonstrate the transgression of physical laws and disrupt the patterns of experience and behaviour determined by them. Suddenly, the human body could move in ways that it was both impossible to do in the 'real world' and impossible to represent in live-action. This spectacle was inherently funny because it illustrated the literal breakdown of social order as it is located in the physical environment. The notion of *surprise* has always been intrinsic to such modes of comedy because the level of engagement with the moment of transgression from the representation of the 'real world' necessitates that the audience perceive reality in a different way. In a sense, the human beings in the films became depersonalised, heightening the audience's relationship to the 'gag' and further legitimising its comic purpose. These effects liberate the viewer into a new visual vocabulary, one that silent film comedy and, more importantly for the purposes of this discussion, the animated film, came to exploit and develop.

Clearly, Blackton and Smith's *The Humorous Phases of Funny Faces* (1906), signals its comic intentions by drawing upon the circus tradition of the clown 'pulling a funny face'. By distorting the expected symmetries of the face, and the normal conduct of expressions, the film, ironically, draws attention both to the limitations of human expression and to the special expressive qualities of small gestures. This is the essence of where the humour lies. A top-hatted man rolling his eyes in impossible ways, surprises and shocks his female companion, who eventually becomes engulfed in the man's cigar smoke, a chalk 'cloud' rubbed out by Blackton himself. This focus on small actions, in many senses, operates in a similar fashion to the comic decentring of the body in physical comedy, because the normal balance and symmetry of the body is challenged, making the subsequent execution of movement unusual and, thus, potentially amusing.

2 The power of personality

The catalyst for amusement in the early 'trick' films was a random moment of often unmotivated physical spectacle, happening to people in locations that the audience had no previously determined relationship with. In other words, the comic moments were largely unallied to identifiable characters or set within a developing story. John Canemaker suggests that it is Winsor McCay who began to change this in his film, The Story of a Mosquito (1912), creating a bonafide character:

> The film's star is a mosquito whose design is a disquieting combination of human and insect elements. He is an anatomically correct bug with six spindly legs, two slender wings, and over-sized eyes. But this mosquito also possesses small, pointed ears, eyebrows and a receding hairline. He wears a hat and short-legged trousers, and carries a valise.
>
> (Canemaker, 1988: 33)

The design of the mosquito, which anticipates Jiminy Cricket in Disney's Pinocchio (1941) (see Thomas and Johnson, 1981; Grant, 1993), begins to display anthropomorphic characteristics and, consequently, this enables audiences to understand the 'insect' on 'human' terms. The design essentially reconciles the 'alien-ness' of the insect with the 'familiarity' of human beings and provides the visual foundation for the character to begin behaving like a human being. Models of comic behaviour during this period were predominantly drawn from clowns and performers on the vaudeville circuit, and serve to inform the development of two related, but distinctive, forms of comic output, one informed by 'gags' in the spirit of the 'trick' film, but personalised by a comic character, and one informed by 'personality', deriving its humour from the recognition of comic aspects within the human character. Inevitably, the two forms overlap, but the latter, 'personality-centred humour directly informs 'personality' animation – 'an art that goes beyond merely moving designs around, and emotionally involves the audience by communicating a character's individualism to them' (Solomon, 1987: 33). The key aspects of this kind of performance which directly influence 'personality' animation and begin to create a vocabulary for comic purposes, may be characterised as follows.

1   The necessity for the illusion of eye contact between the character performing and the audience watching.
2   Facial gestures which obviously signified particular thought processes, emotions, and reactions experienced by the character.
3   Physical traits and behavioural mannerisms common to, and recognised by, the audience, which remain largely consistent to the character.
4   The direct expression of motivation in the character and the immediate execution of the narrational action which achieves the objective signified.

(This 'immediacy' becomes crucial to the speed and execution of cartoon 'gags'.)

5   The creation of a particular physical rhythm for the character which expressed a specific attitude or purpose.

6   The overall treatment of the character as if it were an actor playing a role (see also Jenkins, 1992: 59–72).

Canemaker assesses the personality of the mosquito in The Story of a Mosquito, stressing this comic 'business' describing him as 'an egotistical show-off' who is also 'wary and calculating', 'brave, but ultimately foolhardy', 'a homely reject so distracted by any attention to his antics, that he risks and loses his life' (Solomon, 1987: 35). Though perhaps over-stressing the dimensions of the mosquito's fate, Canemaker clearly identifies the 'personality' of the creature, and makes the crucial point that there is enough significant detail that defines the mosquito as an individual to support the view that he has an off-screen life. McCay properly develops 'personality' animation, however, in the figure of Gertie the Dinosaur (1914), who makes eye contact with the assumed audience and indeed, her creator, McCay, who, using the film in the course of his stage act, appeared to give Gertie instructions, and offer commentary. Gertie also expresses her feelings and attitudes; she smiles, cries, expresses happiness, tiredness and irritation; she dances, eats, plays with a mammoth, lies down and wags her tail, sleeps and scratches. Her motivation is always clear, under-pinning her playfulness, and her relationship both to the environment she inhabits and the audience space beyond it. Her rhythm is determined by her weight and size; her sheer bulk prohibits fast 'leg-work', but she possesses a comic lope, and McCay cleverly used the elastic quality of her neck for addi-tional lateral movement and comic expression, especially when Gertie hurls the mammoth into the far distance. The humour essentially resides in her behaviour and its 'performance' and not the execution of structured 'jokes'. Gertie fully anticipates the wholly rounded personalities of Mickey, Donald, Pluto and a host of others that emerged from the Disney Studios, who inevitably extended this form of animation and its comic possibilities.

Frank Thomas and Ollie Johnson, veteran animators at the Disney Studios, suggest that Disney understood that the fundamental principle of comedy was that 'the personality of the victim of a gag determines just how funny the whole incident will be' (Thomas and Johnson, 1981: 32). Crucially, 'personality' here precedes the 'gag' and, for Disney, personality is informed by status and identity; therefore, it is intrinsically funnier if a king slips on a banana skin rather than a child. In order to properly develop and reveal 'personality', it was necessary to concentrate on the narrative developments out of any one particular situation or context. This imperative to derive humour from specific kinds of behaviour in a plausible scenario supported Disney's overall drive towards the verisimilitude discussed in Chapter One. Though this was not at the full expense of the 'gag', Disney recognised that, to a major extent, the 'gag' was predominantly facilitated

130

by stereotyping and sought to resist this through his broader ambitions for the animated film:

> Walt's ideas of entertainment went far beyond gags: he sought the new, the novel, the unexpected, the beautiful, and the colorful situation with warmth. Instead of thinking of cartoon material as being 'entertaining', one might find a better concept in the word 'captivating'. Audiences have to be impressed, absorbed, involved, taken out of themselves, made to forget their own worlds and lose themselves in ours for cartoons to succeed. Walt had to find actions that were funny in themselves yet easily recognised as something familiar, gags that were plausible even though very imaginative, situations that were based on everyone's experience, and characters that had interesting personalities.
>
> (Thomas and Johnson, 1981: 34–5)

Disney's concession towards the stereotypical, however, did lie in the use of 'caricature' and 'exaggeration', which operated as heightened signifiers of human thought and emotion as they were played out by animal characters. 'Caricaturing' in the Disney canon is largely used to denote human flaws, whilst 'exaggeration' is deployed to stress human foibles, a distinction which essentially delineates the kind of comedy *caused* by the character themself, and the kind of comedy *inherently within* the character. Character flaws create *external* humour drawn from physical events while character foibles represent humour from an *internal* source evident in behaviour.

As has been stressed, 'personality' and 'gag' humour are not mutually exclusive, and both models, especially as they are expressed in the evolution of the animated film, display distinct vaudevillian roots. Norm Ferguson, another of the great Disney animators, had a particular predeliction for the vaudeville style and often employed certain routines in his animation of Pluto (Thomas and Johnson, 1981: 99). Pluto certainly embodied the 'physicality' of the vaudevillian clowns, but erred towards the style of acts described by Henry Jenkins as those which 'combined sentimentality and virtuousity' (Jenkins, 1992: 70). This, in many ways, remains consistent within the Disney canon. The vaudevillian 'gag', however, became the central facet of cartoons made both at Warner Brothers and MGM Studios, and will be addressed later, but it is important to stress that the evolution of personality animation accompanied the evolution of the animated form in its own right, and animators remained concerned with the uses of the graphic space itself, and the origination of humour which self-consciously used that space. Thus emerged the first examples of the 'visual pun'.

3 The visual pun

In Chapter One, the relationship between the comic strip and the early cartoon forms was emphasised. The codes and conventions that characterised comic narratives were soon employed in the cartoon but, more importantly, developments in animated comedy were enhanced by the recognition and exploitation of the graphic possibilities available to animators. As Norman Klein has suggested, while this kind of work 'makes allusion to story, its primary responsibility is to surface, rhythm and line' (Klein, 1993: 5). Best remembered in this spirit are Otto Mesmer's Felix the Cat films, made at the Pat Sullivan studios in the early 1920s, of which Raymond Dugnat says, 'Felix's head, all cheeky points and apexes, and his curly limbs and grin are one degree nearer the doodle line, with all its chirpy freedom, than the oval and circular forms which were to sweep the cartoon in emulation of Disney's developing smoothness' (Durgnat, 1969: 99).

Mesmer himself stressed at the time that other animators were seeking to achieve 'full animation', he concentrated on the visual 'gags' that emerged from defying perspective in the animated drawing.[2] This directly challenged any plausibility in 'the story' at the level of Disneyesque verisimilitude but extended the narrative space by using all of the graphic possibilities that had been established in the mise-en-scène. For example, in Felix in Fairyland (1925), Mesmer, as he did in most Felix films, self-consciously uses the graphic space to achieve visual puns. This essentially means that shapes and forms as they are drawn may represent two or more things, and the transition from one graphic representation to another, when it is deliberately executed by the character in the film, in this case, Felix, becomes funny. The amusement arises through the surprise and recognition that the audience simultaneously experiences in acknowledging the graphic relationship between two shapes or forms that have been drawn to their attention, both by the animator, and the central character. Felix, for example, in attempting to win the affections of a fairy princess on a balcony situated next to a castle (which in perspective terms seems to be in the background of the image), takes the turrets from the castle and makes them into ice-cream cones, while also producing a scoop to fill the cones with ice-cream from what has previously been graphically understood as a cloud. Mesmer's manipulation of the graphic mise-en-scène shifts the emphasis from images which denote things to images which connote things, thus destabilising the visual space, and enabling comic events to continually take place. The initial representational idea that has been established in an image cannot be trusted because it is likely to change, and the chief elements to undergo a shift of emphasis in transition will be notions of size and implied weight. The castle turret, evidently a large construction in the way it is understood in the 'real world', becomes an ice-cream cone in Felix's hand, obviously a much smaller, lighter, object. The 'fluffy' cloud which looks the same as the consistency of ice-cream, is, of course, lighter and more transient. The transition bequeaths 'weight' to the ice-cream. In playing with these typographical perspectives, Mesmer calls attention to the two-dimensionality of the image, and makes audiences realise that 'every object he transforms is flat ink' (Klein, 1993: 5).

This is a significant development in the sense that this type of 'gag' is unique to the animated film, extending the possibilities of what Noel Carroll calls 'the mimed metaphor' in silent, live-action comedies:

> In such cases, humor arises from seeing objects in their literal aspect at the very same time that the miming gesticulation enables us to see them as otherwise: to see cogs as bugs and nails as turkey bones. The operation here is essentially metaphorical; disparate objects are identified for the purpose of foregrounding similes, in this case, visual similes. This abets the play of incongruous interpretations. For the self-same object can be seen either literally or figuratively.
>
> (Carroll, 1991: 31–2)

In the animated film the literal can become the figurative, once more emphasising the nature of the form, and extending the range of the visual simile (see also Leyda, 1986: 57–85). This is particularly so in the way that Mesmer manipulates the conventions of the comic strip and the design of his own character. For example, loving thoughts are expressed through the presence of 'hearts' above Felix's head which are literally pulled from the space above his head to become part of a banjo, while question marks that signify Felix's puzzlement or exclamation marks which signify his surprise and shock are literally transformed into hooks, keyholes, struts for car wheels, a propeller for an aeroplane etc. Even the notes which signify the idea of a musical tune in the silent era could be used for other visual effects. These visual puns were often conjoined with Felix's ability to use his own tail as a prop, it becomes an umbrella or a banjo neck in accordance with narrative necessity. The whole premise of the Felix cartoon is about the fluidity and uncertainty of graphic space, and though this provided 'gags' – *Comicalities* (1928), later foregrounding the relationship between the animator and the film in the way that the Disney and Fleischer Studios had also done – this could not wholly support the premises of the film. As Mesmer realised, it was Felix's playful character that abetted the comic strategies. He notes, 'I found that I could get as big a laugh with a little gesture – a wink or a twist of the tail – as I could with gags' (Maltin, 1987: 24). The drives towards the creation of an appealing character and the adoption of recognisable modes of performance drawn from vaudevillian contexts, as I have already suggested, began to properly inform the cartoon. Felix himself had been profoundly influenced by Charlie Chaplin, who directly worked with the Sullivan studios on a number of animated films specifically depicting Chaplin (see Crafton, 1993; 1992). Even though characterisation became an important aspect of the developing cartoon film, Mesmer's work had gone a long way to establishing a set of comic conventions which operated as a stock set of visual 'gags' which survived into the sound era, particularly in regard to the deployment of the *incongruity* gag (see later).

Felix did not survive into the sound era, his graphic humour usurped and surpassed by the emergent sound 'gag' and character comedy. Both Klein and Durgnat, however, both cite his comedy as the antecedent of the 'Theatre of the

Absurd' especially as it, in turn, becomes located in Eastern European animation. The 'Theatre of the Absurd', exemplified by the works of Ionesco and Beckett, illustrated the oppressive cycles of behaviour that characterise human existence, suggesting that modern patterns of living depersonalise and misrepresent human potential. This depressing scenario, they imply, can only be accepted if it is perceived in the spirit of black humour, recognising the *absurdity* of ever-repeating patterns of behaviour, and, inappropriate notions of order and routine as they are determined by hierarchical power structures in society. All this seems a long way from Felix, but the minimalist inflections of absurdist theatre (a recognition of the 'theatre' space and convention in itself, the use of a few props or settings, primarily for symbolic purposes, etc.) echoed the graphic conception and freedom of expression in cartoon films and the use of the 'gag' as a radical device to reveal or disrupt behavioural and environmental orthodoxies. What the absurdists (and their counterparts, the Eastern European animators) did, was to bring a *philosophic* dimension to the visual pun, and this will be further addressed later, in regard to the incongruity gag, and also as part of the overall working agenda of the Zagreb Studio, and the films of Jan Svankmajer.

4 Expectation and exploitation

The next stage in the evolution of the animated comic form was the consolidation of a vocabulary of 'gags' which *exploited* the form and determined certain codes of *expectation* in the audience. The analysis of *Soda Jerks* in Chapter One, and *Duck Amuck* in Chapter Two, serve as representative examples of the kind of vocabulary that the cartoon constantly employed, and came to use in a predictable and formulaic way. This formula included the following aspects.

- Establishing a recognisable context in which characters have specific roles or immediately identifiable traits or qualities, even if these become subject to quick change or redefinition.
- 'Riffing' a number of comic events by problematising a specific situation (e.g. employing mistakes, coincidence, misunderstanding etc.).
- Compressing the events by the use of elliptical conventions changing the logic of time and space in the narrative, often resisting 'unity' with regard to plot.
- Creating an 'unreliable space'(see Klein, 1993: 7), which destabilises narrative by revealing the mechanisms of the medium (e.g. 'squash-n-stretch' movement, metamorphosis of character and environment etc.).
- Using jokes which had been seen before but which had been subjected to a fresh interpretation or use (e.g. a character standing in mid-air, realising, and then, falling; a character being subjected to some form of violent act etc.).
- Establishing the idea of characters in conflict which would be played out within the narrative parameters of a chase.

134

The seven-minute cartoon essentially required that it foreground its terms and conditions with immediacy and clarity in the same way that the vaudevillian comedian had to quickly establish himself and determine the style in which he was working in order to make his audience engage with him. These formulaic elements served this function but also had the consequence of creating and sustaining particular kinds of stereotype. As Henry Jenkins has noted of the vaudeville context:

> This brutal economy weighed against the exposition necessary to develop rounded characters or particularised situations. Instead, characters and situations had to be immediately recognisable. An elaborate system of typage developed: exaggerated costumes, facial characteristics, phrases, and accents were meant to reflect general personality traits viewed as emblematic of a particular class, region, ethnic group, or gender.
>
> (Jenkins, 1992: 70)

Such a typage also informed the animated cartoon, and its implications with regard to gender and race will be examined later. This visual shorthand runs beyond character, though, and creates the comic aspects of the mise-en-scène. Within the context of this chapter then, it is useful to detail a number of the graphic conventions which came to inform the 'golden era' of the cartoon from the early 1920s through to the early 1950s (see also Pilling, 1984). This will constitute the framework by which other kinds of character comedy, situation comedy and 'gag'-oriented comedy may be addressed. It prioritises 'the visual', illustrates the exploitation of the form, and determines the schemata which underpins an audience's expectation of the cartoon. The examples are drawn from the cartoons of the silent era, and those produced by the Disney, Fleischer, Warner Brothers, and MGM Studios, as well as their smaller imitators in the sound era. Once again, such a list cannot be exhaustive, but does serve to link the comic object or event to its comic possibility or expectation.

Clearly, the iconographic conventions are used as a narrative shorthand as well as comic devices. In establishing a climate of expectation these devices become the lubricant for the engine of other more elaborate 'gags' which individualise each cartoon and the nature of the engagement between its chief characters.

5 'Just a minute, Chubby – you ain't seen half the kid's repertoire-e-e!': Some old saws

Henry Jenkins suggests, 'The fragmented, frenetic, and emphatic style of variety performance spoke to modernists of all nationalities, to many seeking alternatives to the conventionality of theatrical realism and the banality of commercial cinema' (Jenkins, 1992: 63). Conventional live-action films in Hollywood were soon characterised by what has become known as the 'Classical Hollywood Narrative

Table 4.1

Comic object/event (signifier)	Comic possibility/expectation (signified)
ACME	A company supplying unusual inventions
Anvil	Omnipresent, incongruous, dangerous object
Babies	Nappied with large safety pin; able to talk in an adult way
Bandages wrapped around face	Bad toothache
Barrels	Hiding places prone to falling apart
Blackened face	Post-explosion (race) caricature of woe
Blunderbuss	Incongruous old-fashioned weapon; tends to split into ribbons on firing
Bulges	Usually under carpets or within metallic objects when figures are moving
Cauldrons	Cooking pots for characters with added vegetables; often accompanied by cannibals with bones in their noses
Corn on the cob	Fast food eaten as if mechanised
Desert islands	Small, single-palmed, surrounded by sharks
Dollar signs in eyes	Sudden possibility of wealth
Donkey ears on someone's head	Recognition of stupidity or humiliation (character often becomes an ass)
Extended tongue	Profound thirst or exaggerated shock
Eyelids/shirtfronts	Operate like rollerblinds
Fish	Eaten to leave a complete skeleton
Five o'clock shadow beards	Villainy
Flushing red faces/limbs etc.	Contact with heat/extreme pain
Fridge	Completely full with appetising foods
Huge gulps	Recognition of fear in overwhelming odds
Huge sandwiches with olive on a cocktail stick	Picnics; eaten in one bite
Indians	Literally 'red'; complex smoke signals
Large straws	Drinking from vessels quickly/at a distance
Painted tunnel/hole entrances	Illusion to fool victim which becomes three-dimensional
Round black bombs with lit fuses	Melodramatic suspense/explosion
Precarious rock formations	Falling rocks on victim
Prison vans, large nets	Dog-catchers
Pumping heart revealed through the body	Passionate love/lust
Semi-circular mouseholes	Fully-furnished mouse homes
Shattered teeth	Post-assault collapse of teeth; the gag is extended by expressing teeth as falling pieces of glass
Snoring	Suction so strong, it moves objects
Spinning blurred lines and smoke	A fight
Storks in post office hats	The delivery of a baby
Swelling lumps on head	Consequence of assault
Telephone receivers	Vibrates/moves on ringing
Twittering birds and stars	Confused look of being knocked out

Structure' (see Bordwell, *et al.*, 1985). This approach to film-making became its dominant model, using particular kinds of cinematography and editing to create a seamless continuity in the story-telling process, rendering the process of film-making itself invisible. This narrative structure inevitably underpinned what was understood as the closest representation of fictional 'realism' because it corresponded to conventional notions of linear narrative, plausible motivation in the main characters, logical (if over-determined) resolutions to narrative 'problems' etc. Disney strove to achieve this in the animated film and, in doing so, prioritised personality animation and character comedy in the 'folksy' style of old rural populations. Other animation studios, however, strove to develop a vocabulary that legitimised what Norman Klein calls the 'anarchy' of the cartoon, heightening its modernist credentials, and drawing attention to the 'New Humour' of the non-WASP immigrant cultures which became part of the American 'melting pot' at the end of the eighteenth century (see Klein, 1993). Durgnat describes this humour as 'sharp, rapid, cynical, often cruel, reflecting a faster, quicker-witted world' (Durgnat, 1969: 102). It was clearly the humour of the 'gag', known as an 'old saw', the verbal one-liner that was the stock-in-trade of many vaudeville performers, and the central premise, particularly of the Warner Brothers output, especially in relation to the development of characters like Bugs Bunny and Daffy Duck in the sound era.

It also becomes the intrinsic and enduring difference between the approach of Disney and the approach of the animators on 'Termite Terrace' at the Warner Brothers Studios. Disney continued to prioritise the human dimensions of his narratives, finding humour in his characters' vulnerability, while Warner Brothers exploited this vulnerability merely to create 'gags'. As Durgnat suggests,

> The gag represents, in a sense, a depersonalisation of emotional release, it depends on the very rapid recognition of emotional stereotypes. In splitting humour from character, it brings comedy towards the condition of farce. But, unlike farce, it can gear in very exactly with the mental aggravations of realistic social life. The new genre expresses both the brutalisation of comedy and the new shrewdness in farce. Life is becoming a matter of rapid manipulation of feelings rather than a full experience of them.
>
> (Durgnat, 1969: 102)

Warner Brothers' *Looney Toons*, in particular, oscillate between the dominant 'personable' aspects of their characters and the depersonalised style of the construction of gags which involve them. Rather than splitting humour from character, as Durgnat suggests, the Warner Brothers animators play out a tension between character and humour which enables the cartoon itself to oscillate between the construction and collapse of narrative. The vaudevillian aspects informing this process are a 'different performer–spectator relationship, a fragmented structure, a heterogeneous array of materials, and a reliance upon crude shock to produce emotionally intense responses' (Jenkins, 1992: 63). Though it is possible to choose numerous examples from the Warner Brothers canon to illustrate these ideas and issues, a particularly apposite example, which directly recalls the 'vaudevillian' model, and demonstrates the full range of effects available to the cartoon is *Yankee Doodle Daffy*, made as late as 1943, but still engaged with Daffy Duck's aspirations as an entertainer. In a sense, the cartoon operates as war-time propaganda, overtly (perhaps nostalgically) recalling the vaudevillian model, and the contemporaneity of the animated cartoon film itself, as intrinsically American forms of entertainment.

Yankee Doodle Daffy (1943)

Porky Pig, chief casting director of Smeller Productions, attempts to leave his office for his annual holidays, only to be obstructed by 'Actors' Agent', Daffy Duck, 'Personal representative of the most sensational discovery since the sweater girl', one 'Sleepy Lagoo', whom he is eager to promote. Porky refuses to audition him but Daffy refuses to accept this, and demonstrates Sleepy's act himself. Sleepy, meanwhile sits in a big armchair sucking on an oversize lollipop which literally changes the shape of his head from a circular form to an oval shape as he twists it in his mouth. The manipulation of physical form enabled by the animated film is intrinsic to its creation of comic events. Nothing is fixed; everything is subject to its revelation as something else.

Daffy illustrates the performance/spectator relationship by using Porky's office window and curtains as his proscenium space, launching into a version of 'I'm Just Wild about Harry'. Sleepy makes comment on the performance by producing a picture of 'ham'. This sight-gag, shown directly to the viewing audience, simultaneously acknowledges and criticises Daffy's over-the-top style – the joke here is located in the idea that Daffy, in despite of his enthusiasm and energy, is not talented, and it is his crassness and ineptitude which may be laughed at. This is reinforced by a similar sight-gag in which Sleepy produces a picture of a 'corn-cob', suggesting Daffy's style is 'corny', once more a critique of the lack of originality and datedness of his material. The audience is allowed to *laugh at* Daffy, but also *laugh with* him as he becomes the vehicle by which the cartoon demonstrates the vaudevillian traits of 'fragmented structure' and the use of a 'heterogeneous array of materials', described by Jenkins. As Daffy says, before embarking on a breakneck routine, 'Just a minute, Chubby, you ain't seen half the kid's repertoire-e-e!' Daffy plays a banjo solo, solicits laughs through his impersonation of Carmen Miranda, goes tragi-comic with his version of Pagliacci, the clown, and then becomes a singing cowboy in the spirit of Roy Rogers. Such rapid narrative shifts merely reproduce the vaudevillian performance ethos embodied in the skills of the single performer, whether it be a singer, a quick-change artist or an impersonator. Daffy's skills as a singer, musician and performer are abetted by the recognition of 'parody' in his impersonation of Carmen Miranda. Such a moment of overt cross-dressing may be read differently by contemporary audiences. Daffy's performance may be understood as camp spectacle, whereby the humour is located in the ironic recognition of the sexual agenda inherent in the tension between Daffy's uncertain 'masculinity' and the extreme (and highly sexualised) 'femininity' of his appearance. These questions concerning the blurring of gender identity in animation will be addressed in Chapter Five, but here, Daffy's version of the Brazilian bombshell in the 'tutti-frutti hat' may be viewed as funny for the nature of its excess alone, especially as Daffy concludes his performance with an extraordinarily broad smile. Daffy constantly refers to the tableau suggested by theatrical performance and implicitly recognises that his tireless improvisation chimes with the necessary *variety* required by the audience.

Porky arrests his performance by shutting him in a safe, and this initiates the second sequence of the cartoon, which prioritises the expected vocabulary of the cartoon itself. Porky sits comfortably on the plane taking him to his holiday destination, only to discover that Daffy is the pilot, singing patriotically that he is 'Ready to Fly to be Free'. This defies narrative logic and signifies the 'impossible' acts that can only be achieved within the cartoon. Daffy has somehow escaped the safe, got to the airport before Porky, located the right plane, trained as a pilot, taken over the cock-pit etc., none of which is necessary to see, and which is omitted in the customary elliptical cut within the cartoon that stresses the emphasis upon the 'gag' and not its narrative plausibility. Contemporary audiences probably half-expect Daffy to be there, but in many senses, at the structural level, this corresponds to the creation of a 'surprise' gag through the use of 'crude shock for emotionally intense effects', the last of Jenkins' criteria for vaudevillian performance. It is no surprise, though, when the cartoon employs a 'falling' gag, as Porky exits the plane. The surprise comes when the camera pans upward to find Daffy nonchalantly acting as his parachute, as they both float gently on to a roof-top. From here the cartoon engages with its normal frenetic pace as Daffy chases Porky down several flights of stairs to the tune of the 'William Tell Overture', perhaps the most overused chase music in cartoons! Having paid lip-service to the expected chase conventions, the cartoon then returns to its overtly vaudevillian mode, but uses the dynamics of the cartoon vocabulary to present Daffy simultaneously tumbling, juggling, unicycling, back-flipping, spinning, and balancing himself. As Daffy says, 'And now the kid goes into his finale, and what a finale!' This multiplicity of performance styles represents the multiplicity of vaudeville acts and reflects the plurality of tastes and interests in the audience. It prefigures a curious coda, in which Porky finally agrees to see Sleepy, who slowly puts his lollipop into a 'violin' case as if it were a musical instrument (an obvious visual pun in the style described earlier), and starts to sing an operatic aria, only to collapse into a coughing fit. The cartoon's final irony is that, after all Daffy's efforts, Sleepy cannot perform. Of course, it little matters, because the cartoon has foregrounded Daffy's performance, and it is that which the audience expected to see and enjoy.

As Norman Klein has noted, 'At the top of the cartoon industry, virtually every producer and distributor from the twenties into the thirties had worked in

139

vaudeville in some capacity, either as a booking agent, or in art direction, advertising, or simply drawing or providing show-cards' (Klein, 1993: 21). The influence of the vaudeville ethos and output in the cartoon industry was profound and largely expressed the tensions of dealing with the development of mass culture in a newly industrialised nation. The 'modernity' of the fragmentary style reconciled contradictory tensions between the old and the new worlds, heightening the difference between rich and poor; town and country; law and order; us and them; now and then. These polarities were to inform the development of humour in the USA as a perpetual engagement between the 'one-liner' and situational comedy located in character. This reflected the tension between comedy as a mechanism for innocent reflection and comedy as an agent of progress and critique.

6 'Catch that and paint it green!': Adult Avery

Tex Avery radicalised the cartoon by suggesting implicitly and explicitly that the cartoon could be a medium for adult audiences. He clearly understood that children would be appeased by physical slapstick while adults required a more knowing, *self-conscious* approach, which would engage with more mature themes. These included:

- Status and power, and specifically, the role of the underdog.
- Irrational fears, principally expressed through paranoia, obsession, and the re-emergence of previously repressed feelings.
- The instinct to survive at any cost.
- A direct engagement with sexual feelings and sexual identity.
- A resistance to conformity, and consequently, a re-evaluation of the point of anticipated identification and empathy for the audience.[3]

Avery is a chief contributor to the the stock of visual 'gags' listed on p. 136, and his madcap invention did much to invigorate the cartoon and extend its possiblities. Taking up the vaudevillian mode and matching it with the absurdist principles of the visual pun, he directly addressed his assumed audience, calling upon its adult members to engage with something entirely different from Disneyesque 'cuteness'. Avery, in essence, rejected what may be termed the 'culture of cheerfulness' inherent in the Disney cartoon, preferring instead to be less endeared by humankind, and more engaged with the surreal madness of the universe. As Avery himself said, 'I've always felt that what you did with a character was more important than the character itself. Bugs Bunny could have been a bird' (Adamson, 1975: 162). In moving away from the complexities of fully rounded characters, Avery was able to focus on specific kinds of relationship between characters and the very environment of the cartoon. Most importantly, Avery's 'gags', in self-reflexively interrogating the boundaries of cartoon animation, simultaneously revealed the underpinning imperatives of human behaviour as it was expressed through his characters as they, in turn, engaged with their destabilised and uncertain contexts. Avery's disruptions in the narrative became narrative itself. His development of the vocabulary of 'gags' became a perceptive engagement with inarticulable aspirations and unspeakable desires.

Avery's vehemently anti-Disney stance perhaps reaches its apotheosis in *Screwball Squirrel* (1944), in which Screwy Squirrel beats up a Disneyesque bunny, who is just about to embark on a pleasant cartoon story about woodland animals, but his efforts to challenge the aesthetic, narrative, and ideological certainties of the Disney cartoon characterised the whole of his career. This largely entailed recasting the role and function of the 'gag' to reform the cartoon to resist any coherent social or political stance, prioritising what may be termed 'primal motives'. Avery essentially achieved this in five ways:

1 extending the premise of a visual gag;
2 the deployment of *alienation* devices;
3 using the tension between the visual and the verbal to develop the literal gag;
4 integrating unexpected black humour into his narratives;
5 exploiting and exaggerating *psychological, emotional* and *physical* taboos.

These types of gag are illustrated below as specific examples of 'Twenty Five Ways to Start Laughing', with particular examples from Avery's films.

7 Extending the premise of the visual gag

In *Thugs with Dirty Mugs* (1939), (a parodic title echoing Michael Curtiz's 1938 gangster movie, *Angels with Dirty Faces*), Avery uses the typical live-action device of a montage of piling copies of the *Telegraph Post* showing the escalating number of National Bank robberies. Each newspaper's headline says, '1st National Bank Robbed by Killer', '2nd National Bank Robbed by Killer' etc., in an accelerating pace until the papers pause at the thirteenth bank, whereupon the headline says, '13th National Bank Skipped: Killer Superstitious'. The papers then pile once more, before Avery cuts to a robbery in which a car, able to squash-up and stretch-out around corners, and squeeze into small spaces, is used in a raid. A safe, pulled from a bank, also immediately becomes a caravan. The 'punchline' of the sequence is a newspaper headline proclaiming '87 Banks Robbed Today'. Avery cleverly extends the logic of each of the constituent parts of his sequence. First, he takes the idea that the one and only '1st National Bank' could, in fact, be the first of a whole lot of specifically numbered National Banks. Second, he uses the same sequence of numbers to call upon the superstition associated with the number thirteen to break the apparently predictable sequence of robberies. Third, he uses the elliptical cut to a robbery itself, in order to cut once more to the newspaper which says that eighty-seven robberies have taken place in one day, both making a joke of the fact that eighty-seven newspapers may have been produced in a single day, and exaggerating possible events until plausibility is exhausted and disbelief becomes amusing. Even the intervening action of the robbery itself exaggerates the impossible capability of the car, and crucially provides the opportunity for Avery to suggest that this is merely one of an escalating number of robberies that are taking place. Avery looks to exploit and extend each aspect of both the initial 'gag' idea and its ultimate composition and execution. Avery's comedy thus often occupies the space between the improvised 'spot gag' and a coherently plotted form and, as has already been suggested, this constitutes the redetermination of narrative in the cartoon.

By extending the possibility of the 'gag', Avery not merely redefined narrative, but reconstituted established visual jokes. One of the most memorable occurs in *The Heckling Hare* (1941), which includes one of the most protracted 'falling' gags in cartoons. Willoughby, the hunting dog, based on Lenny from Steinbeck's novel, *Of Mice and Men*, pursues Bugs Bunny, only to be tricked into falling over a cliff, after initially avoiding a fall through a hole made by Bugs. Punished for his complacency and arrogance in humiliating Willoughby, Bugs actually falls through the hole, and both fall in parallel towards their inevitable doom. For over thirty seconds, Bugs and Willoughby tumble through the air screaming and shouting, pulling exaggerated faces, before arresting their fall and coming to earth safely. Both then turn directly to the assumed audience and say 'Fooled you didn't we?' Avery's recognition of the audience goes beyond Bugs and Willoughby's direct address, in the sense that he is manipulating the audience's expectations of the 'falling' gag by creating comic suspense, delaying or subverting the gag's predictable outcome.

Extending the premise of the visual gag may be understood, therefore, as:

- compressing subordinate comic possibilities within the basic structure of the dominant comic event, and;
- altering the timing and expected outcome of the dominant (and widely known) comic event.

8 The development of alienation devices

Though seemingly unrelated culturally and intellectually, the work of theorist and playwright, Bertolt Brecht, and Tex Avery, has much in common; chiefly, in what may be described as the use of 'alienation' effects. Brecht's concept of *verfremdung* may be translated as 'distantiation', 'estrangement' or 'defamiliarisation', but in whatever respect, it essentially means the aesthetic strategy by which the creator or performer of the text directly reveals the means and mechanisms of its creation to the audience. This intervention calls upon the audience to recognise the position of themselves as the 'subject' and the textual apparatus they are engaged with as the 'object'. The audience, therefore, is also offered the overt illustration of the shifting points of access and identification that they are normally implicitly asked to adopt (see also Pilling, 1984; Lindvall and Melton, 1994). As Elizabeth

Wright suggests, 'it sets up a series of social, political, and ideological interruptions that remind us that representations are not given but produced' (Wright, 1989: 19). While Brecht's agenda is to reveal the dynamics of *social* relations, Avery is concerned with the machinations of the *individual*, and the comic possibilities available by undermining the codes and conventions of the cartoon. These intentions do not necessarily depoliticise Avery's work, however, particularly in relation to his representation of women, and the ideological intent of his wartime propaganda. Clearly, though, Avery's refunctioning of the cartoon is prompted first and foremost by his desire to engage the audience in the direct participation with the *consciously* contrived aspects of his cartoon text. Interestingly, this finds direct correspondence with some aspects of Brecht's dialectical theatre:

> In order to unearth society's laws of motion this method treats social situations as processes, and traces out all inconsistencies. It regards nothing as existing except in as so far as it changes, in other words is in disharmony with itself. This also goes for those human feelings, opinions and attitudes through which at any time the form of men's life together finds its expression.
>
> (Wright, 1989: 37)

One need only replace the word 'society' here with the word 'cartoon', and Avery's working practice may be clearly understood. Avery uses the unique vocabulary available through the 'laws of motion' in the cartoon as the specific *embodiment* of the ambiguities and contradictions informing an inherently unstable sense of 'the self' and 'the social' in any situation. Perhaps Avery's most significant similarity to Brecht, however, lies in his insistence that his 'comedy' was historically relevant. Avery's 'gags' reflect a modern world aware of the precarious balance between tragedy and comedy. Disney's folksy optimism was in many ways *passé*. Self-consciousness in the cartoon represented self-awareness in its audience. The audience were sometimes literally included in Avery's films (a figure emerges from the audience to aid the stage-swami in *Hamateur Night* (1938), while Cinderella shouts 'Yoo hoo, here I am in the tenth row' to her Prince Charming in *Cinderella Meets Fella* (1938)), or constantly referred to (in *Happy-Go-Nutty* (1944), Screwy Squirrel and other characters rush into a dark cave and the audience hears typical cartoon crashing sounds. Screwy lights a match and says 'Sure was a great gag. Too bad you couldn't see it').

Most importantly though, Avery asked the audience to always remember that they were watching a cartoon, a medium reliant on contemporary technologies. In *Henpecked Hoboes* (1946), George and Junior, whilst chasing a chicken, cross a line with a sign on it which reads, 'Technicolor ends here', and immediately become black-and-white characters. The chase music also grinds to a halt at this point, drawing attention to its relationship to the action. This had already been made absolutely specific in *Screwball Squirrel* (1944), where the convention of the drum roll as the prefiguring sound to the anticipated action of a character, is

143

subverted by the fact that we see Screwy playing it within the course of the action. In the same cartoon, Screwy is able to look ahead to see the outcome of the next sequence by literally 'flipping' a few images in the corner of 'the page'. In *Magical Maestro* (1952), a conductor is literally transformed into a different character by the wave of a wand, but even the most committed viewer is distracted from the main action by the presence of a hair apparently moving in the bottom left-hand corner of the image. The conductor literally plucks the hair, but not before numerous projectionists had lost theirs in attempting to remove it from the projector lens!

These devices all 'alienate' the audience from the customarily settled condition of linear narrative and reveal the construction of the 'gag' in the cartoon by challenging the assumptions of watching a cartoon. Simultaneously, Avery implicitly suggests that the audience laughs at its own sense of certainty, in both the movie-house and the real world (see also Adamson, 1975; Peary and Peary, 1980).

9 Literal, visual and verbal gags

In *The Cuckoo Clock* (1950), Avery literally visualises a number of everyday phrases, rapidly stacking 'gags' to represent the escalating madness of a cat driven crazy by a cuckoo. 'Cuckoo' gags had already featured in *Cinderella Meets Fella*, but here become a *tour de force* of surreal thinking. As the cat imagines 'ringing in my ears', his ears become bells; when he says he 'kept seeing things', coloured squiggles float about in the corner of the screen with a sign saying 'things'; his eyes then grow 'big as saucers', and after doing so, break like china; when he says 'I couldn't keep a thing on my stomach', objects literally bounce off; not knowing whether he is 'coming or going' he simultaneously walks backwards and forwards going nowhere; confessing he was 'down in the dumps', he is seen pacing in a junkyard; his head keeps blowing up when he says 'I kept blowing my top'; his body falls apart when he feels himself 'going to pieces', only to be reconstructed when he admits 'I had to pull myself together'. Yes, he was 'going cuckoo'! These 'spot gags', deliberately play on the gap in the language between the literal and the figurative and essentially extend the vocabulary of the visual pun defined earlier. Nearly all Avery films deploy this device in some way, but some films, including the early mock-documentaries he made at Warner Brothers (*Believe it or Else* (1939), *Detouring America* (1939), *Cross-Country Detours* (1940)), his imaginative views of the future made at MGM (*The House of Tomorrow* (1949), *The Car of Tomorrow* (1951), *TV of Tomorrow* (1953), and *The Farm of Tomorrow* (1954)), and most particularly, *Symphony in Slang* (1951), which literalises 'hip' phrases like 'raining cats and dogs', prioritise the use of this device. The colourful and imaginative aspects of the verbal fuel the surreality of the visual, rendering the literal depiction of impossible similes and metaphors amusing.

10 On black humour

Playing on the tension that, perhaps, informed all of Avery's work, black humour emerges from the narrative preference to heighten the tragical aspects of the fine line between the tragic and the comic in the contemporary world. This usually emerges as an extension of violent conduct in Avery's cartoons but often in unexpected contexts. In *Hamateur Night* (1938), the stage-swami asks a member of the audience to participate in one of his tricks by getting into a basket, which he then spears with a sword. The trick, of course, relies on the man re-emerging, miraculously unharmed. In Avery's world, the trick fails, and the swami passes the basket to an usher saying 'Give this gentleman his money back'. The black humour emerges here from the swami's disregard for the man's death and the apparently ludicrous compensation implied by giving the dead man his money back. In order to create such a gag, Avery often has to empty an image of its associative meanings in order to prioritise the literalism that characterises the humour. For example, in *The Shooting of Dan McGoo* (1951), a man who is allegedly dying is described as having 'one foot in the grave', whereupon he enters with the entire paraphernalia of a grave on the end of his right leg. The tombstone and the plot of ground carry sacred connotations which may render this joke in bad taste in spite of its absurdity. Its use of 'sacred' imagery, though, still determines it as a mode of black humour unexpectedly emerging within this context.

This technique becomes important in the Avery canon though, because comic excess in the expression of black humour essentially renders the implications of the imagery, at best ambiguous, but for the most part, meaningless. A cartoon like *Blitzwolf* (1942) is, on the surface, an engagement with something as unfunny as Adolf Hitler, but becomes an excess of gags that parody the military and ridicule authority, recalling Hitler himself only at the iconic level. Similarly, *Who Killed Who?* (1943), a spoof of horror stories and murder mysteries, employs sinister imagery only redeemed by exaggerated comic effects. As Joe Adamson has noted:

> The grotesque sight of a door opening to let a corpse drop past the camera and thud to the floor is somewhat qualified by the equally grotesque sight of another corpse directly behind it, and then, after it falls, another one behind that. The graphics and the animation draw forth all the horror possible and the effect is genuinely ghastly, but by the time seventeen of them in a row have hit the floor it's just crazy. Finally, one of the cadavers pauses, in his drop, long enough to trill the words, 'Ah yes! Quite a bunch of us isn't it?'. And down he goes, followed by seventeen more.
>
> (Adamson, 1975: 65)

Avery's black humour acknowledges the implicit relationship between horror and humour, carefully playing out the notion that something may be frightening for an individual if it is happening to them, but amusing if the very same thing is happening to someone else. Amusement comes from the alleviation of the terror or anxiety and its projection elsewhere. Avery carefully places his audience in the middle of this tension, soliciting a different emotional source for laughter. This approach directly informs his capacity to interrogate adult concerns.

11 Recognising torment and taboo

Avery's work is based on a consistent refusal to accept the conventional parameters of representational fiction. It is constructed wholly on the terms of a direct address to an audience who Avery assumes shares the same preoccupations and level of understanding. Avery implicitly asks his audience to *recognise* themselves in the codes and conditions of his *revelatory* mode, rejecting the easy narrative continuities of the Disney style or the fluidity of a certain 'dream-state' kind of animation located in cartoons by Friz Freleng, Bob McKimson or Bob Clampett, other major Warner Brothers animators (see Peary and Peary, 1980; Pilling, 1985). It is this style which ultimately draws attention to the thematic consistencies in Avery's work cited earlier. One of Avery's most dazzling illustrations of the tenuous conditions of status and power, for example, occurs in *Slap-Happy Lion* (1947), when a lion at the point of his greatest authority swallows himself in fear of a mouse, diminishing his self-imposed standing, proving, as Durgnat suggests, that 'not even lions should throw their weight about in the jungle, because everyone's neurotic about something' (Durgnat, 1969: 186). Issues arising concerning status and power are intrinsic to the chase cartoon because invariably the characters chasing each other correspond to the following models:

- inept hunter/superior hunted (Elmer and Bugs; Coyote and Road Runner);
- irritating pursuer/fleeing pursued (Daffy and Porky; Sylvester and Tweety);
- equally matched adversaries (Tom and Jerry).

Avery complicates these issues by constantly placing notions of status and power in flux, subject often merely to the whim of the characters themselves, within their delirious universe. Little Red Riding Hood, Grandma and the Wolf, for example, all decide that they are sick and tired of playing out the traditional Little Red Riding Hood tale in *Red Hot Riding Hood* (1943), and recast Red Riding Hood as a night-club 'vamp' fully aware of her sexuality and entirely self-possessed, Grandma as a sexually voracious society madame, and the Wolf torn between his unrequited lust for 'Red' and his deep anxiety over Grandma's relentless pursuit of him! By recasting role and identity, Avery redefines and relocates the notion of status and power in his characters. Because they are entirely free to pursue their most instinctive motives and desires, Avery's characters pay no attention to social etiquette, cultural norms, or prevailing hierarchies of influence and effect. This liberates them to behave entirely 'in the moment' and within the context of the 'gag' itself. Clearly, this liberation not merely redetermines aspects of status and power, but privileges the psychological, emotional and physical imperatives often

146

misrepresented or repressed within 'the social'. Avery lets his characters have free-play with their appetites and *irrational* motives, and as such, reveals the deepest of obsessions, the most primal of instincts, and the most inchoate aspects of the human condition.

By addressing two of Avery's most well-known cartoons – *Little Rural Riding Hood* (1949) and *King Size Canary* (1947) – some brief points concerning the implications of these revelations in regard to the creation and innovation of 'gags' may be made.

Little Rural Riding Hood (1949)

This cartoon, like *Red Hot Riding Hood*, *Swingshift Cinderella* (1945) and *Wild and Wolfy* (1945), may be recognised as a body of work most representative of 'Tex on Sex'. Once more, rejecting the traditional telling of the 'Red Riding Hood' story, Avery plays out the town and country motif, so beloved of Disney in films like *The Country Cousin* (1936). The cartoon begins with a gangly girl telling the audience in the extended drawl of a country bumpkin that she is going to visit Grandma. Avery then cuts to Grandma's house, where the wolf, dressed in Grandma's nightie, says 'Folks, confidentially, I'm not the real Grandma, I'm the wolf, see', and proceeds to confirm that far from eating Little Red Riding Hood, he is going to 'kiss her and love her'. Avery, of course, is merely literalising the sexual connotations of the term 'wolf' in the everyday vernacular, recasting the wolf as a creature driven predominantly by his sexual appetites rather than his physical need to survive. In the film's opening sequence between the two characters, the Wolf chases Red attempting to kiss her, ending up in the first instance kissing a cow! Red dexterously opens doors with her feet, flattens the Wolf's body against the door, and charges through his body, leaving it flapping like two saloon doors. The chase then reaches a hysterical pace as a proliferation of doors suddenly appear in every wall and ceiling created by Wolf and Red as they pursue each other. This merely operates as a prologue, however, for the rest of the cartoon, when their chase is arrested by the arrival of a telegram from the country wolf's city cousin, who suggests he should come and see an entertainer called 'Red' in the city. He encloses a photograph of 'Red' which features a red-headed girl in a basque dress, to which country wolf's eyes widen out of his head to half the size of his body. Country Red, by this time, has rouged her lips ready to kiss him, but finds herself kissing the cow, as he excitedly motors to the city, skidding the car to a halt as if it was a piece of wood ground down to a pile of sawdust. He then meets his city cousin in a hotel suite.

The city cousin is the epitome of control and sophistication, a still character, heightening the total lack of control in his cousin, who is so driven by his lust for Red that he searches under the seat for her, extends his body to search within a lamp, and walks on air from building to building to find her in the adjacent apartments. The country cousin is in essence 'a force' beyond character; a spirit in a body that can operate outside the physical limitations of the body in the on of pure feeling. Avery changes the rhythm and purpose of the cartoon, rily overstating the action in *extremes* to heighten the recognition in the ce of feeling-states beyond articulable words. As Ronnie Scheib suggests:

.he impact of Avery's extremes is perhaps most visible in his celebrated 'takes' – bodies that break apart like a mad contradictory gaggle of exclamation points or zip out limb by limb, jaws that drop open to the floor in shock, necks that sprout multiple hydra-heads of surprise, tongues that jaggedly vibrate in horror or infinitely expand in desperation, eyes that grow to the size of millstones or spring out of their sockets or multiply to form sets popping out in rows towards their object of lust or terror.

(Scheib, 1980: 115)

Avery derives humour from illustrating how the body would react if it did have the capacity to properly express the intensity of its feelings. He uses the cartoon to show the inadequacy of the body in representing the thoughts and emotions that are projected through it. The desire in the country cousin continues unabated when his city counterpart takes him to the club to see 'Red'. The country cousin's wolf-whistle defies being 'corked' by his cousin's finger, and travels through his cousin's arm to emerge out of his cousin's mouth! The city cousin pushes the country wolf's head down beneath his collar, and ties it at the neck, only for his head to re-emerge from his stomach as he pokes through his 'rollerblind' shirt-front. He literally smokes his cigarette and half his face off, and resists having his face pushed in by his city cousin by forcing his face back so vehemently on the rebound that he finds himself within his cousin's shirt collar. His city cousin also attempts to foil his whistling by forcing both his arms into his mouth and out through his ears, while also arresting his charge towards the tempting 'Red' by flooring him with a mallet which he 'fires' from the country cousin's braces. Flattened, the country cousin is pushed away like a wheelbarrow. City life is all too much, it seems, but what Avery is suggesting is that 'civilisation' stimulates desires which it then refuses to appease. The city cousin's every act is one of oppression and suppression, desperately trying to contain the overt public expression of a taboo emotion. Avery has no interest in maintaining the boundaries of the public and private, and this violation is at the core of his humour. As if to reinforce the view that primal impulses will not be inhibited, the cartoon concludes, with a classic Avery reversal when the city cousin expresses the same lust towards the gangly country 'Red', and Avery enjoys a frenetic reprise of the same gags that characterised the demise of the country wolf.

King Size Canary (1947)

King Size Canary represents another evaluation of primal drives in the sense that it is principally concerned with the instinct to survive, whether this be in appeasing hunger or guarding against threat. In Avery's world, these drives become obsessional, leading characters into strange realms which have their own internal logic, a logic which Avery pursues to its uncertain ends. A black cat, scavenging for food becomes desperate when three fish skeletons are stolen by other cats, leading him to break into a house. He foils a dog with searchlight eyes by using sleeping pills and defies gravity by stacking crates in mid-air to climb in a window. Though he imagines the fridge is full, it proves empty, envisaged as a room for let by Avery with a small 'For Rent, Furnished' sign. Even the sardine tin on the shelf proves a disappointment when the cat twists back the lid only to discover a 'Kilroy was here' sign. These deliberate constructions of gags at the expense of the central character, delay the fulfilment of the character's prime need and perpetuate the narrative. Avery's fundamental purpose for including these devices, though, is to escalate the character's paranoia, and to cast the world as a place without order, with no enduring sense or logic (see Peary and Peary, 1980: 121). Both the animator, and the world he represents, persecute the cat, refusing him success or resolution. This provokes a high degree of irrationality in the cat as he completely ransacks the house looking for food, finally happening upon a tin of cat food.

Excitedly opening the can, he tips out a mouse, who, unsurprisingly, in the Avery universe, though seeming to be the underdog in this situation, turns out to be more streetwise than the cat. Once again, Avery draws attention to the character's own self-consciousness about appearing in a cartoon, when the mouse resists the cat's attempts to eat him by saying 'Forget it, see, I've seen this cartoon before, and brother, believe me, if you're smart you won't eat me, 'cos before this picture's over, I save your life'. The cat accepts this, but remembers that he is still hungry. The mouse, leaning completely into the middle of the cat's head through his ear, suggests that he eat the 'Great, big, fat, juicy, canary' in the next room. Frustrated once more, the cat only finds an emaciated canary who says 'I've been sick'. Just at the point of utter defeat, he sees a bottle of 'Jumbo Gro', a plant feed, and after experiencing a literal 'brain-storm' with attendant rain, thunder and lightning, he feeds it to the canary. The canary becomes hugely inflated, and in doing so shifts its status. The cat plucks its leg, initially pursuing the logic of eating the canary as he had intended. He suddenly realises, however, that the canary is now bigger than he is, and thus presents a threat. Gingerly he returns the leg-feathers he has plucked, and adopts a new logic of survival, that of protecting himself from an enemy who may harm him.

The cartoon from here becomes a frenetic chase based on the exchange of the bottle of 'Jumbo Gro', and the ever-escalating size of the protagonists. The cat drinks some, and becomes intimidating to the canary, who in a typical Avery moment, refuses to believe in the presence of the cat, even though he is leaning against his fang-like teeth. He then pulls out the cat's teeth, nose and eyes, reconstituting his face in mid-air, in order to properly accept that the cat is there, only to quickly throw the pieces of face back on to the cat's head in a different order! The ensuing scuffle leads to the bottle being thrown, and it lands in a dog's mouth. He, of course, grows huge, and ultimately dwarfs both a house, and the cat chasing the canary. The bottle is dropped down a chimney by the dog, landing near the feet of the mouse, who originally came out of the tin. He is reading 'The Lost Squeekend' (Ouch!), but inevitably drinks the 'Jumbo Gro' until he dwarfs the dog and, as prefigured much earlier, saves the cat's life. This, though, is not the end. The cat is still hungry, and perceives the mouse as food. The two then continually exchange the bottle as they traverse the world growing ever-larger. When the bottle runs out, the mouse says 'Ladies and Gentlemen, we're going to have to end this picture – we just ran out of the stuff'. The cat and mouse are arm-in-arm, standing on top of the planet. Beat that, Tom and Jerry! Avery pursues the relentless logic of a comic scenario until the idea was exhausted of possibilities. This approach radically changed the cartoon, and even extended the boundaries of film itself.

Tex Avery is one of the undisputed masters of animation. Even though he created the characters of Bugs, Porky, Daffy, Droopy and Screwy Squirrel, his interest was not in character comedy, but the *proliferation* of gags, simultaneously occurring and operating on a number of levels. Avery asks the audience to laugh at what it knows, takes for granted, little understands, and endures. His surreality is merely a recognition of the illusion of control and order in society; his comedy, an indulgence of the inchoate forces informing humankind but rarely engaged with. Curiously appropriate here is Avery's cry of 'Catch that and paint it green!' every time he broke wind. A funny sound, an absurd response, an impossible instruction, a taboo broken, an extended joke!

12 Jones' Road Runner gags

Like Avery, Chuck Jones made significant contributions to the vocabulary of cartoon gags, but unlike Avery, he became more interested in the comic possibilities of limiting the logic of a situation rather than over-extending it. For Jones, 'there are – there must be – rules. Without them, comedy slops over at the edges. Identity is lost'. To this end, Jones created the following specific rules for the Coyote and Road Runner series, which are useful to reprise in their entirety because they serve as a particular kind of comic model (Jones, 1989: 224–5).

1   The Road Runner cannot harm the Coyote except by going 'Beep-Beep'.
2   No outside force can harm the Coyote – only his own ineptitude or the failure of the ACME products.
3   The Coyote could stop at anytime – if he were not a fanatic. (Repeat: 'A fanatic is one who redoubles his effort when he has forgotten his aim' – George Santayana.)
4   No dialogue ever, except 'Beep-Beep'.
5   The Road Runner must stay on the road – otherwise, logically, he would not be called a Road Runner.
6   All action must be confined to the natural environment of the two characters – the south-west American Desert.

7   All materials, tools, weapons, or mechanical conveniences must be obtained from the ACME corporation.

8   Whenever possible, make gravity the Coyote's greatest enemy.

9   The Coyote is always more humiliated than harmed by his failures.

These rules underpin all of Jones' 'Road Runner' cartoons, and show the intrinsic difference between his work and Avery's. Jones cherished character, and consistently showed his affection for characters, even when they endured adverse experiences.[4] In many senses, Jones occupies the space between the cheerful bonhomie of Disney and the anarchy of Avery, combining an intrinsic warmth in his characters with the precision timing of the 'gag'. Unlike Avery's, Jones' gags essentially required that an audience knew the outcome of the gag, and the humour emerged from *when* something happened, rather then *how* it happened. The audience always knew that the Coyote would fail in his efforts to catch and eat the Road Runner, but enjoyed the *repetition* of the formula because what was important was the nuances of the gag rather than possible innovation. The Coyote's reaction to the inexplicable failure of his ACME products or the way in which the environment conspired against him, was just as, if not more, important than the slapstick physicalities of the gag. In numerous respects, though, the Coyote did endure the 'slap-of-the-stick' far more frequently than many of his cartoon counterparts because objects (normally huge catapults) would vent their mechanical malice upon him.

Jones' great skill was in the creation of *comic suspense*, when the audience recognises that the seed of a joke has been planted and they are merely waiting for its inevitable outcome. The tension that this creates liberates laughter with the eventual fulfilment of the gag. For example, on one occasion, Coyote builds an ACME trapdoor in the middle of the road which springs up at the touch of a switch. The Coyote's obvious hope is that as the Road Runner speeds round the corner, he can flick the switch, and the Road Runner will come to a sorry end crashing into the iron door. When it comes to the crunch, the door does not spring up and the Road Runner goes past. Coyote checks the mechanism, nothing appears to be wrong, but the trapdoor still refuses to spring up. The audience think, of course, that it is going to spring up, and harm the Coyote. Significantly, it doesn't. The cartoon passes on to other comic encounters, and just when the audience has possibly forgotten the failure of the trapdoor, or perceived it as a narrative loose-end, it springs up in the middle of another unrelated chase sequence, injuring Coyote. It is the delayed outcome of this scenario that makes it funny, working on the tension between the audience's mutual need for surprise and reassurance.

It is this tension which also informs Jones' 'running gags' which are essentially repetitions of the same scenario but with some comic variations on a theme. Coyote, for example, is constantly attempting to fire himself after the Road Runner like an arrow or within a large piece of elastic band. Similarly, huge catapults conspire against him, and no rock face passes without being the instrument of his downfall. Jones' rules give the audience reassurance, and do not stir or represent Avery's primal motives. The consistency in character, location, action and typology of 'gags' resist social readings, except at the level of the kind of 'fanaticism' that the Coyote represents. The Coyote's relentless imperative to catch the Road Runner is, however, more about pride than paranoia. His obsession is purely related to his own puzzlement concerning why he has never captured or defeated the Road Runner, and not about some primal need to do so – as Jones suggests, he could stop at any time. Jones trusts the internal logic of characters and situations and interrogates their predictability. Avery uses characters as ciphers for gags related to primal motives while Jones creates in Road Runner and Coyote 'single-note' characters who he seeks to employ in subtle variations on the chase motif. The Road Runner's 'Beep-Beep' is both a surprise noise and a call-to-arms, an existential signature of continuous movement and yet, limited progress. The Coyote, it seems, cannot move on, unless he secures this particular prey. The limited conditions of the cartoon, seen in these terms, can have absurdist overtones, but Jones limits the darker connotations of their scenario, by privileging 'humiliation' over 'harm', sustained effort and endeavour over self-conscious defeat and resignation. This largely came about because of the abject failure of *Fast and Furry-ous* (1947), the first Road Runner and Coyote cartoon, which started out as a satire on the dominant orthodoxy of the chase cartoon, a satire which no one recognised, and which wasn't amusing either (Jones, 1989: 226). Satire was left in other hands.

13 Some theories on character comedy

Jones' preoccupation with character and the development of the chase cartoon, leads logically into a proper address of the role and function of character in the animated film. In this section, therefore, I intend to conflate three different theories, with recognisably similar aspects which will serve to inform the study of character, and also to suggest three specific models which might usefully serve as a point of access to extended study in one area. These are essentially a theory of character typology in the cartoon, a theory of character typology in character comedy in general, and the theory delineating the basic tenets of human character in psychoanalysis. Their relationship may be initially understood in Table 4.2.

Norman Klein's theory of cartoon character with regard to role and function suggests that there are three principal roles, the Controller, the Over-reactor and the Nuisance (see Table 4.2). He says 'the Controller is usually indestructible in the cartoon: he may feel anguished but he hardly ever gets hit', while 'the Over-reactor tends to take the lumps, like the fall-guy in a slapstick comedy', and 'the Nuisance usually starts off the cartoon by annoying the Over-reactor, who then keeps the gags flowing', becoming particularly useful because 'he is more like a force of nature than a character that thinks at all' (Klein, 1993: 38). Clearly, Bugs largely controls the action in his cartoons, though Elmer attempts to gain control of a situation and suffers accordingly, while Daffy perpetually plays out his

Table 4.2 Some theories of character

Theory	Character type 'A'	Character type 'B'	Character type 'C'
Cartoon character (Klein)	Controller	Over-reactor	Nuisance
Comedy character (Jenkins)	The clown	Dupe/Killjoy	Counterfeit
		Comic antagonist	
Psychoanalytic characteristic (Freud)	Id	Super-ego	Ego
Example	Bugs Bunny	Elmer Fudd	Daffy Duck

mad-cap self-interest against the tension between Bugs and Elmer. Though these roles predominate, they are sometimes necessarily in flux to facilitate further gags, but their complexity runs deeper than merely structural device, and this is where Jenkins' work becomes of interest.

Jenkins asserts that 'the comedy of social disorder', of which the cartoon must be the most extreme example, features a tension between the Clown and the Comic antagonist:

> The Clown personifies change, encapsulating all that is rebellious and spontaneous within the individual, all that strains against the narrow codes of social life. The Comic antagonist embodies civilisation, all that is stifling and corrupt within the existing social order, all that would block or thwart efforts towards individual self-expression and personal pleasure.
>
> (Jenkins, 1992: 221–2)

Jenkins suggests that the 'Comic antagonist', however, is characterised by three further social types – the Dupe, the Killjoy and the Counterfeit. He describes the Dupe as 'completely bound by conventional patterns of thought', the Killjoy as representative of social stability at the cost of 'individual spontaneity and personal expressiveness', and the Counterfeit as those who 'claim unearned respectability and hold others accountable to standards they themselves refuse to obey' (Jenkins, 1992: 232–4). Once more, when applied to Bugs, his role as Clown is unchallenged, but interestingly within the cartoon, this is prioritised as the controlling rather than oppositional force. The cartoon privileges the Clown without necessarily determining him as a social outsider. Elmer is both Dupe and Killjoy in the sense that his predictability inhibits his ability to cope with 'the Clown' and in order to try and impose control he must attempt to outlaw the pleasure and eccentricity embodied in Bugs. 'Hunting wabbits', after all, is an attempt to control the proliferation of the creatures and act in a spirit of containment. Daffy's double-standards render him as the perfect 'Counterfeit', and the hypocrisy embodied in the sneaky ways in which he attempts to undermine the opposition while according himself great dignity and status is concordant with his role in Klein's scheme because his attempts to think through a situation are always undermined by his more primal motives. He becomes a hysterical 'spirit of nature' because he ultimately cannot sustain his role as a 'Counterfeit'. Daffy would love to be a Clown, but despite all his efforts, he hasn't got the credentials. If these interactions are to be read outside their cartoon or comic context, though, a further set of readings is legitimised through the deployment of psychoanalysis.

In personifying his concepts, the *super-ego*, the *ego* and the *id*, (naming them after mythological figures), Freud brought previously alienated ideas slowly into the public domain. In some of his first models of psychic life, Freud identified the unconscious, pre-conscious, and conscious states, but as his studies developed he localised the workings of the super-ego, ego and id within the unconscious, thus further complicating the psychological mechanisms which seemed to underpin conscious 'external' life. Anna Freud, Freud's daughter, in her introduction to her father's 1923 essay, 'The ego and the id', usefully summarises its key themes:

> The blind search for satisfaction by the drives, which are given at birth and determine the nature of the id, is not compatible with the nature of the ego whose task it is to register conditions, requirements and dangers in the outer world and to take them into consideration. . . . For the ego itself is nothing other than a re-modelled part which, having split off from the id, is adapted to the external world; the super-ego, again, is a precipitate of the child's prolonged dependency on his parents and their demands with regard to drive restriction and socialisation.
>
> (Freud, 1986: 436)

The id is the collective name for the primal forces that constitute instinctive drives in the personality. Tex Avery's films, for example, are essentially an illustration of the free-play of the id, unchecked by other mechanisms in the personality. The id seeks to fulfil itself, and this is known as the pleasure principle, a wholly subjective drive to satiate physical, emotional and psychological appetites. An inherent imperative, it *acts*, resisting attempts to suppress it. This clearly coheres with the symbolic role of the Clown, and the controlling premise of the cartoon as it is embodied in Bugs. Bugs is always provisionally content, satiating his hunger by chewing on his carrot, enjoying a restful life without anxiety or stress. When this is disrupted or challenged, he resists 'civilising' processes which do not fit in with the fulfilment of the pleasure principle that his lifestyle represents. Bugs acts to maintain the free-play of his pleasure principle, using his comic capacity as 'Clown' to liberate him from inhibition or repression. As an embodiment of the id, he represents the drives which achieve his particular wishes – anger, the instinct to survive, the enjoyment of sexual freedom (see Chapter Five) etc. Most importantly, he represents the essential energy and anarchy of the cartoon itself.

The ego may be recognised as a 'reality' principle, inhibiting psychic energy until it finds its proper fulfilment, simultaneously, attempting to hold the imperatives of the ego in check. In many ways, the ego is the psychic drive that balances the antagonistic tension between the id and the super-ego. Daffy, the Counterfeit, is the embodiment of this tension, oscillating between his desire to achieve power, status, and above all, control, and his collapses into madness through frustration or weakness. Daffy's 'ego' is, indeed, fragile, caught in the perpetual bind of wanting to 'do the right thing' but being seduced or distracted from the possibility of achieving it. Daffy tries to think and reason in order to be 'realistic' but he is destabilised by the things that happen to him and his irrational response to uncertainty. If Bugs is the free-playing anarchy of the cartoon, Daffy is his partial counterpart, having to deal, however, with another aspect of his identity, which is about attaining absolute control.

Absolute control is central to the idea of the super-ego, which operates as a kind of 'conscience', punishing transgression, and rewarding complicity and conformity. The super-ego often embodies traditional methods of doing things, and the common ideals and values which underpin the dominant ideology. In a similar approach to the earlier suggestion that Avery's work represents the id, it is clear that the predominant tone of the Disney output is locked into the machinations of the (American) super-ego. The super-ego is a regulator, mediated through the uncertainty of the ego in the attempt to contain the id. Often the super-ego solicits 'guilt' in the transgressor - Disney films are full of conscience figures making characters feel terrible about what they have done (e.g. Jiminy Cricket in Pinocchio, Thumper in Bambi etc.). In the Warner Brothers cartoons, Elmer Fudd is the closest one gets to a super-ego figure trying to impose himself on the world of nature, but suffering, despite all his attempts to punish transgression in Bugs. His role and function are to contain and restrict, but the very spirit of the cartoon resists the imposition of the super-ego. No matter how much Elmer tries to inhibit Bugs' pleasures and instincts, his efforts are doomed to failure, because his authority as the embodiment of the super-ego is constantly under question, or plainly ignored. The 'modernity' of the tension between the ego and the id in the cartoon fundamentally triumphs over the 'traditionalism' of the super-ego.

The cartoon can readily support these kind of interpretations, and these methodologies may be tested and modified against different character types in other forms of animation. Betty Boop, for example, in films made by the Fleischer Brothers, may be the Controller/Clown/id, set against the Over-reactor/Killjoy/super-ego of her principally male counterparts, or in another of the most successful Fleischer creations, it is engaging to play out the tension between Popeye, Bluto and Olive Oyl, as the interaction between Popeye as Controller/

Clown/id, Bluto as Nuisance/Counterfeit/ego, and Olive Oyl as Over-reactor/Dupe/super-ego, though in many respects the role and function of Popeye and Olive Oyl may be reversed; Popeye, it may be argued, only attains the status of Controller/Clown/id when he is helped by a can of spinach! Clearly, these delineations provide theoretical tools for different kinds of analysis, and help to clarify particular roles and functions in cartoon character formation.

14 The shaggy dog story

Having deployed psychoanalytic theory as part of the discussion of character, it is useful also in determining the conditions defining what may be termed the 'shaggy dog story' in animation. As Freud notes:

> The two fixed points in what determines the nature of jokes – their purpose of continuing pleasurable play and their effort to protect it from the criticism of reason – immediately explain why an individual joke, though it may seem senseless from one point of view, must appear sensible, or at least allowable, from another.
>
> (Freud, 1976: 181)

The tension between 'sense' and 'nonsense' is at the core of the 'shaggy dog story', suggesting, as it does, that the logic or expectation used at any one point in the comic narrative may be refuted by a counter-logic or alternative view which differs from the most obvious progression. At one and the same time, the narrative drive appears to sustain reason and rationality, whilst actually supporting utter absurdity. Recognising the space between these two positions results in the understanding of the kind of humour that is being deployed. A specific example illustrating this is *Special Delivery* (1978), made by John Weldon and Eunice Macauley, under the auspices of the National Film Board of Canada, and the sponsorship of the Post Office.[5]

Special Delivery (1978)

Alice Phelps leaves for her judo class, instructing her husband, Ralph, to clear the front walk of snow. Ignoring her, Ralph goes out, only to return and discover that a mailman has slipped on the walk and died. Fearing the 'wrath of the Letter Carrier's Union', Ralph thinks through the situation, remembering a friend who had a similar experience in which his mailman had broken a leg, and concludes, anxiously, that in terms of the possible compensation he may have to pay, 'a broken neck is as bad as ten broken legs'. He decides, therefore, to wear the mailman's uniform, and deliver the rest of the mail, so that no one would know that the mailman had completed his deliveries at the Phelps' house, and no one would accuse him of being responsible for his death. Instead of doing the obvious thing and reporting an accident to the police, Ralph (and the narrative

156

Figure 4.1 Sponsored by the Postal Services, the National Film Board of Canada made the deadpan *Special Delivery*, an excellent example of animation naturally accommodating surreal logic and unusual occurrences as if they were everyday happenings

itself) pursues an alternative logic, resisting the simple course of action, but crucially, consistently *justifying* it. Ralph essentially thinks of himself as someone who has committed a crime, and fearing the consequences of being caught, tries to cover up the evidence. The fundamental joke is that by not doing a simple chore, Ralph casts himself as a serious criminal, and pronounces himself as guilty. Further, the joke is extended by the fact that the sponsors of the film are the Canadian Postal Service, who embrace a narrative which parodies the presence and supposed authority of the Letter Carrier's Union.

The narrative is told in deadpan voiceover, which simply tells the tale as if there was nothing extraordinary in it. This further exacerbates the tension between sense and nonsense because each is delivered in exactly the same tone and register, thus investing it with the same authority. When Ralph undresses the mailman, leaving him slumped naked in his living room chair, and departs to deliver the mail, this is delivered as if it were the *natural* thing to do. The development in the twisted logic of the piece comes when Ralph returns home from his delivery round (mercifully, arousing no suspicion in those people receiving letters) and realises that his door key is in his original trousers. This necessitates that he try and break into his own house – he enters the window only to be spotted by the police who, hearing Ralph's protests that this was his own house, 'were doubtful that a mailman could own such a large house'. At this point, Ralph 'remembered there was a body in the living room and dropped the subject'. Ralph is arrested even though he has yet to commit a crime and is victim of his own self-made circumstances. Absurdly, he is perceived as 'a disgrace to the Letter Carrier's Union', even though he is not a mailman. The film, therefore, sophisticatedly establishes the counterlogic that resists order as its comic premise.

Alice returns to the home and sees an open window, a pile of clothes, an open whisky bottle, and the dead body. She recognises the body because she had an affair with the mailman some months earlier. Like Ralph, she does not take the obvious course of action and call the police. Rather, in a comic strip think-bubble she imagines the scenario that link the window, clothes, whisky and body. She believes that the mailman broke in, trying to rekindle their love affair, got drunk, ripped off his clothes and fell into a stupor – 'It was just like him', she thinks, implausibly. Only when she dresses him and returns him to his apartment does she realise that he is dead, and only then, does another possibility occur to her. She imagines that Ralph discovered the rampant mailman and killed him, and is now preparing to kill her. With sudden deadpan extremism, as a result of this scenario, the voiceover intones: 'Alice drove away to a new province and started a new life under the name, Patricia.' From a small domestic incident, the film has escalated into a neurotic film noir, in which the protagonists consistently imagine themselves as immoral and murderous. Clearly, a great deal of humour resides in the very ordinariness of the situation and the melodramatic morass the characters imagine it to be.

Ralph is released, and after discovering the mailman's body is gone, he burns his uniform and resolves to forget the whole incident. The dead mailman, of course, does not appear at his own trial, and a visit to his address by the police and the coroner finds him dead in his bed where Alice had put him. The police believe he may be a different man but explain away the difference by suggesting that this is merely because a dead body looks different. Similarly, the coroner justifies the fact that the man has died of a broken neck by suggesting that he had been so remorseful about his crime (the alleged break-in!) that he had dreamt he was being hanged, and the subsequent reflex action had caused his death. It is this sustained set of justifications for implausible acts that maintains the idea of nonsense as sense and, as such, implies that the story will carry with it a 'punchline' that further authenticates the whole premise. Instead, the film concludes with the narrator saying, 'After a while, Ralph stopped worrying about the fact that the body had disappeared and his wife had never come back, and in all the long and happy years that followed, Ralph never cleared the walk'. As Freud suggests, though:

These extreme examples have an effect because they arouse the expectation of a joke, so that one tries to find a concealed sense behind the
nonsense. But one finds none: they really are nonsense. The pretence
makes it possible for a moment to liberate the pleasure in nonsense.
These jokes are not entirely without a purpose; they are a 'take-in', and
give the person who tells them a certain amount of pleasure in mis-
leading and annoying his hearer.

(Freud, 1976: 190)

Lest we forget that *Special Delivery* is an animated film, such is its prioritisation of
the story and the story-teller, it is worth remembering that animation is particularly conducive to sustaining such a narrative premise. The film uses the
medium to create a fluidity in the illustration of the tale so that its fundamental
logic and counter-logic are never made obvious. Images evaporate, interiors
metamorphose into exteriors, characters materialise in their environment, lines
and shapes cohere as bridging links between the scenarios being described by the
narrator, and the thoughts being experienced by the characters. The animated
form facilitates a dream-like continuity which combines images in a way which
makes the viewer uncertain of their specific status, particularly in animated films
which aspire to be funny. What images, as it were, should we trust as embodying
'the truth' or the dominant contention of the narrative, when the image itself is
fluid and unstable? Further, when the overt narrative, as it is told in voiceover,
also brings apparent certainty to an absurd premise, it is the audience's suspicion
of the story's questionable authenticity that creates its humour. Animation then,
can bring *equal* symbolic status to any of its images, and it is this, whether used in
a humorous context or not, which enables the animated film to be particularly
successful in the manipulation of its effects. As Peter Munz suggests,

The theory of the symbolic equivalence of images regardless of their
ontological status gains added strength when one considers how arbitrary all attempts to distinguish the ontological status of one image from
that of another really are. One is very hard put to state the difference in
status between a dream and a daydream; between a dream and an
imaginary image. The distinction between a hope and a memory may
be somewhat easier; but we know so many hopes are projected memories
(if one looks at their psychogenesis) that even here the distinction seems
unstable.

(Munz, 1973: 95)

When Munz speaks of 'ontological status', he refers to the source or basis for
the image in the 'real world', and recognises that to establish the intrinsic essence
or distinctiveness of an image is extremely difficult. Animators recognise this as
fundamental in the creation of their imagery, slipping easily between representations of 'the real' and the illustration of 'thought' or 'feeling' without needing to

distinguish between the two. This informs all animated films, but is especially useful in the creation of specific kinds of 'gags', examples of which will now follow.[6]

15 Discontinued lines

Discontinuity is at the very essence of most approaches to creating humour. The rational order of the world and the whole nature of cause and effect must be disrupted by the unexpected. When two ideas that do not seem to naturally relate, meet, and indeed, fundamentally conflict, this can create a comic event. The joke comes out of a resistance to logical continuity. This informs many of the comic scenarios and gag structures already described, but further mention should be made of the work of Terry Gilliam in this context, as it was the incongruities that were at the core of his animated inserts that came to inform the approach to comic construction throughout *Monty Python's Flying Circus*. His cut-out collage animations were essentially 'spot gags' debunking fine art, creating absurd relations between high and low culture, and making fun of narrative conventions. Particularly memorable are his use of a foot from Agnolo Bronzino's painting, *Venus, Time, Cupid and Folly* (1545), which arbitrarily squashes other images to conclude a sketch, or his use of Sandro Botticelli's *The Birth of Venus* (1485), in which Venus' nipple is used as a switch, and when tweaked by a hand which emerges from a shell she is standing within, it makes Venus dance, her leg impossibly spinning in circles. Such comic contempt for great works of art only serves to give the joke a more subversive function. Gilliam's shock tactics also include gags in which a man covers his whole face with shaving cream, only to cut his head off with a cut-throat razor; a hippo jumping up and down on a grave; a small man bouncing up and down on a naked Ruebenesque nude; and an old lady tripping a bus over! Gilliam also demonstrated Fleischeresque surreality in one of his earliest films, *Elephants at War* (1968), in which pulling an elephant's tail immediately reverses its direction, and blowing in its trunk makes its skeleton emerge out of its skin. The style and tone of these short pieces ran over into the sketches that followed in *Monty Python's Flying Circus* creating a surreal world that implicitly satirised the British temperament and tradition.

Similar modes of surreality inform *Bartakiada* (1985), a Czechoslovakian cartoon by Oldrich Haberle, in which a man endures a particularly arduous 'Friday the thirteenth'. That which the viewer assumes to be an open window revealing day and night turns out to be a picture of daylight or a night sky which the main character peels off like a calendar. The man fries an egg, and answers the phone, only to return to his cooking to find a wreath on the egg delivered by two chickens. At breakfast, he reads a sandwich, and eats a book, and so it continues. Incongruity follows incongruity but, unlike Gilliam's work, this is played out slowly, and consequently, Haberle creates a different atmosphere and tone. The speed and zany insanity of Gilliam's animation possesses the spirit of comic anarchy and violation whilst Haberle's jokes are essentially recognitions of the absurdity of humankind's attempts to bring logical order to the world. Eastern European humour like this may be viewed as black irony – the surreality is a philosophic and political statement as well as the vehicle for humour. The incongruity is used for different comic purposes - Gilliam's to shock, Haberle's to reveal. One is the comedy of revolution, the other, the comedy of resignation.

16 Accidents will happen

The logical extension of random events is the idea that they will cause accidental things to occur, things which will be largely of a slapstick, 'destructive' nature. Most cartoons prioritise this as the substance of their narratives – Tom and Jerry, for example, continuously pursue each other, the consequence of which is the wholesale demolition of the domestic environment. Interestingly, this is all done without any real consequence. The home is immediately repaired and ready for its next assault, but the audience never sees the implications of destruction for those who experience or live within it. The same could be said of violent acts, or indeed, physical accidents akin to slipping on a banana skin, which have no enduring effects. The 'slap-of-the-stick' is a purely comic device which brings no harm, but does bring destabilisation and disorder, the space in which the comic flourishes.

The Disney cartoon, *How to Have an Accident in the Home* (1956), cleverly uses 'the accident' for comic purposes, but also to send messages about how to prevent domestic accidents. A small duck with a beard, called J.J. Fate, berates the audience for blaming 'fate' for their own capacity to cause accidents, while Donald Duck more than demonstrates how the contemporary home becomes a minefield of possibilities for accidents to occur. On his way back from work, Donald avoids racing traffic and falling pianos, and arrives 'safe at home, he thinks', but J.J. Fate tells the audience that over 5 million people have been hurt in the home, and the cartoon reveals the gamut of lit cigarettes, hot irons, toys on the stairs, leaking gas pipes and loose rugs on polished floors, all of which cause major accidents. The film is essentially warning the new commodity culture of the 1950s of the dangers of modern conveniences, and employs the engaging device of matching a recognisably dangerous activity with its taken-for-granted equivalent in the home. For example, it is suggested that Donald would never willingly sit in an electric chair, but the film then shows him using an electric shaver in the bath and receiving an excessive shock. Further, Donald would never put his head in a lion's mouth, yet he puts his head in the gas oven while lighting it, and though he would never go over Niagara Falls in a barrel, he negotiates the stairs unsighted because he is carrying something. With quiet irony, Donald, having been severely chastened by his experience of accidents, goes back to the safety of his work at a dynamite factory, while J.J. Fate counsels that average people are failing to use their 'average intelligence', and warns, 'Don't blame fate for your carelessness'. Ironically, by reinvesting the accidents with their real dangers, the cartoon fails to gain the maximum purchase from its slapstick humour. Donald's personality carries the weight of being 'funny' but the caution offered by J.J. Fate only serves to limit the space to laugh.[7]

17 Objects have a life of their own

The 'autonomous' gag may be understood as the comic motif of investing objects and materials with an unpredictable life of their own. This, of course, is the whole premise of animated film, and thus 'gags' created in this spirit in animation differ slightly from their presence in live-action film. When the organic and inorganic worlds collide in live-action film this usually demonstrates a tension between humankind and the apparent autonomy of the physical environment. The joke emerges from the fact that the physical environment is expected to be benign, passive, and in the control of its human occupants, but seemingly conspires to undermine this view. The humour hinges on the belief in the live agency of an apparently inanimate place. Animation makes the 'life' in the inanimate space absolutely explicit and uses the organic and the inorganic as the subject of its basic principles and, thus, redefines the comic aspects of the relationship. For example, Norman McClaren, in his film, *Neighbours* (1952), uses the technique of pixillation to animate objects and *re-animate* the movement of two men. Pixillation is the frame-by-frame recording of rehearsed and deliberately executed live-action movement to create the illusion of movement impossible to achieve by naturalistic means. In this case, for example, figures spinning in mid-air or skating across grass.[8] A small flower, a picket fence, artificial scenery and deckchairs also move of their own accord within the film, and though the film carries with it a serious message, McClaren recalls, 'my memories are of the public laughing from beginning to the end of the film' (McClaren, 1978: 31).

Neighbours actually works on a number of levels. Its comedy largely echoes that of the 'magical surprises' in the trick film, discussed earlier, once more achieving humorous effects through the divergence between the representation of the real world and the presence of impossible events within it. A man appears to spin in mid-air – the man is real enough, but what he does is physically impossible, and thus amusing. The film also works as a piece of developmental animation that derives its humour by directly drawing attention to the conventions of the cartoon, and mounting an implicit critique of its representation of violence. Two neighbours, seated in deckchairs, smoking their pipes, reading newspapers with the headlines, 'War Certain if No Peace', and 'Peace Certain if No War', become involved in a territorial dispute over the ownership of a wild flower. The dispute escalates rapidly, horrible violence takes place between the two men, and the pair eventually end up killing each other.

McClaren alludes to the two-dimensional cartoon by using two-dimensional scenery in a real environment. Two hand-painted cartoon-like house fronts signify two homes in the middle of a field. McClaren creates a balancing symmetry in the *mise-en-scène* which he then disrupts when the men decide to fight over the flower, the fragrance of which each reacts to with ecstatic exaggeration, anticipating the wildly exaggerated movement that parodies the physical excesses of the orthodox cartoon. Similarly, the electronic soundtrack echoes the role of sound effects in the cartoon, creating mood, accompanying actions, and replacing words. The outcome of using these conventions, but reinventing the means by which to create them, is to self-consciously draw attention to them for comic effect. This, in turn, signals that to reinterpret the conventions is to reinterpret the meanings inherent within them. To create cartoon conventions showing violence is to ignore that the conventions are about violence too. Understanding this, McClaren takes the exaggeration of cartoon violence to its logical extreme by showing the primitive barbarism in the two men's actions. By depicting this violence in a highly stylised and artificial way, McClaren examines the tension between the natural and the unnatural, the organic and inorganic, and the animate and inanimate. Objects, materials, and the supposedly civilised, highly ordered, human being, all it seems, possess an unexpected life of their own.

The orthodox cartoon regularly depicts objects with their own identity or personality, of course, whether they be the candlestick, clock or tea set in Disney's *Beauty and the Beast* (1989) or the techno-trousers in Nick Park's *The Wrong Trousers* (1993), but one of the funniest versions of the sustained autonomous gag occurs in Tex Avery's *The Cat that Hated People*, made in 1948, which features a cat fed up with urban life who rockets to the moon for some peace, but as Raymond Durgnat suggests, 'his peace is shattered by a Surrealistic procession of objects gone mad. A pencil-sharpener sharpens his tail, a nappy and safety-pin treat him like a baby, a garden spade buries him deep, a bulb and a watering can brings him sprouting up like a daffodil' (Durgnat, 1969: 185). All the objects possess their own logic and behave in a way which holds the cat (i.e. the apparently controlling figure) in complete contempt. The autonomous gag is, therefore, by extension, ultimately about humankind's precarious hold upon the space it inhabits and the control it assumes it has over the natural order.

18 'The sight of 40-year-old genitalia is too disgusting, is it?': Self-conscious humour

Animation possesses the special ability to render psychological, emotional and physical states, and as such can properly highlight the humour which emerges from self-consciousness. In depicting the frailties and idiosyncrasies of the body; the deep prejudices, concerns and neuroses that inform daily life; and the difficulties inherent in trying to communicate, the animated film properly represents humankind's own recognition of the inherent comedy within the human condition. As the old joke says, 'I've learned to laugh at myself . . . but then, I've got alot of material to work on'.

Bob's Birthday (1995), Alison Snowden and David Fine's Oscar-winning short film, is concerned with Bob's disaffection with life on his fortieth birthday. Bob, a dentist, is troubled by a mid-life crisis, which is characterised by his lack of purpose and the utter boredom of his existence. Unbeknown to him, however, his wife

Figure 4.2 Oscar-winning *Bob's Birthday*, by Alison Snowden and David Fine, derives its humour from the observation of self-consciousness and embarrassment seemingly so deeply embedded in the British character

has organised a surprise birthday party for when he gets home. She suggests that all the guests find a hiding place and spring out when she gives the signal. Bob is too preoccupied when he returns home, though, and despite all his wife's efforts to get him into the living room, so that the party can begin, he starts discussing his problems with her. The viewer has the privilege of having information which Bob doesn't. The more intimate and personal Bob becomes, the more embarrassed his wife gets, and the more amusing it seems for the audience. Bob's self-consciousness leads him to question whether he should change his job and to ask his wife if she had ever been bothered that they had never had children. The revelation of these private issues are essentially being discussed in public because of the presence of the party guests, who can all hear what he is saying. This is exacerbated when Bob comes downstairs with no trousers on, and mistakes his wife's urgency for him to get dressed as a further indictment of his body and says, 'The sight of 40-year-old genitalia is too disgusting, is it?'. This begins a tirade which recalls his sexual prowess, principally through his 'pink elephant' routine, which he demonstrates with the bowl of fruit. He rails that his wife should go off with someone more sophisticated, and suggests one of the men in the room, simultaneously alleging that the man's wife is open to affairs, and that all their friends are boring. Bob's wife, consumed with embarrassment, runs to her bedroom and covers her face with a pillow. Bob, of course, still has no idea that the room is full of these very same friends waiting to spring out and participate in his surprise birthday party. This operates as comic suspense for the audience who want the party-goers to emerge, but this suspense is never relieved as the film finishes with Bob and his wife going out to dinner, leaving everyone still hiding in the lounge. Bob's wife cannot confront her friends, nor can she reconcile Bob's anxiety, and the self-consciousness of the couple remains the governing principle for the film's comedy. They only recognise their deep-rooted fears and foibles, which the audience is invited to laugh at because the private has inadvertently transgressed into the public space.[9]

A yet more self-conscious version of self-consciousness, though, occurs in Will Vinton's clay animation, *The Great Cognito* (1982), which features a middle-aged stand-up comic soliloquising about war and the military in post-war America. His routine explicitly takes personal thoughts into the public context as comic entertainment, his observations operating as satiric comment about the (myth) making of the American war hero. The main humour for the audience, though, emerges from the quick metamorphoses of Cognito's head into well-known figures and events, including Franklin Roosevelt, Winston Churchill, the Andrews sisters, a battleship, a Japanese attack, feuding brothers in the same head, and John Wayne, who is shot down with an arrow. His routine, essentially a neurotic tirade, shifts from personal insight to insane babble, concluding with near collapse at the idea that John Wayne had been shot. What animation achieves here is the conflation of Cognito's descriptive words *and* his inner thoughts, effectively articulating his inner-directed personality and its neurotic solipsistic world. Cognito embodies the collapse of American masculinity as it has been projected by its myths and its global will to power and status. The death of John Wayne caused by an arrow through his head becomes a complex satiric image. John Wayne embodies both the Frontier Cowboy Myth and right-wing militarist confidence – he is killed by an arrow, perhaps signifying the rise of the Native American and revisionist political understanding. At the comic level, though, the image recalls one of those arrow-through-the-head trick hats worn by anyone from Ben Turpin in silent era comedies through to Steve Martin in his 'wild and crazy guy' stand-up persona. This juxtaposition not only heightens satiric intent, but begins to point up the self-consciousness of comedy itself, an issue addressed in Phil Austen's and Derek Hayes' *Binky and Boo* (1988).

Aging music-hall artist, Binky, voiced by veteran British comic actor, Jimmy Jewel, looks at an old scrapbook, reminiscing about his career in variety theatre in a comedy double act, Binky and Boo. Made in cut-out collage, the film prioritises dark contexts and grotesque designs, foregrounding its black humour and its implicit, highly critical view of comedy which has no purpose and remains insensitive to those it offends. Highly correspondent to the rise of 'alternative' comedy and the tide of political correctness, *Binky and Boo* operates as a comedy about comedy. Binky and Boo are red-nosed, boatered, physical clowns, who use a cross-talk repartee, doing clichéd 'mother-in-law' gags in the traditional 'I say, I say, I say' manner. Austen and Hayes highlight the hackneyed, irresponsible nature of the gags, by calling attention to the *structure* of the gag, altering it so that it demonstrates the anticipated formula of the joke but changing its punchline to signify its unfunniness. For example, Boo says, 'I wouldn't say the mother-in-law was fat . . .' to which Binky intercedes with an overemphasised 'But . . .', prefiguring the joke, which Boo concludes by saying 'when she's upstairs she's not downstairs'. The punchline is effectively a non sequitur, and is amusing in a surreal way, but most importantly, it interrogates the gag, rendering its structure and content as stale, predictable and, ultimately, unacceptable.

This treatment of the gag is consistent throughout the film, and informs Binky's revisionist versions of his performances during the war, and when he couldn't get work, his performances in alternative time periods, parallel galaxies and works of literature! Binky's inability to distinguish fact from fiction is facilitated by the animation in the sense that his supposed performances in contexts that he can only imagine he was involved in are treated with the same dark veracity as contexts in which he was plausibly involved, though even these have evidently been subject to shifts of emphasis and omission in his memory. The ontological status of the image, and the narrative which informs it, is once again highly questionable, and serves to enable the film to reveal its purpose by using ever escalating absurd versions of Binky's experience. Binky claims to have entertained 'Stage door Johnny' Louis XIV, those present in the Black Hole of Calcutta and at Custer's Last Stand, and even 'hunter/gatherer societies', 'primitive life forms', and Captain Ahab from *Moby Dick*, insisting that 'every killer whale had its own theatre'. The film's use of exaggeration in this way calls attention to the idea that comedy, as well as being a useful tool to address political ideas, may also be used to ignore or absolve political agendas from their complexity and meaning. The joke, in the variety model that Austen and Hayes criticise, as suggested earlier in regard to some of the imagery employed by Tex Avery, can only succeed if it is emptied of its associations and implications. The surface of the joke may be funny, but will only remain funny if its other meanings are ignored or suppressed. Binky does not see the horrors of war, or the Black Hole of Calcutta etc., because he insists 'you've got to laugh, haven't you', absolving himself from the political implications of his own role in implicitly endorsing those who caused the horror and from whom he is making a living. In short, Binky does not possess conscience or consciousness of his actions, and Austen and Hayes clearly wish their audience to laugh at him, not with him; criticise him, not accept him.

This issues are at their most focused and acute when Binky and Boo get their bookings mixed up, and perform for Adolf Hitler in his bunker during the last days of World War II. Binky and Boo witness and uncritically accept human atrocities, but maintain their mission to entertain. It may be argued that this approach asserts the healing and disinterested aspects of humour, but Austen and Hayes are careful not to let their audience be seduced into accepting this view by suggesting that no one could possibly accept the idea that comics would entertain Hitler himself. Indeed, they also insert critical jokes about Hitler using the premise that Boo can be 'cheeky and saucy'. Boo says to Hitler, 'I wouldn't put you in charge of a Reich that's supposed to last for a thousand years. Don't give up your day job, that's all I can say'. Austen and Hayes carefully foreground these aspects of ex-stand-up comic, Bernard Padden's script, because they effectively reveal the manipulation and redefinition of the variety/vaudeville form in critical contemporary terms. Binky and Boo thumb their nose at Hitler, not because it is a political gesture, but because it's a silly joke. The style of the film makes these moments ambiguous, however, drawing attention to the invalid nature of variety comedy, criticising its misrepresentative stereotypes, its lack of political aware-ness, and its preparedness to ignore the social context in which it takes place. This signifies a self-consciousness not merely about different modes of comedy, but about the changing nature of the contemporary psyche. The film concludes with the demolition of the tower block in which Binky lives. Binky willingly dies because he cannot accept change, nor can he really live in the past. His death only signifies the passing of the vaudeville/variety mode, and the assertion of the New Humour, wiser, more cynical, more ironic.

19 Everything can mean its opposite

The ironic gag creates a framework by which everything can mean its opposite, at once apparently endorsing one point of view, but at the same time undermining it. 'I am happy' may be said in the most doleful of tones, or even whilst crying, and it is unlikely that anyone will accept that this is so. Inevitably, this fine line between what is asserted and what is actually the case, often informs the tragi-comic and the parodic.[10] A good example of this would be the collaboration between the political caricaturist Steve Bell, and veteran British comedy animator Bob Godfrey, called *Send in the Clowns* (1987). The piece, drawn in Bell's style, is a satire on the supposed 'special relationship' between Britain and the USA, particularly during the Margaret Thatcher/Ronald Reagan era. The film uses the song 'Send in the Clowns', sung by a Reagan sound-alike, with some adjustments to the lyrics. Reagan is drawn as if he were a comic strip 'Rambo', and the political arena is defined as a circus or a theatre. The ironic clearly underpins the film's central metaphors – the image of an aging Reagan does not sit with his muscularity as 'Rambo'. Similarly, the 'Iron Lady' image of Margaret Thatcher is re-cast when she is presented as a ballerina. Reagan's datedness is accentuated by the manipulation of the lyric, 'I'll make my entrance again with my usual *flares*', when he literally appears in red flared trousers.

The central premise of the film, though, is to discredit the nature of American foreign policy and military interventionism, ironically redetermining the phrase 'Send in the Clowns' by placing red noses on the faces of American troops who were 'sent in' to Vietnam, Grenada, etc. As the song concludes with the line 'Where are those clowns?', the film shows a line of graves, and the notion of a 'clown' as a physical, playful figure of fun is wholly redetermined as a powerless 'fool' subject to the whims of 'clowns' with political power. One of the most persuasive images in this respect is a large clown's nose placed over Reagan's genital area both *endorsing* phallic power, but *undermining* it as well. Indeed, the clown's nose is the chief signifier of irony throughout the film, playing on the ambivalence of the clown's face as a sinister comic mask, hiding human excess. The clown figure, in general, usefully acts as the chief embodiment of the ultimate collapse of language and the physical expression of the difficulties in maintaining language as a meaningful tool with which to properly communicate. It is this issue that informs the histrionic gag.

20 Yabba-Dabba-Do!!!

The histrionic gag occurs less in the animated film because its comic premises are fundamantally visual. In prioritising the visual over the verbal, the relationship between the two is altered. The animated image either relates directly to voiceover or creates its own conditions for comic events. The histrionic gag emerges from the premise that language can properly express the thoughts and emotions of the speaker. Ultimately it becomes clear, however, that the relative and ambiguous nature of language betrays the speaker, leading to inarticulacy, and the collapse into physical expression, and the hysteria of 'clowning'. In the live-action context, for example in the Steve Martin vehicle, *Roxanne* (1987), Martin attempts to help his inarticulate friend express his feelings to Roxanne. In order to do this, his friend wears a radio receiver within his hat so that he may listen to and use the words Martin suggests. Initially, his friend copies Martin faithfully and expresses himself poetically and eloquently, but his receiver picks up interference and he starts to copy a police intercom system. Rendered totally inarticulate when he removes his hat and the ruse fails, he resorts first to clichés, and then to incompetent physical oafishness – the hysteria of 'clowning'. The amusement comes out of the transition from one state to another.

The primacy of the physical in animation means that this comic construction occurs less often, but within the realms of character comedy it does directly inform characters like Donald Duck and Daffy Duck. Both habitually lose control and the deep frustration they experience renders them speechless, leaving them defined only by their physical expression. In many ways, *Duck Amuck* (see p. 39) perfectly illustrates Daffy's decline into hysteria. Betrayed by his own inability to negotiate, or to come to terms with power greater than his own, Daffy has nothing left to say, and merely becomes the subject and object of the physical gag. In other types of animation that more resemble the situation comedy, the verbal is once more the dominant form, and the histrionic gag gains proper purchase. Even Fred Flintstone's cry of 'Yabba-dabba-do' ultimately represents Fred's desire to express happiness and optimism without the formal language to do so, and triggers his physical liberation from the constraints of work. He slides along a dinosaur's tail in the opening credits of the *The Flintstones*, and jumps into his car, pedalling his feet furiously in order to propel it. These visual jokes are facilitated by the animation, and prompted by Fred's delirious transition into physical expression. Many of the comic moments that occur in quasi-sit-coms like *The Flintstones* and *The Simpsons* emerge from this context. Language fails, physical 'clowning' begins.

21 Telling it over and over again

One of the fundamental structures of comedy (if not life itself) is repetition. Recognising formulaic patterns becomes part of the pleasure of watching comic events because it legitimises the anticipation of expected outcomes, and the further pleasure derived from encountering the unexpected. Repetition constitutes an important structural device because it creates the conditions for a comic event with particular economy. Viewers know that certain events are going to take place and what they essentially await are the variations on the main theme. This may be a matter of changing *emphasis*, an additional *complication* which alters the fundamental premise, the *extension* of the initial premise, or the *resistance* to the established comic logic. These aspects re-focus anticipated scenarios in most cartoons, but some animations use the very concept of repetition as their main comic function. A good example of this is Cordell Barker's *The Cat Came Back* (1988), which takes as its premise the repeated attempts of a man to avail himself of an unwanted, highly destructive cat. While the conventional cartoon operates as a series of comic scenarios in a similar way, *The Cat Came Back* uses the *refrain* of a song to support its simple premise.

The Cat Came Back (1988)

The film begins with what will be its recurrent visual motif – Mr Johnson's house on the hill. A tune is being played on a tuba. The viewer initially assumes that this is a non-diegetic theme, but when the film cuts to the house interior, the viewer sees that it is actually a diegetic sound because it is Mr Johnson who is playing the tuba. The theme he is playing, however, does become the film's recurring song, 'The Cat Came Back', with lyrics that help construct the narrative of the piece and comment upon the action. The very sound of the tuba, in the first instance, though, helps to establish a jaunty melancholia, echoing Mr Johnson's eccentric aloneness. Disturbed by a knock at the door, he irritably answers, bellowing 'What?' at the top of his voice. His anger soon subsides, however, when he notices that a yellow cat has been left on his doorstep in a baby carrier. At first, he behaves with coy sentiment, compassionately playing with the cat as if it was a baby. When the cat breaks his childhood rattle, however, the relationship is at an end, and the cat is unceremoniously dumped outside, the welcome mat he is placed on withdrawn from inside. The cat, of course, refuses to leave, constantly returning to the house to cause increasing havoc. This constitutes the establishing premise of the cartoon and from here, as in the cartoons described earlier, the film becomes a chase cartoon played out in a number of sequences, each operating as a self-contained scenario with a variety of comic events, interspersed by Mr

Johnson's return to his home. With each return, comes a new verse of the song, and the escalation of both the speed of the cartoon and the level of destruction.

As in all cartoons, the very condensation of events serves to exaggerate them further, but in The Cat Came Back, Barker, whilst compressing time in the elliptical manner discussed earlier, makes sure that these events are not merely repetition in the Road Runner/Coyote sense, but repetition with remembering. The Road Runner/ Coyote series, in employing repetition with forgetting can create renewal, but The Cat Came Back pursues the logical consequences of a sequence of events, principally the effects upon Mr Johnson in his attempts to get rid of the cat, and the cat's escalating destruction of his home. When Mr Johnson tries to leave the cat in a dark wood, he returns to his car, only to find the cat in the driver's seat. Attempts to leave the cat deep in the wood fail and result in another leitmotif in the film, Mr Johnson's anguished wail, which in this case, is loud enough to disturb the birds. Returning to the house on the hill, Mr Johnson enters the door dishevelled and covered in sticky pine-cones, only to discover the cat ripping up the wall-paper and tearing his sofa apart. The cat's omnipresence is similar to that of Droopy in North West Hounded Police (1946), and creates like-minded paranoic responses in Mr Johnson. He tempts the cat into a sack with the lure of a fish, for example, and tries to drown the cat at sea, succeeding in nearly drowning himself by clinging on to the anchor as it drops into the water. Humour emerges from his own sense of self-defeat, especially when he blows bubbles at the fish, who return in kind, but then play a game with Mr Johnson's single strand of hair.

Trying to cope with his humiliation, he returns once more to the house, only to find that the cat is scattering the interior padding of the sofa all over his living room. Mr Johnson picks up the cat, cycles to a hill top, places it in a hot air balloon, and in a scene reminiscent of Richard Condie's The Big Snit (1989), attempts to saw away the guide rope. Even as he does this, the balloon shoots off, expelling air after the fashion of a rapidly deflating domestic balloon, and the cat somehow survives again. Mr Johnson, exhausted, and with a fresh black eye, returns home again, collapsing on the floor, some of his teeth falling out of his mouth. The cat, meanwhile, is undoing the thread of both the carpets and the curtains, leaving only the template of carpet where Mr Johnson's body is lying. In the film's most inspired sequence, Mr Johnson grabs the cat, and with renewed vigour, speeds up a mountain on a hand-driven railway truck. Here the film deploys the Comic Rule of Three, whereby the first thing is expected, the second thing is expected, but the third thing becomes funny by not being expected. Barker revises and extends this basic premise. The first thing is the unexpected presence of a woman tied to the railway tracks. The viewer accepts this because it is an image that knowingly references a similar image in Victorian melodrama. The second thing, however, extends the joke by surprisingly showing numerous women tied to the tracks. The third thing, which does operate in the anticipated way of the Comic Rule of Three, is the presence of a cow being tied to the rails. This is made funny by the viewer's anticipation of a third take on the women-tied-to-the-track theme, which Barker adjusts through the use of the cow. The cow also seems a slow, cumbersome, 'comic' creature, utterly different from the cunning relentlessness of the cat. The railway truck somehow transcends all these obstacles but, in a clever variation, is actually thrown off the track by a tiny green beetle who, in a subsequent shot, is seen to be cut in half. Mr Johnson falls over a cliff (naturally) and ends up down a mine. In the dark, the viewer sees two pairs of eyes, and clearly anticipates that it is the cat who is seated alongside him. In a neat *reversal* gag, Mr Johnson lights a match and sees that it is not a cat, but a rat, not merely one rat, but hundreds, who along with a group of bats, chase him home.

Back at the house, the cat is breaking the final taboo by defacing and destroying pictures of Mr Johnson and his wife (absent, and evidently missed). The violation of family mementoes leads Mr Johnson to fill his house with a huge barrel of dynamite. Even his attempts to blow up the cat are foiled by the fact that he lights his own single strand of hair, mistaking it for the fuse. He explodes and, ironically, becomes gleeful when he realises that he is a ghost and, thus, is free from the material world and the presence of the cat. This moment of triumph is soon undermined, however, when in another clever reversal, Mr Johnson's physical body drops on the cat, inadvertently killing it. Not one, but nine ghosts appear, representing the nine lives of the cat, ready to persecute him in the afterlife. The chase continues into the sunset, suggesting that the mode of comic repetition could continue *ad infinitum*. *The Cat Came Back* sustains its lightness of tone through its playfulness, at once recalling the tradition of the cartoon, but finding surreal variations by stressing the time-lessness of the conflict.

Another method of using repetition as a comic structure is in the parodic mode, where the animated film directly takes the familiar characteristics of a live-action *genre* and places them with the animated *context*. This can produce mixed results. One example is particularly revealing about the different sense of humour in Eastern Europe to that in the USA. Puppeteer of renown, George Pal, left Budapest to make animated advertising films in Holland, before going to the USA to make the celebrated 'Puppetoons'. In a film called *Western Daze* (1941), Pal parodies the Western, and depicts a slapstick chase across a prairie, ending with the fall of the villains down a rock face. This physical comedy was clearly the staple of American humour, and fitted comfortably within America's most famil-iar film genre with regard to design and narrative. At the end of this sequence, though, Pal injects a moment of darker, absurdist humour, when a sign appears next to the villains saying, 'There ain't nobody lower than we', a gag that, first, operates at the literal level, given that the villains have fallen to the bottom of the cliff, but second, at the philosophical level, illustrating their status as villains. The two modes of comedy sit uneasily together, as one nearly counteracts the other. Slapstick essentially empties its action of consequence and meaning, while the comic comment reinvests the characters with social position and a moral dimension.

22 25 ways to exaggerate, understand and alienate

Bill Plympton, currently contributing animated links to the American satirical sketch show, *The Edge*, has a distinctive comic style, which makes him the natural successor to Tex Avery as the animator dealing with primal motives and their consequences. Instead of adopting Avery's frenetic style, however, Plympton's work is almost static, concentrating on the limited movements of one or two faces or bodies. Plympton's work often includes a middle-aged, smartly dressed man, whose sheer stillness accentuates the sometimes excessive violence he is subjected to, or imposes on himself. The man often remains largely inexpressive in the face of the things that happen to him, and once again, this is where Plympton takes a deadpan stance instead of the stylised over-reaction of Avery's characters. Plympton's middle-aged man is just as obsessive and paranoid as his Averyesque counterpart, however, and demonstrates extreme behaviour as a consequence of his desire or preoccupation. Plympton's film, *25 Ways to Give Up Smoking* (1988), aptly illustrates his relationship to Avery, and most particularly, shows some of the ways in which he has contemporised similar themes.

25 Ways to Give Up Smoking (1988)

The structure of Plympton's film is simple. Essentially the film consists of twenty-five consecutive 'spot gags', each prefigured by a caption and a laconic voiceover suggesting a method by which someone might give up smoking. Each spot gag features the same middle-aged man, mainly in medium shot, testing out each of the recommendations. Of course, none of the suggestions has any real validity, but all are the logical development of a more plausible method, subverted, distorted or manipulated for comic effect. Plympton's style is one of understatement but, predominantly, he understates already extremely exaggerated actions. His central character is remote, possessing no affecting personality. Consequently, the viewer is alienated from the excessive nature of his actions, never feeling sympathy for the man; enjoying the cumulative effect of the 'gag-stacking' but not the cumulative effect of the physical assault he consistently experiences. Most importantly, like Avery, Plympton is careful to use the unique vocabulary offered by the animation itself, to extend the comic possibilities inherent in the form.

Inevitably, Plympton uses a running gag which occurs at the beginning, near the middle and at the end of the piece, involving a sumo wrestler who falls from the sky flattening the middle-aged smoker. This sets the tone of the piece in the sense that it suggests that even in spite of one's best efforts to lead a healthier life, it may easily be taken away by the most random of events. Plympton takes this 'random-ness' to its logical extreme by using an accidental gag, made more amusing by both its sheer impossibility and its repetition. From here, Plympton's gags may be roughly divided into four distinct comic categories, though all except one are played out though the body of the male figure. These categories are:

1   the deconstruction or manipulation of the physical form;
2   satiric takes on contemporary psycho-therapy;
3   extraordinary events with some degree of plausibility;
4   extraordinary events which are implausible but amusing because of their
    'fantastical' excess.

Plympton's deconstruction or manipulation of the body differs slightly from
Avery's in the sense that his middle-aged protagonist acts upon his own body
rather than merely being a victim of its untrammelled expression. He can 'remove
the orifice of entry' tearing off his own mouth to watch it emit smoke outside his
body; he can pull off his own head and exhale through his neck; he can put a
paper-clip over his face or tie a knot in his neck to prevent smoke entering his
lungs; he can use a 'safer orifice' to smoke, namely, his naval, or confront the
internal workings of his body by literally coughing up a lung or imploding his
head within his body, only to re-emerge and scream with terror. Whilst his body
retains the capacity to do all these things, it also must admit to failure. He
imagines his mouth has been lost to cancer, and eats by sucking food up with
his nostril. Ironically, Plympton reveals the fallibility of the physical, while using
animation to depict its impossible extremes. The animated form enables Plympton to demonstrate the apparent malleability of the body, finding humour in its
shortcomings and in the violation of the body as a fixed, highly controlled,
functional thing.

Plympton mocks the psycho-therapeutic approach to the body by satirising its
terms and conditions. 'Aversion therapy' amounts only to putting a stick of
dynamite in your mouth and blowing your head off. Plympton times the explosion to coincide with the arrival of the next title card, thus effectively staging the
event 'offscreen', but implicitly asking the audience to imagine the consequences.
This is clearly an imaginative development of the 'explosion' gag in cartoons,
which normally show blackened, highly dishevelled characters and environments
which have been completely destroyed. This does not disrupt the overall 'cool-
ness', pacing and rhythm of the piece. In a similar way, when the man attempts to
reach his cigarettes, which he has hidden in a food-blender placed on the top of a
cupboard, the audience can anticipate that his fingers are going to be injured, but
it is not until the viewer sees the blood spattered on the next title card is the deed
imagined to be done. These comic devices prevent the film from moving into
violent excess, and sustain a particular kind of momentum in the timing of the
gags. Whilst the viewer only imagines the outcome to these gags, the film does
not collapse into the kind of distastefulness which would alienate the viewer in
the wrong way. The response is one which maintains the suspension of disbelief
in the service of illogical and previously unimaginable comic events. To over-
indulge, for example, is to fill an ever-expanding mouth with hundreds of
cigarettes, and light them simultaneously, or to engage in self-discipline is to
punch oneself in the face after every 'puff'. Plympton essentially literalises and
exaggerates psycho-therapeutic advice, rendering it spurious and superficial.

173

ipathising with the cigarette' means you dress up as one, struggle to stand up,
1 then get flattened by a falling sumo wrestler.

Plympton's extraordinary events that possess a modicum of plausible motivation operate in a similar fashion. If indeed, one did use heat-seeking missiles
attached to the head to stop smoking, it is entirely likely that they would find the
offending cigarette and blow your head off! Similarly, if one did try to make it
hard to light a cigarette, it would be perversely logical to attempt to do so in a
windy igloo, or underwater, the latter only recognisable in Plympton's vocabulary
by the way a lighter floats to the bottom of the sea and fish swim past. Seeking
divine intervention, or placing oneself at the mercy of fate is equally debilitating.
God merely crushes your head or electrocutes you with a bolt of lightning.
Plympton's advice is sometimes highly practical, though, when he suggests
that a smoker should try different lighters, demonstrating that if you use a
blow-torch you can reduce your head to a cinder and never smoke again. Even
the use of something as practical as a smoke alarm is subverted by Plympton
when the viewer discovers that the smoker has swallowed it, discarding it as soon
as it goes off!

Plympton's use of the extraordinary extends to the 'fantastical', though it does
to some extent rely on allusion. He suggests, for example, that the smoker should
lock his cigarettes 'in a car on a hot day', treating the cigarette as if it were a pet.
The cigarette's pitiful cries of 'help' almost elicit sympathy. The film also suggests
that the smoker should join an African tribe because the wooden embellishments
on the mouths of some African tribesmen prevent the cigarette being smoked
altogether. Though, clearly, the gag itself has some racist overtones, its humour
emerges more from the persistent attempt to smoke the cigarette, despite the fact
that it is impossible. Every time the smoker closes his mouth, its wooden
ornamentation snaps the cigarette to the floor. Keeping a pet tobacco beetle,
however, means that every now and again a huge green insect devours both
the cigarettes and their packet. Having tried all of Plympton's twenty-five suggestions 'you can now walk in the fresh air and breathe free'. This, of course, is
entirely untrue, and reflects the failure of many smokers to give up. Attempts on the
scale of Plympton's violent extremes would result in death anyway, but of all his
twenty-five ways to give up smoking, probably the most persuasive is also the one
which best reveals the economy of the animated form. The brown-haired, ruddy
face of the middle-aged man metamorphoses into the ashen death-mask of an old
man in one extended inhalation of a cigarette. Black humour at its darkest; animation at its most effective in the compression of time and the revelation of effect.

23 Dedicated to those who disapprove but
continue to watch

Plympton's work, some would argue, is on the edge of bad taste. This is an issue
which characterises most discussions of comedy in general. It is extremely
difficult, if not impossible, to establish the limits of comedy, and attempt to

delineate when 'good humour' becomes offensive or inappropriate. It would seem that no subject area is absolutely taboo in comedy, nor does it seem that there are limits to the way in which a comic view is expressed. The reception of comedy is also an entirely relative thing, dependent on so many factors, from being in a conducive mood to being in the right company. How, then, is it possible to define what is acceptable or unacceptable as a 'gag', particularly in animation, where the freedom to express more 'extreme' points of view is validated by the medium itself? Terry Gilliam suggests that 'there is no such thing as good taste, but there might be such a thing as bad timing'.[11] This insight provides a clue to some of the parameters of comic expression. It implies that no subject is sacrosanct, but dealing with it is a matter of *self-censorship* and *sensitivity to context*. The animator should, in the first instance, be entirely responsible only to his/her role as an artist, uninhibited by his/her role as a citizen, but, nevertheless, should be aware of the audience the work is directed to, and the time and place in which it is shown.

Animation further confuses these issues, however, because it still retains the stigma of being a form directed at a children's audience whilst having the facility to show things that are not available to mainstream live-action 'adult' film-making, i.e. nudity depicting genitalia, sexual acts, marginalised codes of sexual conduct (cross-dressing, transvestism etc.), and cross-species coupling. Somehow, graphic or three-dimensional expression in the animated film disguises the apparent explicitness of this imagery and, supposedly, dilutes its impact. In some respects, this is profoundly liberating for animators, but in other ways, does not properly acknowledge the capacity of the medium to address such issues and to find new ways of expressing a view about them. Comic exaggeration in animation, in this respect, is sometimes particularly effective in drawing attention both to a taboo issue and the animated form's unique vocabulary in illustrating it. Whether this amounts to 'bad taste', however, still remains contestable.

Marv Newland's Rocketship animation company, based in Vancouver, addresses this debate explicitly in a compilation film, made by a number of reknowned animators, titled *Pink Konkommer* (1990). The film concludes with the dedication used in the heading to this section, deliberately highlighting the double standards of many viewers, who criticise and disapprove of particular kinds of artistic expression yet continue to watch – the implicit suggestion being that they too are enjoying it, but denying its pleasures; pleasures which often emerge from the breaking of taboos and the questioning of moral boundaries. This may be best achieved through comedy and the imaginative use of animation, a brief which informs the basic premise of *Pink Konkommer*. Each animator uses the same soundtrack as the illustration of a sexual fantasy. These are the fantasies of a little old lady, animated by Chris Hinton, who serves as the narrative link to these short sequences. Though a little repetitive, the format enables Newland himself, Paul Driessen, Alison Snowden and David Fine, Craig Bartlett, Stoyan Dukov, Janet Perlman, and Sara Petty to bring their own comic talents to a supposedly taboo subject.

The musical theme of the film has burlesque overtones and foregrounds the sexual orientation of the images that are to follow. Craig Bartlett's opening 'dream' shows a newly born chick peeping through a large keyhole in a box in which he sees a frying pan cooking two eggs with green yolks and a toaster which simultaneously 'pops-up' a piece of toast and an erect penis. Clearly, any interpretation of such a set of images is purely subjective, and probably indicates more about the viewer than it does the film-maker. As the phrase goes, 'it's a tough job but someone has to do it', so I will offer some tentative analysis. In many ways all 'dream' sequences require psychoanalytic attention but, such is the nature of animation, its image systems, whilst being the most appropriate vehicle to illustrate 'inner-states', also recall other codes and conventions of aesthetic expression which colour any interpretation. As noted in Chapter Three, many images may be understood at the purely symbolic level, and sequences of images may constitute the construction of a metaphor. In regard to Bartlett's 'dream' it is hard to resist the view that the chick, freshly emergent from its shell, directly engages with its first primal scene, voyeuristically recognising the domestic space as a highly sexualised environment. It is in this sense that Bartlett's imagery also becomes amusing, however, because it mocks the idea of the primal scene through the absurdity of the imagery, and by drawing attention to the ease in constructing innuendo. The soundtrack, with its various moans, groans, whipcracks, roars and lip-smacking, directs the audience to think of sexual acts, but Bartlett's imagery also reflects the obvious nature of this direction, by the use of visual puns. The penis 'pops-up' like a piece of toast, the eggs (perversely) resemble breasts etc.

The images from here, though, become a little more complex. The chick pours a drink and re-engages with the pleasures of watching – an agenda taken up by the whole film – and sees a blue car pull into this 'kitchen' area, a large, fishnet-stocking-clad, pink-stilettoed leg crash through the window, and sexual consummation between what turns out to be a chick with human legs (and further, a large concertinaed penis), and the blue car tied to a chair. The more one attempts to describe these images, the more ridiculous it seems, but each image does carry symbolic value. The chick watching these scenes continues to observe the first primal scene between its parents. The viewer watching the film sees a set of images which recall sexual practices and deliberately confuse the boundaries of taste and acceptability. The blue car seems to be gendered 'male'; the leg, with its fishnet stockings and stiletto-heeled shoes is gendered 'female'. When the viewer sees the legs belong to a chick, this challenges expectations, but in the realms of animation, merely highlights the cross-species coupling which characterises many cartoons. By giving this figure a penis, 'gender' is clearly blurred, an issue addressed in Chapter Five, and whilst this may also appear shocking, it recognises the ability of animation to destabilise traditional notions of male/female, and, masculine/feminine. In the eyes of the chick, this is merely the recognition of the indistinct nature of gender in the first stages of socialised sexual identity. When the chick-figure and the car tied to a chair copulate, all manner of sado-masochistic ideas seem to be conflated within one image. A hybrid, loosely gendered creature, physically engages with an inhibited machine and is ultimately consumed by it. Humankind devoured by late industrial capitalism? Surely not, or certainly only on specific terms. Two cars (one pink, one blue – presumably the one with the chick-creature in) on a hoist, suddenly emerge into the same space, only to collapse through the floor, replaced by a highly phallic easel with lots of rapidly changing pictures of works of art and social scenes. The collapse of late industrial capitalism but the maintenance of creativity? Who knows, but if such a set of images is to be coerced into sense and operate beyond its superficial juxtaposition of strangely matched forms, the images must be interrogated as a set of symbols which move towards metaphoric continuity, however forced this may seem. The legitimacy of such interpretation comes out of the simultaneous recognition of the knowing manipulation of the animated form to controversial comic ends and the politicised agenda which often informs the radical imagery of the surreal.

Analysis of this sort is also appropriate to the rest of the 'dreams'. Janet Perlman, creator of a satiric assault on good manners in *Lady Fishbourne's Complete Guide to Better Table Manners* (1976), sophisticatedly uses the figure of a clown mime-artist to physically suggest sexual acts while juxtaposing her character with a shadow narrative of images suggesting sexual activity between a knight and a corseted woman, possibly in jelly! I remain uncertain of what exactly is going on, but a recognisable penis ejaculates at one point, and this is enough to point up the intrinsic difference between animation and mainstream live-action film. Such imagery does of course beg the question of whether this is, indeed, pornography; a question, it seems, that is not posed because of its animated context, and its comic scenario. Bulgarian animator, Stoyan Dukov, director of the controversial *March* (1986), which deals with the effects of a sex shop on a peasant village, contributes a sequence which highlights the fluidity of the two-dimensional space, as a self-flagellating dominatrix in a circus is willingly devoured by a lion that she has artificially stimulated with an aphrodisiac. Such fluidity also characterises Sara Petty's much less figurative response to the soundtrack, deploying abstract cubist designs to echo the penis and vagina, but also to use animation to *illustrate* the feeling of orgasm. This is coitus with, and through, the aesthetic dimensions of 'modernist' experimental animation.

Alison Snowden's and David Fine's 'dream' effectively illustrates two related 'gag' forms, which find particular purchase in the British context. Like Craig Bartlett, Snowden and Fine, point up the notion of *innuendo* in the noises from the soundtrack. Though here demonstrated through sound, innuendo humour is normally verbal, and is essentially the use of a double meaning in words which directs the listener to think not of the dominant meaning of the words, but of their very 'literalness' in suggesting a more taboo meaning. A good example can be found in Bob Godfrey's film about Isambard Kingdom Brunel, *GREAT* (1975), which includes the song, 'What a Big One', literally about his ship but, in the grand music-hall tradition, alluding to the size of a man's penis. The visual version of the innuendo 'gag' is the *substitution* 'gag', where one image which recalls the more taboo image is literally substituted in its place. Snowden and Fine use carrots and sausages instead of an overt depiction of a penis; stuffing a chicken as an image which half-echoes coitus; and the unselfconsciousness of nudists on a picnic to bring innocent shock to the madcap moment when a cat, previously used by a couple in a badminton match, literally devours the woman player! If Petty's interpretation of the soundtrack was erotic, Snowden's and Fine's is playful.

Paul Driessen, also discussed in Chapter Three, probably makes the most explicit sequence in the film, though any real offence that may be caused by the action in the film is undermined by the design. Driessen's flaccid, 'blobbish', over-extended figures de-eroticise numerous acts of copulation, fellatio, cunnilingus and masturbation, and essentially dilute the seriousness associated with sex and sexuality. The scenes appear to be set on clouds in a dark, night sky, and the inclusion of angel figures suggests that this may be heaven. Right at the beginning of the sequence, an angel bites off the penis of a man, and though psychoanalysts may suggest that this foregrounds anxieties about castration (a fear seemingly echoed in many of the sequences), a more controversial reading might suggest that the man is God, and that the sexual acts that follow, performed by men, women and beasts, are merely the physical indicators of an amoral universe. Marv Newland's contribution does not lend itself to similar metaphoric intensity, but locates itself purely in the realm of male sexual fantasy. Nude, winged, fairy-girls burst through a window and ravish a man sitting in an armchair, wearing a pair of rabbit slippers. The most interesting image in the film is the attachment of five 'fairy-girls' to the man's penis. His penis goes through the mouth, body and bottom of each of the girls and seemingly conflates the allusion to oral, coital and anal sex into one image. Though this may be deemed sexist and unacceptable, this compression of actions (beyond their political implications) and the creation of this kind of imagery is only achievable in animation, legitimised by its apparently fantastical context. The comedy here, surely, is about sexual excess and physical extremism, mocking the obsessional quality of fantasy by parodying its perversity.

Chris Hinton's figure of the old lady, who has supposedly had all these dreams, concludes the film by being the central figure in a desexualised interpretation of the soundtrack. Slurps and groans which have previously been the soundtrack to various physical acts are now used merely as the sounds which accompany an old lady having a cup of tea and dunking her biscuit, although she does pluck her pet bird when it breaks the teapot! The whole film is about the fact that attitudes towards sex and sexuality and, indeed, morality, are entirely personal and relative. Its comic daring, and its particular deployment of animation to illustrate this relativity, suggests that perception and understanding is 'all in the mind'. The images couch themselves as funny and ambiguous, thus dismissing any notion that they may be censored. Comedy in animation is clearly a subversive tool.

24 Driessen's comedy of cruelty

> There's a lot of black humour, I think, in my films. There's some kind
> of cruelty I have, I think, and most people probably have, and I can get
> away with in my films, and not in real life, because basically I am a
> nice person![12]

Paul Driessen's contribution to Pink Konkommer is in some ways unrepresentative in
its directness, as Driessen's work is characterised by a certain comic obliqueness.
His vision is entirely his own, and unlike many of the animators who create
specific 'gags', his narratives tend to create unusual comic events out of apparently typical scenarios. His designs do much to simplify these scenes, though,
distantiating them from 'the real', and, in depersonalising the main figures,
enable him to prioritise their actions. These actions sometimes focus on the
hostility inherent in comic acts and highlight the more cruel dimensions of
human life through the role of the victim (the butt of the joke). In Uncles and
Aunts (1993), a small baby approaches the edge of a ledge, and this is described as
'Junior's first steps'; the very same animation is then shown with the caption
'Junior's last steps' as he topples over. Similarly, 'Mother trying out Father' begins
with her punching his face, cutting his head off with a large sword, then striking
his head with a club so that it bounces round the four walls of the room. Only
when she finally decides to put a paper bag over his head is the audience invited
to think that she may have undertaken these actions because she didn't like the
way that he looked, and having failed to get rid of his head, she merely decides to
cover it up! The humour here relies upon the reconciliation of the joke, in the
sense that implausible justification is given to excessive acts which appeared
initially to have no motive at all, logical or otherwise.

Driessen's film, Oh, What a Knight! (1981), takes this kind of cruelty to its logical
extreme by making the butt of the joke someone who does not deserve to be.
Within the traditional story, the knight is expected to save the damsel in distress.
Driessen seeks to subvert this outcome with a particular comic 'twist' – a 'punchline' which differs from the one that has been anticipated and redefines the
previous narrative. The knight in Driessen's film, rides through a storm and
over ravines to save a damsel from a three-headed dragon. Throughout the film,
though, his armour keeps falling apart and reassembling, effectively de-
constituting and re-constituting the knight's 'body' – there is no sense that there
is anyone in the armour; the pieces of armour, it seems, are the man inside.
Defeating the dragon, and a huge frog-like monster holding the damsel captive,
the knight engages in a final confrontation on a cliff-edge, with another dragon
still holding the girl. In a particularly inventive variation on the cliff-edge 'gag',
the little man in the suit of armour climbs out of the back of it and climbs around
the cliff-edge to pounce upon the dragon from behind. As he edges around the
cliff, cars pass incongrously below, destabilising the time period of the film, and
placing it entirely in the realms of fantasy. Once he pounces on the dragon, killing

179

it, the damsel merely pats him on the head, and approaches the knight thinking that he is still standing in front of her. It is only the armour, of course, and the damsel tumbles off the cliff as she attempts to take it in her arms. The man doesn't get the woman, the woman dies, the heroism of the knight gains no reward, and the whole myth has been cruelly satirised. As Michel Ciment comments about Driessen's work, '[he] achieves a fusion of the Hollywood cartoon with its manic rhythms, and the Zagreb studio with its more philosophical concerns' (Bendazzi, 1994: 311). Driessen's comedy of cruelty is rarely without purpose and, like much of his work, serves as a warning against assuming things, and complacency about aspects of existence which may offer revelation and surprise.

25 Techno-titters and post-modern forms

While computer animation clearly offers another visual language in which comic devices may be created, it is, ironically, an ex-Disney animator working in the style of the Warner Brothers cartoon who has achieved a great deal through its use. John Lasseter, using the PIXAR system (see Lee, 1989a), essentially three-dimensionalises the animated cartoon, using the limitations of computer animation in the representation of figures to his advantage in depicting neo-cartoon characters. Computer animation, at the time of writing, is still negotiating the difficulties of creating persuasive human figures with a high range of expression. Computer animation can show the three-dimensionality of geometric forms and physical space to good effect, however, providing a dizzying redefinition of conventional environments. Lasseter thus combines the characterisation and comic structure of the cartoon form with the multiplicity of possibilities in the construction of material contexts made available by computer animation.

In 1989, John Lasseter won an Academy Award for Tin Toy (1988), in which a one-man-band tintoy lives in fear that Billy, a baby, might play with him. In one of the funniest of revelatory gags, his fear leads him to rush under a chair. The film cuts to a whole number of other tin toys also hiding there, all evidently having experienced the same thing. Fear becomes compassion, though, when the tin one-man-band thinks the baby has fallen and has hurt himself. He rushes out, momentarily entertaining the baby, distracting it from its pain, only to be abandoned when the baby prefers to play with the box that the tin toy came in, and then a paper bag. This is merely the film's narrative, however, and not half of its achievement. The figures in the film were first created as drawn figures like cartoons, then modelled like puppets or clay figures, then overlayed with a wire-frame grid so that each element of the body has a reference point which may be electronically traced into the computer, and finally digitally rendered with colour and lighting effects. This method of construction is important to relate because it determines particular ways in which a figure can move, and thus the vocabulary available to the animator for comic effects. This applies not only to the figures, objects and environments within the film, but the simulated movements of a 'camera'. As Nora Lee explains:

Figure 4.3 John Lasseter's *Tin Toy* prefigures *Toy Story* in its experimental use of computer-generated animation, but echoes the earliest 'trick' films in its use of toys as characters and calls upon the slapstick of the Silly Symphonies and the 'gags' from Looney Tunes in its jokes and narrative

> The opening sequence is a nice overhead view of the bag, box, and toys on the floor that ends as the camera cranes down to look squarely at Tinny's profile. When Tinny attempts to escape from the monster [the baby], the camera dollies with him as he flees, which increases the feeling of speed. In another sequence, as Tinny emerges from under the couch, the camera gives an overhead view of Tinny coming out to meet his doom, showing us exactly how small our hero is compared to the enormous baby.
>
> (Lee, 1989a: 82)

These movements are crucial to the construction of comic moments reliant on particular kinds of timing and the recognition of size as possible threat. As also becomes significant in Lasseter's *Knick Knack* (1989), the sense of confinement and entrapment in an apparently vast space is also intrinsic to the comic event. The computer, as mentioned earlier, is particularly effective in producing geometric shapes and forms, and less impressive in its depiction of the organically moving figures.[13] It is for this reason that *Tin Toy* is a great achievement, extending the range of *personality* animation in a different form. Rarely has a sneeze been so amusing, but it is made comic by the recognition of the delay between the baby's realisation that it is going to sneeze and the sneeze itself. Such details characterise

181

real babies, but go unnoticed. The computer baby is a plausible enough character to enable the joke to work, deriving humour from the control imposed upon the moment when the sneeze comes. The timing of a sneeze in the real world becomes the comic timing of a computer generated one.

The poses and direct-to-camera looks of the baby and the tin toy become the stock of Knick Knack, in which a snowman tries to escape from the glass snow-shaker ornament he is part of so as to pursue another girl 'knick-knack' on the mantle shelf. This was the first properly three-dimensional, computer-generated film made by Lasseter, exploiting all the possibilities of time and space for cartoon effects. Lasseter self-consciously utilises the ease of creating geometric objects by having ornaments as his lead characters. Each possesses a rhythm, however, which complements Bobby McFerrin's a cappella soundtrack, and matches the pace of the action. The scantily-clad girl ornament from Florida also has ridiculously spherical breasts which recall previous designs of women in the cartoon from Betty Boop to Red Riding Hood to Jessica in Who Framed Roger Rabbit? (1988). It is the sheer plasticity and artificiality of the objects, though, which computer animation is adept in expressing. The snowman in his snow-shaker is an entirely plausible ornament, but becomes characterful by the manipulation of the pieces of coal and a carrot which constitute his face. Each attempt to escape from the snow-shaker – running into the ornament's glass dome; using the two-dimensional igloo from the arctic landscape to try to break the glass; banging his carrot nose against the glass with a hammer as if it were a nail; using dynamite – all disfigure his expression, signifying his disappointment and frustration. His attempts to escape the ornament, are, of course, a succession of gags in the Avery/Jones tradition, all operating without any explanation of where he gets a hammer, an aestheteline torch, dynamite, etc. When he blows up the ornament though, he spins round in a flurry of snowflakes, toppling the 'knick-knack' to the edge of the mantlepiece, whereupon it falls. Computer animation is particularly effective here in defining the extraordinary drop that the object has. During this extended fall, the snowman sees an exit door in the bottom of the ornament and makes his escape, only to topple into a fish tank. Initially daunted, he then sees a fishbowl 'knick-knack' – a mermaid from Atlantis, and moves to approach her. Unfortunately, the snow-shaker ornament which he thought he had escaped falls on him before he can reach her. The film concludes with a closing iris focusing on the snowman's frustrated look towards the audience.

Post-modern forms

In many ways then, Knick Knack is Road Runner revisited in a contemporary form, using computer-generated imagery to provide a different look and appeal to similar gags in a redefinition of the cartoon. Animation, in this sense, is a deeply self-conscious medium, but clearly, because of its self-defining purpose in relation to live-action film-making, it always has been. When it is not calling attention to the limitations of photographic realism, it is recalling its own codes and conventions and, most significantly, developing new ones. This intensifies the progressive nature of the form and resists the retrogressive reliance upon post-modern codes of pastiche and reiteration that have informed artistic practices in the post-war period. In many ways, animation insists upon its *modernity* even in the post-modern era (see Lindvall and Melton 1994).

Norman Denzin suggests that post-modernism is defined as:

> A nostalgic, conservative longing for the past, coupled with an erasure of the boundaries between the past and the present; an intense preoccupation with the real and its representations; a pornography of the visible; the commodification of sexuality and desire; a consumer culture which objectifies a set of masculine cultural ideals; intense emotional experiences shaped by anxiety, alienation, ressentiment, and a detachment from others.
>
> (Denzin, 1991: vii)

Though such a generalisation may be directly challenged by the specifity of an alternative model which refutes these tendencies, this list of dominant cultural processes provides a set of conditions which may be tested against the animated film itself, and the role of comedy within it. Contemporary animation is characterised by so many different styles and approaches that it is impossible to say what its dominant mode of engagement is, but even if it may only be measured by its most obvious proponent, the Walt Disney organisation, it is clear that the animated film is still subject to a progressive agenda which doesn't necessarily sit easily with Denzin's summary of post-modern preoccupations. This is partly because some of its conditions have *always* been crucial issues in the construction of the animated form in general. Clearly, animation has always exhibited 'an intense preoccupation with the real and its representations' because it has fundamentally resisted 'reality' as its governing aesthetic agenda, and even when expressing the kind of 'realism' defined in Chapter One, it necessarily creates alternative conditions for its expression. The temporal agendas of the animated film also correspond to the conflation of past and present, but as a necessary condition of creating a *timeless* space rather than as a particular recognition of the past's place within the present. For the most part (although there are obvious cultural codings which would challenge this view), the cartoon does not signify a particular historical moment. In prioritising comedy as its agenda within a highly simulated space it looks to resist the realistic premises which locate the film in a certain time in a certain place and limit its possible effects. It must be remembered that these agendas *precede* the post-modern era, yet exhibit its characteristics. Other animated films, not in the cartoon mode, and not attempting to be funny, also look to create this unstable notion of time and space in order to interrogate and refute the logic imposed by time and space, and the naturalised conditions of expression and existence attendant to them.

The form itself then, offers resistance to inhibiting consistencies which, in turn, also means challenging 'the pornography of the visible' and 'the commodification of sexuality and desire'. The very ambiguity of the animated image and the in-built contradictions which inform the codes and conventions of representation in animation constantly re-evaluate 'the visible' and redetermine its 'exploitation'. Even a film like Pink Konkommer is an exploration of the image and the relativity of the pornographic, not merely a reproduction of the seen and known, and this is fundamentally achieved through the 'open-ness' of animation as a form as much as it is the personal expression of the film-maker. Animation also undermines the commodification of sexuality and desire because it redetermines how sexuality and desire may be expressed, blurs representations of gender and its socialised identities, and is a medium which has produced a genuine feminine aesthetic. These issues will be discussed in detail in Chapter Five, but they are also fundamental to the ways that patriarchal norms have been challenged in animation, by both men and women. It is mostly in the area of 'intense emotional experiences shaped by anxiety, alienation, ressentiment, and a detachment from others' that animation has provided a particularly appropriate vocabulary. As suggested in Chapter Two, animation has become a vehicle by which inarticulable emotions and experiences may be expressed. Most importantly, with regard to this chapter, though, it is the way that anxiety, alienation etc. have been used as the fundamental tools in the creation of comic forms that is of special interest.

The avant-gardist notions of post-modernism in the USA during the 1960s and after, provide a useful focus to briefly discuss the comic aspects of the post-modern in animation, a 'post-modernism' intrinsic to the form, even out of its modernist roots. The avant-garde determine the post-modern as outlined below (Smart, 1993: 19).

- Future oriented, innovative temporal imagination.
- Iconoclastic attack on the institution, organisation and ideology of art.
- Technological optimism, bordering at times on euphoria.
- Promotion of 'popular culture' as a challenge to high art.

Whilst the post-modern condition itself remains an illusive concept, despite all the critical theory engaging with the topic, it is broadly recognised that post-modernism posits the idea of an end to the discrete narrative, and the proliferation of discourses resisting modes of closure. It is further recognised that these discourses often relate specifically to previous models of representation and exchange. Animation, from its earliest developments, has prioritised the 'temporal imagination', predominantly in the comic mode, and as a liberating form of expression in the face of the institutionalisation of mainstream live-action cinema. Its agenda from the outset has been to challenge the ideological certainties naturalised in photographic realism, and the emergence of classical Hollywood narrative. This was further enhanced by the use of different kinds of animation as a resistance (conscious or otherwise) to the industrialisation of the form, and the hyper-realistic consistency of the Disney Studio in the late 1930s and 1940s, though Disney, ironically, had been the embodiment of 'technological optimism' as it revolutionised the industry. The cartoon did much to sustain the *anarchic* mode which refused orthodox discourses, and opened up a multiplicity of agendas through the formulation of the 'gag' as it has been discussed in this chapter. Not merely did it define, promote and engage with 'popular culture', but it undermined high art while possessing many of its graphic and aesthetic qualities. Other forms of animation, for example, puppet animation and clay modelling, took up this agenda, locating *personal* expression within the popular form, sustaining its innovation while recalling some of its key premises. Animation seems, therefore, to occupy the space between modernity and post-modernity, and the comic is the central feature of its ability to sustain a multiplicity of discourses yet maintain aesthetic focus.

Ironically, a interesting example of these tendencies comes from, of all places, the Disney Studio, in its recent version of *Aladdin* (1992), which featured stand-up comic improviser, Robin Williams as the genie. Amidst the technical innovations of combining traditional cel-animated movement with computer-generated imagery, the customarily obvious representations of moral adversaries, and accusations of racism concurrent with new debates about orientalism (see Said,1978; Felpin-Sharman 1994; Griffin 1994), Williams' performance as the genie was accommodated by the Disney animators in ways which broke with traditional modes of Disney story-telling. Williams' cameo as the stall-holder who tells the story of Aladdin uses a direct to camera address, and even uses the illusion of the camera itself, when the stall-holder asks the audience to come closer, only to find his nose jammed against the implied lens/screen. 'Too close', he says nervously, prompting the withdrawal of the camera, and the apparent presence of the audience who share its point of view.

This merely prefigures Williams' improvisations as the genie, which include impressions of popular figures such as Jack Nicholson, Arnold Schwarzenegger, Ed Sullivan, Peter Lorre and Groucho Marx; references to William Buckley and the character of Travis Bickle as played by Robert De Niro in Martin Scorsese's film, *Taxidriver* (1976); and references to the Disney canon itself in the inclusion of the elephants from *Fantasia* (1940), a Goofy hat worn by the genie when he becomes a tourist and, most specifically, when the head of Pinocchio emerges on the genie's neck, when the genie assumes that Aladdin is lying when he promises to set him free. The genie, of course, can metamorphose into anything he wants to – he becomes a Scotsman, a dog, a one-armed bandit, a rocket, a barber, a magician, a dragon, a dresser, a bee, a sheep, an orchestra, a submarine and a set of cheerleaders, all comically redetermining his body. Uncharacteristic in a Disney film, though, are his Averyesque leanings – bug-eyes, dropped jaw, cross-dressing, and the support of 'Red'-like girls.

Like *Who Framed Roger Rabbit?*, the genie works as a compendium of comic cartoon expression, but it is Williams' contemporary wit and delivery which defines the modernity of the animation through the post-modernity of its terms of reference (see Canemaker, 1988). The speed of the visual changes matches Williams' verbal delivery and even extends beyond it. Such rapidity of visual invention, over and beyond its recall and deployment of cartoon conventions, and the assurance of its execution, takes the animated form a stage further in its development. The genie is located in the contemporary era and directly addresses a contemporary culture aware of the terms of reference Williams brings to the character – the 'laughs', as it were, often occur outside the context of the narrative. The genie, though, is also the definitive embodiment of the possibilities inherent in the animated form and an expression of the capacity for animation to resist conventional modes of expression. At once he is confirmation of the form's modernity and a demonstration of its post-modern credentials. Even his last line of dialogue confirms this. He says, 'I'm history, no, I'm mythology; I don't care what I am, I'm free!' As this chapter has hopefully illustrated, only in an animated comedy could that be said.

5

ISSUES IN REPRESENTATION

The idea that animation is an *innocent* medium, ostensibly for children, and largely dismissed in film histories, has done much to inhibit the proper discussion of issues concerning *representation*. The modes of narration and the strategies for comedy described in previous chapters have deliberately concentrated on the structural premises by which certain ends may be achieved in the animated form. Though some attention was paid to the ostensible content of certain films, the complex ways in which animation problematises the representation of gender and race have yet to be discussed and that is the focus of this chapter. As is by now obvious, the distinctive language of animation raises some important questions which are as much about the unique parameters of expression available to the animator as they are about socio-political issues. The conventional methods by which such issues are addressed will always be further complicated by the use of animation which, almost by definition, transforms the codes and conditions by which traditional or dominant modes of representation are considered.

Like many art forms in the twentieth century, animation has been subject to the revisionist readings of the lobby for political correctness, and has inevitably been found wanting, particularly in its use of racist caricature and in its sexist bias. Clearly, there always remains the apparent defence that these kinds of representation were innocent in their intention and did not mean to cause offence. Further, it is sometimes argued, for example, that female and black artists were involved in aspects of production, and contributed to the creation of works which are now criticised for their misrepresentation of these people. These codes of representation, of course, occurred mainly in the American animated cartoon, and it is important to remember that this kind of work prefigured the lobbies of the Civil Rights and Feminist movements who demanded political sensitivity in all aspects of society and, critically, in popular art forms. It would be easy to perceive the animation industry in the West as pathologically male, run by men in the spirit of expressing the interests of men, creating patriarchal hierarchies in major studios. In many senses this is true, but part of a historical orthodoxy, that is now subject to revisionist research, and which is reclaiming the place of marginalised or unrecognised figures in the evolution of the animated form (see Pilling, 1992; Langer, 1993; Allan, 1994; Klein, 1994). Though this does much to properly

187

reconstitute the place and influence of neglected artists in the creation of important animation work, it does not necessarily redress problematic issues of representation within the films themselves.

Issues of representation are complicated, first, by the purpose of the representation, and second, by its expression. Cartooning has always been informed by the tradition of caricature, that both operates as a satirical mechanism which makes comment through its exaggeration of certain physical traits, and as a design strategy, which concentrates on redefining and exaggerating aspects of the body or environment, for purely aesthetic purposes. It is here that any discussion of representation properly begins, because animation is unique in its address of the body and, as such, in its creation of the codes and conditions by which masculinity and femininity may be defined, and by which questions concerning race may be advanced. Animation has the capability of rendering the body in a way which blurs traditional notions of gender, species and indigenous identity, further complicating debates concerning the primary political agendas of men and women, and enabling revisionist readings which use the ambivalence and ambiguity of the animated form to support the view that traditional orthodoxies in society itself must be necessarily challenged. It is in this sense that animation as a form is acknowledged as having a potentially radical vocabulary, even in spite of some of its earlier tendencies towards insensitive caricature. Women in particular, as will be discussed later, have especially benefitted from the open-ness of the animated form in the development of a feminine aesthetic unique to animation and not available in the live-action context. It is this tension between animation as a radical language, and the necessary reconciliation of the representational embarrassments in its evolution as a form, that will be discussed, first, by engaging with the issue of the body.

The body in question

Some of the narrational and comic dimensions of animation already addressed are clearly predicated upon an attitude about the body, whether it be the body of a human being or an animal or, indeed, where these two states meet as an anthropomorphised creature. Orthodox animation and developmental animation, in largely engaging with the figurative, are perpetually concerned with construction and symbolic expression of the body yet, ironically, it is in the design or narrational use of the body that most orthodox or developmental animation moves towards the condition of the experimental. The figurative aspects of the body substantially collapse into the abstract. Bodies merely become forms subject to manipulation, exaggeration and reconfiguration. The capacity and capability of the body in animation may be broadly defined in the following eight ways:

1 The body is malleable – it may be stretched over long distances, be compressed or extended, take the shape of another form, fit into incompatible spaces, etc.

2   The body is *fragmentary* – it can be broken into parts, reassembled and conjoined with other objects and materials.

3   The body is a *contextual space* – it can be a physical environment in itself, which may be entered into and used as if it were ostensibly hollow.

4   The body is a *mechanism* – it may be represented as if it was a machine.

5   The body has *impossible abilities* (i.e. it can fly, lift heavy objects, experience violence without pain etc.).

6   The body directly expresses *explicit emotions* (i.e. it fragments in surprise, contorts in terror etc.).

7   Bodies of humans/animals/creatures which are apparently incompatible are rendered equable in size, strength, ability etc.

8   Bodies may redetermine the physical orthodoxies of gender and species.

These conditions are principally considerations of the form the body may take in any animated scenario and ignore the social or political implications of the body's formation as a *character*, or interaction with other characters and the environment. Clearly, the ability for the body to take on many forms and adhere to many conditions often places its actual meaning in flux. The animated body frequently becomes a fluid form which, even when it closely adheres to the codes of realism defined earlier, still exhibits an instability when scrutinised at the level of ideological coherence. Significantly, Eisenstein has suggested that this level of mobility cannot wholly be recognised as the pure domain of form, and inevitably extends to subject matter and theme. Citing early Disney, he admires the destabilising effects of the animated form, and the implicit resistance to the 'logical case', but states that this fundamental premise necessitates that the subject is not rigorously interrogated. He says, 'Disney doesn't go to the roots, but has fun and entertains, mocks and amuses – jumping like a squirrel from branch to branch somewhere along the surface of the phenomenon, without looking beneath to the origins, at the reasons and causes, at the conditions and pre-conditions' (Leyda, 1988: 23). In recognising this tendency, Eisenstein articulates the chief problem of addressing representation through the body in animation. The animated form itself enjoys engaging with the 'surface of the phenomenon' and resists the agendas of the historical source, the cultural position, and the acceptable limits of representing the subject. Whilst suggesting that Disney is not guilty of obliviousness or a lack of responsibility, Eisenstein still, in a sense, excuses Disney by asserting, 'Disney is simply "beyond good and evil". Like the sun, like trees, like birds, like the ducks and mice, deer and pigeons that run across his screen' (ibid.: 10).

Eisenstein is essentially seduced by the purity of form in Disney's work, which leads him to conclude that it is in some way part of a *natural* order, an order which is self-evidently acceptable and beyond political scrutiny. He thus endorses the view that by sustaining its engagement with the 'surface of the phenomenon', the animated form remains ideologically neutral. This seems naïve, and is an argument which only retains credibility if animation is perceived as an *innocent* form. The reclamation of the status of animation beyond its self-evident aesthetic

189

credentials as an art form, thus necessitates that all the things that Eisenstein suggests Disney excludes – origins, reasons and causes, conditions and preconditions – become the crucial premises of enquiry, not merely in how the body is constructed, but in what it means, even in despite of its mutability. To a certain extent, this level of analysis has already been engaged with, particularly with regard to films like *Girl's Night Out* and *Daddy's Little Bit of Dresden China* in Chapter Two. The focus of the discussion here, though, is on the issues raised by notions of masculinity and femininity in animation, and the questions raised by the facility of animation to blur gender distinctions.

'Faster than a speeding bullet . . .': Men and masculinity

Rather than understanding the muscular male hero as either a re-assertion, or parodic enactment of masculinist values, we can examine the ways in which he represents both, as well as being produced by the ongoing and unsteady relationship between these, and other, images of masculinity.

(Tasker, 1993: 109)

Writing here about the relationship between gender, genre and contemporary mainstream action cinema, Yvonne Tasker stresses the tensions informing the reading of the (muscular) male body in live-action films. Since the animated male body, in aesthetic terms, has been principally defined by muscularity, with its connotations of power and strength, these issues also fundamentally inform the animated form, where the 'unsteady relationship' of various modes of representation is compounded further by the fluidity in the construction of the body cited earlier. Masculinity as it is directly expressed through representations of men is actually remarkably stable and consistent, however, largely playing out modes of excess and spectacle in a similar manner to models offered by the live-action movie. Masculinity, as it is expressed anthropomorphically through animals, is a little more complex, though, and will be addressed later. The Fleischer Brothers Studio created the two best-known animated versions of masculine heroism in their adaptation of the comic book figures of Popeye and Superman. Popeye, with his appeal to the common man and the blue-collar ethos, spoke to parochial interests during the Depression, and was the perfect antecedent of Superman, the American everyman, suitably empowered to champion not merely the USA, but the democratic principles of the West during World War II. The different models of muscularity on offer here serve as important examples of the dominant kinds of masculinity in the animated film.

Popeye, created by cartoonist Elzie Segar for King Features, first appeared in comic strip form on 17 January 1929, where he joined the cast of the Thimble Theater on a journey to Dice Island. Reputedly based on Frank 'Rocky' Feigle, a local character in Segar's hometown of Chester, Illinois, Popeye was initially a

190

bit-player in the strip, often characterised by small acts of cowardice, but soon he developed into a character with moral certainty who fought to defend his point of view. As is well known, Popeye's transformation into a highly muscular, super-human figure was catalysed when he ate spinach, a choice made by Segar on the basis of its promotion by the medical profession in the late 1920s. Such is the mark of Popeye's popularity, and his persuasiveness as an ideological influence, spinach consumption in the USA rose by 33 per cent between 1931 and 1936 (Sagendorf, 1979: 43). In 1932, the Fleischer Brothers Studio started to make Popeye cartoons. In 1933, newspaper proprietor, William Randolph Hearst, ordered that King Features monitor Popeye's behaviour in the light of his popu-larity with children, and the stories that followed, both in comic strip and cartoon form, represented Popeye as a much less randomly antagonistic character, fighting only as a last resort, and self-evidently for the right cause. Though the spinach motif was not regularly used by Segar, the Fleischer Brothers used it throughout the nine years in which they made Popeye cartoons, defining his awesome strength through ever more exaggerated extensions of his muscular prowess. As Fleischer historian, Leslie Cabarga, has noted:

> With each new cartoon the bicep gag became more outrageous. The muscle might grow into the form of an anvil, a horseshoe or a machine gun. As the camera came in for an extreme close-up there might be a super-imposed image (in motion, no less) of a battleship cutting through the ocean waves or a speeding locomotive.
>
> - (Cabarga, 1988: 87)

Popeye's masculinity is predominantly defined by the association between his own organic expansion and the strength of hard metal and machines. In the comic strip, and to a certain extent in the cartoons, Popeye's manliness was also determined by the exaggerated view of his own heroism, and the idea that he was indestructible. Segar, writing in the character of Popeye in 1936, says 'I been shot a hun'erd an' twenty times, an' I ain't dead yet. When a bullit does go through me tough hide it don't bother me none', but assures the reader 'I never hits a man as hard as I kin on account of it ain't right to kill peoples' (Sagendorf, 1979: 43). What is important about this kind of character construction is that it is far more legitimate in animation because animation has the capacity to render figures indestructible in a more plausible way than in any live-action fantasy. The capacity of the animated body to assume any shape or form ironically de-physicalises the body in the corporeal material sense. Popeye's character transcends the things that actually happen to his body. As such, his exaggerations are supported by the capability of the form, and simultaneously, his mode of masculinity is defined through his ability to live through, and emerge victorious from, the conflicts he inevitably becomes part of. Though also only a bit-player in the original Thimble Theater cast, it is Bluto who becomes Popeye's masculine adversary. Though Bluto is on the face of it bigger and stronger than Popeye, he is never the champion of the proper cause, seeking to undermine Popeye as he competes for the affections of Olive Oyl.

If Popeye is rarely undone in conflict, his masculinity, as it is expressed through his sex and sexuality is always threatened by Olive's fickleness. Cabarga notes that this is one of the key themes in the Popeye oeuvre, along with more absurdist stories concerning wasted effort and failed purpose, and the overt compassion for children (like Swee'Pea) and animals (Cabarga, 1988: 93–6). Significantly, he also mentions what happens if animation of this sort is interrogated beyond the surface of the phenomenon mentioned earlier:

> If anyone could eat spinach, one might ask, why didn't the vengeful Bluto keep a supply on hand and why did Popeye always wait until the last moment before he ate it? These questions are as silly as asking why Popeye and Olive never consummated their relationship, or who actually parented Popeye's 'nephews', Peepeye, Pipeye, Pupeye and Poopeye? One simply must not question cartoon conventions after all!
>
> (Cabarga, 1988: 98)

Perhaps unwisely ignoring Cabarga's advice, it is interesting to address what the cartoon conventions ignore or marginalise in not paying attention to logical narrative questions like the ones he raises. The spinach, for example, becomes a metaphoric talisman that actually defines Popeye's masculinity. It is the catalyst in the creation of a heightened muscularity that spectacularises his manhood, in a distinct mechanism that enables him to make the transition from put-upon comic oaf to a heroic common man. Popeye's heroism has to emerge from the very urbanity of his culture and, thus, must be prevented from assuming mythic dimensions. This is achieved by emasculating Popeye through his association with Olive Oyl. By not reconciling the act of consummation, and creating characters who appear to have no plausible ancestry, animation once more de-physicalises the narrative space in the *sexual* sense, but re-physicalises it in the *kinetic* sense. Important biological agendas are marginalised by prioritising the intrinsic capability of the animated form to extend and exaggerate Popeye's physical *action* and not burden his character with the complexities of physical *relationship*. Questioning cartoon conventions, therefore, only reveals how much men are defined through the obvious agency of action, and that women are located as complex embodiments of *difference* either through the overtness of their sexuality or through its implicit denial. These issues will inform the rest of the discussion, but it is worth noting here that by the time Popeye is required for propaganda purposes in *Fleets of Strength* (1942), Olive Oyl is not present, and Bluto's role as the enemy is assumed by the axis powers. As the viewer would expect, Popeye defeats his adversaries single-handed with one slug of spinach, along the way *becoming* an aircraft. Feminine absence only heightens masculine strength, especially as it is extended by the ability for animation to plausibly redefine the body. It is this very fact, however, which has encouraged women

192

animators to redefine the body in their own light and in the face of masculine hierarchies like those often defined in the Fleischer Brothers' *Superman* series.

Joe Shuster and Jerry Steel created Superman in 1938. Even though the comic strip was concerned with a fantasy character, the stories were set in a real world populated by human beings, and little emphasis was placed on humour. The Fleischer Brothers' *Superman* series was thus a radical departure from the ostensibly 'cute' sensibility that characterised animation by the end of the 1930s, largely due to the influence of Disney. Paramount agreed to substantial funding for the series, and considerable effort was made to create a feeling of darkness and foreboding in the cartoons, reflecting some of the deep-rooted anxiety in American culture during the war period. Whereas the early Fleischer cartoons revealed fears and phobias in a distinctly *surreal* approach, the conditions of war necessitated a *new realism*. The Fleischers abandoned the squash-n-stretch caricaturing of the Betty Boop and Popeye films, prioritising a design strategy predicated on sharp angles and dark wedges of colour. Clark Kent, Superman's everyday alter-ego, was often rotoscoped from the actions of an actor to properly authenticate his identity as a real human being *not* subject to cartoonal logic. This further accentuated the space between Kent's ordinariness and Superman's extraordinariness. Whereas cartoonal logic had primarily been applied for comic effects, here the capacity for animation to relocate the body is merely to extend human capability *believably* to its imaginable *super*human extreme. If Clark Kent is the helpless, well-meaning, inadequate, defined by the limitations of his human-ness (a condition shared by the ordinary American male in regard to the threat of war), then Superman is a mythic role model. Popeye is only a parody of muscular achievement. Superman is the hysterical (if understated) return to the necessary muscularity required to oppose alternative ideologies, and any sense of *otherness*.

This is especially the case in *Jungle Drums* (1943), in which an Allied spy plane is shot down by Nazis secreted in an ancient temple. On board is reporter, Lois Lane (the chief emasculator of Clark Kent), who is given some important papers by the dying pilot, Commander Fleming, who insists she must 'destroy them'. These papers are concerned with the movements of an American convoy; information which the Nazis are eager to secure. Inevitably, Lois doesn't obey Fleming's instruction and hides them. She is then captured and tortured by the Nazis, who are thwarted by her 'American stubbornness', and prepare her to be burned at the stake in a native ritual. It is here that the film betrays a range of anxieties, both in relation to modes of masculinity and with regard to codes of race and ethnicity. As Joan Mellen has suggested:

> In a primitive, ritualistic manner movies have defined manliness in terms of getting the 'enemy' before it gets you. It is a set of values designed to nurture suspicion, fear of one another, and the need to rely on authority, as well as to exorcise through images of male prowess the sense of helplessness that life in America really induces in us.
>
> (Mellen, 1977: 11)

The 'enemy' in *Jungle Drums* is not merely defined as the Nazis. It is clearly, all notions of *otherness*. The Nazi commandant poses as an ancient god, dressed to resemble a member of the Klu Klux Klan, and in silhouette, the devil himself. The natives of the jungle are in his thrall, and obey his every command, so they build the fire in preparation for Lois' ritual death. The film increases the tension by depicting the natives' actions as the descent into primitive delirium and madness. The dark-skinned warriors pummel drums and dance around the fire, the embodiment of uncivilised, irrational forces of destruction. During this sequence, the commandant finds the papers Lois has hidden and, seemingly, she is left without hope. This is compounded by images of the raging fire, threatening native faces complete with nose-bones, and the general sense of chaos evoked by flying spears and deafening drums.

Thankfully, Clark Kent and his air-force compatriot are flying overhead, and notice both the jungle fire and the crashed aircraft. Clark parachutes into the danger zone only to transform quickly into Superman and pluck Lois from the fire. Significantly, Superman emerges through the fire, eliciting shocked silence and awe in the natives, who perceive him as a new god. This only reinforces the mythic credentials of Superman to the home audience, and represents Superman's actions as the forces of reason in the face of unchecked barbarity. When fired on by the Nazi commandant, Superman bends back the gun barrel in what may be read as a moment of castration in view of a preferred masculine agenda. Lois manages to escape and warn the American convoy of the approach of Nazi submarines. The submarines are duly destroyed and the film ends with Hitler angrily switching off the radio bulletin informing him of the defeat.

Whilst in a period of war, it is entirely credible that propaganda will deliberately represent the enemy in a derogatory and threatening way, but here, the Fleischer Brothers Studios very much determine the unacceptable nature of the Nazis by associating them with the highly charged enactment of bodily sacrifice and ritualistic violence in primitive cultures. It is apparently a violence without reason, yet stylised and choreographed but, most importantly, it is allied with the open expression of physical pleasure and celebration, and in this case directed against a woman. Devoid of its cultural and historical context, and portrayed in highly stereotypical terms, a native ritual is deployed to heighten the alien-ness and distastefulness of the 'enemy'. It might further be suggested that the 'enemy' includes women, because the film is clearly ambivalent about the fact that Lois disobeyed the order to destroy the papers, and half-fetishistically enjoys her torture and endangerment. It may be argued that there is an acceptable sexism and racism within the codes of expression foregrounded in propaganda, but here the Fleischers go beyond acceptable limits in championing not merely Superman's implied defence of democratic principles but, contradictorily, his embodiment of white (American) supremacism.

The film clearly recognises a hierarchy of masculinities, and seeks to perpetuate that hierarchy by resisting the 'unsteady relationship' between masculinities which these codes of otherness clearly represent. Similarly, though Lois displays her normal feistiness and courage, she is not allowed the customary ending to the film common throughout the series, in which she gains kudos for writing an exclusive story. She, like the men in the film, is contained and ultimately excluded. Like Popeye, in *Fleets of Strength*, Superman is allowed no possible dilution of his prowess within the context of war. Much animation enjoys the resistance of the easy binary of 'masculine' and 'feminine', but the neo-realist approach of the *Superman* series during this period, does much to insist that few factors remain in place which suggest any insecurity about the identity and ethos of the white male, and the dominant mode of masculinity he represents.

Interestingly, this kind of masculinity, predicated on physical spectacle and activity, is sometimes redefined in moments of crisis. In the mid-1960s, at a time when the USA found itself at a historic crossroads in the face of the assassination of John F. Kennedy, the war in Vietnam and the escalation of a youth-oriented counter-culture championing new modes of civil liberty, an animated curiosity entitled *Norman Normal* (1967), directed by Alex Lovy, shows the corporate WASP American subject to introspection and a crisis of identity. All models of socially acceptable and/or successful codes of masculinity are challenged, leaving Norman uncertain of his role and function in society. Norman feels perpetually self-conscious, located in a morally unstable world, half-nostalgic for a former idyll, half-directed at a cosmopolitan idyll. The kind of racism directed at the enemy that was acceptable during World War II was not acceptable in the newly enlightened 1960s. The kinds of unchecked antagonism towards the Japanese exhibited in cartoons like Friz Freleng's *Bugs Bunny Nips the Nips* (1944), or towards Stalin and Hitler in the chaotic surrealism of Bob Clampett's *Tin Pan Alley Cats* (1943), could not be repeated in an age uncertain of just exactly who 'the enemy' were, and sceptical of the kind of macho agenda endorsed by central government. Further, as has been persuasively argued by Amy Lawrence, historical moments, like the fall of communism in Eastern Europe, in which the enemy, or self-evidently unacceptable codes of otherness disappear, codes of masculinity become confused and directionless. She says, 'masculinity is depicted as the product of a difficult, contested relationship between a subject and his body, and between the body and the state' (Lawrence, 1994: 33). Discussing Jan Svankmajer's *The Death of Stalinism in Bohemia* (1990) and *Darkness, Light, Darkness* (1991), and Polish director, Piotr Dumala's *Freedom of the Leg* (1989) and *Franz Kafka* (1992), Lawrence stresses how men are torn between their psychological and physionomical lives, and their anatomical and socio-mythic functions and, further, wholly distantiated from their sex and sexuality in relation to women and the family. Seemingly, then, depictions of masculinity as it resides in representations of neo-realist male figures is intrinsically bound up with issues concerning the limits of the body and its ideological identity. To remove or complicate masculine function is to problematise male identity.

Significantly, one of the most popular forms of contemporary animation, the Manga films from Japan (see McCarthy, 1993), maintain the heroic tradition of masculinity by couching the violent Samurai codes of honour and sacrifice in tales of apocalpytic mayhem, where technological advances result in urban chaos and socio-cultural collapse, most notably, in Otomo Katsuhiro's *Akira* (1987). Masculinity in this context is concerned with the survival of the fittest in the face of change and challenge, whilst engaging with a historically determined agenda about what it is to be Japanese. Folk-tale and fantasy meets a science-fictional cyber-world where identity is uncertain but largely determined by a technological power base. Interestingly, female characters in such stories are normally characterised by a mythic, and sometimes highly sexualised sense of magical power, which the urbanised, techno-literate male cannot deal with, for example, as in Takayama Hideki's *Urotsukidoji: Legend of the Overfiend* (1987). As David Vernal has suggested, though, some aspects of these narratives are related to the post-war generation's perception of World War II in the light of the quasi-appropriation of Japanese culture by Western (American) influences, and inform salutary stories which play out the reasons for ideological conflict and rehearse (ultimately) peaceful resolutions, for example, *Mobile Suit Gundam* (1979) and *The Mobile Police Patlabor* (1988) (Vernal, 1995: 56–84). Once again, male identity is at the service of nationalist agendas but, significantly, in pursuit of a *specific* sense of Japanese being which is being eroded by other influences, and constantly undermined by the increasing presence of man-made (man-like) machines.

The concept of 'everyman'

If masculinity is not coded through role and function, it is often played out through the universalising concept of 'everyman', in which male figures, or figures which are assumed to be male, become the symbolic embodiment of humankind. This is still at its most prominant when the masculine figure operates in the service of function, but also informs scenarios in which a male character represents a victim alienated from civilised codes of society, i.e. a figure like Trnka's Harlequin in *The Hand*, which symbolises both the oppressed artist and the oppressed human being.[1] In other words, this universal role is coded masculine, and assumes to represent the interests and outlook of women, while mainly operating in a way that expresses the ideas and interests of men. This idea may be briefly discussed with regard to Disney's most distinctive icon, Mickey Mouse.

In his (psycho) analysis of Mickey Mouse, Martin Grotjahn suggests, 'Mickey Mouse symbolises the small, invincible, invulnerable, utterly victorious and triumphant, old and omnipotent child' (Grotjahn, 1957: 220). Arguing that Mickey triumphs over the age of the machine, humanising all before him, Grotjahn further notes that he is 'the mechanised symbol of the little and victorious phallus' (ibid.: 222). Disney historian, Brian Sibley, suggests this idea of achievement and victory is bound up with the idea that Walt Disney projected his own desire and ambition through Mickey, and perceived the character as one who would absorb and reflect the progressive aspects of popular culture.[2] This is evident in early films like *Steamboat Willie* (1928), which echoed Buster Keaton's film, *Steamboat Bill Jnr* (1928), or *Galloping Gaucho* (1928) which was inspired by the Douglas Fairbanks vehicle, The Gaucho (1928), and Plane Crazy (1928) which was based on the pioneer aviator, Charles Lindbergh. This was further advanced when Mickey became the chief character in a number of genre parodies, and thus became a cowboy or an exploror depending on the story. As such, Sibley argues, that Mickey:

> . . . is symbolic of everyman. He is simple in outlook and expectations; he is unceasingly curious, as most of humanity is. He's prone to all failings, hopes and fears that all of us experience, but he is also, I suppose, the new man – the Renaissance man, because he is not content with life the way it is, any more than Disney was content with the medium of animation in the way he found it.[3]

While some aspects of this argument are persuasive, it is clear that Mickey is played out in purely masculine terms, an agenda which Eric Smoodin suggests was wholly concerned with the construction of cinematic exhibition in the early 1930s that used male characters to reinstate 'mythologised stereotypical American values, both contemporary and historical' (Smoodin, 1993: 66). Mickey essentially became heroic, and intrinsically male, the more he came to supposedly represent ideological certainty in the USA. Simultaneously, he became 'a star', and achieved 'growing importance as an aesthetic object rather than the mouse-next-door' (ibid.: 66).

This idea became even more important when Mickey became a 'real' character in Disney's theme parks, because the masculine integrity of Mickey's body takes on an obvious material status, whether played out through an actor or a mechanised puppet. Mickey's physical status as 'everyman' in this context may therefore be threatened by his actual presence and the possibility of interaction with real adults and children. To this end the Disney organisation forbid photography of back-stage tours at Disney World because, as Susan Willis notes, 'the "magic" would be broken if photos of disassembled characters circulated in the public sphere' and adds, sardonically, 'children might suffer irreparable psychic trauma at the sight of a "be-headed" Mickey; Disney exercises control over the image to safeguard childhood fantasies' (The Project on Disney, 1995: 196). This point is particularly significant when placed within the context of the representation of the body. Masculinity in animation is predominantly determined by the maintenance of the physical/material definition of the male body. Any mode by which it is deconstructed, acted upon and changed, or merely destroyed, inevitably refutes its masculinity, and its status as 'everyman' on purely male terms. Anticipating the subversive agendas of the feminine aesthetic and queer politics, to be addressed later, Susan Willis also suggests:

> As I see it, the individual's right to imagine and to give expression to unique ways of seeing is at stake in struggles against private property. Mickey Mouse, not withstanding his corporate copyright, exists in our

common culture. He is the site for the enactment of childhood wishes and fantasies, for early conceptualisations of the body, a being who can be imagined as both self and other. If culture is held as private property, then there can only be one correct version of Mickey Mouse, whose logo-like activity is the cancellation of creativity. But the multiplicity of quirky versions of Mickey Mouse that children draw can stand as a graphic question to us as adults: Who, indeed, owns Mickey Mouse?

(The Project on Disney, 1995: 197)

Willis' approach attempts to redefine Mickey through the availability of his image as a site for personal expression and interpretation. This, however, would inevitably refute the corporate and ideological conception of Mickey as a white, American, male figure, and make him the subject and object of other projections. Instead of being 'everyman' on masculine terms, he would be, ironically, 'everyperson' on more democratic terms than patriarchally determined commercial interests will allow.

Wayward girls and wicked women: The feminine aesthetic [4]

Though it is fair to suggest that men have been predominant in the creation of animated films, and the subject of many of them, it is ironically, women filmmakers who have recognised animation as a form in which they can work and achieve significant ends that are not available in any other film form. If men, in general, have used animation to echo and extend the premises and concerns of men in live-action film-making, then women have used animation to create a specific *feminine aesthetic* which resists the inherently masculine language of the live-action arena, and the most dominant codes of orthodox hyper-realist animation which also use its vocabulary. Evelyn Lambart, who worked with Norman McClaren at the National Film Board of Canada, stresses that 'derivative work was absolutely hated. We didn't do any cel work at all, in fact, we were highly contemptuous of Disney' (Pilling, 1992: 30). It is this which provides some of the first clues concerning the development of a feminine aesthetic. Lambart implies that the Disney industrial and aesthetic ethos was inherently informed by a lack of individuality and a fixedness in approach. Indeed, Faith Hubley, an American animator best known for her collaborations with her husband, John Hubley (ex-Disney and UPA animator), and her family, stresses the importance of 'eliminating the hard-cel and the hard line that I've always felt was ugly' (ibid., 1992: 26). The fluidity of line; the creation of an original design concept; the engagement with different narrational approaches that challenged lineal orthodoxies and the address of specifically personal, *gender*-led issues resulted in the direct politicisation of some women's animation, an example of which, would be the work of the Leeds Animation Workshop in England, of whom founder and ex-member, Gillian Lacy says, 'The work continues to be committed to issues and still embodies the aims of the workshop – use of a style that is accessible to a wide audience combined with the creation of cartoon women who do not have huge tits and eyelashes' (ibid.,1992: 36).

The resistance to 'Boopism' (see Cabarga, 1988: 53–81; Hendershot, 1993; Smoodin, 1993: 30–9) is more than just a rejection of highly sexualised design. It is a direct response to the male representations of women; masculine codes of composition and narrational construction; and personal, social and political agendas concerning men. It is also a recognition of the possibilities available to women once these codes have been overturned. Essentially, animation, more than any other form of film-making, offers the opportunity to operate in a safe space and create auteurist cinema outside the constraints of patriarchal norms, both with regard to the means of production, and the modes of representation. Outside the industrial context, animation can be achieved relatively inexpensively, dependent upon the style and approach of the film, and once the location, materials and time have been secured to make the film, it is possible for women to have full control over the production process. This type of film-making is sometimes reliant on external arts funding or an educational context in which to start but because, in the first instance, it is intrinsically outside the commercial arena, it offers the possibility of being more radical, more experimental, and more irreverent. Fundamentally, it creates the context in which the absolutely personal becomes inevitably political, because it becomes defined through its gendered aesthetic, and is self-evidently opposed to male-dominated orthodox animation.

Perhaps most importantly, women's animation is less censored in its concerns, even when working in forms that move beyond hyper-realism, and seek to be more subjective. Women animators more readily seek to express themselves in ways that trust and exploit the ontological equivalence of imagery. The creation of animated dream-states mixes easily with subjective interpretations of fairytale or poetry, which in turn sits comfortably with the use of the documentary tendency, or the overt use of abstract symbolism. This enables women animators to address topics which many male animators could not deal with. Marjut Rimmenen and Christine Roche examine sexual abuse, incest and murder in The Stain (1991) (see Pilling, 1992: 38–40); the Leeds Animation Workshop address the phallocentric aspect of language and naturalised patriarchal norms in Out to Lunch (1989); American Suzan Pitt looks at female desire and its relationship to creativity in Asparagus (1979) (see Pilling, 1992: 57–61, 71–5); Emily Hubley, daughter of Faith Hubley, addresses sexual confusion, rape, pregnancy and social alienation in The Emergence of Eunice (1980); while Alison De Vere addresses how a woman becomes more conscious of herself as a woman by interrogating the roles she has imposed upon her and actively engages with, in The Black Dog (1987) (see Law, 1995: 39–49). All these films demonstrate a feminine aesthetic which could not have been achieved in live-action film-making. Such an aesthetic may be defined in the following terms.

Figure 5.1 Suzan Pitt's extraordinary film, *Asparagus*, uses dynamic colours, an alienating
soundtrack and challenging, highly sexualised imagery to: illustrate the feminine aesthetic; re-envisage the domestic space; and redefine the concept of 'the
phallus' as the determinant of power in the contemporary world

- Women's animation recognises the shift from the representation of woman
  as *object*, to the representation of woman as *subject*. This seeks to move away
  from traditions in which women are merely erotic spectacles or of marginal
  narrational interest.
- The feminine aesthetic mistrusts language, perceiving it as the agent of masculine expression, preferring to express itself in predominantly visual terms,
  using a variety of forms, and reclaiming and revising various traditions.
- In order to construct a feminine aesthetic, it is necessary to abandon
  conservative forms, and create radical texts which may demand greater
  participation from the viewing audience.
- The feminine aesthetic seeks to reveal a woman's relationship to her own
  body; her interaction with men and other women; her perception of her
  private and public role; her social and political identity within the domestic
  and professional space, as determined by law; and also, the relationship
  between female sexuality, desire, and creativity.

The feminine aesthetic has become more recognisable, and more self-conscious,
since the 1970s, when it informed the overt politicisation of female artworks *per
se*, but it is important not to underestimate the importance of the female animation

pioneers who preceded this more politically driven work. In a sense, Lotte Reiniger's unparalleled works of silhouette animation, based on Chinese shadow theatre, exhibit a feminist tendency in that the language of such work is couched most specifically in the lyrical movement of the figures, and the emotional intensity of gesture – a profound departure from the (male) agendas of the evolving cartoon. This lightness of touch, this subtlety of expression, this desire to delineate emotional states in films such as The Adventures of Prince Achmed (1923–1926), (where she worked with Walter Ruttman and Berthold Bartosch, other renowned animators), The Stolen Heart (1934) and Papageno (1935), were clear statements of intent. Of Disney, she said, 'his films are technically perfect; too perfect' (Pilling, 1992: 15), hinting at the impersonality of industrialised, masculine cel-animation, and secure of her own femininity as an expressive tool in the creation of her own work. Reiniger's work seems a long way from the abstronics of Mary Ellen Bute, who suggests that her work is concerned with 'a method for controlling a source of light to produce images in rhythm' (Russett and Starr, 1976: 104). Combining 'abstractions' and 'electronics', Bute created animated patterns on an oscilloscope, and in doing so not merely made engaging abstract experimental films, but also dispelled myths concerning women and the use of technology. Like Reiniger, Bute enjoyed the control and rejection of functionalism in creating personal works. Similarly, she perceived her work as art and the expression of feeling, fully distantiating herself from cartoonal humour.

Female animators like Faith Hubley (see Peary and Peary, 1980: 183–192; Priestley, 1994: 23–32), Joy Batchelor (see Manvell, 1980), Sally Cruickshank (see Pilling, 1992: 51–3), and Kathy Rose (ibid.: 62–3), continued this tradition from different points of view and artistic perspectives. Constantly blurring lines between different cultural, artistic and performance traditions, each created a distinctive agenda which sought to distantiate itself from masculine forms and interests. The work of American animator Jane Aaron will be discussed below in the context of the feminine aesthetic as it is defined and expressed in one of her most personal films, Interior Designs (1980).

Interior Designs (1980)

Jane Aaron's first film, A Brand New Day (1974), perhaps includes one of the quintessential images within the feminine aesthetic. A lone woman within the domestic space opens and closes a window blind, revealing different landscapes in the outside world. On one occasion, she observes a snake in the desert and a blooming cactus flower. In a single image, Aaron encapsulates the restrictions imposed upon, and the liberties available to the female artist. Seemingly trapped by the domestic space, and subject to the inhibitions and intrusions of the phallic landscape – a frontier, both final and terminal – the central female figure seeks physical and poetic solace in the freedom of personal creativity. Aaron's profound desire to liberate her imagination further, and work beyond the confines of purely drawn animation, led her to address and animate the environment around her, combining the two styles in the same frame. The interaction between these two modes of animation is revealing and serves to combine many of the narrational strategies defined in Chapter Two. Aaron deploys *metamorphosis* and *synecdoche* in her drawn style in order to maintain a tension with the *fabrication* and *associative relations* in her use of live-action footage. This results in a mode of *penetration* where one form of animation interrogates the other, drawing attention to the *choreographic* principles at large in the work, and the sparse deployment of sound, which serves to create particular moods and atmospheres.

Interior Designs begins in a bedroom filmed in live-action, but superimposed upon it is a frame of drawn animation featuring a couple apparently twisting, turning and rolling in space. As the frame starts to move across the room, however, and principally across a bed, it is clear that the movement is correspondent to the kind of restless movement which takes place during sleep. The objects and materials in the bedroom move as if they are being acted upon, but there is no sign of any live-action figures. Immediately, this calls attention to the mode of fabrication described earlier in relation to Svankmajer and the Quay Brothers, in which the tangible elements of the environment recall their function and inherent life. There is energy and kineticism in the bed which relates to the vitality of those people who use it. The figure, who appears to be the feminine figure in the couple, metamorphoses into a full-colour person who immediately fragments into lines and shapes, becoming a primitive, child-like drawing of a house and tree, set against a live-action urban background. The drawn aspect of the animation represents a recall of childhood innocence and the ease of expression, while the urban environment within which it is contextualised represents an inappropriate and oppressive reality. In deploying this technique, Aaron successfully uses *counterpoint* to simultaneously recall personal associative relations and juxtapose them with contexts which inhibit their expression or operate as the embodiment of change and constraint. The drawn aspects of the film thus increasingly represent the liberation afforded to the artist by transforming images through the free association of colour and form. Significantly, it is the female body which evolves into a range of shapes, signifying the primacy of the feminine aesthetic.

Aaron's image system then moves from the bedroom and urbanity into the Death Valley desert in California, in which she plays out further aspects of her creative sensibility by making animated Land Art, superimposing self-evidently paper shapes resembling cacti on to the rugged backdrop of rock formations and mountains. The quasi-plants appear to grow, and further draw attention to the disparity between nature and civilisation, between organicism and artifice, and between reality and illusion, and as Bendazzi has noted, this is 'Land Art where nature is not modified, but rather invited to act and assume attitudes and meanings' (Bendazzi, 1994: 253). The images fragment once more and contract back into the shape of a woman, but the drawn element of the frame is used to make the transition from the original scene in the bedroom to a new scene in the kitchen. The drawn figure appears to actually tear the frame, revealing a kitchen scene, whereupon the camera withdraws, revealing the real kitchen environment on which the image is superimposed. Aaron plays upon the associative relations of the kitchen as a stereotype of containment for women and, most importantly, the scene of habitual domestic routines. She uses the synecdoche of numerous coffee cups to reinforce this point, half-historicising the space by the recall of the hundreds of domestic moments of drinking coffee, having meals and snacks etc.; half-criticising the banal and mundane execution of everyday existence. The sound of a dripping tap accompanies this sequence and further emphasises the passing of time and the sense of waste. A figure reads a newspaper and exits. Spaces that were once occupied become empty. Life goes on.

Aaron once more calls attention to her key theme of the role of the woman artist within both the spheres of influence determined by contemporary existence and the natural world, when the film again moves into this environment. She draws the changing shadows of some real trees which are filmed in live-action time-lapse photography, revealing the presence of the artist, and the artist's resistance to time passing. The feminine aesthetic particularly reveals itself here, in the sense that it is about the woman artist attempting to take control of, and redefine, the supposedly familiar and supposedly naturalised codes of existence. Thus, in the final sequence of the film, the woman figure resists the routines created within the domestic space, and with it the assumed agendas of an order fundamentally imposed by men, and enters her studio. To the sound of fairground music, created artefacts and drawings (mostly of women and objects seen earlier in the film) come to life and, in a blaze of light, acknowledge and endorse the female artist and the feminine aesthetic. These themes have been pursued in her subsequent work, Remains to be Seen (1983), Travelling Light (1985) and Set in Motion (1986) (see Pilling, 1992: 55–6), and all seek to expand the vocabulary of both animation and cinematography in the service of expressing the personal agendas of a woman artist and rejecting the dominant codes of expression and representation established by men. It is this aim which has created a feminine aesthetic in animation which is at once unique to the form, a progressive development in the form, and a radical addition to the conventions of film-making in general.

Cross-dressing, transvestism, gender-bending, cross-species coupling and other unusual trends

Anthropomorphic characters are a step removed from human characters and require a certain degree of imitation or impersonation of human traits in order to succeed. Thus, Bugs and Daffy are, in a sense, impersonating male humans with respect to their values and behavior, just as Petunia (Pig), Minnie (Mouse) and Daisy (Rabbit) are impersonating female humans in respect to theirs. The major difference is seen in the degree and type of abstraction: whereas the male characters are abstracted to actions and 'masculine' traits (for example, cunning,

203

aggressiveness), the female characters are abstracted and reduced to physiological characteristics and recognizable 'feminine' traits (for example, shrewishness, passivity).

(Delgaudio, 1980: 211)

Sybil Delgaudio usefully summates the dominant traditions of representing masculinity and femininity in the anthropomorphised characters of the animated cartoon. Simply, 'male' characters are defined by what they are, and how they behave, while 'female' characters are essentially understood by what they look like and through a vocabulary of stereotypical mannerisms. These codes were not confined to the Warner Brothers output. Disney animator, Fred Moore, who drew Mickey and Minnie Mouse, located key differences in the design of the two characters, even though Minnie was 'drawn the same as Mickey' (Thomas and Johnson, 1981: 553). In order to make one mouse female he used lace underwear, high-heeled shoes, a small hat and eyelids and lashes. He recommended that Minnie's 'poses and mannerisms should be definitely feminine' (ibid.: 553) and that a certain 'cuteness' be achieved through having 'the skirts high on her body – showing a large expanse of lace panties' (ibid.: 553). Most importantly, though, Moore suggested:

> In order to make Minnie as feminine as possible, we should use everything in her make up to achieve this end. Her mouth could be smaller than Mickey's and maybe never open so wide into a smile, take, expression etc. Her eyelids and eyelashes could help very much in keeping her feminine as well as the skirt swaying from the body on different poses, displaying pants. Carrying the little finger in the extended position also helps.

(ibid.: 553)

It becomes clear that the cartoon female, as defined through the assumed traits of femininity, is designed in relation to the primary representation of the male character. Further, the female is predominantly defined as a set of signifiers of femininity, i.e. skirts, panties, high-heeled shoes, etc., which also function as additional signifiers of character differentiation from the male model. Particular attention is drawn to genital difference through the exposure of panties, but the chief mode of physical differentiation lies in the design of the face – most notably, in this case, Minnie's eyes. Unlike Mickey, she has eyelids and eyelashes, and a smaller mouth for smaller expressions and reactions. This stress on the suggestion of petiteness and prettiness in Minnie, as in the representation of Betty Boop, is a common design strategy for the idea of the child-woman in animation, and is significant in that it defines juvenilisation as feminine.

This issue becomes of particular note when, as Stephen Jay Gould argues in a reiteration of some of Konrad Lorentz's theories, that it is Mickey who has been progressively juvenilised in the attempt to give him the appealing characteristics of a baby to court the affections of adult audiences (Gould, 1987: 500–8). This argument may be extended further by suggesting that Mickey has not merely been juvenilised but also *feminised*, and that the modes of *feminisation* inform the shifts of gender position in the apparently masculine contexts and agendas in the animated cartoon. Before embarking on a particular case study on this issue addressing the Tom and Jerry cartoons, it is useful to further examine how such *gender-blending* may be anticipated in the work of a number of key animators, and how this creates a context in which certain subversive readings may be legitimised.

Patrick McGilligan, writing about Warner Brothers animator, Bob Clampett, discusses the specific idiosyncrasies that defined each of the main directors' contributions to the Warner Brothers ethos and output. He examines Chuck Jones' liberal tendencies and Tex Avery's madcap comedy (see Chapter Four), but pays particular attention to a comparison between Frank Tashlin's 'subversive naughtiness' and Clampett's ultimate conservatism:

> While Tashlin taunted the censors and leered at the flesh and exulted in characters such as the overripe Petunia Pig – who, as Greg Ford has observed, is 'a Jayne Mansfield-progenitor' – Clampett veered closest to open sexuality by having Daffy Duck striptease before surrendering to an oven in *The Wise Quacking Duck* (1943). . . . Sex? It either embarrassed – as when the silkworm knits a brassiere for Porky Pig in *Porky's Party* (1938), triggering a mortified blush – or disinterested him. Sex was played strictly for laughs. Thus Clampett's secondary characters inclined towards bland sexless androgyny, in disposition as well as anatomy.
>
> (McGilligan, 1980: 153)

These are significant observations and serve to raise a number of issues. As has been stressed, the representation of the body constitutes the basic vocabulary by which particular aspects of masculinity and femininity may be expressed. The depiction of sexuality is clearly a dominant methodology by which to locate gender but it is also the most destabilised and ambivalent arena of representation in the animated cartoon. Tashlin *over-determines* the gender of Petunia Pig through some of the codes cited by Fred Moore, but chiefly, through her fleshly voluptuousness, and her sexual knowingness. Clampett, however, in being less overt reveals the ambiguous space in the animated cartoon which incorporates a number of complex gender discourses. Daffy's striptease engages with the idea of the body as a costume and the necessary vocabulary of feminised gestures which eroticise a dance. Consequently, he highlights the *performance* of gender practices. Porky's embarrassment about a silk brassiere fetishes the thought of *cross-dressing*, a practice which is explicit in many Warner Brothers cartoons, perhaps, chiefly in Chuck Jones' seven-minute distillation of Wagner's Ring Cycle, *What's Opera, Doc?* (1957), in which Bugs becomes Brunnhilde, complete with all the overt signifiers of femininity like eyelashes, lip-stick and long blonde plaits.

These are appendages, of course; merely the accessories required for the impersonation, but, as Kate Davy has noted, 'female impersonation, provides in short, a seemingly endless source of fascination because, unlike male impersonation, the man who appropriates his "opposite" is not simultaneously effaced by it' (Meyer, 1994: 137). Bugs remains 'male', and retains his masculinity, yet looks 'female' and clearly affects his posture and gesture in a feminine way. This is both the performance of gender practices and the significant blurring of gender distinctions, offering the opportunity for humour but also for subversive appropriation.

In recent years, for example, queer politics, the evolution of gay and lesbian ideological critique, has sought to create and appropriate texts which reinforce the idea of redefining historically determined, socially restrictive, definitions of sex and sexuality. As Moe Meyer stresses,

> Queer sexualities become, then, a series of improvised performances whose threat lies in the denial of any social identity derived from any participation in those performances. As a refusal of sexually defined identity, this must also include the denial of the difference upon which such identities have been founded. And it is precisely in the space of this refusal, in the destruction of the homo/hetero binary, that the threat and challenge to bourgeois ideology is queerly executed.
>
> (Meyer, 1994: 3)

The animated cartoon is predicated on such conditions. At any one time Bugs and Daffy *et al.* are merely involved in momentary performances which demonstrate that the definition and recognition of gender representation is in flux. Consequently, both the physical and ideological boundaries of the anthropomorphised body as it exists in the cartoon are perpetually in a state of transition, refusing a consistent identity. As Meyer implies, not only are aspects of masculine and feminine sometimes made indistinguishable, but the received notion of what constitutes the conditions of homosexuality and heterosexuality is also made ambivalent. This is not to say that character representation becomes fixated around the sexless androgyny McGilligan cites as the disappointing credential of Clampett's secondary characters. Rather this places 'sexlessness' and 'androgyny' as arenas in which discourses remain active and constantly open to interpretation.

What further complicates these discourses is the recognition of species. For example, novelist E.M. Forster once posed the question, 'But is Mickey a mouse?', and answered his own question by concluding that 'It is his character rather than his species which signifies'.[5] This view tends to desexualise, and in some senses, de-anthropomorphise the cartoon, prioritising the recognition of behavioural tendencies and outcomes as if the characters were indeed without proper identity. This way of viewing the cartoon essentially returns it to the domain of innocence and the free play of the 'surface of the phenomenon' cited by Eisenstein. It limits the ways in which the characters can be viewed because, once more, it resists the significance of species and sexuality, and most particularly insists upon the acceptance of the Disney cartoon as innocuous, disavowed of political intent or possibility. One only needs, however, to place a Disney cartoon in an explicit political context to see how this apparent innocence merely disguises a whole gamut of ideological possibilities and assertions. Julianne Burton-Carvajal's exemplary work on Disney's part in the USA's war-time 'Good Neighbour Initiative' in Latin America, reveals that *South of the Border* (1941), *Saludos Amigos* (1943) and *The Three Cabelleros* (1945), films made in partial collaboration with Latin-American artists, and constructed with the intention of showing Latin-American culture, all exhibit subversive tendencies. As Carvajal notes:

> Cartoons are an unlikely vehicle for propaganda. Disney is an unlikely locus for lasciviousness. Yet in addition to the predictable fun, frolics and fireworks, *The Three Cabelleros* (1945) indulges its audience in scenes of cross-dressing and cross-species coupling, of blatant sexual punning and predation, in tales of conquest in which the patriarchal unconscious and the imperial unconscious insidiously overlap.[6]

Whilst Donald Duck indulges himself in a highly sensualised *otherness*, which is not unrelated to the physical decadence of *Jungle Drums*, he exhibits, along with his Latino companion, José Carioca, a tendency to define himself through physical experience. The animation codes the excesses of this indulgence in the abstraction of the body and the sexualisation of the environment, another strategy which serves to blur the masculine/feminine boundaries in each scenario. Though Carvajal suggests that these images serve to mask and insinuate 'a patriarchal unconscious' allied to an imperialist sensibility in the films, the imagery may also be identified as the collapse of socio-sexual certainty. Gender and species become almost arbitrary constructions and performances which constitute a number of transgressions and points of contradiction. *Saludos Amigos* and *The Three Cabelleros* (like much cartoon animation) *de-historicise* characters, so Donald, for example, is only a set of personality traits and not a fully rounded, experientially determined character. His expected physical bluster and belligerence is extended to incorporate the rhythm of Latin America, and its attendant association with sensual pleasure. Donald is literally played out through his bodily functions and imperatives, which sometimes operate in ways that render gender and species as unstable, legitimising unusual and excessive modes of behaviour unchecked by social norms. It is difficult to define, for example, what is implied by Donald's desire for a live-action woman, yet it is clear that a number of possible meanings are being generated. Donald's lasciviousness, for example, may be read as an adulterous act if he is re-historicised as Daisy's 'husband'. Similarly, his implied sexual coupling with a woman recalls the tradition of 'animal groom' stories, of which, *Beauty and the Beast* is the best known, and complex notions of bestial sexual taboos (see McLaughlin, 1993; Warner, 1994). This possible excess of meanings is a highly significant factor in the reading of animated films, and requires further address.

Case study: Is Jerry a girl?[7]

From 1940 to 1967, 161 Tom and Jerry cartoons were produced in three distinct eras of production. For the first seventeen years, now seen as the classic period, the films were created by William Hanna and Joseph Barbera at MGM Studios. For a two-year period from 1960 to 1962, the films were made by UPA graduate, Gene Dietch, while from 1963 to 1967, Chuck Jones took on the challenge of sustaining the appeal of the series at the point when the animated cartoon itself seemed in a period of terminal decline.

Throughout these periods, however, Tom and Jerry remained ambiguous in the specificity of their gender, or, rather, in the ways in which the apparent certainty that both Tom and Jerry are 'male' has been manipulated to contradictory and often challenging ends. The instability of form, an intrinsic credential of the animation medium itself, has led to an instability of representational norms, particularly in the creation of comic effects. This is important because the comedy in the films distracts the viewer from noticing how the characters actually look and behave. The audience tends to laugh at what the characters do, not at what they particularly look like, and this serves to further mask the flux of gender positions in the narrative that this case study wishes to foreground.

Over-determining gender

Patrick Brion suggests that one of the most enduring questions raised by the Tom and Jerry cartoon series is 'Was Jerry a Female?' (Brion, 1990: 38). This question clearly arises from the number of occasions in the cartoons when Jerry overtly looks and behaves like a girl within the context of his relationship with Tom. Brion notes:

> The relationship of Tom and Jerry is very curious. It vacillates between hostility and friendship. The complicity of a latent love is carefully sustained by the ambiguity of Jerry's sex. The game between them evolves from teasing to violence. Despite the explosion of several hundred sticks of dynamite and bombs and innumerable blows of all sorts, the two characters keep – and this is in the tradition of the animated cartoon – the same appearance.
>
> (Brion, 1990: 38)

Whilst Brion is correct in his assertion that a latent (heterosexual) love is sustained by the occasional overt signification of Jerry as a female, this overlooks the possibility of a homo-erotic sub-text and, indeed, notions of cross-species coupling and the blurring of gender caused by cross-dressing. Brion also suggests, here, that these sexual concerns become submerged beneath conflict and the maintenance of the same enduring appearance. This neglects the changes which inform their conflict before the resumption of physical continuity, and which are intrinsic to the idea of destabilised gender identities in cartoons in general.

The best, and yet most ambiguous, example of Jerry becoming a female occurs in *Baby Puss* (1942). Interestingly, the cartoon also uses the idea of juvenilisation as feminisation and, ironically, applies it to Tom. Only identified by her legs and skirt, a little girl plays at being 'mother', dressing Tom in a bonnet and nappy, placing him in a cot, and giving him a bottle of milk. Jerry, like three alley cats later in the cartoon, openly mocks him for his childishness and lack of apparent 'toughness'. This initiates the anticipated chase across the child's playroom. Jerry scampers into a doll's house, where (inexplicably) he takes a bath, only to be observed by Tom, as he looks through an upstairs window. While in the bath, Jerry behaves in a highly feminised way, and even sings in a high-pitched tone. Once he notices Tom at the window, he covers his body as if he were covering breasts and genitalia, turning his legs away as he screams in shock, before beating Tom on the nose with a loofah as punishment for his voyeurism. Jerry here is clearly coded as a girl and the intrusive factor of (peeping) Tom's gaze is emphasised. Running from Tom, however, Jerry leaps into bed with a girl doll, who cries 'Mama' in surprise. Perversely, it is now possible to code Jerry as male because he is embarrassed to be next to 'a girl' (coded in bonnet, skirt and frilled panties after the style of Minnie Mouse). Perhaps even more perversely this may be read as an extremely transgressive moment in which the feminised Jerry finds *herself* in a moment of lesbian exchange. The issue is further complicated by the fact that, following a cut-away to Tom, Jerry emerges from the doll's house wearing the doll's clothing, and masquerades as a 'Southern Belle' in the hope of deluding Tom that he is not Jerry. Important to note here is that it is implied that Jerry has undressed the girl doll. There appears to be no sexual implication in this, except perhaps Jerry's recognition that he has colluded with 'a doll', a material artefact which is ostensibly sexually innocent. Her clothes become 'props' for his disguise, but Jerry authenticates his femininity by remaining consistent with his gesture and posture in the bath. He is exposed, however, when his dress falls down, revealing his frilly panties and high heels. Distracted by the little girl's return, Tom lets Jerry escape. Jerry then goes to the playroom window, still wearing the panties and high heels, and overtly displays himself as a pretty young girl to the alley cats by 'showing an ankle', inciting wolf-whistles and lustful stares. At this juncture, it is clear that Jerry has transcended the assumed the knowledge that he is a 'male' rodent, and has become a 'female', made attractive to the maleness of the cats through this highly feminised sexual ritual.

The alley cats then mock Tom for his subjugation by the little girl. They hit him, steal his milk, inflate his face, play catch with him, throw him into a goldfish bowl and finally, in a mock operation, change his wet nappy. Consistently hitting him over the head with a mallet to anaesthetise him, the cats use Tom as a musical instrument, playing his whiskers as harp strings in a wild routine of madcap celebration. This routine relates Tom to the other cats, and is significant in the sense that Tom is coded as a feminised domestic 'kitten' as opposed to a streetwise, sexually knowing, alley 'cat'. His assumed masculinity is normally only judged by his relationship with Jerry, in which his coding as an over-determined male seems consistent. However, it is the lack of consistency in these areas already illustrated which enables legitimate subversive readings. This is further reinforced by the 'carnivalesque' dimensions which characterise the alley cats' invasion of the playroom. Discussing the regenerative aspects of Bakhtin's conception of 'carnival', Karnick and Jenkins stress that 'through carnival, fixed social roles were abandoned in favor of a more fluid conception of identity, the hierarchy was shattered . . .' (Brunovska Karnick and Jenkins, 1995: 271). This is clearly the case in the playroom where the cats subvert dominant sexual codes in the midst of their song and dance. One cat kisses Tom, another (over)dresses as Carmen Miranda (a model for cross-dressing adopted by Daffy Duck in *Yankee Doodle Daffy* (1943)), and also dances with a doll dressed as a maid. This mode of play is entirely subject to its own self-determining laws, creating a fluidity of gender positions which service the sureality of the gag sequences by providing constant surprise. This is largely through violating expectations and the forma-tion of incongruous relationships. Jerry's unexpected over-determination as 'female' incites libidinous rebellion in the cats, and undermines Tom's masculi-nity. The carnivalesque notion of a world turned upside down serves only to further enhance the representation of an ambivalence in orthodox sexual identity (see Lindvall and Melton, 1994).

Jerry's 'femininity' is largely determined by costume or moments of 'delicate' behaviour. In similar scenarios to that in *Baby Puss*, Jerry becomes feminine through his movements as a dancing girl in *Mouse for Sale* (1955), once again protecting his top half as if it were naked after having his disguise as a white mouse washed away revealing his real brown fur. This is taken to its logical extreme by Chuck Jones in *Snowbody Loves Me* (1964), when Jerry becomes a ballerina and dances in a tutu. Jones' more lyrical approach to the Tom and Jerry series is exemplified here. It also demonstrates the redesign of Jerry in Jones' films to good effect. Jones gives Jerry bigger ears, makes him a little plumper and accentuates his 'sweetness' in smaller, more deliberate gestures. The slower pace of the films supports the softer 'feminised' Jerry in essentially 'gagless' sequences which prioritise the grace of the animated movement for its own sake. In many ways, the narrative and context, as well as Jerry, are gendered feminine in Jones' films.

Whilst it is rarely in doubt that Tom is 'masculine', even if sometimes 'fem-inised' in the presence of other cats, he occasionally cross-dresses in the spirit of deceiving someone. This 'disguise' motif occurs in *Fraidy Cat* (1942), where he wears a set of curtains as a dress when he sits afraid after listening to 'The Witching Hour', and in *Flirty Bird* (1945), in which he disguises himself as a female eagle to distract a male eagle protecting Jerry. This is especially pronounced in the Jones' vehicle, *The Brothers Carry-Mouse-off* (1965), when Tom becomes a perfumed female mouse, the catalyst once more for carnivalesque delirium. Jerry is initially attracted to Tom as a mouse, thus coding himself 'male', but he is deterred by the presence of more overtly masculine mice, who are also in pursuit of Tom. In trying to escape from the mice, Tom is then also pursued by cats believing him to be their prey. Ironically, the cartoon, thus reverts to its normal orthodoxy as a cat and mouse chase narrative, but with the main characters being redefined either by species or gender. The 'gags' in this sequence thus either result from the over-determination of gender, or the revision of Tom and Jerry as a set of dehistoricised character traits.

Significantly, though, some of the most poignant moments of gender destabilisation happen when Tom is behaving in a specifically masculine way, directing his lust towards an over-feminised (usually) white kitten. This brings out a particular kind of jealousy in Jerry, and, as he is reminded by the little green devil of envy in *Smitten Kitten* (1952), 'Everytime Tom meets a kitten, he falls in love, and that means you have problems again!' Tom is at his most Averyesque in these scenarios, and his gender is secure. Interestingly, however, in *Puss 'n' Toots* (1942), *Texas Tom* (1950) and *Casanova Cat* (1951), all Tom seduction scenarios, Jerry is presented as a possible competitor with Tom, especially as in all three he kisses the kitten in a spirit of victory over Tom. In *Solid Serenade* (1946) and *Salt Water Tabby* (1947), though Jerry is not identified as a masculine competitor, he does much to distract Tom from his attempted seductions, in the spirit of both spoiling his chances and winning back his attention. Such jealousy is also foregrounded in the narrative of *Springtime for Thomas* (1946). Jerry writes a forged love note to 'Dream Boy', the alley cat, from 'Toodles', the white kitten, to initiate conflict with Tom. Allied with Tom against Dream Boy, Jerry asserts their relationship, before he, in turn, is distracted by a passing female mouse. In *Blue Cat Blues* (1956), an unusually bleak episode, both Tom and Jerry contemplate suicide over lost loves and take solace in the inescapable and eternal bond that their relationship represents. It is no wonder that Tom kisses Jerry after a horrible nightmare in *Heavenly Puss* (1949) and after an extended chase in *Sweet Mouse-story of Life* (1965), the latter illustrating Jones' desire to romanticise the couple by temporarily feminising Jerry's response to Tom's kisses by giving him coy eyes, shuffling feet and a Disneyesque bashful demeanour. Simultaneously, then, the Tom and Jerry texts generate readings which can support both a cross-species heterosexual bond, a cross-species homosexual bond, and same species heterosexual bonds.

Contextual gendering

If certain moments represent over-determination in gender design discourses, other sequences imply a subtler view of gender positioning. This, once more, informs aspects of Jerry's narrative function in certain films. If Jerry is sometimes highly feminised in relation to Tom, he is determinedly masculine when he is being pragmatic in relation to the protection of others, most particularly, Nibbles (sometimes called Tuffy), a little mouse, which featured in thirteen films, and the little duckling, which featured in eight films. Jerry becomes more muscular, walks with an upright confident stride, and less attention is paid to his face as a mechanism of 'cuteness', especially with regard to half-closed or wide eyes, or fluttering eyelashes. Rather, this is transferred to his highly juvenilised compatriots, the little mouse and duckling. His assertion and practicality are coded 'masculine', at least in so far as it informs his more overtly physical presence, echoing the muscular design of his cousin in *Muscles Mouse* (1951). It is in these moments that Jerry transcends size and appears to take on Tom on his own terms. As I stressed earlier, it is the condition of the cartoon that creatures have abilities and powers that they do not possess outside of a cartoon vocabulary, but the scale of abilities and powers does not necessarily equate with the creature that has them. Jerry can wield heavy objects as well as Tom and can take equal punishment; his size rarely impinges on his ability to combat Tom's aggression.

The notion of size, which is central to gender coding in the 'real world' relates more to sight gags in these cartoons. For example, in one episode, *Jerry and Jumbo* (1953), Jerry befriends a lost baby elephant who, despite his size, relies on the help and protection of 'a mouse'. He becomes instrumental in the deception of Tom, however, when he curls his trunk into a knot, paints it black, and superficially looks like a larger mouse. Tom is driven mad by the playfulness of Jerry and Jumbo as they constantly exchange places frustrating Tom's efforts both to capture Jerry and to understand why he apparently keeps fluctuating in size. This is compounded by the arrival of the baby elephant's mother, who joins in the game, and looks like an even bigger 'mouse'. In this situation, the rapid shift in power and status relations diminishes Tom's 'masculinity', especially when something taller and wider (including 'a mother' and 'a baby'), is coded as being more 'masculine' in moments of conflict. The premise of the 'gag' here – the escalating size of a small creature – overrides the necessity for gender certainty. The cartoon environment recontextualises gender by deploying established and expected gender codes in destabilised and unexpected modes of character behaviour and narrative necessity.

This *contextual gendering* also informs the redefinition of Jerry as a mermaid in *The Cat and the Mermouse* (1949) when Jerry loses his feet and gains a tail. In Susan White's discussion of the role of the mermaid in contemporary film, most notably in Disney's *The Little Mermaid* (1989) and the Disney/Touchstone vehicle, *Splash* (1984), she deploys psychoanalytic theory in determining that the mermaid's tail 'despite its phallic shape . . . is not easily defined as either male or female, as threatening or reassuring' (White, 1993: 186). This ambivalence further complicates readings of Jerry as mermouse, readings already confused by the fact that he violates the notion of a mermaid as half human/half fish, by being half animal/half fish, a cross-species hybrid. Jerry may be read as either male or female in many of the Tom and Jerry texts, but this ambiguity is further compounded by the gender indeterminacy of the tail. This proves threatening for Tom when he encounters Jerry underwater, at first rubbing his eyes with disbelief, then having his eyes pop-out in Avery style, as he cannot come to terms with the ease of Jerry's behaviour in circumstances so distant from and different to their 'normal' domesticity. Reassurance only comes at the climax of the film with Jerry's return to his normal state. This only occurs as the viewer discovers that the whole of the underwater sequence is in fact a hallucination that Tom has experienced while being unconscious, evidently having been pulled from the water after nearly drowning. Tom's hallucination clearly reveals his fears of a reconstituted 'Jerry'; fears located in the otherness of Jerry as an ambivalently gendered or genderless creature. Contextual gendering, in this instance, is about the blurring of gender and identity, a destabilisation which, once again, facilitates the comic exchanges resulting from the recognition of 'difference'.

Body and identity

As suggested at the beginning of this chapter, the body in animation is a form constantly in flux, always subject to redetermination and reconstruction. In the Tom and Jerry series, body formations carry with them particular agendas about identity. Tom, for example, is perpetually taking the shape of an object during particularly violent exchanges or chase sequences. He becomes a set of bowling pins in Jerry's Cousin (1951), a waterfountain in Hatch Up Your Troubles (1949) and Posse Cat (1954), a string of paper dolls in Cat-napping (1951), and a doormat in The Brothers Carry-Mouse-off (1965). It may be argued that when Tom becomes an object he is rendered both genderless and without identity. He is merely the subject and object of the 'gag'. This is achieved by violating the consistency of Tom as a character through relocating him as an infinitely flexible two-dimensional form. When Tom is hit by an iron, his character experiences pain, provoking sympathy in the viewer, while his form instantly changes into the shape of an iron, provoking laughter. This process of temporary depersonalisation diffuses the extent of the violence and legitimises the comic aspect of the incident. It is possible, however, to also argue that once Tom becomes a 'form', then his shape is redetermined in gender terms also. If it is possible to gender the whole visual environment of the animated film, then this is clearly an area which can be fruitfully discussed.

It may be suggested, for example, that dark colour codings and angular shapes possess masculine credentials while lighter pastel shades and curved lines are more feminine. Though these superficial extremes reflect stereotypical gender orthodoxies, they are useful starting points in the further address of contextual gendering. Is Tom 'masculine', for example, when he becomes an iron or a door-mat, but 'feminine' when he is a string of paper dolls or a waterfountain and, further, does this reflect upon his status in the narrative at the time? Obviously, these are questions which need to be addressed within a broader framework of enquiry, but clearly inform the view that the animated body can facilitate a number of readings that place gender orthodoxies in crisis, a factor, as has already been

213

stressed, which favours the representation of the 'feminine', challenging, as it does, broadly masculine agendas and design discourses, in both the live-action and animated forms.

This also becomes especially interesting when the body is portrayed as a costume in its own right. Tom and Jerry strip away their outer fur as if it was a set of clothes, often revealing a set of underwear or naked skin. In *Of Feline Bondage* (1965), directed by Chuck Jones, Jerry becomes invisible and starts to shave Tom, who inevitably retaliates in kind. By the end of the cartoon, Tom sits with the top of his head and upper torso shaved, wearing an undervest, his hair intact on his legs and face, while Jerry sits shaved, appearing half-undressed in a fur bikini, his remaining hair resembling a fur swimming cap. Here body-as-costume clearly codes Tom as male and Jerry as female, their (romantic) intimacy acknowledged in the final sequence as they break into laughter in recognition of the ridiculousness of the situation. The film also features a female fairy, drawn like Jerry, but taller and dressed in the mode of costume-as-gendered appendage (i.e. blue blouse, green skirt, and high heels). The animated form essentially determines that the body-as-costume and the costume-as-gendered appendage have equal status. That is to say, the physical materiality of the body (in the cartoon) operates in the same way as any representation of clothing or accessory. This still raises the question, however, of nakedness. When, as it were, is a cartoon character naked? It may be argued that all cartoon creatures are naked if they have no costume, but this is clearly undermined by the example above in which bodily fur is treated as an outer garment, a frequent occurrence in many cartoons. If the skin beneath the fur is a cartoon character's ultimate nakedness, then nakedness is without gender because no physical signification of male or female remains. That said, the hair that remains on the skin after the body garment has been removed may still constitute a gender determinant. A 'stubbled' skin may still signify maleness while 'smoothness' may be understood as intrinsically female. The first largely leaves the body subject to a comic reading while the latter significantly juvenilises and/ or eroticises the body, sometimes, once again, redetermining gender, for example, in Daffy's striptease in *Wise Quacking Duck* cited on p. 205.

The body, naked or otherwise, in the cartoon, is fundamentally free of the aging process. Tom and Jerry were perennially the same age in the Hanna Barbera period, unless aging itself could be used as a gag, for example, in *The Missing Mouse* (1953), when Tom rapidly ages with worry as he realises that the white mouse he is vigorously washing isn't Jerry, but an explosive mouse who has escaped from a laboratory, and who will 'go off' at the slightest touch! It is certainly the case, however, that in the post-Hanna Barbera period, Tom does seem to age while the perennially youthful Jerry seems even more baby-like. Chuck Jones, by his own admission, never really comfortable with the kinetic violence of the characters (see Peary and Peary, 1980: 131–2), gave Tom and Jerry a lyrical, almost nostalgic feel and, in doing so, humanised them to the point where Tom, in particular, had intimations of mortality. In *Year of the Mouse* (1965), Tom is placed in a series of situations, contrived by an invisible Jerry and his friend, where he seems to be committing suicide – by shooting, hanging and stabbing himself – and, although he finally turns the tables, the cartoon posits the real notion of death within its text. Tom is also seriously injured in *The Cat's Me-Ouch* (1965), and far from instantly recovering in the spirit of the Hanna Barbera cartoons, he is covered in bandages, uses crutches and is hospitalised. It is the final irony that in the last Tom and Jerry cartoon, *Purr-chance to Dream* (1967), Tom actually takes sleeping pills to help him sleep – a sleep from which, of course, he never wakes.[8]

Tom and Jerry are merely one model of animated animals playing out the complexities of gender identity and social positioning, and the model of address used here raise more issues than it has properly engaged with. Over-determination of gender, contextual gendering, and the body and identity are appropriate starting points, however, because they are posited upon the intrinsic link between the fluid language of animation and the *inevitable* engagement first, with the representation of men and women, but second, and more complexly, with the representation of creatures, objects and environments which are playing out masculine and feminine agendas, both by accident and by design. The more removed animation is from representations of the real world, the more its texts are subject to the kind of fissure which locates gender in a contradictory and ambiguous way. Issues concerning the representation of race in the cartoon operate a little differently, however, largely because the representation of African-Americans, the Japanese etc., has been crude, perpetuating racist stereotypes which do not allow alternative readings. Importantly, though, contemporary scholarship is attempting to properly contextualise these works, address the role of the National Association for the Advancement of Coloured People (NAACP) in America with regard to animation, and promote the evolution of national cinemas as a mode of resistance to these dominant forms.

Race in context

The issue of the representation of race in animation is essentially clouded by the self-evident racism of cartoon caricaturing from the early teens of the century to the late 1940s.[9] Klein has usefully delineated the sources of graphic caricature in the depiction of black people, and suggests that American animators used E.W. Kemble's illustrations of the freed slave; the Dogtown lithographs of Currier and Ives; images from the popular *Uncle Remus* tales; jokes from the minstrel shows and black cast musicals like *Showboat*; one-reel films of black swing-bands in the 1930s and 1940s; and finally, the comic strip and radio incarnations of *Amos 'n' Andy* (Klein, 1993: 191). These stereotypes found fresh purchase in the light of the general agendas about 'race' during World War II. With the imperative to properly delineate 'the enemy' came the inevitable delineation of 'the other'. Interestingly, though, the war was also a period in which the NAACP made proper claims for the recognition of racial equality as a principle in the light of the ways in which the Axis powers had mobilised racial hatred as one of their major political agendas (see Cripps, 1993: 52). Racial stereotyping in the USA was familiar, almost reassuring to white audiences in its popular fictions and entertainment, and continued to be so until the 1950s. While such stereotyping is inexcusable, it may be understood as a product of an insensitive climate so naturalised in its political inequalities that these kind of representations were perceived as an aesthetic orthodoxy, operating as a playful rather than malicious presentation of black tropes. The perpetuation of such representation, ironically, seemed a manifestation of the status quo that the USA was drawn into the war to maintain. However, the ideological questions raised by the outbreak and conduct of war, did aid the black political cause. Indeed, it may be argued, that black artists had already subverted white orthodoxies by insinuating black culture in previously white-only domains of expression in the 1930s. Those artists who worked with the Fleischer Brothers or at the Warner Brothers Studios were recognised as important figures, bringing a different mode of entertainment into a popular form, still perceived and dismissed as part of low cultural ethos. This, in many ways, explains their acceptance, and their featured presence.

Clearly, the Fleischer Brothers, and their predominantly white audience, only partially understood the sinister scenarios of 'Minnie the Moocher' or 'St James Infirmary Blues', sung by renowned orchestra leader, Cab Calloway, when they appeared in albeit more adult cartoon noirs, featuring Betty Boop. Similarly, the ambiguity of the line, 'You gave my wife a coca-cola, so you could play on her vagola', as sung by Louis Armstrong, from a song called 'I Wish You were Dead, You Rascal, You', escaped both the censors and the Fleischer Brothers, who merely couched Armstrong's live-action presence in the cartoon within a stereo-typical scenario featuring cannibals chasing Koko and Bimbo in the jungle (see Cabarga, 1988: 64–72). While the character of Bosko, the black boy, who featured in the first Warner Brothers Looney Tunes, cannot be considered a subversive representation, once more, the presence of black-oriented musical forms in films like Sinkin' in the Bathtub (1930) and Box Car Blues (1931), determined an ethos in the cartoons which half-promoted the codes and conditions of black aesthetics (see Beck and Friedwald, 1989). It was this aesthetic that was actively deployed, enjoyed and exploited in Bob Clampett's films, Coal Black and De Sebben Dwarfs (1943), an obvious parody of the Disney film (see Klein, 1993: 192–6), and Tin Pan Alley Cats (1943), in which a character, based on pianist, Fats Waller, is literally blown away by the raucous exuberance of the jazz idiom into a surreal heaven. Here Stalin kicks a blue-bottomed, long-necked Hitler; huge red lips operate independently of a face or body; legs walk independently of their owner; and a 'string' band made of elastic plays a tune!

By the end of the film, the Fats Waller figure finds that he cannot ultimately cope in jazz heaven and joins the neighbouring gospel choir singing 'Gimme that old time religion'. This epitomises a recurring motif of the containment of black idioms which, as Klein has suggested, 'cloaks White anxiety about modernization' (Klein, 1993: 188). Further, it signifies a deep ambivalence about 'otherness', half-attracted to its freedoms, half-frightened of its ultimate repercussions. In *Minnie the Moocher* (1932) and *Betty Boop's Snow White* (1933), for example, Betty Boop is drawn into the dark, mysterious underworld, characterised by trans-gressive behaviour and taboo imagery. Even in its crudest forms, representa-tions of black-ness or black-oriented contexts, operate as signifiers of danger and cultural threat. Its *potency*, however misunderstood, is not ignored. The sensuality and abandon of certain black caricatures is simultaneously frighten-ing and profoundly appealing to white audiences (see Watkins, 1995: 207). When couched as part of an inevitably destructive 'otherness', as in the Fleischer Brothers' *Jungle Drums*, black characters have no identity but as the cannibalistic savage native. When absorbed into white mainstream culture, however, the black idiom works as a mechanism by which white animators and audiences can rehearse their fears and play out scenarios which are suppo-sedly outside WASP society. These include the temptation of excessive physicality, over-determined sexuality and sexual practice, gambling, drinking etc. Black caricature is ultimately the reflection of the apparent prohibitions placed upon white desire. Black stereotypes are essentially the symbolic embodiment of white hypocrisy.

As Smoodin has argued, though, the representation of black people in film texts bore close relation to representations of other marginalised and oppressed social groups, and most specifically, women and the working classes (Smoodin, 1993: 44–71). Consequently, film bills were constructed in a way which appeased these social groupings, simultaneously locating such groupings as discernible markets, and operating as a mode of social control. For example, in 1934, the Frank Capra feature, *It Happened One Night*, was paired with *The Lion Tamer*, one of only two Van Bueren cartoons featuring Amos and Andy, black characters played by two white performers, Freeman Gosden and Charles Correll. *Amos 'n' Andy* was the most popular radio comedy of the 1920s and 1930s and was characterised by Amos' and Andy's attempts to improve their social and financial status in numerous madcap scenarios, normally involving their manipulative friend, Kingfish, and usually resulting in Andy falling prey to his absurd schemes. This kind of story had great comic purchase, and in a similar way to Depression-era comedies like *It Happened One Night*, provided both identification and escapism. Those most affected and disenfranchised by poverty, were encouraged to find solace in laughing about their predicament. The success of the *Amos 'n' Andy* radio series persuaded the Van Beuren studios to make it as a cartoon in the hope that its popularity would be maintained in another medium. Unfortunately, for the studio, this proved not to be the case, and like the later *Amos 'n' Andy* television series, suffered because blackface caricature ultimately undermined the persua-siveness of black *characters* in the sound idiom. Even though the Van Beuren cartoons are well executed (though far behind the Disney works of the same period), their form fundamentally distracted from the quality of the writing in the radio series, and the necessity for the public to *imagine* what the characters looked like. Even though it may be argued that the radio series was still informed

217

by racist traits, it self-evidently could not create an image of the characters, and clearly presented Amos and Andy with a degree of complexity and streetwise cunning not present in the cartoons. Inevitably, the cartoon sought to present the characters in *cartoonal* terms and prioritised the visual and physical over the verbal, and thus, diminished the established personas of the couple. Further, this drew attention only to their stereotypical representation which, however necessary to the cartoon, merely highlights its racist dimension.

In *Rasslin' Match* (1934), Andy is persuaded by Kingfish to take part in a wrestling match with 'Bullneck Mooseface'. Already humiliated by his own shadow when 'shadow-boxing' in the gym, and wholly out of condition when training, Andy, still wearing his hat and smoking his cigar, attempts to fight Bullneck, who in the course of the match metamorphoses into a moose. Their bodies become knotted and Andy bites his own leg in the ensuing attempts to liberate himself. He bounces off the ropes a number of times, and after an accidental head-clash, falls on his opponent and wins the bout. In *The Lion Tamer* (1934), Andy is this time persuaded to be a lion-tamer at the circus on the basis that it will not be a real lion that he is supposedly taming, but 'Brother Crawford and Lightning dressed up like a lion' in pantomime style. Inevitably, Andy ends up attempting to tame the real lion, but before he realises, he puts his head in the lion's mouth and is surprised when he does not find Brother Crawford and Lightning! An interesting dimension to these cartoons is that there are audiences at both the wrestling match and the circus, and perhaps unsurprisingly, they are wholly populated by black characters, but obviously, the cartoon played to principally white audiences. Despite the prevailing social distinctions between black and white, the everyday conditions that they actually shared informed these simple stories and the contexts in which they were seen. Sometimes, therefore, the race dimension may be seen as a less important aspect within some stories when the dominant narrative concerning *common* experience overcomes the possibly negative aspects of its presentation.

Unquestionably, there are few arguments that justify or legitimise the kinds of representation of black characters that we may witness in the cartoons addressed here. Beck and Friedwald remain coy, for example, when they cite Bugs Bunny's adversary in Tex Avery's *All This and Rabbit Stew* (1941) as 'a lazy hunter' (Beck and Friedwald, 1989: 121). This is a self-evident caricature of the thick-lipped 'lazy darkie' which prevailed as a popular stereotype. Watkins argues that the perpetuation of such images was partially as a result of an ignorance of black history, and therefore, the possibility of more accurate representations was unlikely, (Watkins, 1995: 192), but interestingly, the response to this by white artists in this period, is not to revise their view and depiction of black characters, but to ignore or marginalise them, or find new victims for their jokes. One might suggest that some degree of race sensitivity had taken place, for example, when the same sequence in which Bugs humiliates the black hunter in a routine with a hollow log, in *All This and Rabbit Stew* is re-used in Bob Clampett's last Warner Brothers cartoon, *The Big Snooze* (1946), in which the black hunter is replaced by

Elmer Fudd. Equally one might suggest that by this time Elmer was properly established as Bugs' adversary, and that the sequence suited their scenarios, and thus, was used to save time and money, and engage the popular audience on purely commercial terms.

This notion of 'absence' is often coupled with allusion to black stereotypes in marginalised roles. For example, in Disney's *Three Orphan Kittens* (1935), a black maid is depicted only by her legs and long anticipates a similar representation of 'Mammy Two Shoes' in the Hanna Barbera *Tom and Jerry* cartoons of the 1940s and 1950s. MGM's version of racial sensitivity in this case was to merely make her an Irish maid in later cartoons (see Adams, 1991; Brion, 1990). Perhaps one of the most influential aspects of change in the animated cartoon, however, was the shift of emphasis in representation in comic strips. Pre-war strips like *Joe and Asbestos* and *The Spirit* became more realistic and, therefore, more racially and ideologically sensitive. Similarly, with the escalating popularity of comic books during the war, there was a recognition that their influence could be profound. Parental groups mobilised to form the Parents Institute and produced *True Comics*, while the Writers' War Board released *Master Comics* and the National Urban League brought out *All-Negro Comics*, all of which demonstrated more sensitive, revisionist attitudes towards the representation of race (Cripps, 1993: 154). The crass caricatures of George Pal's puppetoons featuring Jasper were recognised by Pal himself as poorly judged, and *John Henry and Inky Poo* (1946) and *Tribute to Duke Ellington* (1947) were made in what Cripps describes as a spirit of 'atonement for his guilt' (ibid.: 186). The chief agent of change, though, was the NAACP, and its response to the post-war insensitivities of Disney's *Song of the South* (1946), a part-cartoon, part-live-action feature based on the *Uncle Remus* stories.

Though lobbied by black political groups and academics, Disney perpetuated a highly sentimentalised version of the 'good darkie' stereotype in the film, but the enormously endearing performance of James Baskette as Uncle Remus only served to confuse the political issues raised by the very making of such a self-evidently regressive narrative in the post-war period. Critical lobbying for an Oscar for Baskette proved more successful than the political lobbying which could not properly clarify its objections to this system of representation, when the character seemed so dignified, clever and appealing. This apparently 'positive' representation ultimately seemed, however, to once more diminish the status and identity of black people by still couching them in a plantation-era idiom and, thus, a mode of behaviour which was subservient, and inevitably 'other'. The modern black person; the modern black, *middle-class* person; the modern black *academic*; the modern black *parent*, saw no place for this persona in contemporary society. As a generational anomaly it was not part of a progressive black agenda, nor part of the educational premises that it was necessary to bring to previously disenfranchised black children. *Song of the South* was thus a crucial element of the debate, not merely to revise the representation of race in animation, but in film-making in general (see Cripps, 1993: 187–94).

In many senses, debates about 'good' or 'bad' representation are not particularly useful, but clearly discourses about *misrepresentation* are very important. Though the depiction of black characters is a dominant racial trope, it is matched in cartoon animation by a preoccupation with the Arabian or Oriental stereotype. In Chapter Four, Disney's *Aladdin* was addressed, suggesting that it had chimed with timely debates about Orientalist representation. Said suggests that Orientalism is a discourse through which the West has colonised and reinvented the Orient as a mode of 'otherness' which simultaneously distantiates the dangers and complexities within the alien Eastern culture and encourages a belief in the identity and ideological superiority of the native Western culture (see Said, 1978; Said, 1994). This occurs in cartoon animation from the Fleischer Brothers' *Popeye Meets Ali Baba and his Forty Thieves* (1937) and *Aladdin and his Wonderful Lamp* (1939), through to the version of *Aladdin* made by Disney. The dark, sensual, often despotic, mysteries of the Orientalist identity in these films is once more the cloak for a multitude of Western anxieties about the loss of control and power. It is no accident that Disney's *Aladdin* may be read as a thinly veiled metaphor for the USA engagement with Saddam Hussein and the Iraqi military in the Gulf War. Indeed, it is almost the perfect vehicle to represent the enlightened, technologically advanced, self-evidently just rationale of the West, not only in its acts of political intervention, but in its popular entertainment.

Such texts often emerge at a point of national crisis but, more importantly in the contemporary era, such films indicate an anxiety about the collapse of global imperialism and decolonisation. The easy polarities of moral and political opposition between capitalist and communist nations have broken down. Political independence, achieved through the increasing fragmentation of territories worldwide, has resulted in the drive towards modernisation, and the reconstruction of cultural identities through the reclamation of regional and national traditions. Ironically, this agenda has always informed the field of animation, because studios in many nations, dedicated to the preservation of a national identity have had (1) to resist the influence of political agendas and censorship imposed on the creative context by authoritarian or totalitarian regimes, and (2) produce work which denies the ideological and aesthetic influence of Disney animation. In order to become distinctive, animation studios have had to look back and reclaim their own graphic and performance traditions and reinvent old myths and folk-tales from their own countries for new audiences. This has led to a number of countries creating work which is for, and about, their own history, culture and socio-political identity, and serves to constitute a *national* animated cinema dedicated to the particular and specific orientations of its people, and their creative heritage.

Even though no conception of *national* animated cinema could possibly encompass the range and purpose of animated films in any one country, there is a sense in which the mobilisation and definition of creative work which is an expression of a variety of national interests both identifies the work and prevents its assimilation into other areas of aesthetic style or cultural recognition. For example, in the post-perestroika period of national fragmentation in the former Soviet Union, animator and former Poet Laureate, Andrei Khrzhanovsky, creator of such extra-ordinary films as *The Grey Bearded Lion* (1994), *The King's Breakfast* (1985) and *There Was a Man Called Kosyavin* (1966), argues that animated work in Russia has survived periods of despotic rule, bureaucratic and military oppression, and the loss of any discernible national ethos, better than any other creative apparatus. He further suggests that the animated film should, therefore, be instrumental in the recovery of cultural coherence because the diversity of works in animation made by such luminaries as Yuri Norstein (see Chapter Three), Rein Raamat, Priit Parn, and Gazmend Leka (see Bendazzi, 1994: 367–82) represents the historical continuity of art and culture *in spite of* social and political change. Similarly, in China, the work of the Shanghai studio has operated in ways that have emerged as anything from a resistance to Japanese invasion through to a rejection of the Disney style. In returning to traditional texts in children's literature, the theatrical conventions of the Beijing Opera, and the six principles of Chinese painting conceptualised by Xie He (see Farquhar, 1993: 4–28), the animators of the new school of Chinese animation were able to recall what Marie-Clare Quiquemelle calls 'the originality of Chinese culture' (Quiquemelle, 1991: 182) through new technical forms. These were, principally, animated paper-folding techniques and animation achieved through an ink and wash style similar to that of Caroline Leaf (see Chapter Three), but more akin to older traditions of Chinese watercolour paint-ing. These differing approaches self-evidently produced works in which *national character* may be viewed in a completely different way than that played out in Disney features. Such distinctiveness ensures that representation may only occur upon the terms and principles of the animators themselves, and the aesthetic and cultural traditions they are working in, rather than in the hyper-realist terms of global Disneyfication.[10]

6

ANIMATION AND AUDIENCES:

'My mother used to call me Thumper!'

Cinema and the spectator

The relationship between cinema, both as an institution and a practice, and the assumed movie audience has been a rich and complex one, provoking many areas of enquiry and discussion. Film theorists have addressed 'the audience' in a number of ways, and invoked arguments about the influence and effect of movies themselves and the cinematic apparatus in which the audience participates.[1] These debates constitute an important prologue to the primary research undertaken for this chapter, but will only be summarised here in order to contextualise the particular discussion about the relationship between the spectator and the animated film. Though audiences had previously been directly addressed through the supporting publicity materials, journalism, and film-related publications that specifically related to the release of certain films and the promotion of particular stars, it was not until the 1970s that 'the audience' was properly theorised in a *conceptual* way. Following the discourse theory of Althusser and Barthes, theorists essentially determined the audience as a *subject*, and not as a set of undifferentiated individuals and, thus, engaged with the idea of cinema as an *ideological* apparatus, and one which created certain structures of address which demanded that an audience recognise and participate in certain narrational codes and conventions, informed by a number of possible discourses (i.e. political, representational, psychoanalytical etc.). These terms and conditions were further complicated by the idea that cinema enabled particular kinds of viewing practice, ranging from the voyeuristic to the culturally empowering, dependant upon how one viewed the very construction of films, or their contextual apparatus. Key issues emerged which have characterised some of this book, thus far, chiefly, that cinema facilitates the male gaze, constructs particular models of socialised identification out of Western practices, and determines dominant and preferred agendas concerning representation and modes of permission, power and order.

Implicitly, it has been suggested that animation, as a form, subverts many of the orthodoxies of mainstream live-action cinema and, indeed, even operates in a more radical way than various kinds of counter-cinema have sought to do. This is not to argue that all forms of animated film intrinsically challenge these codes but, clearly, some of the narrational and comic structures discussed earlier do work in a number of different ways. The points raised as matters of definition and interpretation are essentially couched in the assumption of the audience as a specific kind of *subject*, which differs from the assumed subject of the live-action film because of the unique conditions created by animation. Equally, the discussion has largely been predicated on particular approaches to animation as a text, and as such does not engage with other types of address which may look, for example, at the cognitive affects of the animated film, and the specific role of the *individual*. Inevitably, work on the effect which cartoons and animated advertising have on children has been carried out (see, for example, Ellis and Sekyra, 1972; Stutts *et al.*, 1981), but little has been done in regard to ethnographic studies of particular audiences, or the study of audience reception of cartoons and animated films in particular historically determined periods. It is clear that many governments and agencies have used the animated film for educational and propaganda purposes for many years, and particularly in periods of war and crisis. Further, animation has always figured in commercials – the Fleischer Brothers Studio, for example, allied their 'bouncing ball' singalong cartoons of the late 1920s and early 1930s to the advertising needs of the Oldsmobile Car Company – and animation still features in many product campaigns worldwide in the contemporary era.[2]

Animation self-evidently reaches large audiences, appeals to them, and has an effect, but the specificity of this effect needs further research, and some of the points raised in the following analyses are merely preliminary ideas which anticipate such work. It has already been suggested, for example, that audiences are reclaiming and revising the meanings of animated films with regard to their own gendered, ethnicised or sexual gaze, and that other kinds of critical interpellation are achieved by addressing how post-modern reflexivity necessitates the viewer to engage with the text in a different way. Obviously, more work will follow, but the following case studies, first, recontextualise animation within a historical moment, and second, address the influence and effect of animated films that were viewed as a child, but remembered as an adult. These case studies are specifically concerned with the feature films from the Walt Disney Studio.

The Disney version

We know that they are . . . drawings, and not living beings.
We know that they are projections of drawings on a screen.
We know that they are . . . 'miracles' and tricks of technology,
that such beings don't really exist.
But at the same time:
We *sense* them as alive.
We *sense* them as moving.
We *sense* them as existing and even thinking.

(Sergei Eisenstein, quoted in Leyda, 1988: 55)

Everyone, it seems, has a childhood memory of seeing a Disney film. This is such a taken-for-granted, yet uninterrogated fact, that it seems absurd that little attention has been given to Disney films and the nuanced responses of their audiences. Statistics mount concerning how many people worldwide have seen Disney feature films, or purchased them on video, implicitly suggesting that commercial success is a self-evident barometer of enjoyment and acceptance. Critical reaction to the Disney canon has always been mixed, and largely constitutes the discourse about animation itself (see Peary and Peary, 1980: 49–58, 90–2; Smoodin, 1994), but scant address has been given to the actual agendas of the viewing public who attend Disney films. One might presume that this is part of the overall neglect of animation, but also add that such work might suggest certain disparities between particular responses and the eagerness to promote a specific highly idealised model of innocent, ideologically sound, relentlessly optimistic, family entertainment, somehow safe from the vagaries and difficulties of the world. It has probably always been the case that the particular experience of watching Disney films has been much more complex, testing a range of psychological and emotional issues in spectators.

My own early reminiscence, seemingly not untypical, testifies to this, in the sense that it demonstrates the affective aspects of Disney films, and their enduring potential to influence and inform later life. I was provoked into deep sobs of terror by the wicked Queen in Snow White and the Seven Dwarfs, and refused to be cajoled out from beneath my seat in the cinema, despite my mother's pitiful assurances that the dwarves would be back soon. The dwarves had been amusing, if a little strange, and I had clearly invested my empathetic eggs in their comic basket. I remember thinking that Snow White herself was 'yuck', once again, a not unrepresentative response to anything romantic or sentimental that intervened in the comedy routines. As my study, discussed later in this chapter, proves, however, this was only because I had yet to discover the imperatives of the loins, or the desire to be more beautiful, standard responses by others to the same agenda. The terror inspired by the Queen, though, was a more universal dimension, and does inform a number of people's subsequent views about their girlfriends, sisters, mothers and grandmothers alike. For me, that early traumatic moment clearly relates to a particular aesthetic about certain women that still fills me with dread and uncertainty. Indeed, I vividly remember not completing a particular jigsaw with the Queen's face on it because I couldn't confront the image again. Similarly, on one occasion, a sudden glimpse of a woman who looked like the wicked Queen on the bus home also gave me a considerable shock! Thankfully, I am not alone in such reactions, and it is this phenomenon which will be discussed in this chapter.

The quotation that begins this section, by Eisenstein, properly identifies that the empathetic and cathartic effects caused by Disney films are all the more extraordinary in the light of the fact that these are merely drawings, and not even as purportedly 'real' as characters in live-action films. Distinguishing between the representative fantasies and fictions of the cinema and the exactitudes of the real world has always been problematic, largely due to the spectator's desire to confuse the codes and conditions of their experience. The spectator is intrinsically bound up in a particular relationship to a film, identifying, sympathising, resisting, endorsing, dismissing, etc. in the course of a film narrative. The interaction between the film, with its highly constructed, deliberately manipulative strategies to engage and affect the viewer, and the spectator, who brings a personal perspective to matters of interpretation and experience, is a relative and some-times complex process. Numerous theories have emerged which engage with this process (see Brannigan, 1984; Mulvey, 1989; Hansen, 1991; Mayne, 1993; Denzin, 1995), but few take account of the special circumstances created by animation, and most particularly, do not take account of the *adult* response to animated films. It is obvious that animation that has been especially created for television since the 1950s takes account of the adult audience which engages with such pro-grammes, and an animated sit-com like *The Simpsons* contains a great deal of adult content which has been instrumental in stimulating numerous debates about the programme in the culture of the internet. Similar exchanges have occurred in relation to *Ren and Stimpy, Beavis and Butthead, Duckman* and *The Critic*, but this is a long way removed both from classical animation and the animated films of indepen-dent artists. These debates are more concerned with the recognition of cultural cross-referencing rather than meaning and affect, and no animation produced for television bears proper comparison to the omnipresent and historically charged influence of Disney.

While this in no way properly addresses how an audience relates to animated films *per se*, it will provide a useful platform from which to interrogate the effects of different forms and styles of animation upon different audiences in the future. The Disney film is self-evidently operating on terms which the broad spectrum of audiences recognise *as* animation, i.e. cel-animation characterised by human/ animal figures who play out plausible, if highly fanciful fictions. Other kinds of animation are, indeed, now reaching a wider audience, and further research will reveal how the reaction to what we have defined as orthodox animation differs from the response to developmental or experimental animation. Obviously, there will be considerable difference in the ways audiences respond to different kinds of orthodox animation, most notably, perhaps, in the experi-ence of watching the conflicting styles of Disney and Warner Brothers cartoons but, here, it is important to stress that the two studios may only be compared with regard to the creation of the short form. Disney essentially defined the parameters of the full-length animated feature and, consequently, the requirement to move beyond the gag-oriented structures of the cartoon short. This inevitably means that the range of intentions and possibilities is immediately widened and offers audiences a number of different narrative premises which, in turn, provoke a greater number of possible responses. The primary research conducted for this chapter, therefore, predominantly prioritises an address of the response to Disney features, in the sense that they offer the most scope for analysis, but are also the focus of most people's early memory of a Disney film viewed at the cinema.

Prefiguring my own research in this area, which is directly concerned with a contemporary audiences' first memory of a Disney film experience, aspects of the work undertaken by the Mass Observation group working in Britain during the late 1930s and early 1940s will also be discussed. Jeffrey Richards' and Dorothy Sheridan's *Mass Observation at the Movies* (1987) (hereafter, Richards and Sheridan, 1987) details the experience of a sample of the film-going public during this period, and includes quantitive and qualitative information concerning the presence and affect of Disney cartoons. This is a useful model because it demonstrates a particular attitude about animation in a specific period; offers unmediated responses to Disney films in the 'Golden Era'; and properly contextualises the study I have undertaken, with a piece of research which privileges the adult response to the films as they emerged, rather than as a retrospective analysis of a childhood experience. The two differing approaches, however, are revealing, and foreground a number of key issues and questions which are intrinsically related to the animated form, the determination of the place of the spectator in relation to the films, and the terms and conditions which define the understanding of, and response to, the films.

Disney and mass observation

Tom Harrisson's Mass Observation Unit produced over fifty reports on the viewing practices and preferences of a sample of the British cinema-going public in Bolton, Lancashire, during World War II. Known as the Worktown project, the research sought to address how cinema informed different social and cultural paradigms, and directly reflected the mores, morale and material agendas of the people in the face of war. The study is concerned with the complete range of cinematic experience, and in many senses only touches upon animation in passing, as merely one aspect of the film-going menu available to the Bolton public. The surveys undertaken, however, often contain insightful remarks concerning cartoons and, most specifically, Disney features. The work of other studios is mentioned but clearly carries less credibility as a representative example of the animated film. The critical and commercial agenda that quickly accrued around the Disney product immediately gave it a kudos which set it apart from its competitors. Considerable research is required to properly establish the extent and frequency of cartoon showings during this period and, most importantly, what particular cartoons proved to be most popular but, for the purposes of this discussion, it is suffice to say that both cartoon shorts and full-length animated films featured regularly on bills in the late 1930s and early 1940s, but were clearly constituted as part of the programme, and most often merely supported a more prestigious production from Hollywood. In the USA, the animated cartoon was often specifically related to the 'A' feature, and was chosen as part of a bill which sought to reflect and appease an implied hierarchical configuration of the audience on class, race and gender terms (Smoodin, 1993: 44–71). Within the British context, this is much harder to determine, but it is clear that animated

226

propaganda films made by the Halas and Batchelor studios in Britain for British consumption did appear on some bills which featured other Ministry of Information short films and feature films wholly concerned with the British experience of the war (see Wells, 1995). It is clear, though, that British audiences fundamentally preferred American films, and recognised a Disney feature in this light, as much as in its distinctive character as an animated film. It is difficult to determine, therefore, if any ideological or political coherence informed bills in British cinemas during the war or, further, whether the animated film played any significant role in the construction of the bill, except at the level of being self-evidently, an example of 'propaganda', or defined as simply escapist entertainment.

Mass observation proved, however, that even if 'cartoons' had a place in a broader ideological scheme, they still remained the least preferred kind of entertainment in the Bolton cinemas (Richards and Sheridan, 1987: 34), but there is some evidence to suggest that they were indeed, universally enjoyed (ibid.: 52), if slightly preferred by female audiences (ibid.: 35–6). It is probably the case that audiences recognised no particular importance in the animated cartoon at the level of *relevance*. It may be assumed that the cartoon was largely seen as an amusing diversion and wholly separate from the earnest, often emotionally intense, live-action cinema. Interestingly, both men and women wanted to see more humorous films, but while acknowledging the cartoon as an amusing fiction, audiences seemed to recognise a different purpose for, and aesthetic sense within, the animated form. Disney's influence in this respect should not be underestimated because viewers came to properly acknowledge that animation offered something different and distinctive. One viewer writes:

> Perhaps the only films certain to please me are Disney's *Silly Symphonies*. Disney, in my view is the first man to go up to a cine camera and say 'Here is a new instrument, it has possibilities for a new mode of artistic expression. Let's *invent* a new mode of expression'. This, I feel he has done and I never feel it so strongly as when I see his imitators. . . . Apart from Disney and the producers of the documentary film, who must be a class apart because of their different object, film producers, I feel, are still hide-bound by the tradition of stage craft. The stage and the screen are, I think, as the poles apart.
>
> (ibid.: 233)

This extended comment acknowledges the *modernity* of the animated film, and the innovative mode of expression that animation legitimises, and readily accomodates. The viewer clearly endorses the way in which animation has the capacity to abandon or resist outmoded notions of theatrical performance or documentary realism in fictional narratives. In recognising that animation has a different *aesthetic* agenda, he/she implicitly supports the idea that the animated form can carry with it alternative *ideological* imperatives. Disney's *Silly Symphonies* seem progressive in the way that they negate the presence of didacticism and overt modes of performance, preferring to encourage engagement with the material not merely at the level of being an amusing diversion, but as a piece of work which is so different in its outlook and approach that it may be distinguished as obviously in the vanguard of technical and artistic achievement. That is to say, that audiences took pleasure not only in the antics of Mickey Mouse and Donald Duck, but in their fundamental recognition of the skill and expertise in the execution and construction of the animated form.

Michael O'Pray (1993) has noted,

> In this virtuousity where form and content reach a perfection there is the deepest pleasure because we are confronted with a control and importantly the very phantasy of the control in the animated figures. In other words, in the plasmatic element – the sheer virtuousity of the lines . . . we have an objectification of our own desire for omnipotence. Our desire to will something without in fact acting upon it, is acted out in the animation itself through the virtuoso use of the forms.

O'Pray argues here for the idea that the audience is significantly *empowered* by the control inherently imbued in the virtuoso constuction, and ultimate freedom, achievable within the form. Shades of Terry Gilliam's 'impish god', cited earlier, inform this view. The animator plays out the fantasy of control and free expression in the work and, by successfully enacting this fantasy, achieves material success. A completed animation represents an example of an entirely controlled environment which is a symbolic space wholly predicated on the whim, intention, and bravura of the animator. This is the fantasy of uninhibited creativity given *substance*, and as such becomes a model by which viewers may enjoy the pleasures offered in the perfect conception of the piece. There is somehow an innate pleasure in the recognition of the exact achievement in aligning an absolutely personal intention with the particularity of its execution, and it is this that the animated film implicitly offers in a language which only operates on its own terms.

This level of engagement is not shared by all viewers, of course, but significantly, one viewer in the Mass Observation survey, who abstains from aesthetic recognition does so on the basis of seeing a *Popeye* cartoon, which he perceives as 'unnatural and silly' (Richards and Sheridan, 1987: 51). This viewer clearly resists the opportunity to move beyond the confines of realistic representation or naturalistic performance and, indeed, sees no purchase in virtuoso artistry as it was also practised by the Fleischer Brothers Studio. This perhaps supports the view that the possible liberation offered by the animated form is only possible when it is recognised as *different*, and addressed in a spirit which recognises that its art is informed by its intrinsic capacity to accomodate a variety of approaches and to create significantly different effects. The two viewers represent two models of spectatorship. The first, a model informed by the objectification of the *artwork* and the subjective empowerment it offers; the second, a model of denial, which only objectifies the limitations and inappropriateness of the *cartoon*. These positions create a polarity which usefully defines the limits of the discussion. Within the context of the Mass Observation surveys, it provides a framework by which to discuss the British public's response to *Fantasia* (1941).

One hundred and sixteen men and 104 women responded to a questionnaire which asked them to record their favourite six films in the viewing period between 1942 and 1943. A 28-year-old entomologist from Horley lists *Fantasia* in all six positions and suggests that it is 'very nearly art' (ibid.: 222). A 52-year-old musician and journalist, however, felt that it was 'desperately tasteless in parts' (ibid.: 225), while a secretary from Epsom had a mixed reaction, partly enjoying the film, partly detesting it, but ultimately concluding that 'it is all most unsuitable for children' (ibid.: 288). Many correspondents cited the originality or uniqueness of the film and saw it a number of times, and some of the best endorsements for the film, perhaps not unsurprisingly, came from an art student (ibid.: 274), a student draughtsman (ibid.: 242) and an architect (ibid.: 228). These responses reinforce the idea that Disney's *Fantasia* aspires to art, even if there is an uncertainty that it has been achieved. This falls neatly into the paradigm of spectatorship defined earlier in the sense that the work has clear aesthetic credibility, but its very originality or intention creates doubt about the *actual* nature of its achievement. Those versed in particular kinds of expertise about creative artforms represent a specific mode of recognition which is intrinsically related to the agenda which we will assume they are bringing to the film; this is the address of *Fantasia* as a *comparative* art form whose credentials make it appropriate to critical interrogation in respect of other aesthetic approaches known to the viewer. Their emotive response is, therefore, to some degree tempered by the imperative of their analytical judgement.

Two extended audience accounts, though, best exemplify the issues raised by *Fantasia*, and serve to inform the paradigm of spectatorship being developed. A 26-year-old charities organiser from Glasgow says:

> *Fantasia* I liked because of the beauty of the music and the ingenuity and genius with which Disney matched actions and pictures to the spirit and phrasing of the music. There was a great deal of this film which I disagreed with violently, but there were so many moments of pure joy that it more than compensated for the bits I disliked and even these were interesting. It is a film I can see over and over again without being bored.
>
> (ibid.: 277)

Once again, the viewer notes the coincidence of beauty and ingenuity in the Disney text, fully endorsing that some of the film's best effects involve the embodiment of a perfected relationship between sound and image, one sensitively reacting to, and revealing the meaning of, the other. There is the implicit recognition that the way in which the animated image relates to the sound signifies the specific differences afforded by the visual codes and conventions available in the animated form. When the film is less successful, the viewer recognises a disparity between his/her own perception of the intensity and elusiveness of the music and the way it has been interpreted and illustrated in the film. Here, O'Pray's 'phantasy' of control breaks down, even when there is an acknowledgement of virtuousity. This is interesting because it enables the paradigm of spectatorship being defined to extend in a way which acknowledges that animation, unlike the majority of live-action film, is informed by an intrinsic *plurality* and *ellusiveness*, which refuses certainty and notions of the absolute. In whatever style, approach, or condition that the animated film works within it is *innately* suggestive. Its very form invites interpretation and participation, a condition which the viewer acknowledges by saying that even those parts of the film which he/she rejects as matters of taste, still remain 'interesting' by virtue of their implied intention and the virtuoso manner of their execution. The viewer oscillates between 'pure joy' (the exact achievement of the artwork) and parts of the film he/she 'disagreed with violently' (the breakdown of, and disengagement with, notions of aesthetic credibility, and an implied rejection of the form). Ultimately, this also operates as a model which simultaneously perceives animation as both an incontrovertibly original art form, with the possibility of achievements unique to the medium, *and* as a form in which aesthetic ambition can easily collapse into banal and naïve modes of expression, and thus reinforce the stereotype of animation as an immature mode of creativity fit only for consumption by children.

Though this idea simultaneously praises and damns the animated form, it probably accurately reflects the predominant trends in those who watch it, half dazzled by its art, half embarrassed by its assumed status. A second viewer – a 33-year-old sales manager from Blackburn, has no such ambivalence, however, but does acknowledge that progress does not occur without cost, and that aesthetic aspiration is not necessarily understood or endorsed by all:

> Yes, Disney did something which from my own experience baffled the public, they did not seem to be able to absorb the real significance of the film. Who could have devised the small intermission where a huge Symphony Orchestra becomes so human as to start a small 'jam' session. *Fantasia* was sheer art from beginning to end – and in spite of the fact that it was drawn and painted and photographed, it was above all – Very Human.
>
> (ibid.: 235–6)

This evaluation views the Disney text as an artwork, but one made even greater by its grounding in the human dimension which informs both its technical achievements and its possible failings or lapses in taste. In many ways this viewpoint chimes with Walt Disney's own qualms about attempting to raise the status of the animated film. Seemingly threatened by the idea of 'high culture', yet persuaded of animation's capacity to become high art, Disney found himself in a quandary, and said:

> [. . .] the horrid feeling persists that, perhaps, Dopey is as well qua-
> lified as I am to discuss culture in America. As a matter of fact, at times
> I have caught myself viewing the word 'culture' with suspicion. It
> seemed to have an un-American look to me, sort of snobbish and
> affected, as if it thought it was better than the next fellow. Actually,
> as I understand it, culture isn't that kind of snooty word at all. As I see
> it, a person's culture represents his appraisal of the things that make up
> life. And a fellow becomes cultured, I believe, by selecting that which
> is fine and beautiful in life and throwing aside that which is mediocre
> or phoney.[3]

It may be argued that it is the very tension between beauty and banality which informs much of Disney's work, often creating images of profound intensity and technical and artistic achievement, but, at the same time, scenes of great super-ficiality and over-determined sentimentality. This, ironically, means that the films can operate on a number of levels and facilitate the appreciation of the art critic and the disapproval of the cultural cynic. Disney's view of culture essentially promotes the idea of a classless agenda underpinned by moral and aesthetic integrity, and it is this code which informs much of the contemporary debates about Disney's work and, indeed, the views of the sample of people involved in the second case study under discussion here.

In this primary research, it was my intention to address how the Disney film had affected and influenced children, but instead of constructing a more clinical approach to studying this phenomenon, I decided to ask adults of varying ages and backgrounds to respond to a simple question, which merely required them to state their first memory of a Disney film in as much detail as possible, i.e. where did they see the film, who were they with, why did they go, what did they recall about the film, the occasion etc. Essentially, I wanted to evaluate the *actual* experience of viewing Disney films from the adult perspective which ultimately shaped and expressed the memory. In my view, this process helps to reveal the real influence and effect that the film had because the memory was being articulated in a way which had already subconsciously determined its signifi-cance. Such an approach necessarily assumes that the viewer has chosen what to recall, repressed what seems inappropriate to admit, heightened or marginalised aspects of their memory, partially evaluated or interpreted it etc. In other words, the viewer has already prioritised the important aspects of his/her spectatorship, and signified how and why the Disney text has connected with the individual's *formative* gaze as a child viewer, and the individual's *mature* gaze as an adult fully conversant with a Disney ethos which has imbued itself within a global popular culture.

Table 6.1

Age group (Years)	Participants	Percentage of sample
15–25	158	36.3
25–35	117	26.9
35–45	67	15.4
45–55	53	12.2
Over 55	40	9.2

Nostalgia's not what it used to be: Disney, then and now

The sample for my research was taken from a number of events which directly related to aspects of animation, i.e. festivals, cinema showings, lectures, workshops, etc. and, therefore, assumed that the people present had some previously determined interest in the animated film. Each person was given a brief questionnaire, and requested to provide as much detail as possible about their first recollection of watching a Disney film. The sample amounted to 435 people, and was composed as shown in Table 6.1.

The gender division was approximately 55 per cent female, 45 per cent male, and the sample represented a broad spectrum of occupational and material experience. I consulted each of the 435 questionnaires, noting the film that the viewer had remembered. Inevitably, there was a wide diversity of films recalled, and some thirty-five Disney films were cited. The top ten films were as shown in Table 6.2.

These figures are inevitably affected by the age of the participants and the particular Disney films which were released during their childhood, or the period in which they actually encountered a Disney film. A large proportion of the sample did remember viewing a Disney film when they were children, but some

Table 6.2

Disney film	No. of citations	Percentage of sample
Snow White and the Seven Dwarfs	87	20.0
The Jungle Book	78	17.9
Bambi	50	11.5
101 Dalmatians	31	7.1
Dumbo	17	3.9
The Rescuers	15	3.5
Lady and the Tramp	13	3.0
Mary Poppins	13	3.0
Sleeping Beauty	10	2.3
Pete's Dragon	10	2.3
Others (25)	86	19.8
Not a Disney film/couldn't remember	25	5.7

suggested that it was much later when they saw one, perhaps as part of a student peer group, or as parents themselves. Though it is unsurprising that *Snow White and the Seven Dwarfs* (1937), *The Jungle Book* (1967), and *Bambi* (1942), feature strongly in the survey, it is interesting to note the small percentage of people who could not remember seeing a Disney film ever, or who confused the Disney style with that of another animated film – in this sample, chiefly, *Watership Down* (1978), or remembered a part live-action film like *Mary Poppins* (1964) and *Pete's Dragon* (1977). The predominant trend shows that the Disney 'classics' have entered the popular domain on more occasions and thus, would inevitably constitute the dominant aspect of the sample.

Having consulted the sample to note the cited films, I further categorised the responses to the films under some broad headings, largely those which reported an emotional engagement with the films; those which prioritised aspects of the event or occasion over and above the effect of the film; those which cited particular elements of the films like characters, songs or scenes; and those which proffered opinion or evaluation of their experience. Having noted key phrases, incidents and detailed memories, I then proceeded to construct a framework by which these responses could be evaluated and interpreted, and discovered some dominant themes which would usefully structure my discussion. These are as follows:

1   empathy and identification;
2   fear and concern;
3   treats and occasions;
4   codes of contentment.

'Oo-be-do, I wanna be like you-oo-oo': empathy and identification

Notions of empathy and identification among the Disney memories largely fall into three categories. First, those which determine how the animated film is actually perceived and, consequently, how this determines and creates the parameters of acceptance and, therefore, defines how these films may be understood. Second, those that recognise particular kinds of empowerment on offer in the films and, finally, those which enjoy the idea of playing out projections and fantasies in an uninhibited way. Saira (25), provides an interesting example of how these issues are unconsciously conflated when she suggests that 'I had read the book [of *Cinderella*] about a million and one times and it was amazing to see [the characters] in "real life"'. Here animation becomes the most appropriate vehicle for the projection of a child's imagination into a mode of 'reality'. The animated form both represents a similarity to the ways in which literary narratives have been illustrated in children's books, and the ways that a child starts to conceive some aspects of the real world before they have been socialised to specific kinds of order. Disney's *Cinderella* (1950) essentially becomes a symbolic embodiment of the formative construction of perceived existence into

233

representational forms. Alan (30), a joiner, shares this recognition of the animated space as a 'real' world in relation to characters, but experiences difficulty when his perception of the real world is violated by the capacity for animation to change its conditions. Of *Snow White and the Seven Dwarfs*, he says, 'The Wicked Queen didn't frighten me, but the trees coming alive did'. Here it seems that the viewer can cope with the frightening excesses of the Wicked Queen because he has a point of identification with the fact that the Queen is ostensibly human, but as soon as something seemingly unnatural or unrealistic occurs this becomes the source of fear and threat.

The perception of the animated space as a recognisable and familiar environment, yet one which can operate on other terms, underpins many of the responses, and suggests that there is an understanding that animation constitutes a self-evidently non-live action space which is at once related to the real world but different enough to facilitate other kinds of projection. Consequently, this legitimises anything from the desire never to grow up and be an adult, like *Peter Pan* (1953), through to the wish to have a haircut like Mowgli's in *The Jungle Book*. The sample revealed a number of dominant modes of projection, however, and particularly those associated with appearance and identity. Leeann (23) says 'I always wanted to look like Snow White and live in a cottage', while Alexandra (32) agrees that '[I] always wished to be as beautiful as Snow White', and some, like Sophie (20) 'wanted a dress like hers'. Dresses, it seems were highly coveted in Disney films. Charlotte (21) wanted Sleeping Beauty's dress, which she remembers 'keeps changing from red to blue'. Indeed, Amanda (41) remembers 'envying Cinderella' over her dress, while Tessa (25) also says 'I wanted the dress' and continues, 'I wanted to be Cinderella!' Interestingly, these are all expressions of need from women who all recognise a particular role model for women in the figures and forms of Snow White, Sleeping Beauty, and Cinderella.

Significantly, men also recognised early stirrings of sexual attraction towards these women. Mark (31), a sales assistant from Doncaster, remembers 'becoming infatuated by the lovely Ms White', and felt that the Prince was 'a lucky bleeder' because he was able to be with her. Similarly, Sean (29) from Belfast, recalls 'falling in love with Snow White', but in general, men recalled more aspects of their experience at the cinema, or prioritised ideas about significant role models. This is probably more of a comment about the ways in which men repress the articulation of their sexual feelings as it is about the specific provocations of a Disney text at this level. Certainly, women were much less inhibited in this respect. Jane (17) says 'I fancied the Prince' in *Sleeping Beauty* (1959). Leeann, cited earlier, also 'had a massive crush on the Prince', but Karen (22), takes this kind of projection further, by unconsciously aligning significant aspects in the part-live-action Disney film, *Bedknobs and Broomsticks* (1971), when she says 'I wanted to have a magic bed too, and I also wanted to marry the eldest boy – Charles? – when I grew up'. Arguably, the latter reception may signify a greater degree of pre-sexual maturity as she alights on the real figure within a fantasy environment. Conversely, Lalage (21), rather than moving beyond the frame of the text to redetermine a possible realignment with the real world through the direct identification with a real figure, plays out a range of empathies in her response to The Jungle Book:

> I went with my mother to a beautiful old local cinema in Africa – maybe a friend came. I fell madly in love with Mowgli, and modelled myself on the little girl. Vowed I was a Red Indian (I thought the two were the same). Baloo the bear reminded me of my Grandad in appearance. I always remember my mother came with me to all my early films – we didn't have a TV 'til I was 8 – only radio, so it was my only visual experience.

This particular memory is rich in implications in the sense that the Disney text here constitutes a very significant model of primary cinematic experience. Not versed in the vocabulary of televisual imagery, this viewer brings a strong investment to the imagery she witnesses, playing out a romantic fantasy in relation to Mowgli, the little boy in the film; seeking an identificatory role model in the little girl at the end of the film who Mowgli falls for; recognising an error in her understanding of gender/race representation, believing the African girl to be a Native American (especially ironic given the background and viewing context of the viewer, and, thus, perhaps an indictment of the Disney aesthetic regarding race); and achieving empathy with characters in the film by relating them to familiar adults, in this case, her grandfather. An acknowledged prefiguring of gay empathy was recalled by Adam (31), also concerning Mowgli, who suggests, 'I remember seeing those scary animals and that amazing boy. I loved that boy, I wanted to be that boy'. Mowgli's aesthetic didn't quite meet everyone's approval, though, as Jason (28) recalls: 'I do remember thinking the boy was really skinny and would never make a rugby player, as I used to play rugby myself'. Clearly, even in these formative viewings, ideas about masculine and feminine identity were being formed, and Disney characters used as particular figures by which early preconceptions of the self in the viewer were compared and contrasted.

Indeed, some of the most amusing reflections that the sample revealed were related to how viewers saw aspects of themselves in Disney characters, or recognised elements of their family. Jenny (32), found particular purchase in Dumbo (1941), suggesting, 'I empathised as I have big ears', and continues 'my sister took the mick about my ears for three weeks afterwards'. Colin (66), from Tunbridge Wells, noted 'I laughed at Dopey – probably associated with him!', while Emma (24), especially enjoyed the Siamese cats in Lady and the Tramp (1955), as she went to the cinema with her sister, and 'there were two of them and two of us!' Significantly, however, key moments of empathy occur when viewers are seeking particular ways of expressing criticism or displeasure with regard to members of their family. Rugby-playing Jason, when not dismissing Mowgli, finds useful comparisons by which to view his father: 'The head elephant reminded me of my dad, as it was mainly my dad that had a lot to say, and most of the time, he thought it was important.' Ben (36) 'didn't like Bambi's dad, '[I] thought he was a snob', but this may have been related to the fact that 'Dad made fun' because Ben had cried over Bambi's mother's death. More fervent criticism attends the use of Disney villainesses, who are regularly used as role models by which to convey particular disapproval of other female family members. Angela (22) says of the Queen in Snow White and the Seven Dwarfs, that 'she was dark and ugly and evil, a bit like my step-mother', while Rachel (35) calls the Queen's incarnation as a witch, 'the Grot Granny', who is apparently, 'alive and well and still living in Reading'. Particular focus attended the antics of Cruella De Vil in 101 Dalmatians (1961), which I will address in the next section.

Unsurprisingly, the more extreme the caricature, and the more the character was coded as unpopular or evil, the more it was identified with people that the viewers did not like, and served as a useful vehicle by which to play out aggression and bitterness unarticulated in verbal terms. All of this is inevitable, of course, and perhaps, desirable, especially it seems if you are Edward (29), who was nicknamed 'Thumper' by his mother after the viewing of Bambi. For the record, Edward says, 'I don't really remember much about him except that he had a crappy, flat, pink nose, and didn't really look like a rabbit at all'. Just as well. . . .

'Who's afraid of the big bad wolf?': Fear and concern

Of the 435 viewers sampled, 107 (24.6 per cent) noted that they had cried or had been in some way afraid when watching a Disney animation. Comparatively, only 41 people (9.4 per cent) registered overt pleasure and happiness. Three particular moments of trauma figured again and again in varying degrees of affect; first, the actions of Cruella De Vil in 101 Dalmatians, second, the death of Bambi's mother in Bambi, and third, the scenes involving the poisoned red apple in Snow White and the Seven Dwarfs. Further anxieties also revolved around the incarceration of Dumbo's mother, Pinocchio and Geppetto being swallowed by a whale in Pinocchio, and fears for animals in danger in a number of films. As a simple overview, a statement by Rebecca (20) probably best reflects the earnestness and intensity of some of the recorded memories: 'I took everything really as a matter of life or death.' In many ways this supports the idea that the Disney hyper-realist text clearly engages with the fluid tension in childhood development between the recognition of persuasive, authentic conceptions of character and environment, and some of the primary psychological and emotional sites which animation can concretely portray and rehearse.

Faye (25) reports 'I'll never forget how upset I was when Dumbo's mum was locked up'. This represents a common and long-lasting feeling in a number of participants in the survey, and clearly relates to the deep-rooted anxiety in many people about the violation of maternal bonding with a child. This finds its profoundest correspondence in the scene from Bambi in which Bambi's mother is shot, which reduced boys and girls to tears in equal measure. Simon (23) from Port Talbot, admits 'I remember weeping profusely when Bambi's mother was killed', while Barry (39) remembers 'screaming and being dragged out after the death', and Rachel (40) recalls going with her best friend and then 'bawled our eyes out when Bambi's mother got shot'. Robyn (22), perhaps best summates the symbiotic relationship between what is occurring on the screen and what was happening in the cinema:

> The first Disney film I saw was Bambi, with my mother and brother. [It was a] very emotional film. [I] cried lots at the age of six. I can't remember much of the story but it was very sad, especially when Bambi's mother was shot. Having my mother there was comforting to me – a shoulder to cry on.

The inevitable anxiety caused by the loss of a mother figure is assuaged by the comforting presence of the viewer's own mother, and the reassurance of continuity in her own life in spite of the trauma she has experienced. It is in this sense that a character such as Cruella De Vil causes heightened anxiety in the audience because she represents a different and cruel code of maternity which confuses a young audience. Emma (23) remembers 'hating' Cruella, and thought 'someone would make my cats into a coat'. Angie (31) also remembers 'hating her for wearing a fur coat', and in her politically aware mode as an adult, asserts 'which I still do'. Stuart (25) demonstrates his anxiety about her identity and behaviour when he suggests, 'Cruella plucking out eyelashes filled me with horror and disgust', while Paul (26), freely admits 'the woman scared the crap out of me'. More troubling for Sue (34), was the fact that her 'mother wore a red coat with a synthetic fur collar' and this reminded her 'of the red coat in the film and scared me'. Unlike the viewer above, Sue was clearly not reassured by her mother's presence and, indeed, her mother's role was undermined by the representation of the evil 'mother' on the screen. Rachel (24), even recognised that the power of the emotion she experienced in relation to Cruella led her to completely forget that 'this was an animated movie, or even that it was a movie', and to her 'hiding behind a chair', and later having nightmares. Cruella's identity and actions usefully conflate a number of anxieties which might occur in children, chiefly, that she is prepared to harm animals in the creation of her maternal persona. This both undermines the supposedly benign nature of motherly affection and the protective agenda which should attend the care of pets. Practical concerns do sometimes override this issue however – Helen (28), though scared of Cruella, 'wondered how the two people who rescue the dogs were going to feed them all'. She, like a number of others, reported that the film also prompted a request for a puppy. Tina (29), who saw the film with an all female group composed of family and friends, also wanted a puppy, mainly because she 'felt quite emotional when [the] dog had puppies'. It may be suggested, therefore, that sometimes, the greater the violation of benign maternity, the more certain projections by the viewer seek to reassert motherly instincts and values.

If Cruella embodied the threat of the 'bad mother', the poisoned apple in *Snow White and the Seven Dwarfs* operates as a particularly potent signifier of foreboding. A number of mothers must have experienced great difficulty with their children after the film, because having probably attempted to convince their offspring that 'an apple a day keeps the doctor away', they now found that it did not necessarily prevent an evil witch arriving on your doorstep. Alicia (29) said, 'I wouldn't touch an apple for weeks afterwards', a common refrain, and probably, one which was informed by the view forwarded by Lisa (19), who said, 'It looked delicious but was deadly'. The apple thus symbolises the tension between pleasure and pain, and is an object which determines the limits of permitted behaviour and modes of punishment. For some, this level of symbolism persists – Alan (35) said, 'I don't think I've ever eaten a shiny red apple since then'. Others voiced their fears for Snow White when she is being tempted to eat the apple. Gordon (55) noted, 'I wanted to tell her not to take it to eat', thus clearly indicating a recognition of 'forbidden fruit' and the harm that may come as a consequence of taking it. Wanting to protect Snow White was a common dimension of male responses, but the predominant response by women was to feel unhappy that she had been deceived. A feminist reading of this phenomenon would probably suggest that female viewers wish that the heroine would be intelligent and aware enough not to be tempted, and critical of the male conception of feminine duplicity, and the supposed necessity of masculine patronage.

Fear is a prominent emotion for a number of people watching certain scenarios in Disney films. If the image of the apple was concerned with *what* was consumed, the moment in *Pinocchio* when Pinocchio and Geppetto enter the whale is about the fear of being consumed wholly oneself. Sally (40) 'screamed so much when Pinocchio was swallowed by the whale that [she] had to be brought out and taken home'. Brian (42) says he was 'worried' by the whale, Peter (22) was 'concerned' about it, and Sarah (28) only remembers Pinocchio's father being swallowed and, after a hasty and extremely distraught exit from the cinema, to this day she has 'never seen it all the way through'. It may be argued that children have a certain understanding of the things that they can do, and the aspects of existence of which they are in control. They also recognise the limits determined for them by their parents, but when things occur which are beyond their experience, and even the defining laws of parental authority, then extreme effects can happen. Obviously, the power, size, strength and sheer 'otherness' of the whale might be disarming, but it is also a crucial characteristic of animation itself that it can create images outside the experience of human beings, and thus challenge their innate and inherent perception of the world. This can be particularly traumatic for a child, especially if the animation aspires to a close approximation of reality only to subvert the codes and conditions upon which the real world is materially constructed and predicated. Ironically, children can accept this fluidity in the extremes of a cartoon short made by Warner Brothers, MGM *et al.*, because they quickly come to terms with the elastic, comic premises of the characters and stories. The fear of the whale in *Pinocchio* is ultimately the fear of a loss of control in a recognisably real, but suddenly strange world, where even parents have no jurisdiction or effect. Fiona (24), summarises this kind of moment:

> [. . .] the death of Bambi's mum made us all cry, including my mother, which embarrassed her, but the effect it had on me stopped me watching Walt Disney films because I always thought I would cry. I also didn't like the fact that the animals died, and I stopped watching them.

Here the viewer recognises that nothing, not even her own mother, can offer order and reassurance in the face of difficulties problematically raised within the supposedly safe haven of the Disney text. Even knowledge in adulthood cannot revise childhood experience and merely endorses the idea that some Disney texts create formative moments when notions of 'wholeness' are disrupted forever, and innocence is fundamentally lost.

'My, oh, my, what a wonderful day': Treats and occasions

The experience of seeing a Disney film in childhood is largely contextualised within the family outing, often on a specific occasion like a birthday or at Christmas. In whatever context, the idea of seeing a Disney film is very much couched within the assumption that the inevitable pleasures (and pains) of seeing the film are a reward for good behaviour by the child and, coincidentally, a celebration of 'togetherness' among family and friends. Some people find this experience difficult to handle of course – Helen (28) reports that 'my dad fell asleep five minutes into the film and snored really loudly until the usher came and woke him up', and it is this incident that constitutes her memory of The Jungle Book. Such distractions are common in the survey, but so too are examples of collective catharsis in which whole families succumb to the effects of the film. Ann (36) details her own experience as a parent with her children:

> [I saw] The Little Mermaid last year at the Odeon, with three young children and my husband. At the end, [the] middle child was bored, lying on the floor. The older child was weeping piteously. On the screen the little mermaid and her prince were together – my glasses were steamed up with tears. I turned to my husband for a hankie – no chance – he was awash with salt water, and we both still weep now when we even just hear the soppy song.

Viewing a Disney film together is probably one of the few occasions when this kind of collective weep might occur. Wholly legitimised by the sentimental stimulus and the sense of mutual comfort, reassurance and shared experience, the family enjoy their emotions in ways which other contexts would not accommodate. Unlike the occasion which removes the participants from engaging with

239

the film, this kind of experience is almost unique in familial experience, coming as it does, spontaneously and, seemingly, without embarrassment or loss of face. The chief pattern which emerges from these occasions is, therefore, one of either *informal distraction* or *formal attraction*.

Informal distraction can occur in a number of ways. Abigail (19) enjoyed *Alice in Wonderland* (1951), but was preoccupied throughout the film, resenting the fact that 'my dad took my brother to see a Science Fiction film on the same afternoon'. Seething about an apparently sexist agenda in cinema going, however, is nought when compared to Natasha (22), who merely resents that her youngest brother was taken to see a Disney film at the cinema while she never was. If seeing a Disney movie is a treat, then not seeing one at all seems like a punishment. Had Natasha gone with her brother at any one point, she would have no doubt enjoyed a similar scenario to the one experienced by Julie (25) whose 'brother climbed over the back of [the] cinema seat, landing on [a] bloke's lap behind, in an attempt to hide from [a] character'. These incidents become the memorable aspects of the occasion and not the film itself. Sheila (45), perhaps, summarises this best:

> I went to the Saturday rush when I was a kid and the experience was in the audience not the film. Disney cartoons were there to respond to with cheers, boos, throwing sweet papers on other friends, and generally, joining in the chaos that was the audience. I don't remember much about the films, they were just a background prompt to the events between neighbourhood gangs within the audience.

Many in the sample report this energy and excitement both in anticipation of the film, within the audience itself, and with regard to the time when they saw the film. Jeremy (28) remembers *Robin Hood* (1973) because 'it was the special Christmas showing [so] now [I] always associate it with Christmas even though the film contains no Christmas images'. This sense of event is often compounded by extra-filmic but related events like competitions. Jennifer (24) from Belfast won free tickets to *Mary Poppins* in a radio competition and, further, walked off with a Fun Boy Three record because she could sing 'Supercalifragilisticexpialidocious'. Unfortunately, she didn't like the film. Clare (21) valued the experience of being at the cinema in Newport Pagnell more than actually seeing *Dumbo*. The blue and red seats, stewards shining torches, blue and purple tickets, slippery floors and tubs of ice cream take precedence over the aurally-advantaged elephant. Food, in fact, figures on numerous occasions, and often popcorn is enjoyed more than Poppins. Premieres cannot sometimes outweigh the effect of a Macdonalds burger or, indeed, prevent fights. Derek (31) had been given tickets to see *Snow White and the Seven Dwarfs*, but he and his mother and brothers were ejected because they fought – 'my brother bust my nose and I blackened his left eye'. Family catharsis of a different sort.

An extraordinary array of events accrue around the experience of witnessing

Disney films but, ultimately, some of the most engaging are those which provoke incident after the film. Amie (21), for example, watched The Aristocats (1970), and noted 'they danced on a roof, which I quite fancied the idea of, and have done since'. Jo (17), part of a group who had seen Alice in Wonderland at the cinema, also enjoyed its video version. She recalls, 'During the film we all got very stoned and repeatedly rewound the video to watch the caterpillar smoking. We found this hilariously funny and laughed so much we cried'. Inevitably, any text is open to subversive use or different kinds of reading, and this is only one example from the survey which suggests that animation may be enjoyed differently under different conditions. Dean (20) has managed, however, to turn the Disney text into reality. A long-time admirer of Herbie the Volkswagen, he now has one of his own.

'With a smile and a song': Codes of conflict and contentment

A number of participants in the survey note the pleasure of Disney songs, and several, completely unsolicitedly, included the lyrics of their favourite tunes, most notably, 'Bobbing Along' from Bedknobs and Broomsticks, and 'Little April Showers' from Bambi, which Naomi (26) recalls provided the soundtrack for 'Sunday afternoons thundering around the living room, making the needle jump, being fawns to the melody'. Carla (24) 'listened to the tape compulsively and knew all the songs' from The Jungle Book, and suggests that this was her 'first introduction to The Beatles and jazz'. Melanie (30) enjoyed the ape-King singing 'I wanna be like you' and notes that '[it] still makes me cry with laughter because of his big bum'. Cerys (21), however, experienced sheer wonder that an ape could sing and dance at all! Gail (21) failed to remember the words when she attempted to singalong during The Jungle Book, but remembers the occasion as 'being a kind of milestone really. I felt really independent going out with just my friends'. These anecdotes represent aspects of the Disney film as a liberating rite of passage. Indeed, all the responses in some way inform this view, either as models of wish fulfilment and desire, or as projections which are negotiating particular complexities around growing up, coming to terms with personal identity and familial relationships, or rehearsing new feelings and experiences. In many ways, animation as a form presents events in a way in which both children and adults can address the familiar as otherness and, conversely, difference and unfamiliarity as the mechanisms towards knowledge and understanding. The very 'otherness' of the dwarves in Snow White and the Seven Dwarfs is reconciled by the emotions and qualities they represent, and in several responses prompted questions concerning their status and identity – Andrew (34) reports he was 'in awe' of them, while Chris (22) took pleasure in the fact that the 'dwarves are small and so was I'.

'Otherness' can occur in different ways, of course, perhaps, most notably in the way children perceive their parents in this context. Esther (26), for example, said 'I remember my father crying. I'd never seen that before'. It is clear that some of the normalities and orthodoxies that inform real-life existence are transgressed

241

through the experiences of watching a Disney text, and this is merely one example of the ways in which a previous understanding of someone or something changes in this context. Sarah (21), for example, had the limits of her own sense of right and wrong challenged in *Fantasia*, when she 'didn't want [Mickey Mouse] to get into trouble' because he had disobeyed the wizard, and she recalls 'how worked up I got as he flooded the wizard's house'. Some people overcome their previously held anxieties, though, and several, like Laura (25), suggested that *101 Dalmations* helped her overcome her fear and dislike of dogs. Real life and fantasy can sometimes get too close in a child's imagination, though, as Bhagvati (25) recalls about her viewing of *Bambi*:

> [The] most memorable scenes were of the fire in the forest because a few days before our neighbour had a bonfire in his garden and we'd watched the flames grow and he'd thrown in something like antlers. My brother turned to me and said that our neighbour has roasted Bambi and his mum alive in his bonfire.

Arguably, the film had enabled the children to properly address taboos about violence and death, and in effect, had offered a therapeutic discourse by which particular kinds of social and familial anomaly could be experienced and discussed. Equally, it may have compounded a particular trauma that remains unresolved. As the sample shows, each person obviously has a specific relationship to the films, some find solace, some find pleasure, some find explanation, some expose deep-rooted fears, but many essentially reconcile tensions between reality and fantasy. Some, like Lucy (27), having seen *Mary Poppins*, will always want 'a disappearing suitcase that held hat stands', and some, like Jacqui (40), a mother with three young children, desperately wishes that 'you could clean your room by clicking your fingers'. The Disney text, of course, is not necessarily innocent, heart-warming or magical for some viewers. Joe (32) said, 'I loathe Walt Disney. The majority of his work is so sickly sweet as to be unsuitable for diabetics. The man himself was off the scale in terms of being anti-semitic, misogynist and right wing'. This one response alone surely proves that animation should be regarded as a medium which needs proper and careful interrogation.

Towards a conclusion

Understanding Animation is merely the beginning of an address of the animated film. It has attempted to analyse the spectacle, meaning and contextual apparatus within the animated form, and offered suggestions for modes of study and additional research. It *cannot* be definitive in the sense that for every animated film produced there is possibly a different mode of address and another way of understanding its creation and purpose. This merely confirms the diversity and range available in the medium, and will hopefully inspire in the reader the desire to watch familiar films in a different light or seek out new kinds of animation to view and discuss. In many ways, there are deep frustrations about trying to capture in words the elusive, but deeply affective, qualities of the finest animation, and further, trying to provide a number of theoretical models of study by which such films may be viewed. An even deeper frustration lies in the fact that the pressure of space has prohibited the address of some of the world's best animation – work from the Zagreb studio by Dusan Vukotic; the lyrical ecological films of veteran Canadian animator, Frederic Back; the challenging narratives of Nina Shorina; the Italian good humour of Bruno Bozzetto; and the new animation emerging from nations like Africa and Australia. This is the work of another book, but on this occasion, if the reader sees an interesting agenda for discussion in Donald Duck looking at a striptease in a circus peep-show machine in *A Good Time for a Dime* (1941); or experiences a certain provocation when cowboys have sex with their horses in Phil Mulloy's *That's Nothing* (1990); or finds the colours and forms of Luigi Veronesi's *Film N.6.* (1941) a thing of joy and beauty, then this book will have been successful.

NOTES

1 THINKING ABOUT ANIMATED FILMS

1 The first two chapters of *Understanding Animation* are revised, updated and expanded discussions of ideas and issues first addressed in a chapter titled 'Animation: Forms and Meanings' in Nelmes, J., *Introduction to Film Studies*, London & New York: Routledge, 1996.

2 Quoted in *The Magic Art of Jan Svankmajer*, BBC broadcast, 1992.

3 Ralph Stephenson describes the Phenakistoscope as 'a revolving disc with slits at the edge and figures drawn on it which came to life when viewed in a mirror through the slits with the disc revolving' (Stephenson, 1967: 25). Richard Leskosky suggests 'Zoetrope refers to any sort of rotating drum device with strips of sequential images positioned within the drum which produced the illusion of motion' (Leskosky, 1993: 2); while Thomas Hoffer describes the Kinematoscope as 'a viewing device consisting of a series of photographs mounted on a wheel and rotated in front of a viewer. When the wheel was rotated the illusion of movement was created'. For further discussion of these proto-cinematic devices see Robinson, 1990 and Leskosky, 1993.

4 Cohl's life and work is fully explored in Crafton, D., *Emile Cohl, Caricature and Film*, Princeton: Princeton University Press, 1990. The concept of *incoherent cinema* aptly describes the fluidity and diversity afforded to the freely directed graphic line, which may be used to create the figurative and abstract; to fix form and meaning and to challenge it; to bring narrational suggestion in the most minimal yet affecting way.

5 The Fleischer Brothers' 'Out of the Inkwell' series and Disney's early 'Alice' films are examples of many early animated films which suggested the freedom available to the animator within the medium by counterpointing animated characters and environments with the real world and, most often, the studio environments in which they were created. This tension has prevailed in the animated film and readily constitutes a level of reflexivity which is fully explored in Lindvall and Melton (1994), where many examples are given, not merely of cartoonal interaction with live-action, but of self-referentiality in animation from Winsor McCay's *Little Nemo in Slumberland* (1911) to *Who Framed Roger Rabbit?* (1988). When animation interacts with live-action representations of the real world, it essentially defines the limits of space, the weight of objects, and the incapacities of human beings, thus drawing further attention to the expressive qualities of animation in exploring aspects of the real world beyond their perceived parameters and historically naturalised functions and meanings.

6 Though the Disney Studios created the first sound synchronised cartoon in *Steamboat Willie* (1928), the Fleischer Studios were actually the first to experiment with sound synchronisation, but failed to perfect their system. The Fleischer Studios used sound to good effect, however, when they created animated films which were essentially simple

texts of popular song lyrics, whereupon a bouncing ball would move from word to word as the cinema audience sang along. This also proved an effective tool for advertisers when the Fleischers produced promotional cartoons for companies like Oldsmobile in which audiences sang along to a song about the 'Merrie Oldsmobile' after enjoying a cartoon prologue. See Cabarga (1988) for a full discussion of the Fleischer Studios' work.

7 Although *Snow White and the Seven Dwarfs* (1937) is most readily acknowledged as the first full-length animated feature, this accolade actually belongs to *The Apostle*, made in Argentina in 1917 by Quirino Cristiani. For a full account see Bendazzi (1994: 49–52).

8 This concept is explored by Darley in relation to John Lasseter's computer animation, *Red's Dream* (1987), and is part of an extended discussion of the redefinition of imagery in the light of post-modern forms of hybridity and simulation which redetermine the authenticity and status of visual forms (see Darley, 1993).

9 For a full discussion of Disney's squash-n-stretch style of character design and movement based on the relationship and compression of circle forms, see Thomas and Johnson (1981).

2 NOTES TOWARDS A THEORY OF ANIMATION

1 For accounts of the development and consequences of the industrial process, see Hoffer, 1981; Maltin, 1987; and Crafton, 1993.

2 Arguably, all animated films can be constituted as acts of deconstruction in the sense that the form self-consciously signifies its artificiality as a medium and, consequently, some of the attendant ironies available through the extended vocabulary, in being heightened or intensified, draw attention to particular kinds of construction and execution. More directly, a number of animations actually reference an animator as part of the act of creating an animated film, for example, Daniel Greaves' Oscar-winning short, *Manipulation* (1991), which foregrounds the broad range of possibilities available to the animator with regard to the representation of character and the execution of movement. The film is ultimately an object lesson in the complete control that the animator has over the final work, and a model of how particular kinds of power relation can be played out in the medium. A more humorous treatment of deconstruction is Bob Godfrey's *Do It Yourself Cartoon Kit* (1961), which literally offers the viewer the objects, sounds and stories which constitute the typical cartoon. The simple style of the film, using minimal animation techniques, ironically challenges the myth of animation as a work-intensive, obsessive medium of expression, but also champions its creative freedom and possibilities for humour.

3 *Theories of Authorship*, London & New York: Routledge, 1993, edited by John Caughie, discusses many aspects of the concept of *auteurism*. The term is directly concerned with the actual authorship of the film text, but is subject to many interpretations. Arguably, all film-making practice is informed by the skills and efforts of a number of people and, therefore, fundamentally discredits any notion that the director of a film is its sole creator. Equally, *auteurist* theory has championed the director as the dominant presiding force both in a specific film, and across a canon of work, outweighing the claims for authorship of the screenwriter, cinematographer, editor, actor etc. The *personalisation* of the work sometimes ignores the conditions of its creation, its industrial context, its purpose and intentions, and its cultural and historical position etc., preferring instead to play out the achievements of the text against the aesthetic, intellectual and technical sensibility of its nominal creator. It may be claimed that animation is one of the most auteurist mediums available to the film-maker, in the sense that many animators are, indeed, the sole creators of their works, writing the scenario, drawing the images or manipulating the clay or puppets,

filming the movements, editing the material etc. The complete control that the animator can wield over the work has made the form especially appealing to many artists, and most particularly women, who have been estranged from both the cinematic apparatus and the predominant codes of the (patriarchal) film text. Animation has offered women film-makers a distinctive aesthetic which has fulfilled particular thematic and artistic agendas in a way not available to them in mainstream live-action contexts. Throughout my discussion, I have assumed that the film-makers addressed work in the closest spirit of auteurism, in the sense that they can credibly claim as much control over creative work as is possible in the contemporary commercial and industrial setting.

4 Chuck Jones tells an amusing story which confirms the blurred lines between the perception of reality and synthetic forms. A 7-year-old boy was furious when Jones was introduced to him as the man who drew Bugs Bunny. 'He does not draw Bugs Bunny', he insisted, 'he draws pictures of Bugs Bunny' (Cholodenko, 1991: 59). Bugs Bunny's existence as a *real* phenomenon negates the notion of his creation, and endorses his iconic value in a way that makes it only subject to replication. 'Bugs Bunny' has the same ontological equivalence as any natural, found or constructed phenomenon and, thus, may be perceived as just as 'real'.

5 Denzin, (1995) usefully lists the developments and challenges to Mulvey's approach, pp. 42–63.

6 Frierson notes that 'Clay Replacement Animation follows the method developed in the 1930s by George Pal, who used wooden puppets and a series of interchangeable body parts that were substituted over successive frames to suggest movement. Instead of turning and carving the parts from wood as the Pal Studio did, clay replacement merely sculpts a series of figures or body parts in clay to create the incremental visuals' (Frierson, 1994: 26). He adds 'Clay *painting* is a two-dimensional technique that creates subtly changing colors and a unique fluid motion very different from animating cel or drawn figures' (ibid.), while *clay slicing* or *strata cut*, works in a way that requires the construction of 'long clay "loaves" with three-dimensional visuals embedded within them that are slowly revealed through sequential one-eighth of an inch slices across the loaf when it is filmed' (ibid.: 27).

7 Interview with the author, February 1995.

8 Interview with the author, February 1995.

9 Starewicz's daughter, quoted in a Channel Four documentary about her father, called *The Insect Affair*, Screen First, broadcast in December 1994.

3 ONCE UPON A TIME: NARRATIVE STRATEGIES

1 See Cabarga, 1988: 81, and Hendershot, 1993: 1–15.

2 ASIFA is the international organisation for professional people working in the field of animated cinema.

3 For a full discussion of the Harlequin figure, see Nicoll, A., *The World Of Harlequin*, Cambridge: Cambridge University Press, 1976.

4 Quoted in *The Magic Art of Jan Svankmajer*, BBC broadcast 1992, and fully discussed in Hames, P., 1995.

5 Quoted in *Profile of Yuri Norstein*, TV Films/Eclan, Sofia, Bulgaria, broadcast on Channel Four, 1992.

6 Quoted in Rosenberg, K. 'The World View of Yuri Norstein', from *Animator* no. 28, p.15.

7 Quoted in *Profile of Yuri Norstein*, TV Films/Eclan, Sofia, Bulgaria, broadcast on Channel Four, 1992.

8 Ibid.

9 Yuri Norstein uses this technique for serious purposes, but a similar dislocatory use of forms, shapes and patterns that appear to have only abstract aesthetic signification, but then which gain associative and configurative meanings, occur in Alison Snowden's and David Fine's playful animation, *Second Class Mail* (1984).

10 The use of sound in animation is worthy of an extended study of its own, since many animated films are predicated on particular strategies about the use of song, dialogue, diegetic and non-diegetic sound etc. The intrinsic relationship between sound and image in the animated film is explored by Norman McClaren in his film, *Synchromy* (1971), in which the animated music track itself is displaced on to the picture area and constitutes the abstract movements of the film as the sound is produced. This was achieved by the use of a special optical printer, which also enabled the animated music track to be coloured using filters. Thus the music is actually *seen* and *heard*.

11 Even though the UPA studios have been acknowledged as the pioneers of an innovative visual and aural style, Disney historian, Brian Sibley, claims that the Disney Studio anticipate this kind of work in the late 1940s and early 1950s, in films like *Make Mine Music* (1946) and *Melody Time* (1948), and culminating in their history of music in *Toot, Whistle, Plunk and Boom* (1953) (see Holliss and Sibley, 1988).

12 Quoted in 'A Spoonful of Sugar', BBC Radio Four, transmitted 25 October 1973, transcript p. 8.

13 Erica Russell's Oscar-nominated film, *Triangle* (1994), takes these principles further in a complex configuration of associative and abstract movement. The vocabulary detailed in this chapter usefully aids the description and possible interpretations of the film, over and above its self-evident technical and aesthetic expertise.

4 25 WAYS TO START LAUGHING

1 Interview with the author, February 1995.

2 John Canemaker has made a short documentary on the work of Otto Mesmer called *Otto Messmer and Felix the Cat* (Phoenix Films Inc., 1975), which properly acknowledges him as the creator of Felix and includes an interview and examples of his work.

3 These ideas were foregrounded in a BBC documentary on Tex Avery broadcast in 1990.

4 A particularly useful analysis of the development of one of Jones' earliest characters, 'Nibbles', was given as a video lecture by David Williams at the Fifth *International Conference of the Society For Animation Studies*, Farnham, Surrey, 1993. (See also, Jones, 1989; and Kenner, 1994.)

5 British animators, Alison Snowden and David Fine, readily acknowledge the influence of films like *Special Delivery* and *The Big Snit* in their own working practices, particularly in a film like *George and Rosemary* (1984) made at the National Film Board of Canada. (Interview with the author, October 1995.)

6 These six categories are drawn from Charney, M., *Comedy: High and Low*, London & Oxford: Oxford University Press, 1979.

7 Many of Disney's sight gags are predicated on notions of sustained incompetency and the proliferation of accidents, rather than overt slapstick played out in a spirit of conflict. Goofy, Pluto and Donald Duck are prone to falling foul of their environment or their inability to interact successfully with artefacts and materials. Indeed, their efforts can be broadly read as an ineffectual response to the increased perils of modernity as it is played out through new technologies and social pursuits. Many of the *Silly Symphonies* demonstrate this clearly – *Clock Cleaners* (1937), for instance, shows how Mickey, Pluto and Donald fail to deal with mechanism, and is merely one example of films where the Disney characters cannot cope with machines.

8 Norman McClaren describes Grant Munro's dance in mid-air in an interview in

Sequences no. 82, October 1975, published in the *Canada House Gallery Guide* for the exhibition of his films and paintings mounted in the same year. Munro had to take a rest after every twenty-five jumps, and McClaren achieved the effect by cutting his film using the frame which recorded the high point of each jump.

9 See Law, 1995. Candy Guard's narratives play out self-perpetuating situations in which women are constantly entrapped by their own self-doubt in the face of failing to attain the image and identity expected of them by a male-determined society. Guard's female characters are frustrated by their own attempts to come to terms with the received knowledge that defines them in contemporary culture. These narratives may be seen as detailed analyses of gendered ennui which provoke particular kinds of recognition in female audiences, who acknowledge the use of humour as a critique of passivity and socially determined oppression.

10 For a discussion of cartoonal parody, see Cohen, M., 'Looney Tunes and Merrie Melodies', and Lowry, E. Obalis, L. & Black, L., 'Cartoon as Ritual', both in Pilling, J., *'That's Not All Folks!': A Primer in Cartoonal Knowledge*, London: BFI Distribution, 1984. Many types of animation have parodic elements, which often inform the self-reflexive aspects of many films. For example, Nick Park's Oscar-winning film, *The Wrong Trousers* (1993), includes a train chase in the silent film style, (actually based on the chariot race from *Ben Hur*) and numerous film noir effects, all given an eccentric English twist by being 'played out in a front room in Wigan'. (Interview with the author, February 1995.)

11 Interview with the author, February 1995.

12 Quoted in a Screen First Documentary, *Going to Work on an Egg*, broadcast on Channel Four, 1994.

13 See Bishko, 1994; Darley, 1993.

5 ISSUES IN REPRESENTATION

1 In a range of films including Mimica's and Marks' *Alone* (1958), Marks' and Jutrisa's *The Fly* (1966), and Dragic's *Passing Days* (1969), the Zagreb Studios have addressed the 'everyman' character, as a victim of loneliness, alienation and oppressive social and supernatural forces. This very much characterises work appearing in creative environments in Eastern Europe, subject to the political intervention from the former Soviet Union. For a full discussion, see Holloway, 1972.

2 Interview with the author, March 1988.

3 Ibid.

4 *Wayward Girls and Wicked Women* was the title given to a series of video releases featuring the work of female British animators. For an overview of these films, see Kotlarz, 1992; and Winterson, 1992.

5 See E.M. Forster, 'Mickey and Minnie' in *Abinger Harvest*, London: Penguin Books, p. 64 (first published by Edward Arnold, 1936).

6 Burton (Carvajal), J., 'Don Juanito Duck and the Imperial Patriarchal Unconscious: Disney Studios, the Good Neighbour Policy, and the Packaging of Latin America' in Parker, A., Russo, M., Sommer, D., and Yaeger, P. (eds), *Nationalisms and Sexualities*, London & New York: Routledge, 1992, pp. 21–42. Updated as '"Surprise Package": Looking Southward with Disney' in Smoodin, E. (ed) *Disney Discourse: Producing the Magic Kingdom*, London & New York: Routledge, 1994, pp. 131–48; see also Dorfman, A. and Mattelart, A., *How to Read Donald Duck: Imperialist Ideology in the Disney Comic*, New York: International General, 1975.

7 This case study concerned with Tom and Jerry was first addressed in Kirkham, P. (ed) (1996) *The Gendered Object*, Manchester: MUP.

8 *Tom and Jerry – The Movie* (1994), and further television spin-offs followed the original

series, but with the continuing showings of the original Hanna Barbera cartoons still in regular circulation worldwide, the predominant and influential canon of work is still regarded as the 1940–1958 period. (See Adams,1991; Brion, 1990; and Sennett, 1989.)

9 Some cartoons during the 1930s and 1940s cannot be reclaimed as in any way defendable or celebratory in their representation of race stereotypes. A particularly offensive example, is Walter Lantz's cartoon, *Scrub Me Mama – with a Boogie Beat* (1941), which depicts exaggeratedly indolent slave caricatures, who shoe-shine, eat melons, and blow cotton, as a seemingly half-caste young woman stimulates music and mirth while a large washer-woman scrubs clothes at the laundry.

10 Animation is produced worldwide in many contexts, and in many nations may be constituted as a particularly *national* cinema in the sense that it properly represents the national preoccupations and aesthetic traditions of that country, resisting the influence of Disney, and creating distinctive works. This is only partially referenced in my discussion, but is addressed in Bendazzi, 1994; and in various monographs, essays and articles looking at particular cultures of animation (see the Bibliography, p. 250).

6 ANIMATION AND AUDIENCES

1 For an accessible discussion of these issues, see J. Mayne, *Cinema and Spectatorship*, London and New York: Routledge, 1993.

2 Animation is particularly appropriate to the needs of advertising in the sense that its language is wholly correspondent to the short form. The very 'look' of various kinds of animation is distinctive; previously inanimate lifeless brands become colourful characters; impossible scenarios are executed with persuasive authenticity. Animation effectively dramatises the 'fantastic' premise/promise of the product beyond the limits of its actual capacity. This may be made literal through changing the scale, scope, and function of the product itself, or the objects/environment associated with it, in order to spectacularise the concept which effectively sells the product. From the Tetley Tea Folk to the Creature Comforts animals of the Heat Electric advertisements to the Canon Copier Man, animation has facilitated memorable and enduring product identity. For brief discussions of animated commercials by Richard Purdum, Nick Park, and Joan Ashworth, see Wells, P. (ed.), *Art and Animation*, Academy Group/John Wiley, 1997, and a range of animated campaigns involving new technologies in Noake, R., *Animation*, London and Sidney: Macdonald Orbis, 1988.

3 From *America – The Movie*, Reel Four: Utopia Unlimited, BBC Radio Four; broadcast June–July 1988; researched and compiled by Paul Wells; script and narration by Christopher Frayling; produced by John Powell; original source: BBC Archive: Walt Disney in conversation with Fletcher Markle.

BIBLIOGRAPHY

References

Adams, T.R. (1991) *Tom and Jerry: 50 Years of Cat and Mouse*, New York: Crescent Books.

Adamson, J. (1975) *Tex Avery, King of Cartoons*, New York: Da Capo.

Allan, R. (1994) 'Sylvia Holland: Disney Artist', *Animation Journal*, Spring, vol. 4, no. 2, pp. 32–42.

Beck, J. and Friedwald, W. (1989) *Looney Tunes and Merrie Melodies: A Complete Illustrated Guide to Warner Brothers Cartoons*, New York: Henry Holt & Co.

Bendazzi, G. (1994) *Cartoons: 100 Years of Cartoon Animation*, London: John Libbey.

Bishko, L. (1994) 'Expressive technology: The tool as a metaphor of aesthetic sensibility', *Animation Journal*, Fall, Vol 3, No. 1, pp. 74–92.

Biskind, P. (1995) 'Win, lose but draw', *Premiere*, July, pp. 80–8.

Bordwell, D., Staiger, J. and Thompson, K. (1985) *The Classical Hollywood Cinema*, London & New York: Routledge.

Brannigan, E. (1984) *Point of View in the Cinema: A Theory of Narration and Subjectivity in Classical Film*, Berlin, New York & Amsterdam: Mouton.

Brion, P. (1990) *Tom and Jerry: The Definitive Guide to their Animated Adventures*, New York: Crown Publishers.

Brophy, P. (1991) 'The animation of sound.' In Cholodenko, A. (ed.) *The Illusion of Life*, Sydney: Power Publications & The Australian Film Commission.

Brunovska-Karnick, K. and Jenkins, H. (eds) (1995) *Classical Hollywood Comedy*, London & New York: Routledge/AFI.

Cabarga, L. (1988) *The Fleischer Story*, New York: Da Capo.

Canemaker, J. (ed.) (1988) *Storytelling in Animation: The Art of the Animated Image Vol. 2*, Los Angeles: AFI.

—— (1994) 'Vladimir Tytla – Master Animator', *Animation Journal*, Fall, Vol. 3, No. 1, pp. 4–32.

Carroll, N. (1991) 'Notes on the Sight Gag'. In Horton, A (ed.) *Comedy/Cinema Theory*, Berkeley, Los Angeles & Oxford: University of California Press, pp. 25–43.

Cholodenko, A. (ed.) (1991) *The Illusion of Life*, Sydney: Power Publications & The Australian Film Commission.

Corliss, R. (1985) 'Warnervana', *Film Comment*, Vol. 21, pp. 11–19.

Crafton, D. (1993) *Before Mickey: The Animated Film 1898–1928*, Chicago: University of Chicago Press.

Cripps, T. (1993) *Making Movies Black: The Hollywood Message Movie from World War II to the Civil Rights Era*, London & Oxford: Oxford University Press.

Culhane, S. (1988) *Animation: From Script to Screen*, London: Columbus Books.

Darley, A. (1993) 'Computer animation: Second order realism and post-modernist aesthetics', a paper given at the *Fifth International Conference of the Society For Animation Studies*, Farnham, England, November.

Denzin, N. (1991) *Images of Post-Modern Society: Social Theory and Contemporary Cinema*, London, Thousand Oaks & New Delhi: Sage Publications.

—— (1995) *The Cinematic Society: The Voyeur's Gaze*, London, Thousand Oaks & New Delhi: Sage Publications.

Durgnat, R. (1969) *The Crazy Mirror: Hollywood Comedy and the American Image*, London: Faber & Faber.

Eco, U. (1986) *Travels in Hyper-reality*, London: Picador.

Ellis, G.T. and Sekyra, F. (1972) 'The effect of aggressive cartoons on the behaviour of first grade children', *Journal of Psychology*, Vol. 81, pp. 37–43.

Farquhar, M. (1993) 'Monks and monkey: A study of "national style" in Chinese animation', *Animation Journal*, Vol. 1, No. 2, pp. 4–28.

Felperin-Sharman, L. (1993) 'New Aladdins for old', *Sight and Sound*, Nov, Vol. 13, No. 11, (NS) pp. 12–16.

—— (1994) 'Down the white road', *Sight and Sound*, May, Vol. 4, No. 5, (NS), pp. 20–2.

Fraser, J. (1979) *Artificially Arranged Scenes: The Films of George Méliès*, Boston, Massachusetts: G.K. Hall & Co.

Freud, S. (1976) *Jokes and their Relation to the Unconscious*, London: Pelican Books.

—— (1986) *The Essentials of Psychoanalysis*, London: Pelican Books.

Frierson, M, (1993) 'Clay comes out of the inkwell: The Fleischer Brothers and clay animation', *Animation Journal*, Fall, Vol. 2, No. 1, pp. 4–20.

—— (1994) *Clay Animation: American Highlights 1908 to the Present*, New York: Twayne Publishers.

Garcia, R. (ed.) (1994) *Frank Tashlin: A Retrospective*, Locarno: Editions du Festival International du Film de Locarno: BFI/ Indiana University Press.

George, R. (1990) 'Some spatial characteristics of the Hollywood cartoon', *Screen*, Autumn, Vol. 31, No. 3, pp. 24–44.

Gilliam, T. (1978) *Animations of Mortality*, London: Eyre Methuen.

Gould, S.J. (1987) 'A biological homage to Mickey Mouse'. In Comley, N., Hamilton, D., Klaus, C., Scholes, R. and Sommers, N. (eds) *Fields of Writing: Reading Across the Disciplines*, New York: St. Martin's Press.

Grant, J. (1993) *Encyclopaedia of Walt Disney's Animated Characters*, New York: Hyperion.

Griffin, S. (1994) 'The illusion of "Identity": Gender and racial representation in *Aladdin*', *Animation Journal*, Vol. 3, No 1, pp. 64–74.

Grotjahn, M. (1957) *Beyond Laughter: Humor and the Sub-Conscious*, New York: McGraw Hill.

Halas, J. (1987) *Masters of Animation*, London: BBC Books.

—— and Batchelor, J. (1949) 'European cartoon: A survey of the animated film'. In Manvell, R. (ed.), *The Penguin Film Review*, London: Penguin Books.

—— and Privett, B. (1958) *How to Cartoon*, London & New York: Focal Press.

Hames, P. (ed.) (1995) *Dark Alchemy: The Films of Jan Svankmajer*, Trowbridge: Flicks Books.

Hansen, M. (1991) *Babel and Babylon: Spectatorship in American Silent Film*, Cambridge, Massachusetts & London: Harvard University Press.

251

Hendershot, H. (1993) 'Secretary, homemaker, and "White" woman: Industrial censorship and Betty Boop's shifting design', Unpublished Paper, University of Rochester.

Henderson, B. (1991) 'Cartoon and narrative in the films of Frank Tashlin and Preston Sturges'. In Horton, A. (ed.) Comedy/Cinema/Theory, Berkeley: University of California Press.

Hodgeson, J. and Preston-Dunlop, V. (1990) Rudolf Laban: An Introduction to his Work, Plymouth: Northcote House Publications.

Hoffer, T. (1981) Animation: A Reference Guide, Westport, Connecticut: Greenwood Press.

Hoffman, E.T.A. (1952) Eight Tales of Hoffman, trans. by J.M. Cohen, London: Pan Books.

Holliss, R. and Sibley, B. (1988) The Disney Studio Story, New York: Crown Publications.

Holloway, R. (1972) Z for Zagreb, London: Tantivy Press.

Holman, L. (1975) Puppet Animation in the Cinema: History and Technique, Cranberry, New Jersey: A.S. Barnes & Co.

Jenkins, H. (1992) What Made Pistachio Nuts?: Early Sound Film and the Vaudeville Aesthetic, New York: Columbia University Press.

Jones, C. (1989) Chuck Amuck: The Life and Times of an American Cartoonist, London: Simon and Schuster.

—— (1991) 'What's up down under?: Chuck Jones talks of The Illusion of Life Conference'. In Cholodenko, A. (ed.) The Illusion of life, Sydney: Power Publications & The Australian Film Commission.

Kenner, H. (1994) Chuck Jones: A Flurry of Drawings, Berkeley: University of California Press.

Klein, A. (1994) 'La Verne Harding: Hollywood's first woman animator', Animation Journal, Spring, Vol. 2, No. 2, pp. 54–68.

Klein, N. (1993) 7 Minutes: The Life and Death of the American Animated Cartoon, New York: Verso.

Kotlarz, I. (1992) 'Imagery of Desire', Sight and Sound, Oct, Vol. 2, No. 6 (NS), pp. 26–7.

Laban, R. (1963) Modern Educational Dance, London: Macdonald & Evans.

Langer, M. (ed.) (1993) Film History – Special Issue of Animation, June, Vol. 5, No. 2.

Law, S. (1995) 'Putting themselves in the pictures: Images of women in the work of selected female animators in the UK', Animation Journal, Fall, Vol. 4, No. 1 pp. 21–56.

Lawrence, A. (1994) 'Masculinity in Eastern European animation', Animation Journal, Fall, Vol. 3, No. 1, pp. 32–44.

Leskosky, R. (1993) 'Zoetrope: History and uses', a paper given at the Fifth International Conference of The Society For Animation Studies, Farnham, England, November.

Lewis, D. and Greene, J. (1983) Your Child's Drawings, London: Hutchinson.

Leyda, J. (ed.) (1988) Eisenstein on Disney, London: Methuen.

Lindvall, T. and Melton, M. (1994) 'Toward a post-modern animated discourse: Bakhtin, inter-textuality and the cartoon carnival', Animation Journal, Fall, Vol. 3, No. 1, pp. 44–64.

McClaren, N. (1978) 'Exhibition and Films', Canada House Gallery Catalogue, 26 October to 25 November 1978.

McClaughlin, D. (1993) 'Beauty and bestiality', a paper given at the Fifth International Conference of The Society For Animation Studies, Farnham, England, November.

McGilligan, P. (1980) 'Robert Clampett'. In Peary, D. and Peary, G. (eds) (1980) The American Animated Cartoon: A Critical Anthology, New York: E.P. Dutton, pp. 150–8.

Maltin, L. (1987) Of Mice and Magic: A History of American Animated Cartoons, New York: New American Library.

Manea, N. (1992) On Clowns: The Dictator and the Artist, London: Faber & Faber.

Manvell, R. (1980) Art and Animation: The Story of the Halas & Batchelor Animation Studio 1940–1980, Keynsham: Clive Farrow Ltd.

Mast, G. and Cohen, M. (eds) (1974) *Film Theory and Criticism*, London, Toronto & New York: Oxford University Press.

Mayne, J. (1993) *Cinema and Spectatorship*, London & New York: Routledge.

Mellen, J. (1977) *Big Bad Wolves: Masculinity in the American Film*, London: Elm Tree Books.

Merritt, R. and Kaufman, J.B. (1993) *Walt in Wonderland: The Silent Films of Walt Disney*, Baltimore & Maryland: John Hopkins University Press.

Meyer, M. (ed.) (1994) *The Politics and Poetics of Camp*, London & New York: Routledge.

Moritz, W. (1988) 'Some observations on non-objective and non-linear animation'. In Canemaker (ed.) (1988) *Storytelling in Animation*, Los Angeles: AFI.

Mulvey, L. (1989) *Visual and Other Pleasures*, Bloomington: Indiana University Press.

—— (1992) 'Visual pleasure and narrative cinema'. In *Screen* (eds) (1992) *The Sexual Subject*, London & New York: Routledge. pp. 22–35.

Munz, P. (1973) *When the Golden Bough Breaks: Structuralism or Typology?*, London: RKP.

O'Brien, F. (1984) *Walt Disney's Donald Duck: 50 Years of Happy Frustration*, London: Walt Disney Productions.

Ohmer, S. (1988) '"Who Framed Roger Rabbit?": The Presence of the Past'. In Canemaker, J. (ed.) *Storytelling in Animation*, Los Angeles: AFI, pp. 97–105.

O'Pray, M. (1989) 'Surrealism, Fantasy and the Grotesque: The Cinema of Jan Svankmajer'. In Donald, J. (ed.) *Fantasy and the Cinema*, London: BFI.

O'Sullivan, J. (1990) *The Great American Comic Strip: One Hundred Years of Cartoon Art*, Boston: Bullfinch Press.

Peary, D. and Peary, G. (eds) (1980) *The American Animated Cartoon: A Critical Anthology*, New York: E.P. Dutton.

Pilling, J. (ed.) (1984) *"That's Not All Folks!": A Primer of Cartoonal Knowledge*, London: BFI Distribution.

—— (ed.) (1992) *Women and Animation: A Compendium*, London: BFI.

Priestley, J. (1994) 'Creating a healing mythology: The art of Faith Hubley', *Animation Journal*, Spring, Vol. 2, No. 2, pp. 23–32.

Quiquemelle, M.C. (1991) 'The Wan Brothers and sixty years of animated film in China'. In Berry, C. (ed.) *Perspectives on Chinese Cinema*, London: BFI, pp. 175–187.

Richards, J. and Sheridan, D. (1987) *Mass Observation at the Movies*, London & New York: RKP.

Robinson, D. (1990) 'Animation, the first chapter 1833–1893', *Sight and Sound*, Autumn, Vol. 59, No. 4, pp. 251–6.

Romney, J. (1992) 'The same dark drift', *Sight and Sound*, March, Vol. 1, No. 11 (NS), pp. 24–8.

Russett, R. and Starr, C. (1976) *Experimental Animation: Origins of a New Art*, New York: Da Capo.

Sagendorf, B. (1979) *Popeye: The First Fifty Years*, New York: Workman Publishing.

Said, E. (1978) *Orientalism*, London: Penguin Books.

—— (1994) *Culture and Imperialism*, London: Chatto and Windus.

Scheib, R. (1980) 'Tex arcana: The cartoons of Tex Avery'. In Peary, D. and Peary, G. (eds) *The American Animated Cartoon: A Critical Anthology*, New York: E.P. Dutton.

Schenkel, T. (1988) 'Storytelling as remembering: Picturing the past in Caroline Leaf's *The Street*'. In Canemaker, J. (ed.)(1988) *Storytelling in Animation*, Los Angeles: AFI.

Screen (editor's collective) (1992) *The Sexual Subject*, London & New York: Routledge.

Smart, B. (1993) *Post-Modernity: Key Ideas*, London & New York: Routledge.

Smoodin, E. (1993) *Animating Culture: Hollywood Cartoons from the Sound Era*, Oxford: Round-house Publishing.

—— (ed.) (1994) *Disney Discourse: Producing the Magic Kingdom*, London & New York: Routledge/AFI.

Solomon, C. (ed.) (1987) *The Art of the Animated Image: An Anthology*, Los Angeles: AFI.

—— (1989) *Enchanted Drawings: The History of Animation*, New York: Alfred K. Knopf.

Stanislavski, C. (1980) *An Actor Prepares*, London: Methuen.

Stephenson, R. (1967) *Animation in the Cinema*, London: A. Zwemmer Ltd. Press.

Tarkovsky, A. (1986) *Sculpting in Time*, London: Bodley Head.

Tasker, Y. (1993) *Spectacular Bodies: Gender, Genre and the Action Cinema*, London & New York: Routledge.

The Project On Disney (Karen Klugman, Jane Kuenz, Shelton Weldrep and Susan Willis), (1995) *Inside the Mouse: Work and Play at Disney World*, London & Durham: Duke University Press.

Thomas, B. (1991) *Disney's Art of Animation: From Mickey Mouse to Beauty and the Beast*, New York: Hyperion.

Thomas, F. and Johnson, O. (1981) *Disney Animation: The Illusion of Life*, New York: Abbeville Press.

Thompson, R. (1980) 'Pronoun trouble'. In Peary, D. and Peary. G. (eds) *The American Animated Cartoon: A Critical Anthology'*, New York: E.P. Dutton, pp. 226–34.

Vernal, D. (1995) 'War and peace in Japanese sci-fi animation: An examination of *Mobile Suit Gundam* and *The Mobile Police Patlabor'*, *Animation Journal*, Fall, Vol. 4, No. 1, pp. 56–85.

Warner, M. (1994) *From the Beast to the Blonde*, London: Chatto and Windus.

Watkins, M. (1995) *On the Real Side: Laughing, Lying and Signifying*, New York, London & Toronto: Simon and Schuster.

Wees, W. (1992) *Light Moving in Time*, Berkeley: University of California Press.

Wells, P. (1993) 'Body-consciousness in the films of Jan Svankmajer', a paper given at *The Fifth International Conference of The Society For Animation Studies*, Farnham, England, November.

—— (1995) 'Dustbins, democracy and defence: Halas and Batchelor and the animated film in Britain 1940–1947'. In Kirkham, P. and Thoms, D. (eds) *War Culture*, London: Lawrence and Wishart, pp. 61–73.

White, S. (1993) 'Split-skins: Female agency and bodily mutilation in *The Little Mermaid'*. In Collins, J., Radner, H. and Preacher Collins, A. (eds), *Film Theory Goes to the Movies*, London & New York: Routledge/AFI, pp. 182–96.

Winterson, J. (1992) 'Outrageous proportions', *Sight and Sound*, Oct, Vol. 2, Issue 6 (NS), pp. 26–7.

Wright, E. (1989) *Post-modern Brecht*, London & New York: Routledge.

Yampolsky, M. (1987) 'Norstein and Khrzhanovski: The space of the animated film', *AfterImage 13: Animating the Fantastic*, Autumn, pp. 93–117.

Further reading

Adamson, J. (1974) 'Suspended animation'. In Mast, G. and Cohen, M. (eds) *Film Theory and Criticism: Introductory Readings*, London & New York: Oxford University Press.

—— (1985) 'What's cooking in *The Black Cauldron'*, *American Cinematographer*, Vol. 66 No. 7, pp. 60–8.

Allan, R. (1985) 'Alice in Disneyland', *Sight and Sound*, Spring Vol. 54, No. 2: 136–8.

—— (1987) 'The fairest film of all', *Animator*, No. 21, pp. 18–21.

—— (1994) 'EuroDisney: *Snow White, Pinocchio*, and a European artist', *Sight and Sound*, July, Art in Film Supplement, Vol. 4, No. 7 (NS), pp. 8–10.

Avery, G. (1989) *Child's Eye: A History of Children's Books Through Three Centuries*, London: Channel Four Publications.

Babbitt, A. and Williams, R. (1974) 'Goofy and Babbitt', *Sight and Sound*, Spring, Vol. 3, No. 2, pp. 94–6.

Beams, M. (1994) 'Subverting time: A woman's perspective', *Animation Journal*, Spring, Vol. 2, No. 2, pp. 42–54.

Beck, J. (1994) *The 50 Greatest Cartoons*, Atlanta: Turner Publishing Co.

Benshoff, H. (1992) 'Heigh-ho heigh-ho, is Disney high or low?: From silly cartoons to post-modern politics', *Animation Journal*, Fall, Vol. 1, No. 2, pp. 62–85.

Brophy, P. (ed.) (1994) *Kaboom!: Explosive Animation from America and Japan*, Sydney: Museum of Contemporary Art/Power.

Bryman, A. (1995) *Disney and His Worlds*, London & New York: Routledge.

Care, R. (1976) 'Cinesymphony: Music and animation at the Disney Studio 1928–1942', *Sight and Sound*, Winter, Vol. 46, No. 1, pp. 40–5.

Cawley, J. and Korkis, J. (1990) *The Encyclopaedia of Cartoon Superstars*, Las Vegas, Nevada: Pioneer Books.

Charney, M. (1978) *Comedy: High and Low*, London & Oxford: Oxford University Press.

Curtis, D. (1987) 'Len Lye', *Watershed Gallery Catalogue*, 24 October to 29 November 1987.

Dale, S. and Tritsch, S. (1990) *Simpson Mania: The History of TV's First Family*, Lincolnwood, Illinois: Publications Inter Ltd.

Deidre Pribram, E. (ed.) (1988) *Female Spectators*, London & New York: Verso.

Delgaudio, S. (1980) 'Seduced and reduced: Female animal characters in some Warners' cartoons'. In Peary, D. and Peary, G. (eds) *The American Animated Cartoon*, New York: E.P. Dutton, pp. 211–17.

Dobson, T. (1989) 'Confluence and conflict in Norman McClaren's Synchromy,' a paper given at the First International Conference of The Society For Animation Studies, Los Angeles, October.

Eliot, M. (1994) *Walt Disney: Hollywood's Dark Prince*, London: Andre Deutsch.

Felperin-Sharman (1994) 'Animatophilia', *Sight and Sound*, July, Art in Film Supplement, Vol. 4, Issue 7, (NS), pp. 14–16.

Finch, C. (1988) *The Art of Walt Disney: From Mickey Mouse to Magic Kingdoms*, New York: Portland House.

Fisher, B. (1993) 'Off to work we go: The digital restoration of *Snow White*', *American Cinematographer*, Vol. 66, No. 9, pp. 48–54.

Fjellman, S. (1992) *Vinyl Leaves: Walt Disney World and America*, Boulder, San Francisco & Oxford: Westview Press.

Forster, E.M. (1967) *Abinger Harvest*, London: Penguin Books.

Halas, J. (1947) 'The film cartoonist'. In Blakeston, O. (ed.), *Working for the Films*, London & New York: Focal Press.

—— (1989) 'Animation and Art', *Animator*, No. 25, p. 21.

Harryhausen, R. (1989) *Film Fantasy Scrapbook*, London: Titan Books.

Heuring, D. and Turner, G. (1991) 'Disney's Fantasia: Yesterday and today', *American Cinematographer*, Vol. 72, No. 2, pp. 54–65.

Horton, A. (ed.) (1991) *Comedy/Cinema/Theory*, Berkeley: University of California Press.

Jackson, W. (1995) 'Cecile Starr: A pioneer's pioneer', *Animation Journal*, Spring, Vol. 3, No. 2, pp. 40–4.

Jefferson, D. (1991) 'Aardman Animations: The plasticine puppeteers', *Animator*, No. 28, pp. 28–32.

Kaufman, J.B. (1988) 'Three little pigs – big little picture', *American Cinematographer*, Vol. 69, No. 11, pp. 38–44.

Lee, N. (1989a) 'Computer animation comes of age', *American Cinematographer*, Vol. 70, No. 10, pp. 78–87.

—— (1989b) 'Computer animation demystified, Pt II', *American Cinematographer*, Vol. 70, No. 11, pp. 98–106.

Leskosky, R. (1989) 'The reforming fantasy: Recurrent theme and structure in American studio cartoons', *The Velvet Light Trap*, Fall, No. 24.

—— (1993) 'Two-state animation: The Thaumatrope and its spin-offs', *Animation Journal*, Fall, Vol. 2, No. 1, pp. 20–36.

Levi, A. (1996) *Samurai from Outer Space: Understanding Japanese Animation*, Illinois: Open Court Publishing Co.

McCarthy, H. (1993) *Anime!: A Beginner's Guide to Japanese Animation*, London: Titan Books.

—— (1996) *The Anime!: Movie Guide*, London: Titan Books.

MacQueen, S. (1992) '*The Lost World*: Merely misplaced?', *American Cinematographer*, Vol. 73, No. 6, pp. 37–44.

McReynolds, W. (1971) *Walt Disney in the American Grain*, University Microfilms, Michigan: Ann Arbor.

Merritt, D. (1990) *Television Graphics: From Pencil to Pixel*, London: Trefoil.

Moritz, W. (1992) 'Resistance and subversion in the animated films of the Nazi era: The case of Hans Fischerkoesen', *Animation Journal*, Fall, Vol. 1, No. 2, pp. 4–33.

Mosley, L. (1985) *The Real Walt Disney*, London: Grafton Books.

Musculus, M. (ed.) (1994) 'A sincere tribute to Roy O. Disney', *Storyboard/Art of Laughter*, Vol. 5, No. 5.

Nicoll, A. (1976) *The World of Harlequin*, Cambridge: Cambridge University Press.

Noake, R. (1988) *Animation: A Guide to Animated Film Techniques*, London: Macdonald/Orbis.

O'Brien, F. (1985) *Walt Disney's Goofy: The Good Sport*, London: Ebury Press.

O'Connell, K. (1993) 'The missing films: UPA Studio and Modern Art', a paper given at the *Fifth International Conference of The Society For Animation Studies*, Farnham, England, November.

O'Pray, M. (1993) 'Eisenstein, Stokes, and Disney: Animation and the omnipotence of thoughts', a paper given at the *Fifth International Conference of The Society For Animation Studies*, Farnham, England, November.

—— (1994) 'Between slapstick and horror', *Sight and Sound*, September, Vol. 4, No. 9 (NS) pp. 20–4.

Richter, H. (1986) *The Struggle for the Film*, Aldershot: Scolar Press/Wildwood House.

Rosenberg, K. (1991) 'The world view of Yuri Norstein', *Animator*, No. 28, pp. 14–16.

Rovin, J. (1991) *The Illustrated Encyclopaedia of Cartoon Animals*, New York: Prentice Hall.

Salt, B. (1987) 'Snow White meets Giovanni Morelli', *Animator*, Issue 21, pp 29–31.

Schickel, R. (1986) *The Disney Version*, London: Pavillion/Michael Joseph.

Seldes, G. (1956) 'The lovely art: Magic'. In Mast, G. and Cohen, M. (eds) (1974) *Film Theory and Criticism: Introductory Readings*, London, Toronto & New York: Oxford University Press.

Sennett, T. (1989) *The Art of Hanna Barbera: 50 Years of Creativity*, New York: Viking Studio Books.

Shay, D. and Duncan, J. (1993) *The Making of Jurassic Park*, London: Boxtree.

Stutts, M.A., Vance, D. and Huddleston, S. (1981) 'Program–commercial separators in children's television: Do they help a child tell the difference between Bugs Bunny and the Quik Rabbit?' *Journal Of Advertising*, 10, pp. 16–25.

Taylor, J. (1987) *Storming the Magic Kingdom: Wall Street, the Raiders and the Battle for Disney*, London: Viking Press.

Thompson, F. (1994) *Tim Burton's Nightmare Before Christmas: The Film, the Art, the Vision*, London: Boxtree.

Turner, G. (1988) 'Who Framed Roger Rabbit?', *American Cinematographer*, Vol. 69, No. 7, pp. 44–60.

Wells, P. (1997) *Around the World in Animation*, London: BFI/Momi

—— ed. (1997) *Art and Animation*, London: Academy Group/John Wiley.

White, T. and Winn, E. (1993) 'Allah vs Disney in the South China Seas', a paper given at The Fifth International Conference of the Society For Animation Studies, Farnham, England, November.

Williams, D. (1991) 'Whatever happened to Sunflower?', *Animator*, Issue 28, p 13.

Wilson, A. (1992) *The Culture of Nature: North American Landscape from Disney to the Exon Valley*, Cambridge, Massachusetts: Blackwell.

Yoe, C. and Morra-Yoe, J. (eds) *The Art of Mickey Mouse*, Los Angeles: Hyperion.

Zipes, J. (1989) *The Brothers Grimm: From Enchanted Forests to the Modern World*, London & New York: Routledge.

INDEX

FILMOGRAPHY